Image and Argument
in Plato's *Republic*

SUNY series in Ancient Greek Philosophy
_____
Anthony Preus, editor

Image and Argument
in Plato's *Republic*

Marina Berzins McCoy

Cover art: Still Life—Violin and Music, 1888 by William Michael Harnett
The Metropolitan Museum of Art, New York

Published by State University of New York Press, Albany

For information, contact State University of New York Press, Albany, NY
www.sunypress.edu

Library of Congress Cataloging-in-Publication Data

Name: Marina Berzins McCoy, author
Title: Image and Argument in Plato's *Republic* / McCoy, Marina Berzins, author.
Description: Albany : State University of New York Press, [2020] | Includes
   bibliographical references and index.
Identifiers: ISBN 9781438479132 (hardcover : alk. paper) | ISBN 9781438479149
   (ebook) | ISBN 9781438479125 (pbk. : alk. paper)
Further information is available at the Library of Congress.

10 9 8 7 6 5 4 3 2 1

Contents

Acknowledgments

I am grateful to the many people whose assistance with this book helped to improve it. Nickolas Pappas read much of the first half of the manuscript and provided beneficial feedback on the project as a whole. Jacob Howland, Anne Marie Schultz, and Bill Wians gave invaluable responses to the material on Glaucon and Gyges's ring. Thanks to Franco Trivigno, who gave commentary on the section on comedy and the "three waves." Jill Gordon, Christopher Long, Arthur Madigan SJ, Rachel Singpurwalla, Nicholas D. Smith, and Jason Taylor all gave constructive commentary on various parts of the manuscript, and conversation with Cristina Ionescu helped me to think through the project and its contours early on. Thanks to Max Wade for developing an index. I am also grateful to the Ancient Philosophy Society, and to the faculty at Emory University and St. Francis Xavier University for comments and discussion at lectures I gave related to the book. A conference at the University of Toronto hosted by Lloyd Gerson also helped me to consider more deeply Platonic dialogue form and its methodology. A writing retreat sponsored by Boston College's Mission and Ministry Program assisted at a critical juncture in the project. I am especially grateful to Dean Gregory Kalscheur SJ for a funded yearlong research sabbatical that provided ample time to write. Thanks to my editor, Andrew Kenyon, who was a pleasure to work with. I appreciate his generosity and dedication to the project. Thanks also to Diane Ganeles and Dana Foote for their careful preparation of the manuscript.

Several students at Boston College assisted with the development of this book. Research assistants Drew Alexander and Lydia Winn deserve special thanks for their painstakingly careful work, and both Benjamin Miyamoto and Tyler Viale provided valuable assistance in earlier stages of research. The many students who took a semester-long course on the *Republic* over the years also helped me to understand the dialogue better. Although it has become a truism that we learn from our students, it's still also simply true. Thanks also to John McCoy and Mary Troxell, who offered moral support and encouragement in the course of writing the book.

A few sections of the book were previously published: "Myth and Argument in Glaucon's Account of Gyges's Ring and Adeimantus's Use of Poetry," a chapter in *Logoi and Muthoi*, edited by William Wians (Albany: State University of New York Press, 2019), forms part of chapter 4. An abbreviated version of "The City of Sows and Sexual Differentiation in Plato's *Republic*," a chapter in *Plato's Animals*, edited by Jeremy Bell and Michael Naas (Bloomington: Indiana University Press, 2015) is part of the beginning of chapter 5. "Freedom and Responsibility in the Myth of Er," *Ideas y Valores* special issue of *Plato and Socratic Politics* 61, no. 149 (September 2012), is part of the last section of chapter 9. Thanks to State University of New York Press, Indiana University Press, and *Ideas y Valores* for permission.

Introduction

Plato's *Republic* abounds with imagery. The dialogue opens with Socrates's words "I went down yesterday to the Piraeus" (327a).[1] This language of descent is reminiscent of Odysseus's descent into Hades in Homer's *Odyssey* and of the tradition of *katabasis* poetry more generally.[2] The main argument of the dialogue models the soul on the city, which itself is imagined distinctly from any real, concrete city. In the middle of the dialogue, Socrates describes the forms in terms of the sun and a divided line. The philosopher is freed from his chains in a cave and forced to climb a rugged path to discover the outside world, only later to descend again to rule (514a–20d).[3] The book concludes with the myth of Er, which speaks of souls who are ascending and descending (614b–16b). Throughout the dialogue, there are numerous citations of poetry from Homer, Simonides, Aeschylus, Pindar, and references to comedy. Even the Platonic dialogue itself is an image of Socrates and his friends, gathered together and discussing the nature of justice, a discussion that never took place except in the imagination of Plato and his readers.

At the same time, Socrates is highly critical of images at numerous points in the *Republic*. He tears down the Homeric tradition of poetic education; argues that the *mimēsis* of bad men is morally destructive; explains that artistic and poetic images are thrice removed from the truth; and places images at the very lowest section of the divided line, in contrast to *noēsis* and hypothetical reasoning.[4] Socrates criticizes *mimēsis* more generally, and even banishes poetry from the ideal city. And yet images are central to the arguments within the dialogue. We might ask, for example, what difference it makes that Socrates uses an image of the city as a "paradigm" for the soul, and how we understand Socrates's conclusions about justice as a result. Or if Homeric images are an insufficient form of education, why does Socrates use other images to describe the forms? Why do stories

1

such as the noble lie or myth of Er form part of Socrates's own argument? While some commentators have argued for a more sophisticated interaction between philosophy and poetry in the dialogue, more can be said about how images function as part of argument in the *Republic*.[5]

On the one hand, simply to regard Socrates's arguments against the problems inherent in imagery as ironically undermined by Plato's authorial use of images would be insufficient. Socrates is forcefully critical of traditional poetry, especially Homer, and its educational role in the formation of citizens. On the other hand, Socrates's frequent use of images suggests that imagery has a significant part to play in philosophical practice despite its limitations and dangers.

One solution to the difficulty is to argue that the use of images plays a rhetorical role. For example, James Kastely has recently argued that the dialogue educates in a preparatory way those people who are unprepared to undertake the more difficult work of dialectic, which alone counts as true philosophy. On this view, Platonic imagery functions as a species of rhetorical argumentation but not philosophy.[6] Other authors have argued that contrast between the dialogue's imagery and its arguments are instances of Platonic irony or that the dialogue should be read as developing its ideas over the course of its ten books.[7] While poetry may stand in tension with philosophical practice, philosophy cannot and should not free itself of images entirely. Each of these positions has its merits and helps us to better understand the subtleties of the dialogue.

What has been less widely explored is to describe how images form a part of philosophical argument in the *Republic*. Indeed, image making is central to the dialogue's argument at nearly every turn, and not only in rhetorical or pedagogical ways. That Plato uses particular images—such as the image of the ship as a model for the state—is not disputed. What is not often sufficiently recognized is that the main philosophical arguments of the text about central matters such as justice or the nature of the forms are highly reliant on images. Through examining the use of imagery in arguments, we can learn better how Plato philosophizes with images, and thereby something more about how Plato understands philosophical language itself. For Plato, the aim of philosophical language is not merely to create reality through words, as do the poets, nor to manipulate reality for the sake of power, as do the sophists. Rather, philosophical language seeks to disclose the nature of being in the process of its being sought. However, because being always exceeds and partially eludes the capacity of human beings to grasp its nature, our language likewise must reflect that human limit. The language of images arises at the intersection of being and the human being. Images of the right sort can disclose being to us, but partially and perspectivally. When we recognize that these images *are* images, rather than treating the images as perfect representations of being, we also grow in self-knowledge in how we understand ourselves as seekers of truth. Plato's Socrates uses the language of imagery and paradigm to make arguments and philosophical claims, but then also offers cogent arguments as to why an image needs to be understood as an image. Plato thus includes in this dialogue an assessment of imagistic philosophical language and its limits.

From the arguments in Book One with Cephalus, Polemarchus, and Thrasymachus, to the images that Socrates uses to describe the forms, and onward to the myth of Er, Socrates uses images to make his arguments.[8] The dialogue as a whole is also an image insofar as it constructs an imaginary dialogue between a group of people that goes beyond verbal interchange to include a vivid setting: the mention of races at a festival, the description of a slave pulling on Socrates's cloak, the seat upon which Cephalus sits, and so on. If one were to say that images are not and cannot be properly philosophical for Plato, then the rather peculiar conclusion at which one might arrive would be that the *Republic* does not show Socrates practicing philosophy at all. And yet such a conclusion is unacceptable. For one, the *Republic* not only prepares its readers to take up philosophy by, for example, encouraging the philosophical journey through the image of the cave, although this is part of its work. It also makes numerous positive claims about the nature of justice in both the city and soul. Socrates not only offers arguments that break down the insufficient ideas of his interlocutors in Book One, but also constructs positive models of the just soul and just city. The dialogue is rich in moral and political content. When examined carefully, we find that the development of this content is highly reliant on images for its construction. There is no section of the dialogue in which the reality of the forms is described in image-free language, or another Platonic dialogue in which the nature of justice is described apart from images and paradigms. Thus, the images in the *Republic* do not teach content that elsewhere has been arrived at through some image-free method of coming to know. Instead, images are part of the very development of some of the most significant moral and political claims in the dialogues.

Philosophy as Socrates practices it within the dialogue includes a variety of modalities that are appropriate to the particular task at hand. His use of images encourages his interlocutors to live better lives, practically and concretely. His image of the tyrant's soul, for example, helps to argue for the claim that the just person is much happier than the unjust person and makes the tyrant's life look unappealing in contrast to that of the just person. The imagination also has epistemic value, insofar as the highest objects of knowledge—the forms—are beyond images, but ordinarily, human beings must rely on images in order to make sense of and to talk about these forms. This limit of language is not merely negative, however: intelligible images can assist human beings in coming to know the forms. Moreover, many of Socrates's images in the middle books teach his interlocutors—and Plato's readers—*that it is the case that* images are insufficient to grasp everything about the forms. And this understanding of imagination's own limits is itself crucial to being a philosopher, insofar as the philosopher's growth in self-knowledge and human limit is part of what distinguishes her from the poet.

Images can serve as part of a slow and gradual movement of Socrates's interlocutors—and also Plato's readers—toward the forms. The forms themselves are not reducible to images, and not every image is helpful for learning more about the forms. However, human beings do not simply access the forms all at once, through using the right image-free philosophical technique. Instead, Plato shows Socrates using images as part of the practice of philosophy. Such images need not be understood as entirely truthful or entirely false. Rather, we can understand the image as a way of accessing the reality of the forms partially and incompletely. As Jill Frank argues, philosophers are spectators who look to the forms and their images, and who therefore may not see the whole of that which they seek. Instead, philosophers in the *Republic*, no less than in the *Symposium*, occupy a middle ground.[9] Images allow a seeker of truth to embark on a path that may slowly lead to a philosophical vision of the forms.

Socrates's use of such images is not merely rhetorical or pedagogical, but rather heuristic. Socrates does not teach others with images from the point of view of being a master of an area of knowledge, and then use images that can convey his knowledge to a beginner. Rather, Socrates uses images to *discover* more about the nature of justice, how and whether justice is beneficial, and other philosophical problems. Indeed, images are a pervasive part of his philosophical argument. Images can distract or mislead when they are of the wrong kind or when they are not properly understood *as* images. However, the right sorts of images, such as intelligible images, can lead to a process of discovering more about the forms. The early books of the *Republic* display how images are used to discover the nature of justice. The middle books then provide a series of images in which images are treated in terms of a larger ontological and epistemological whole. Later books then explore the limits of images, further reinforcing their limited and partial nature.

Before beginning, Socrates's use of terms for image and imagination ought to be further explained. Classical Greek has no single word that adequately captures the entire range of meaning of the English term "imagination." I take our contemporary sense of "imagination" to include both, more narrowly, the human faculty by which images are presented in the human mind to represent objects and, more broadly, the representation of images that inform how a social group interprets the world and its meaning. Poetry and works of art are both works of the imagination in this latter sense. To ask how the imagination functions as part of argument is not limited to a problem of philosophy of mind—indeed, Plato's Socrates says next to nothing about how images function as part of a thought process, along the lines of how Aristotle treats image making as a mental faculty in *De Anima*. Rather, his concern is focused on how the imagery found in a shared language, whether poetic, philosophical, or "ordinary" language, affects how we think about the nature of justice or other moral and political goods. Homer's imagery, and the imagery of many other traditional poets, is found wanting for its incapacity to address fundamental claims about the nature and value of justice. However, Plato develops alternative images that do claim to unfold and elucidate the nature of justice, while also reminding his own audience of the limits of his subsequent claims.

A variety of Greek words are used to describe the imagination. Socrates uses the term *eikasia* to describe the lowest portion of the divided line. *Phantasia* is also used to describe the faculty of image making, but the term could also be translated as "appearance," due to its close connection to sensory experience. However, in the *Republic*, Socrates speaks more often of images than of the faculty of imagination itself. An *eikōn* is a copy or an image that may either reveal or distort some aspect of that which it copies. An *eikōn* can refer to art, or even shadows or clouds, as well as to an internal mental representation of an object. Socrates frequently uses the language of paradigms (*paradeigmata*) or type (*tupos*) to describe the subject matter under consideration, such as the image of the city as applied to the individual soul in the discovery of justice. Paradigms and models are often used in order to give conceptual form to a complex or elusive concept. Sometimes the term "paradigm" is used more informally only to designate an argumentative example. Thus, another added difficulty is that Socrates does not always give a precise account of what his own Greek terms for "image" or "imagination" mean. Thus, understanding how images work as part of argument requires looking at each place that Socrates uses images with some care for its specific and contextual use, rather than relying on a single operational definition of image and then applying it to all cases of argument within the dialogue.

Socrates's engagement with images is not limited to how the individual human subject mentally represents objects. He is also deeply interested in the question of how his own Greek world's poetic and dramatic culture communicates moral and political ideals to a whole community, and the effect that dramatic performance has on the souls of those who listen. Plato's concern with poetry in the *Republic* is not primarily aesthetic, but rather with how the educational practices of his own day use poetic imagery in a way that is insufficient for the formation of true wisdom. Thus, *mimēsis* or imitation is also relevant to the discussion of images. The active imitation of an epic, tragic, or comic character may result in the imitating subject becoming like the person whom he imitates. As Andrea Nightingale has demonstrated, Plato as author writes in the form of a dialogue that is partially reliant on these same genres that Socrates criticizes.[10] Any examination of the various ways that Plato treats the images best includes an analysis of their use, the diverse ways that Socrates and his interlocutors talk about their use, and how Plato as author uses images in his own practice of writing a dialogue.

Plato's treatment of the imagination is not systematic but rather seen best through examining his practice. In the absence of a unified account of how the imagination may function positively, this book's approach is to pay greater attention to the praxis of using images and his words about their use.[11] My approach here is primarily to examine a range of ways that the text uses images in the course of the argument of the *Republic*. While this may be less satisfying than an account that unifies in a clear and comprehensive way a single theory of images, Plato's treatment itself is more varied than will allow it.

In this work, I do not seek to provide a comprehensive interpretation of every image in the *Republic*, although a wide range of images and arguments are examined. I also set aside many controversies about points of textual interpretation that do not bear directly on the question of imagery. Still, my claim is that Plato's use of images is pervasive and part of the *Republic*'s main arguments, not limited only to a few well-known images such as the pilot of the ship, the myth of metals, or the cave.

This work takes up the main lines of argument in the *Republic* from Books One to Four, which use imagistic language heuristically, in order to discover the nature of the justice to the human being. I then turn to the middle books, where Socrates uses images in order to show how they can either distort or disclose reality, but *if understood as images*, they can be crucial in a person's seeking to understand the forms. The sun, divided line, and cave images are themselves images that situate the idea of a visual image into a larger context.[12] Last, I take up the later books' discussion of degenerate cities and souls and the critique of *mimēsis*. Socrates's revisiting the nature of *mimēsis* further reinforces the partial and limited nature of image making, including philosophical imagery.

The following chapter begins with a broader look at Plato's relationship to poetry and how the dialogue form itself is responsive to Socrates's concerns about poetry in Books Two and Three. The remaining chapters proceed chronologically, taking up how Socrates uses images as argument beginning as early as Book One to develop a notion of justice. Images can either offer access to intelligible reality or potentially distort; often our particular images of ideas such as justice both disclose being and partially distort its nature. Philosophy can only be practiced well if the philosopher is aware of the ways in which images both conceal and reveal—a self-awareness lacking in many earlier poetic practices before Plato. In the *Republic*, there is no image-free way of speaking about philosophical objects. That is, there is no philosophical language that can wholly free us from the limits of images. Socrates treats images as limited but necessary for philosophical insight. In this way, Plato's understanding of what counts as philosophical language challenges many contemporary understandings of philosophical language as precise and non-imagistic because capable of capturing reality. For Plato, a central task of philosophy is to help us to understand ourselves as image-makers who need the imagination to access reality and yet must be cautious of not too easily accepting our images uncritically.

Socrates even gives us images, such as the imagery of the cave, that can teach us to consider a reality beyond the imagination's own limits, thus encouraging self-knowledge and a sense of self-limit. Such self-knowledge has political value in discouraging tyrannical action. Individuals and an entire culture alike can be imprisoned by unthinking false images of reality that prevent them from properly understanding reality, yet images are part of the journey upward to the forms. The imagination is both a cause of human ignorance or limit, and a potential source of liberation. The *Republic* is best understood as a means of educating its own readers in how to imagine justice philosophically, rather than as an exact political plan for a state.[13]

The order of the book's arguments proceeds as follows.

Chapter 1 begins with the criticisms of poetry in Books Two and Three as a larger context for understanding the dialogue and its more specific arguments. Socrates's treatment of poetry and the initial criticisms of *mimēsis* are explored. I argue that the main objections to poetry in Books Two and Three are unified around the problem of poetic education. Among his concerns are audience passivity, the failure to communicate a hidden sense, and moral harm that arises from the imitation of bad characters. However, while Socrates wishes to eliminate certain kinds of poetry from the city, Plato as author finds ways to reincorporate certain elements of *poiēsis* into his own form of writing. However, Plato does so in ways that take account of these sorts of criticisms. For example, he builds in features to the dialogue that encourage his audience to engage in a more critical hermeneutic rather than to remain passive. The Platonic dialogue also includes both narrated and mimetic elements, but its *mimēsis* asks the audience to imitate Socrates and his mode of philosophical argument, thus strengthening rather than weakening the exercise of reason.

Chapter 2 examines how images are central to the arguments offered by Cephalus, Polemarchus, and Socrates. Instead of seeing Book One as containing three "definitions" of justice that are each in turn refuted by Socrates, these arguments are better understood as a series of paradigms of justice. Cephalus and Polemarchus use paradigmatic images, that is, they give verbal descriptions of justice that present an iconic picture of what the just life looks like. Socrates does not insist on moving to greater abstraction, but instead responds to them with a series of counterimages that help move them to a better understanding of justice. His method is dialectical in the sense that while their views of justice are not adequate, Socrates responds by expanding the scope of justice, without completely rejecting some of the insights brought out by these initial descriptions.

Chapter 3 examines the argument between Thrasymachus and Socrates. Here, paradigmatic argument again is central to the exchange between the two figures. However, because Socrates and Thrasymachus have such fundamentally different values and beliefs, this approach to argument proves to be ineffective. The paradigmatic examples on which they each rely to show that rulers either do or do not care for those over whom they rule remain fundamentally in conflict. For this reason, the remainder of the dialogue takes a different approach to the argument. This chapter also explores how Plato as author uses imagery at the level of the dialogue's drama. For example, a reference to Polemarchus's death at the hands of the Thirty invites the further exploration of questions about justice by Plato's reader. While audience passivity is among Socrates's criticism of traditional poetry, Plato as author asks his own audience to be critically engaged and not only passive recipients of his message.

Chapter 4 takes up Glaucon and Adeimantus's new formation of the challenge posed by Thrasymachus. Glaucon frames the problem by offering two opposing arguments, in a kind of *dialexeis*, with the just and unjust man on either side. The argument continues in terms of images, most notably Glaucon's use of narrative in offering the myth of the shepherd's ring, Adeimantus's poetic images, and Socrates's own city-soul analogy. The chapter takes up each of these three kinds of image making in turn and shows how the imagery contributes to the argument. For example, the narrative about the shepherd's ring invites the listener to increased self-knowledge through a process of identification and disidentification with the shepherd. The chapter also explores the nature of the city-soul analogy and argues that it is both rhetorical and heuristic in its approach.

Chapter 5 begins by briefly examining the image of the "simple" city that Socrates proposes. Although Glaucon rejects it as a "city of pigs," I argue that his main objection is not to its animallike nature but rather on account of it being an overly feminine city that lacks a place for masculine activities of war and political honor. The chapter then looks at how the main models of justice in the city and soul ought to be understood as models, rather than as exacting descriptions of justice itself. While these images of city and soul help us to learn more about justice, Socrates's language about his own process shows that these paradigms are meant to bring insight into the nature of justice itself and to encourage his listeners to want to live a just life. This visual language emphasizes a Socratic concern with knowledge as insight, in which verbal models are used to encourage knowing as seeing.

Chapter 6 examines the "three waves" with special attention to their comedic nature. Socrates's proposals are presented as both comic and as serious critiques of his society. However, rather than stopping where comedy does with critique, the dialogue also invites us to consider *why* we find certain ideas funny. He thus encourages a form of social self-criticism intended to help the polis to see its own limits and to reenvision its own possibilities.

Chapters 7 and 8 offer a detailed analysis of Socrates's images of the sun, divided line, and cave. I argue that Socrates's main focus in these books is not to offer a detailed metaphysics so much as to help his listeners imagine the forms and what it would mean to come to know them. Images are used not only because they are pedagogically useful but also because the forms themselves can only be known partially and perspectivally. Socrates's visual images offer a picture of knowing as intellectual seeing, in which the objects of knowledge are stable and enduring, while our own access to them is limited. Moreover, the epistemic value of images is complex. They are the lowest element on the divided line, but intelligible images can also point us to the forms. Socrates's images of the forms are themselves examples of such intelligible images. Thus, the idea of the form as a "look" (in the most literal sense of the word) remains crucial. The divided line and sun images offer an omniscient viewpoint of the forms and other ways of encountering the world. In contrast, the image of the cave takes on the perspective of an individual person who comes to seek and to contemplate the forms over time.

Chapter 9 finally turns to the remaining books, in which Socrates offers a variety of images about imperfect cities and souls. Socrates offers images of degenerate regimes and their corresponding souls, and of the image of the tyrant's soul in particular. He tells a myth about making choices within the constraints of necessity in the myth of Er. These images do not flesh out the nature of the ideal city, but instead offer ways of conceptualizing and responding to living in imperfect cities. Socrates encourages self-knowledge and the development of justice in one's own soul as the best ways to respond to living in a nonideal or even corrupt regime. This chapter also takes up the critique of *mimēsis* in Book Ten and argues that its late placement is carefully situated. Socrates's audience is better positioned to reflect on the distinction between poetic and philosophical imagery. Unlike the divine craftsman, who possesses full knowledge, the philosopher occupies a middle epistemic position. Images are useful when they help us to grow in understanding of being (the forms) but these images are limited. Part of good philosophical practice is to recognize the limits of the images used in order to argue and to discover more about the forms. The myth of Er is an instance of a myth that explores a topic beyond human knowledge— death and life after death—by addressing the human longing for truth and goodness. Liminal spaces, such as the border between life and death, do not easily lend themselves to precise descriptions. However, imagery understood *as imagery* allows us to encounter and to develop narratives about such liminal aspects of human experiences. The Platonic use of images reflects a Platonic engagement with the human being as "in between" the mortal and the divine.

Chapter 1

Poetry and the *Republic*

Before examining specific ways that Socrates uses image making as argument in Book One, it is helpful to begin by examining the dialogue's larger relationship to poetry. Socrates takes up this topic in Books Two and Three. There, Socrates is quite critical of poetry and earlier poetic education. At the same time, the dialogue form is itself a form of poetry that overcomes many of the limits Socrates articulates regarding earlier poetic education. Plato as author engages with poetry in a manner that is distinct from both the approach taken by his character Socrates and that taken by earlier poets. Whether or not the historical Socrates objected to the poetic education of his day,[1] Plato's writing indicates that his own engagement with poetry is more nuanced than the view that the character Socrates offers. Instead of banishing all poetry and drama, Plato goes a step further than Socrates in developing a *new* way to incorporate poetry into educative practice that is intended to overcome some limits of his predecessors.[2] In particular, Platonic dialogue reincorporates some positive features of *mimēsis* in ways that take account of some of its limitations. The *Republic* itself is a work of both narration and *mimēsis*. Through attending to the ways in which *mimēsis* is reformulated as part of the dialogue form, we can see that the mimetic capacities of the imagination remain central to philosophy.

There is considerable evidence that ancient authors understood the Platonic dialogue as performative.[3] Nikos Charalambopolous notes that Albinos's *Prologos*, a second-century CE introduction to the Platonic dialogues, characterizes the Platonic dialogue as a *logos* in which the characters must speak in accord with their characters (*ēthopoiias*). Albinos takes it for granted that the text will be performed rather than silently read. A student of Olympiodorus likewise writes in a prolegomena to Plato that the work is composed of unmetrical speech in which characters engage in question and answer.[4] It is his lack of meter that is most distinctive, not a shift away from character-based speech. Thus, the dialogue has not always been read in ways in which the content is incidental to the form.

Before Plato, other works of "Socratic dialogue" featuring Socratic ideas also existed—not only Xenophon, but also now lost works by authors such as Antisthenes, Aischines, Aristippos, Eukleides, and others. These authors sometimes recorded Socratic ideas without themselves claiming to adhere to the ideas contained within them. Charalambopolous shows that Plato is exceptional among them for his greater inclusion of performative elements than is found in many Socratic "dialogues."[5] In other words, one cannot assume that the arc of philosophical history is one in which Plato moves away from performance, and Aristotle still further, in their mode of composition as philosophy "progresses." The historical evidence instead suggests that Plato, among the many writers of Socratic dialogue and other prose forms, is deliberately far more dramatic and inventive among his cohorts for his inclusion of dramatic elements compared with other dialogical works about Socrates.[6]

In Books Two and Three, Socrates and Adeimantus criticize traditional poetry on largely moral grounds. While Book Ten will return to a criticism of poetry on ontological grounds, arguing for a distance between artistic imitation and what truly "is," Books Two and Three focus on the moral and theological content of poetry and its power over the soul to do harm. (For the moment, I put off the discussion of Book Ten and its criticisms of *mimēsis* until a later chapter, as I argue that their later placement is important to their interpretation.) Controversy abounds among commentators as to the exact nature of Socrates's criticism of poetry. Some take the main criticism to be the form of poetry, while others the content.[7] Some read Plato's text as rejecting dramatic and performative forms of poetry in particular, while others see the criticism as applicable to all forms of *poiēsis*, which are rejected in favor of philosophical reasoning. Still others see the attack on poetry as directed primarily at Homer and traditional education as practiced in Athens, or at the sophists' particular way of educating with poetry, or both.[8] Indeed, Socrates's and Adeimantus's criticisms are not easily categorized in part because they move both between different authors (e.g., Homer, Hesiod, Aeschylus) and genres (epic, tragic, comic), and they make a variety of claims about the poems. Some poems are criticized because they have negative psychological results in those who listen. Others are problematic because their claims, for instance, about the nature of the gods, are untrue. The imitation of bad characters and its effect on those who perform is also explored.

A common thread of Books Two and Three that unites these criticisms is found in the motive for their becoming the subject of discussion in the first place: education. Socrates raises the issue of the problem of poetry in the context of the education of the guardians. This educational context remains central to the proper interpretation of all else that is said about the form, content, and effect of poetry, for Socrates's points are grounded in the quest for a city whose citizens are just, moderate, courageous, wise, and pious. Socrates's aim is to better understand the best education for the formation of virtuous citizens, and especially children and young people whose souls are still "plastic" and malleable at an early age (377b). In his analysis of education, Socrates's points are multiple because the desired effects in shaping the souls of its young citizens are multiple. Guardians must be more than only both spirited and gentle, the initial qualities with which Socrates begins (375b–c). They must also be courageous, be restrained in their grief and moderate in their emotions, love the truth and hate lies, be capable fighters, be as self-sufficient as possible, honor gods and ancestors, and not love money too much. Socrates's criticisms center around the question of the educational value of traditional poetry and poetic performance.[9] If the goal of poetry is to educate citizens to be just, then the system of education in place thus far has failed.[10]

In Book Two, Socrates criticizes much of the theological and ethical content of Homeric and Hesiodic stories, although such criticisms also extend to later poets. Book Three gives attention to comedy and tragedy, as well as the difficulties that arise with performance/imitation, in contrast to narrative forms that distance the performer from a work's characters. Socrates critically engages with a variety of genres, but especially epic and tragedy. Socrates is not giving a full-fledged account of everything that could be said about the merits and problems of poetry, however. For example, he does not undertake to explore the structures of plays such as plot, diction, or character; or a whole range of topics often addressed in epic, tragedy, and comedy, such as fate, the nature of the hero, punishment, revenge, human vulnerability and limit, the nature of sexual attraction, or other subjects. Socrates homes in on poetry as education and its problems in the restricted context of trying to understand how to form good citizens. While other elements of the traditional system of education such as gymnastics and grammar are not given as much time and attention, Socrates finds poetic education to be in serious need of criticism and reformation.

Socrates's conclusions about poetry here are different in other contexts, for example, where the aim of inquiry is to better understand the nature of *eros*, beauty, or good rhetoric. Other dialogues such as the *Phaedrus* and *Symposium* present a more positive view of poetry as capable of moving the human being toward beauty. For example, the lyric poets receive high praise in the *Phaedrus*, when Socrates says that the very origin of his own speeches is "Sappho the fair," "Anacreon the wise," or perhaps a prose writer, whose words have been like water poured from a pitcher into his ears and whose ideas have filled his chest (*Phdr.* 235c–d). In authoring Agathon's speech about *eros*, Plato extensively imitates this tragic poet as part of a forward movement toward better understanding the nature of love. As author, he imitates Apollodorus imitating Aristodemus, who in turn imitates Agathon. In so doing, Plato is his own kind of poetic imitator. Although Agathon's ideas are limited, some of them inform Socrates's speech about *eros*, as do some of the ideas found in the comic Aristophanes's presentation. Plato's *Ion* praises the inspiration of the poets while criticizing their lack of knowledge. The *Laws* seems to make room for comedy as part of the education of its citizens. The Platonic treatment of poetry is varied, and uniting the claims made across all of the dialogues into a single, unified doctrine is a difficult undertaking, without at least attending to the context in which each of the individual claims are made.[11] Here, I will not attempt to give such a unified view of poetry across the dialogues but will simply point out that the claims made about poetry in the *Republic* arise from the perspective of educating the guardians in an ideal city.

The critique of poetry in the *Republic* is additionally problematic for an interpreter at several levels. First, Plato's use of poetry and frequent allusion to it throughout the dialogue seems to stand in contrast to a total ban on poetry in the ideal city.[12] For example, Socrates makes numerous allusions to Homer throughout the discussion.[13] If the perfect city is banned from its use, why does Plato incorporate it into his own text? In other dialogues, such as the *Protagoras*, Socrates even interprets poetry, albeit with some caveats.[14] Second, Socrates seems to assume a lack of even the slightest sophistication on the part of the audiences of poetic performances, which are assumed always to passively receive the poetic tradition as authoritative. While this worry about audience passivity may be partially warranted, audience reception of Homeric poetry was more complicated than Socrates implies.

Poets before Plato were not naïve practitioners lacking any theories about their own practices. Grace Ledbetter argues that poets before Plato offered theories about their own poetry.[15] Homeric poetry engages its audience with self-conscious awareness of what it is doing, but in a manner that is distinctive from the Platonic approach. For Homer, the audience is meant to have a "sensually immediate experience of apprehending the poem."[16] Such an experience does not call for an interpretation of the poem; rather, it seeks to engage the audience in a sensual apprehension of its content. However, as Ledbetter argues, from the Homeric point of view, this apprehension is a *way* of knowing. Homeric knowing is "quasi-perceptual," insofar as Homer uses imagery that not only reminds his audience of perceptual reality but indeed awakens those sensory faculties to experience a sensual reality in the reception of listening to poetry—an effect enhanced by the fact that the poetry was also sung.[17] We can glean that such theorizing about poetry was present to the developers of Homeric epic through the dramatization of the effect of poetry on its audience by its internal characters. For example, when Odysseus listens to the poet Demodicus and is unable to restrain his tears, we see a listener under the sway of a poet's influence.[18] Ledbetter emphasizes that the Homeric mode of discourse encourages a passivity of reception and the authority of the poet. Rather than encouraging interpretation, the poet attempts to control how the poem will be experienced and received.

Yet one can further complicate claims of audience passivity by noticing how frequently poets and tragedians alike constantly engaged in retelling and reformulating character, plot, and devices. The reformulation of the mythic tradition—often in ways that contradicted, or at least seriously changed, the moral and political meanings of these myths—is commonplace in Greek poetry and drama. Moreover, how poetry was received and interpreted changed over time; for example, allegorical interpretations of Homer by Theagenes, Anaxagoras, and Metrodorus demonstrate an explicit concern with diverse hermeneutical possibilities of a text.[19] There was no uniform poetic view about the gods, nor even about whether particular character traits were emblematic of a good person, despite a largely shared mythology. For example, Odysseus's trickery is largely praiseworthy in the *Odyssey*, but Sophocles's *Philoctetes* treats such deceit as lacking nobility and as far less praiseworthy than the truthfulness, pity, and courage of Neoptolemus. Helen receives quite varied treatment as a character and in terms of her moral responsibility across different poetic works from Homer to Euripides. Greek audiences would have encountered not a single monolithic view of ethical questions, but a variety of views in conversation and in conflict.

Such varied presentations encouraged Greek audiences to examine the same problem from multiple perspectives, thus discouraging passivity and encouraging criticism. Especially in light of Athenian practices of competitions in speech for prizes, and the wide audience of Greek tragedy and comedy as part of public religious festivals, poetry and drama constituted a significant part of civic life. Citizens were regularly exposed to a variety of viewpoints both within and across dramatic works.

Moreover, the sophists had already begun to offer alternative forms of education that included poetic criticism by the time Plato was writing, albeit with mixed reception, in Athens and other cities. In Plato's *Protagoras*, a poem by Simonides that criticizes the poet Pittacus places two poets in direct opposition and potentially in conversation with one another on the nature of human excellence. Their opposition also provides Socrates with an occasion to present his own views of human excellence, which stand in contrast to both Pittacus and Simonides.[20] While Socrates argues that literary criticism is as insufficient as a mode of seeking wisdom, the sophists themselves do not treat poetry as wisdom simply to be passively received. Rather, for figures such as Protagoras, poetry can be a starting point for the listener to explore questions such as the nature of virtue, in conversation with the poetic tradition.

Plato's very inclusion of Homer, Hesiod, Simonides, Pittacus, Musaeus, tragedians, and comedians into the dialogue—as material to be examined by Socrates and his friends—displays the necessity of distinguishing between Platonic and Socratic practice. Socrates and Adeimantus criticize the traditional poets for the inadequacy of their moral and theological views, and Socrates bans certain kinds of stories from the ideal city of perfect justice. The ideal city constructed in speech has no need of poets who examine human weakness, vulnerability, moral failure, and the like because it assumes—for the sake of understanding justice conceptually—a city in which all citizens will be perfectly educated and therefore no moral failure will take place. However, no such cities exist in fact, nor does Socrates claim that they are likely to exist in the future. Socrates emphasizes that he offers this model as a paradigm (472c–d), one that is unlikely to exist unless philosophers rule as kings (473c–d). Real cities, however, do include human ethical and political imperfection, and human beings struggle to make sense of death, chance events, and question the nature of the gods in light of human evils. Perhaps poetry about evil is not needed in a city in which all of its citizens are good and its history ideal, but it can be helpful to those who seek virtue while residing in a city of imperfection. The community of those who discuss these matters in the *Republic* is a case in point. Polemarchus will be killed without a trial in the midst of civic war. Thrasymachus possesses a character that Socrates names as "like a wild beast," similar to the image of the tyrant's soul and its many-headed beast (330b, 588c–89a). Socrates later will be killed as a result of his own city's inability to fully understand his philosophical practice as anything other than impiety and the corruption of the youth, when force overcomes persuasion, just as Polemarchus hints that it might (327c). The drama of the dialogue does not allow us to forget the difficulty of evil in the real city. Therefore, the dialogue describes not only ideals of justice but also departures from justice, as in Book Nine's descriptions of multiple cities and souls in decline, or Book Ten's mythical description of choosing a just life among others who choose injustice. The poetry of Plato's *Republic* does not limit itself to ideal figures because its audience does not live in an ideal world.

In Book Two, Socrates returns to the notion of paradigms and images. Socrates says that in the "greater" stories, they will see the "lesser" ones, "for the pattern (*tupos*) must be the same and have the same power in both the greater and the smaller" (377c–d). Socrates uses the term *tupos*, which can be used to describe a figure or an image in sculpture, or more abstractly, a pattern or a model reproduced in many instances in an identical way. Just as the English word "type" can mean an impression of a letter that is made the same way every time—perhaps truer in the days of mechanical typewriters than in the age of computers—but also describe a "character type," as in a play that has a hero, a villain, and set roles, *tupos* communicates something regular that displays a common pattern across many instances. Socrates says that Homer and Hesiod have the same kind of *tupos* or pattern of the gods as the lesser-known poets. Yet their pattern is not a good representation of the gods, any more than a painter who paints something badly and does not represent it well, although he wanted to do so (377e). Here, Socrates borrows from the language of the arts in order to make a metaphysical claim.

Socrates objects to the manner in which the gods are portrayed by Homer and Hesiod for two distinct reasons in these early books.[21] First, he says, young people cannot understand the difference between tales with a "hidden sense" and those that lack one. These tales misshape souls when heard by those who are too young to discern their deeper meaning (378a–e). Second, tales about the god that describe the god as anything other than good are not *true*, and the god must be described as he is, that is, as good and never as the cause of harm or evil things (379a–c). The god does not cause everything, but only good things (379c, 380c). The god does not "step out of" or depart from his own *idea* but instead remains in his own shape, since the god is best and therefore would not become worse through change (380d–81c). Clearly, Socrates wishes to subject at least some theological claims to rational judgment, such that if the claims of theology are against reason, we have reason to reject those claims.

But it is not only the logical content but also the apparent beauty of these poems that Socrates takes to task.[22] As Gabriel Lear has argued, Socrates shows that the beauty of poetry attracts its audience so that what it presents might seem to be good, even if it is not good, because some of its elements are harmonious or it otherwise induces pleasure in an audience.[23] Heroes and gods are especially attractive topics, too, and might lead a listener to think that certain virtues or values are good simply because the gods or heroes possess those particular traits. As Lear puts it, "Beautiful poetry about beautiful people has a tendency to direct our aspirations."[24] Lear persuasively argues that in place of the traditional heroes, Socrates presents the person of virtue as the standard of poetic beauty (see 402c–d). The just person then becomes the "pattern" of beauty, the true hero. Beauty *can* awaken desire for the good. The problem is with what is being described beautifully. Thus, Socrates's discussion does not completely eliminate mention of beauty nor deny that the poets create works that are powerful. Later in his discussion of the good, Socrates will say that the good is the creative cause of what is truly beautiful. Thus true beauty and true goodness ought to harmonize. The problem will not be to get rid of all images or paradigms but rather to find the right kind of image as a paradigm of beauty.

Socrates also has a concern with the hidden sense or *huponoia* of poetry. What is visible in a superficial experience of a poetic work may not be the poem's fullness. In Xenophon's *Symposium*, Socrates briefly makes mention the difficulty of poetry's hidden sense.[25] Socrates states that the rhapsodes seem not to know the *huponoia* of the poetry that they recite (Xen. *Symp.* 3.6). Another character, Niceratus, boasts of his own capacity to teach others to be excellent. He claims to have memorized all of Homer and says he can recite both the *Iliad* and *Odyssey* by heart (Xen. *Symp.* 3.5). Niceratus claims that his knowledge of this poetry can be useful to those who consult with him: "If any of you want to become a householder, political speaker, or general, or become similar to Achilles, Nestor, or Odysseus, consult me" (Xen. *Symp.* 4.6).[26] Niceratus thinks he exceeds the rhapsodes that Socrates has described, insofar as he has internalized the knowledge conveyed by the poet to be his own. Niceratus gives concrete examples: he claims to know how to drive a chariot close to the goalpost without mishap, how to be king, and even how the right use of an onion allows one to enjoy one's drinks more (Xen. *Symp.* 4.6–4.7). Xenophon's text implies that there were at least some individuals who really took Homer to be a manual for life in all sorts of ways, as almost a kind of scripture. Indeed, as Struck has argued, allegorical readers of poetry often regarded the poet more as a "deep well of wisdom" into the basic structures of the cosmos rather than being concerned with the poet's context, historical concerns, or formalist considerations.[27] Niceratus displays this kind of view of Homer as a figure of universal wisdom. (Niceratus's companions, however, do not share his enthusiasm for memorizing Homer and go on to brag about their own, different gifts.) The character of Niceratus is mentioned early on in Plato's *Republic*. He is present with Glaucon and Adeimantus when they first stop Socrates and then go to Polemarchus's house (327c).[28] It is therefore possible that Socrates's comments about an underlying sense are in part directed at Niceratus and others like him. In Xenophon's account, the rhapsodes lack a sense of the *huponoia*, perhaps because they simply recite the material but may not comprehend all of its details. Niceratus is at the other extreme: having memorized and considered the material carefully many times, he claims multiple areas of expertise not normally available to most people, since specializing in a particular craft takes time. In the *Republic*, Socrates rejects this kind of claim that one can be a master of all trades. Each person in the city can only master one craft well, and poetry does not remove the need for the time and care required for such mastery. An approach to poetry like that of Niceratus would seem to make the poets more than human.

Socrates's criticism of the problem of a "hidden sense" suggests a still subtler engagement with Homeric and Hesiodic theology, however. Socrates also implies that poetry may have a greater depth of meaning than its surface sense, and that the underlying sense may be of value if it is accessible. Yet audiences are not always prepared to understand such deeper meanings. To this extent, Socrates shares something with allegorical interpreters of his time who were concerned with symbolic and enigmatic interpretations of poetry.[29] At the start of Book Two, Socrates's main objection is not yet to *mimēsis* more generally. To begin, he only objects to whether tales that have a "hidden sense" can be harmful to those who are young (378c–d). Socrates claims that not everyone is capable of understanding the true meaning of a particular poem, and so the poem can mislead those who listen. In his interpretation of this passage, Bernard Freydburg attends to Socrates's use of the term *huponoia*. He argues that if one looks to some of the passages that Socrates wants to ban—such as Achilles's description of the world of the shades as a terrible, unhappy existence—their deeper meaning is often directly opposed to the meaning that Socrates highlights within the *Republic*. For example, Achilles's famous words as cited in the *Republic* are not primarily about how terrible it is to die but rather "a song of praise for a life oriented toward truth and being," writes Freydburg.[30] The problem is not always with the poem itself but rather with the skillfulness of its interpreters, who may miss a more expansive meaning in favor of a more constricted interpretation.[31]

In developing the just city, an important question is whether we can adequately prepare citizens to discern the *huponoia* of poetry or of *any* form of discourse that has multiple layers. The educative value of any work lies not only in the content of what is being stated but also in the ability of the audience to receive it, to make sense of it, and to engage with the material meaningfully in light of their own social and political context. Socrates expresses considerable skepticism about the capacity of the average citizen to be able to approach poetry in this way. If an audience does not bring a sufficiently sophisticated hermeneutical framework to bear on the content of the poem, the *form* of poetry does not do enough to encourage a critical engagement with its content or to correct misinterpretation.[32] There is little that its author can do.

One possible response to these difficulties is to ban poetry altogether as dangerous. This is the direction in which Socrates goes when he bans the poets from the ideal city. However, even Socrates does not ban all forms of speech that include images, pictures, or stories in favor of some sort of nonmythic language—for he includes myths such as the myth of the "noble lie" in his city and later tells the myth of Er. We know that Socrates thinks about myth as poetic since, in his discussion of Hesiod and Homer, he describes them as "mythmakers" (*muthopoiois*; 377b). Yet to his own Athenian community, still learning about the good and other ideas, Socrates uses imagery to describe the form of the good and the relationship between forms and the objects that they imitate. Thus, rather than eliminating all myth from his philosophical discourse, Socrates reincorporates certain features of poetry, such as myth and imagery, into it. Other features of poetry and drama—such as meter—are abandoned.

The Platonic dialogue also does not banish some problematic elements found in poetry from its discourse; it includes bad characters who offer reasons for their immoral views (e.g., in the character of Thrasymachus);[33] and there is no gymnastics, music, or mathematical education to be found anywhere in it for its audience to practice. Thus for a reader of the dialogue, it is worthwhile to ask this second-order question about what Plato intends for us to experience in reading the dialogue, and what its educative effects might be, in ways that are separable from Socrates's proposals for the ideal city. Plato, after all, lives not in an idealized and constructed just city, but in a real and living city with many kinds of people and views of what a good life looks like. His form of writing, then, needs to try to bring his own reader to learn about justice.

Platonic dialogue encourages active criticism rather than the passive reception of ideas. To this extent, the theoretic vision of justice, in which competing paradigms are presented, is counterbalanced by logical and discursive criticism. Socrates's interlocutors often go along with what Socrates says, but because the arguments are laid out step-by-step according to a logical order, a reader may question the argument's validity anywhere along the way. At times, the interlocutors do object to Socrates's claims and demand further reasons for them, or lead the argument to go in a different direction, as was the case with Glaucon's objection to the "city of pigs."[34] Traditional poetic structures do not in their *own* textual formulations encourage the same kind of departure from an author and his conclusions, although particular interpreters or schools of interpretation may do so. For the most part, readers of Plato have, indeed, responded to the text by looking for what is incomplete or missing in the argument, rather than by passively accepting its ideas. For example, a student of Plato may notice that Socrates gives relatively little reason for his claims that the gods are the "best," an idea that he relies upon for his later claims that the gods must be changeless. This idea that a god is wholly good is simply assumed. Especially in the context of traditional Greek theology, a listener might ask whether the gods are, in fact, perfect, and what kind of basis there might be for this belief. Or, a reader might explore a different option: In what sense is a god who is changeless a being to whom to make sacrifices at all? How could an economy of sacrifice function in light of divine perfection? Socrates does not address these questions, but at each juncture in his argument, a reader may demand further argument or exploration of any particular point. The dialogical form in which each step in the argument is laid out encourages the rational engagement of the audience at each juncture of the argument in a way that traditional poetic claims about the gods do not. While this is a familiar feature of philosophical argument for modern readers, in the early context of Platonic philosophy, it is a notable departure from usual poetic forms—even though it also stands in continuity with allegorical and symbolic approaches to poetry that had a degree of sophistication in their care for the "hidden sense" of poetry.[35] Thus, active criticism is a good for at least two reasons: First, the claims of poetry may be untrue, and without the capacity to respond actively to false claims, an audience will fail to learn what is true, or to at least reject falsehoods so that truth might later be pursued. Second, with respect to matters of justice, the Platonic reader lives in a world that is not perfectly just. But recognizing injustice itself requires the capacity to be critical of one's own social and political context. Thus, to desire to be just in a political context that is not yet just also requires this critical capacity.

At the same time, the retention of characters and the multivocity of the dialogue brings certain features of drama into philosophy that are no longer common to much of our own contemporary practice of philosophical argument, at least in its written form. Plato's juxtaposition of characters who stand in disagreement with one another—about questions like justice and even about the good of poetry itself—encourages his own audience to take up a critical stance, rather than merely passively receiving Plato's poetic creation.[36] The reader has a choice to make about which argument is better, and why, among different options offered.[37] While it is clear that Socrates is a better thinker than, say, Cephalus, no claim is made that Socrates's arguments are complete or that they must be accepted as such. As Blondell has argued, Glaucon and Adeimantus remain friendly and interested in the positive construction of ideas but also resistant where they think it appropriate.[38] (As such, they represent the mix of friendliness and enmity that characterizes the philosophical "dog" metaphor [373d]!) The Platonic audience is invited into an exercise of criticism by the form in which the work is written, in which the joints of its arguments are laid out to be seen and characters are responsive to one another. As Frank argues, the dialogue is a written text that is not bounded by the constraints of a performed theatrical piece and therefore can be read and reread, inviting a deeper engagement and criticism.[39] Moreover, Socrates also interjects comments about his own doubts at different points along the way that discourages dogmatic reception of the ideas.[40] Indeed, the form of the dialogue shares more in common with oral conversation than with either a passively received performance of a play or a written manual that is to be read and understood dogmatically. While a degree of passivity may be philosophically useful for education—as when one listens to another person and tries to learn from his suggestions—the capacity to reflect on the ideas that others present is also crucial for the exercise of rationality.

As Segal shows, some characteristics of Socratic poetry are shared in common with Homeric poetry: (a) a quest and drive for unity and simplicity out of multiplicity;[41] (b) the use of specific figures of speech such as similes and metaphors to characterize human life in a prelogical way;[42] and (c) the use of mythological language to address topics that are at the margins of human knowledge and experience. At the same time, Plato places such mythological language in the context of a larger philosophical discussion that explicitly raises epistemological questions about poetry, imagery, and myth in a way that Homer does not.

As in both tragedy and comedy, Plato's form of writing includes the portrayal of characters who are to be actively imagined by the reader. The characters sometimes undertake dramatized actions in relation to one another—for example, when the slave boy pulls on Socrates's cloak (372b) or Cephalus exits the scene in order to go perform a sacrifice (331d). The reader is thus encouraged to form a mental image of those who speak and those who listen in the dialogue and not only to absorb the abstracted ideas in propositional form. The arguments are presented not as disembodied arguments but rather as arguments spoken by characters who have histories, whether those histories are real or invented by Plato as author. Along with an idea, we are given a *voice*. The *Republic*'s arguments arise within from life—in this case old age as well as the dramatic context of civil war informs the general import of the question of justice and whether it is a good.[43] Ideas are shown to arise out of the lived experiences of the characters, as will be shown in the cases of Cephalus, Polemarchus, and Thrasymachus. The reader is invited to integrate word and deed, speech and character, through acts of the imagination.

Platonic dialogue departs from the modes of the tragedians and comedians in requiring the audience's rational engagement with the topics at hand in several ways. Platonic dialogue demands active interpretation. Disagreements between the ideas of characters within the dialogue and tensions between the ideas of some of those characters and other elements of the text require a critical, actively hermeneutical approach to the text. An audience member who listens both to Thrasymachus's claim that the unjust life is happier and to Socrates's argument that the just life is happier must himself enter more deeply into the argument than she would be required if only the Socratic argument were present. For example, she must ask herself whether the charges that Thrasymachus leveled against Socrates—that he is naïve and simple in his belief that justice is always better—are ones that

Socrates answers adequately. She may even find additional reasons not offered by Socrates to respond to the Thrasymachean point of view, mimicking the argument and counterargument of the dialogue. Of course, there are numerous examples of argument and counterargument in both Greek tragedy and comedy. For example, in Sophocles's *Antigone*, Creon and Haemon argue back and forth about whether Antigone ought to be punished, in ways that also lead to a more general discussion of the role of a good king, and whether flexibility is a virtue for a ruler. The *Philoctetes* features the youth Neoptolemus actively struggling with the moral question of whether to be obedient to his commanding officer or to act with mercy toward a wounded man. Aristophanes raises serious questions about the value of war in plays such as *Lysistrata*, and the *agōn* is a constant structural feature of comedy. Reflection on political and moral values through the use of argument and counterargument is by no means the sole purview of the Platonic dialogue.

However, the dialogue form differs from tragedy and comedy in that the amount of argument relative to dramatic action is far higher in Platonic dialogue than in tragedy or comedy. Perhaps this goes without saying, but the question of the proportionality of word to action is itself of interest. Plato continues to include affective and rhetorical elements in his dialogues, but in a way where the exercise of reason is supervisory over affect rather than allowing affect either to dominate or to disappear. For example, many of the bawdiest and most banal aspects of comedy are absent from the dialogue, even if moments can be humorous. Just as Socrates will go on to say in the just soul, each part gets its due, but reason rules over *how* those different kinds of desire are to be given their due, in the dialogue form, we also see reason integrate affect. It is precisely in the experience of the dialogue through acts of the imagination that reason and affect come together, as one takes up not only abstract arguments, but arguments embodied by the characters in which the engagement of many different aspects of their soul is visible—for example, in Glaucon's repeated concern with honor, or Cephalus's reference to the effects of old age on his body's appetites. The dialogue form is integrative of intellect, spirit, and desire in ways that continually reinforce that rational judgment of these interior forces must predominate. This is different, however, than saying that affect or spirit have *no* place to play for the dialogue's audience. Indeed, at the end of Plato's *Symposium*, we hear that Socrates insists that a skillful person might be able to write both comedy and tragedy (*Symp.* 223d), perhaps a reference to the kinds of aims Plato himself possessed.

In rhetorical practice, *ēthopoeia*, or the creation of character, takes place when a speaker attempts to make his own character look virtuous in order to gain the sympathy of his audience and to make his own ideas more persuasive. Plato sometimes uses this technique with his own characters, as when Socrates compares himself to Achilles in the *Apology*.[44] Sometimes, the reverse is true: we are presented with a bad character who possesses some defect—for example, Thrasymachus. However, Plato as author does not simply present such characters unfavorably so that we will be less likely to adopt their views, the way a politician might cast aspersions on his opponent's character so that his ideas will be less persuasive. In the *Republic*, Plato undertakes something different: he offers lengthy reasons as to why a character's ideas are inadequate and, through dramatizing something about their character, also asks us to consider how the holding of such ideas has practical consequences for the character who holds them. That is, the Platonic dialogue asks us to look at specific beliefs and ideas and to note the connections between ideas and character formation. Whereas traditional *ēthopoeia* uses the development of good or bad character in order to elevate or to malign a person's ideas, Plato's dialogues begin with ideas in such a way that we see the good or bad consequences of these ideas for a life well lived.[45] He practices a kind of *ēthopoeia* in reverse: rather than suggesting that bad people's ideas should not to be believed simply because they are bad people, Plato demonstrates how poorly defended ideas produce problems in the characters of people who hold these beliefs. We can partly evaluate Thrasymachus's arguments by seeing that his beliefs about justice have not led him to become a happy person, despite his claim that the unjust life produces the greatest happiness. Making these connections between idea and life takes place by acts of imagination in which the reader envisions a particular life—that of Cephalus, Polemarchus, Thrasymachus, Glaucon, Adeimantus, and Socrates—and so can imaginally grasp the connection between belief and action.[46]

Plato's manner of inclusion of this critique of poetry only heightens a demand for sensitive interpretation. As audiences of the *Republic*, we *do* hear myths of the gods behaving immorally in a way that the citizens of the perfect city would not be allowed to hear them. If hearing these ideas is so dangerous, an audience member may wonder, Why am I hearing these ideas discussed now, and what differentiates my own experience of poetry from that of these hypothetically naïve citizens? Plato does not provide exact answers to such a question but rather sets up a hermeneutic of dissonance.

Members of the Platonic audience may experience a kind of dissonance between the political rules set out for the idealized city in speech and the practice that Socrates seems to be following in offering myths as part of his own critical discourse. The dialogue thus encourages mythological language to be received differently than in the passive manner in which Cephalus and Polemarchus treat it, that is, as automatically authoritative.[47]

Socrates's discussion of truth telling and lying also helps us to better understand his evaluation of poetic images. Socrates rejects some poetry because it is not truthful in content. He possesses a deep commitment to seek the truth. However, this commitment to the truth is not about the rejection of all nonpoetic ways of speaking, as his discussion of the *pseudos* (lie) makes clear. Socrates says that all gods and human beings hate a lie (*pseudos*), especially a lie in the soul, which is "ignorance in the soul of the man who has been lied to. For the lie in speeches is a kind of imitation (*mimēma*) of the affection of the soul, a phantom (*eidōlon*) of it that comes into being after it, and not quite an unadulterated lie" (382b–c). Lying is bad, but apparently not because the liar violates a moral rule, for instance, some kind of Kantian categorical imperative. Rather, Socrates rejects lies because they reflect a bad image (*eidōlon*) in the soul. Socrates's main concern is with the way in which the soul itself is changed by lying, and how lying indicates a problem in the soul. Indeed, it is surprising to find that for Socrates, the problem is not so much with false words as with "false souls," on the grounds that false speeches are mere imitations of a state of the soul. Here, Socrates reverses the primacy of speech to soul that one might expect in discussing truth value. On one contemporary understanding, we might identify a lie as a proposition that is false that the speaker knows to be false. A person that speaks such a false proposition might be said to be "false" on the basis of both this intention and the truth value of his statement. But here Socrates's main concern is with how a lie in speech reveals a corresponding defect in the soul of the person who *speaks* the *pseudos*. Telling a lie indicates that the soul is not appropriately formed. The lie's status as mere *eidōlon* comes from its emergence from a soul's limits, and how it images a faulty soul, more than how it is a false image or representation of states of affairs in the exterior world. The state of the soul is primary.

Socrates also excludes from the city stories that harm the souls of those who *listen* to them. For example, young people must not hear that the gods are the cause of strife and the destruction of a house, as Aeschylus insists in saying, "God plants the cause in mortals when he wants to destroy a house utterly" (380a–b). A thoughtful playgoer might understand Aeschylus's claim as metaphorically articulating the seemingly insurmountable difficulty of escaping from a cycle of retributive violence. A young child, however, might have a different experience. We can imagine one that comes away from such a play fearful that a god wishes to destroy his own family, or who cynically comes to believe that human responsibility is meaningless in the face of fate. Socrates's discussion of poetry and falsehood emphasizes the states of the soul of both those who speak and those who listen, more than the factual content of propositions.

Socrates allows for the *pseudos* also to have a role in the city in two kinds of situations. A tale in speeches may be used against one's enemies or to talk about things of which we do not know the truth—but in which we try to make the lie as much like the truth as possible (382d). In this second kind of case, the term "lie" is perhaps not an ideal translation of *pseudos*, as the *pseudos* seems to refer to an account that stems from a lack of knowledge rather than deliberate deception about a truth that we do know. Mythological speech is not completely eliminated from Socrates's own discourse but instead continues to be an important part of his philosophical practice when the precise nature of something is not fully accessible. He tells us that the demonic and the divine are wholly free from lies, that they have no use for them, since they are neither ignorant nor fearful (382e). But falsehoods are fitting, at times, to those beings living in between the divine and the demonic: namely, for us human beings. Here, Socrates does not seem to have in mind only cases where deceptions are acceptable for moral reasons, for example, in order to stop a mad friend from doing something evil (382c). There also exists a need for a manner of speaking that is not exacting because no precise description is or could become fully available to human beings.[48] For example, as I will argue in the last chapter in this book, the myth of Er is not a precise, literal account of what occurs to the human being after death. Yet such images are better than more exacting attempts at description since there is no precise account of life after death available, and yet to talk meaningfully about death is necessary to fully address the nature of justice. A *pseudos* there is not intended to deceive but rather to express through imagery the limits of what cannot be definitively known.

In Book Three, Socrates explores the ways in which listening to or performing poetry can change and shape the soul, in a way that can help us to better address these sorts of philosophical difficulties. Socrates begins by looking at whether listening to poetry helps us to acquire moral virtues. According to Socrates, men should not hear stories that will make them fear death, since these stories will not make them courageous (386a–b).

Fearful images of death and instances of men weeping and grieving will be removed from the ideal city, since such things discourage self-sufficiency and encourage bearing up with misfortune (387d–e). Only bad men and women are allowed to partake in such actions in poetic works (387e). Neither should great men or the gods be allowed laughter as it demonstrates being overpowered by emotions (388e). Moderation must be demonstrated in poetic works, so that citizens will be both obedient and moderate in their pursuit of appetitive pleasures (389d–e). Moreover, actions such as Achilles's dragging the body of Hector around by chariot, which show disdain for gods and human beings alike, and poetry that shows the love of gifts and money must also be excluded (390e–91c). No god or child of a god can be shown to commit crimes such as rape, since the gods cannot be a cause of such evils (391d–e). Thus poetry ought to avoid impiety. Neither should poems or prose writers state "that many happy men are unjust, and many wretched ones just, and that doing injustice is profitable if one gets away with it, but justice is someone else's good and one's own loss. We'll forbid them to say such things and order them to sing and tell tales about the opposites of these things" (302b). In short, Socrates argues that poetry ought to encourage justice, piety, courage, and moderation and discourage their opposing vices.

Socrates's claims may raise for the reader a number of objections, although Adeimantus eagerly agrees with Socrates's assessment. For one, we might reasonably question whether excluding certain ideas in poetry would, in fact, remove or moderate emotions such as grief or the fear of death. Would a father not passionately mourn a dead son if he had never heard poetry about Priam's abject grief in mourning Hector? One might understand poetry to be expressive of a common, if not universal, human experience of grieving the death of a loved one rather than as the cause of grief. Plato's *Phaedo* itself displays such a picture, when Socrates's friends mourn his passing despite his consoling recommendations against tears. There, Socrates is the only one who does not cry. Or, could a person cease to fear death altogether simply by removing poetry about Hades? Socrates seems not to consider the possibility of poetry as expressive of emotions rather than as their cause. Indeed, in Book Ten, Socrates notes a pleasure associated with grief mediated through such imaginary accounts (605d–e), but such a deeper access to grief and its meanings might well prepare one for anticipating and making sense of grief when experienced firsthand.

Neither does Socrates consider the possibility of poetry as cultivating a deeper understanding of bad behavior in others without undertaking bad actions ourselves. Later, he will speak of the importance of judges who can understand evil, but not through committing evil acts firsthand (409b–c). Poetry has the power to provide such a mediated experience to those who witness it; one need not have personally suffered a loss quite like the loss of Patroclus that Achilles has suffered in order to understand the depths of his rage in the river Scamander. Moreover, one may witness such rage with a mix of sympathy and distancing, recognizing both a degree of understanding of Achilles's raging anger in his grief, and its destructive power. Few will walk away from listening to Achilles and decide it would be good to rage senselessly against loss or to impiously mistreat an enemy's body. However, one might walk away with a better understanding of anger or rage, and the problems with resisting our vulnerability to loss and mortality.

Socrates does not address such objections in this section of dialogue, nor does Adeimantus offer them. However, Plato as author does include within the dialogue that he writes precisely the kinds of passages that Socrates excludes from his ideal city, for Socrates and Adeimantus quote the very passages that he wishes to eliminate, and we as readers of the dialogue listen to them. Yet these miniature performances of snippets of Homer, Hesiod, or Simonides are interwoven into a philosophical analysis of what sorts of virtues they might encourage or discourage. They are not performed but rather are mediated through the acts of reading and criticism. This intermixing of poetic content and detached analysis is a significant shift from the simple performative presentation of poetry to an audience who passively listens.[49]

Socrates next takes up the problem of the style (*lexis*) of poetry, contrasting narration (*diēgēsis*) with imitation (*mimēsis*), while acknowledging the possibility of a mixed form. Narrative style is one in which a poetic work describes, for example, what various actions Achilles did in a battle in the Trojan War, whereas a mimetic style directly takes on the voice of a character. While *mimēsis* will later be used in a slightly different sense in Book Ten to describe the work of painters who copy or represent the objects that they paint, here in Book Three, Socrates seems to mean by *mimēsis* a form of speech in which either an actor or speaker takes on the role as if he is the person in question—mimicry of another's voice or actions.[50] As Golden argues, *mimēsis* can include creative acts beyond what the English "imitation" implies. Its earlier usages refer to activities such as dance, or interpretive and creative acts. *Mimēsis* can refer to much more than mere mimicry or making a copy.[51] It can include embodying, imitating, enacting, and creating the presence of a person in a vivid way. Gerald Else has argued that Socrates's specific use of *mimēsis* in distinction from narrative style is his own invention: while *mimēsis* was used to refer to a mimelike character, as in comedies, before Plato it was not previously used to refer to tragic actors.[52] According to Else, this categorization of *mimēsis* and narration as two mutually exclusive styles by which different forms of performed *logos* are to be conceptually distinguished is formulated in the *Republic* itself.[53]

In his account of mimetic style, Socrates does not clearly differentiate between the poet's act of composition, the actor's work in performing a dramatic work, or the audience's reception of such performed works. Making such distinctions might be helpful. After all, actors experience performed works differently than do the poets who compose them, and reading a text is a different experience as well. Perhaps an actor who plays the part of a vicious character is affected differently than one who witnesses it in live performance, or one who reads the same work without a performative element. Such nuances are left unexplored.[54] However, their treatment as a whole may be related to the close connection between written texts and speechmaking in Greek intellectual culture in Plato's time. Rosalind Thomas has argued that late fifth- and early fourth-century written texts were "servants to the performance"—even written texts were read aloud in groups more than silently, and writing often presented as a mere reminder of the oral and interpersonal performance.[55] Epic along with tragedy and comedy were performed, although the sophists included the analysis of poetry as part of their educational practices in ways that may have required some reliance on the written text.[56] But even here a text might be read aloud as part of a discussion or recollected from one's having previously heard its content, rather than from having read it. As Thomas has shown, in the *Parmenides*, Zeno's text is read aloud and then discussed, and Socrates treats the ideas of Anaxagoras similarly, not read privately so much as heard aloud in the marketplace. Moreover, Plato presents sophists such as Gorgias, Protagoras, and Hippias mostly in terms of their oral *epideixis*. Even some Hippocratic medical texts are epideictic.[57]

Especially in light of such a primacy of oral performance over writing, we can understand this unified treatment of *mimēsis* to be found in a shared commonality between poet, performer, and audience: in each case, the person in question mentally takes on and, to some extent, sympathizes with a character whose words are performed. Authors naturally develop a kind of understanding and even sympathy with the characters that they write—even if they are immoral—if the presentation is to be realistic. So, too, do actors, even those who focus on the mechanics of dramatic actions and are not what today would be called "method" actors. Audiences become imaginatively engaged in the characters whose performances are witnessed through a limited kind of mirroring of emotions that takes place in seeing and hearing others' emotions.[58] If we take Socrates's main concern to be less with the formal qualities of written poetry and more with the psychological experiences of poet, actor, and audience, then we can see a basic difference between narration and imitation. Third-person narrated accounts engage our imaginative sympathetic identification far less than first-person performances where an individual speaks as if he is another person. Thus, for example, when Socrates says that many poems give a "bad image" (*eikazēi kakōs*) of the gods and heroes, just as a painter offers a poor image of what he paints (377e), we can take this to describe the image in the audience's *imagination* and not the representative content of the poem (though Book Ten will also go on to explore this aspect of painting and images).[59] This imaginative identification has significant effects on those who perform, witness, and even those who write poetry.

One problem with dramatic imitations is that they are not true: the speaker disguises himself as if he is a character that he is not. As Pappas has argued, *mimēsis* is also treated as morally problematic in other works such as Aristophanes's *Frogs*, which treats *mimēsis* in terms of representational acts that are fraudulent, artificial, and obscure one's authentic identity.[60] Of course, when watching an actor act or a poet recite, we *know* that the disguise is a conceit; we are not actually deceived into thinking that the actor is the character that he portrays. Neither does an actor really think that he is Strepsiades or Achilles. However, the danger of imitation, Socrates argues, is that it leads the person who is speaking as if he were a character to *become* more like that character, through the very act of imitation. By taking on the words and actions of the character, the imitative actor becomes more like the character that he imitates and can be deeply changed by the experience, just as someone who repeats many dance moves eventually might become a dancer herself. If the person being imitated is a bad man, then there is a particular danger of corruption in the process of taking on these traits, and the guardians especially ought not to undertake such risks.[61] Therefore, only entirely good men may be imitated. Moreover, the reception of such poetic acts is essentially passive: in imitating another without intervening relevant questions as to whether such imitation is good to undertake, the soul becomes passively shaped rather than determined according to philosophical evaluation.[62] Here we see demonstrated the power and danger of the coupling of acts of the imagination with embodied performances that increase their mimetic power.

Even if acting were to be limited to only some of the population, this skill would disrupt the scheme of one job for each citizen. Socrates says it must be banned (394d–95c). No single person can be skilled at many things that require specialization, yet the poet pretends to do exactly that. To this extent, he is deceiving both others and himself about the scope of his knowledge. Similarly, Socrates also argues that no poet is a skillful writer of both comedy and tragedy. Different actors, rhapsodes, and poets are also usually skilled for performing different genres. Socrates says that if we were to find a man who *could* imitate many things, "we would fall before such a man as sacred, wonderful, and pleasing; but we would say that there is no such man among us in the city, nor is it lawful for such a man to be born there. We would send him to another city, with myrrh poured over his head and crowned with wool, while we ourselves would use a more austere and less pleasing poet and teller of tales for the sake of benefit, one who would imitate the style of the decent man and would say what he says in those models that we set down as laws in the beginning, when we undertook to educate the soldiers" (398a–b).

However, Socrates's claims about *lexis* in the ideal city and Platonic *lexis* can also be distinguished from one another. Plato's dialogues depart from traditional poetic performances while retaining some features of poetry that are reappropriated in order to address some of these Socratic objections.[63] Here, let me focus on three ways in which Platonic *lexis* overcomes some of the difficulties with both passive listening and imitative performance: through devices of irony, character-based argument, and narrative that displays a care for appropriate responses to emotions.[64] These devices suggest that there is a different way to respond to poetry than to ban it altogether. Instead, one can harness some of the powers of poetry for philosophical purposes—where philosophy is understood as not only a particular activity of rational calculation, but the exercise of reason in relation to the whole of one's soul and the whole of one's world in its often imperfect reality.

First, Platonic irony is a central feature of the dialogue.[65] Instances of irony need not be understood simply as total reversals of the Socratic position within a dialogue. As Griswold has argued, irony exists when Plato's practice departs from the ideas of its characters, or when the audience knows something about the characters that is unknown to them.[66] Such ironic moments are meant to be understood by the audience of the dialogue and are not merely lapses in the author's noticing of a conflict or tension.[67] As the next chapter will discuss, an audience of Plato's contemporaries would know that Polemarchus will die when the oligarchy takes over the city, not long after this dramatically enacted conversation, though none of its characters can know this fact. Knowing of his death in a civil war informs a more robust reading of his definition of justice as helping friends and harming enemies. Here in Book Three, there is also an enacted irony when Socrates raises legitimate and important questions about poetry when poetry also forms a significant part of the Platonic dialogue. Homer and Hesiod are banned from the ideal city but included in the dialogue. Plato describes a *katabasis* that opens the dialogue when Socrates speaks in the first person of descending into the Piraeus, one that is reminiscent of *katabasis* poetry and mythology, even though imitative style and poetic images are rejected as inappropriate in the same text.[68] In other words, in the *Republic*, poetic criticism takes place at two levels: First, in this conversation in the Piraeus, poetry is *neither* banned nor passively received but rather presented for rational analysis and criticism. Second, we can note places where the specific matters banned by Socrates persist in the Platonic text: for example, in presenting Thrasymachus who advocates an unjust life, a person who is exactly the sort of character who will be banned from any poetry in the ideal city.

What is an audience meant to do with such textual irony? First, it is important to acknowledge that some of the problems with poetry that Socrates expresses are real problems for the genesis of justice in the city or soul. Irony is not a reason to reject all of these Socratic claims as superfluous. Clearly, Homeric education is seen as destructive in the way that it is currently received, as the basis of moral and civic education. Still, the Platonic audience is being asked to consider Socrates's arguments with care: perhaps children ought not hear stories of parricide, or deceitful gods, if we wish them to become just adults. Perhaps some adults are also ill equipped to interpret poetic performances and their hidden senses. However, our consideration of Plato's meaning should begin, but not end, there. We can also approach the performance of poetic works with a more critical hermeneutic in mind. Rather than banning all poetry, as the perfect city in speech will do, we the Platonic readers are asked to do as Socrates and Adeimantus do: to approach all poetic expressions with a critical set of questions about their content and style. In other words, rather than receiving poetic performances passively—either as authoritative sources about the life of virtue, or as mere entertainment—the Platonic reader can imitate Socrates's and Adeimantus's enacting of a philosophical approach to poetry.[69] Socrates models for us a procedure of moving between the passive experience of a poetic work—since his capacity to speak aloud many passages from memory suggests close familiarity—and the philosophical discussion of such passages. Socrates does not shelter himself from experiencing poetry but rather engages it with rational discourse.

Thus, Platonic irony does not necessarily reverse the Socratic position about problematic values regarding gods or the heroes, or the dangers of imitation. It rather invites a different approach to addressing what we are to *do* about the power of poetry, especially as a question of politics. One political solution is to ban all instances of such poetry, but another approach is to prepare citizens to encounter bad ideas, even beautifully presented bad ideas, and to educate others in the resources to analyze what the difficulties are and why. Socrates, Glaucon, Adeimantus, and the rest do not reside in a perfect city with perfectly educated citizens whose world has been prestructured by Socrates to include no harmful practices. In fact, they reside in a city that is more or less in a state of civil war, with radically divided ideas of what constitutes the just and the good. These citizens (and noncitizens) of Athens, arguing with one another in the world of the Piraeus, need to learn how to respond to poetry, rhetoric, and claims to wisdom. It will not be enough for them to be educated to be good and yet stay unprepared to defend against an argument like that of Thrasymachus. Glaucon and Adeimantus may not have had the perfect education of the guardians, but they are basically committed to a life of justice. They are sons of Ariston, children of a man whose name literally means "good." Yet they find themselves unprepared to defend Socrates's claims against those of Thrasymachus. Would a guardian who had been sheltered from all such arguments be any better off? We can suppose that such guardians will be habituated to desire and to choose the good but not especially well prepared to counter bad ideas. To this extent, Plato seems to recognize a difficulty that Socrates his character does not: philosophical thought requires a capacity for hermeneutics, for interpreting rather than only passively receiving poetry. As Gadamer has argued, irony opens us up to be capable of deeper hermeneutics of questioning in whatever speech, art, or text we might encounter.[70] Irony is not the only means by which our philosophical questions might be deepened, but it is one means that Plato uses.

Second, Platonic dialogue is performative, although not in the same way as a staged play or a sung epic.[71] As far as we know, Platonic dialogues were not performed with costumes, music, or a stage. To this extent, some of the emotionally arousing elements of dramatic performance are absent from the dialogue. However, it is likely that the dialogues were read aloud by Plato's students rather than only read by solitary readers.[72] In this case, the reader-students are simultaneously those who "perform" and those who inquire into the topics about which the performance concerns itself. There is an identity between the "actor" (if one may use the term loosely) and the "audience." In the case of a solitary reader, this identity would be complete. Readers will also imaginatively take on *all* the different "parts of the play" and so move between identifying with Cephalus, Polemarchus, Socrates, Thrasymachus, Glaucon, and Adeimantus. In Plato's *Sophist*, thought is described as "the soul's conversation with itself." Plato provides for the reader/performer of his dialogue an example of philosophical thinking to imitate. That is, by moving between not only argument and counterargument but also between one character's weltanschauung and another's, the reader/performer comes to understand different philosophical positions and so can deepen the possibilities of thinking through problems and the various dimensions of a particular question, such as "What is justice?"

Moreover, since these positions are presented as belonging to persons, and not as disembodied arguments, the Platonic reader/performer has occasion to understand the psychological as well as logical motives behind holding various views. Plato writes the character of Thrasymachus as an easily angered, disrespectful, beastlike person who also is more skilled in argument than, say, Cephalus. A reader/performer can perhaps see that there is a connection between the character of Thrasymachus and the views that he espouses: perhaps, most noticeably, Thrasymachus is not happy, despite his pursuit of a manner of living that he claims ought to make a person happy. Cephalus focuses on mercantile notions of justice because this is the day-to-day life that he leads, that of a merchant. His actions inform his concepts as much as the reverse is true. Plato's skillful combining of character and philosophical argument allows for some of the benefits of performative works—such as audience identification and sympathy for taking on views that are not one's own—with the rational analysis of philosophy, which in other forms of *poiēsis* can only take place after the play or performance has ended. Performance and criticism are never separated for long within a Platonic dialogue.

Plato's approach to the emotions is also different from the approach that Socrates proposes for the ideal city, although Plato clearly favors the Socratic view of courage, wisdom, self-mastery, and other virtues. The dialogue moves dialectically between human emotions and passions, and a rational engagement with such emotions, that is, with the thoughts and presuppositions that can respond to and guide the emotions. As Schultz has argued, Socrates himself demonstrates good emotional self-regulation in a number of dialogues, when he serves as the narrator of events. Socrates displays for the Platonic reader how he responds to different emotional experiences, such as being frightened by Thrasymachus's sudden shouting (336b, 336d), by asking Thrasymachus to be gentler and to correct any of Socrates's mistakes with argument rather than to act harshly (336d–e). The dialogue shows a different way to respond to the emotions, with responses grounded in rational argument presented as the best. Thrasymachus becomes enraged and suggests Socrates needs a wet nurse and someone to wipe his runny nose (343a–b). Cephalus finds the argument beyond him and so leaves (331d). At the beginning of Book Four, Adeimantus interrupts, pulling on Socrates's sleeve the same way that Polemarchus's slave had pulled on Socrates's cloak in order to forbid him from leaving (327c). In contrast, Socrates responds to Thrasymachus's anger calmly and with the use of reason. Later in the dialogue, he even calls him a "friend," thus demonstrating in his own action that responding to injustice by remaining just is a better way to respond than to trade one injustice for another. He asks Polemarchus to consider reason instead of force as a way to convince Socrates to stay and talk longer (327e). Socrates is patient with his interlocutors, and he willingly follows the argument where it goes, even into unexpected places, like the wind (394d). Whereas Socrates eliminates from all poetry good men who have complex emotional responses, Plato includes his own brothers, Glaucon and Adeimantus, who are both committed to seeking and understanding justice and yet also at times overly passionate, perhaps too willing to choose war and luxury over peace and simplicity—in short, imperfect people with not yet fully perfect souls. The reader of the Platonic dialogue has many places to "enter in" to this discourse, both through argument and through mimetic identification and exploration of a variety of characters.[73] Such character exploration is more than the mere trading of one value for another, however, since reason itself is portrayed favorably as a capacity to respond skillfully to emotion. Just as in Book Four, Socrates will argue that in the just soul, reason rules over the appetites and over spirit. Socrates as a Platonic character displays what this might look like in an imperfect city with a variety of different, imperfect citizens who comprise it. Philosophical argument serves as a kind of *therapeia* for the passions, and the poetry of the dialogue form allows us to see this in action.

The Platonic dialogue's approach to *mimēsis* is also different than Socrates's total banishment of it from the city. The *Republic* itself as a Platonic dialogue is a form that is *both* narrated and imitative.[74] On the one hand, Socrates tells us the whole story, narrating it to an unnamed interlocutor. He begins with telling his own audience that he went down to Piraeus and describes his own action and the actions of other characters. On the other hand, the *Republic* is also imitative at many points, insofar as there are lengthy passages told in the voices of the characters rather than being told entirely in the third person, as Socrates thinks would be best when concerning oneself with vicious characters. A reader takes on the voice of the characters as he reads the text—at least until the myth of Er, when its characters' stories are told via indirect discourse. While Socrates allows for the imitation only of good men in the perfect city and narrative descriptions of all others, Plato's Thrasymachus speaks in his own words as he advocates the transgression of all ordinary boundaries of justice if one can escape the penalties.[75] Thus, Plato must have seen *some* value in imitation, even if it is bad men who are being imitated. The mimetic quality of reading Thrasymachus's words as if one were Thrasymachus, for example, is psychologically more affecting than, say, reading a one-paragraph summary of Thrasymachus's views. Depending on the reader, a particular character's understanding may feel especially insightful, or problematic, or challenging, or disturbing, when such a voice is taken on.

Platonic dialogue thus includes *mimēsis*, but its mimetic quality encourages the reader to undertake a process of critical distance, especially by imitating the character of Socrates. Perhaps a reader who initially most identifies with Thrasymachus when first reading the dialogue over time will be shaped through mimetic imitation to be more like Socrates after time spent in the dialogues. Indeed, the *Republic* itself makes reference to this phenomenon among Socrates's living followers: many young people who followed Socrates *imitated* him, comparing them to puppies who delighted in tearing to pieces others' arguments (539b). However, these young people eventually grew to be cynical of the possibility of learning anything true, remaining only with the destructive potential of argumentation that can tear down arguments. Platonic dialogue engages its readers in *mimēsis* that differs from these youthful imitations of Socrates. For a Platonic reader mimetically imitates both the construction and discovery of new ideas. Some ideas are torn down, but others are built up, such that real learning takes places, even when a problem ends in aporia. In addition, this mimetic engagement with Socrates takes place through the mediation of a written dialogue rather than through verbally attacking one's fellow citizens, as some of the historical Socrates's young followers seem to have done. Socrates may aggressively expose the problematic views of his companions in conversation, but as an author, Plato approaches teaching in a manner different from both the historical Socrates and the poets. Plato does not eliminate *mimēsis* from his dialogues but rather harnesses the power of *mimēsis* so that we can practice being more philosophical in our approach to the opinions and beliefs that we encounter in others and in ourselves. Sufficient imitation of a philosopher's way of thinking about ideas helps one to become a philosopher oneself.[76]

At the same time, narration has its place. Socrates's narrative gives the Platonic audience information that is not otherwise available, such as noticing that Thrasymachus looks almost like an animal, an image that the many-headed beast imagery of Book Ten will also pick up on. Perhaps the Thrasymachean view is less appealing if the one who holds the view is shown to be at the mercy of his own emotions, easily set off and angered, while the more moderate, justice-loving Socrates remains calm. The narrative is, of course, informed by Socrates's own way of seeing things. To this extent, the dialogue is perspectival and told from the point of view of an idealized philosopher. As Schultz has argued, different characters in the *Republic* show different ways of attempting to master their emotions, with varying success.[77] The result is that the mix of imitation and narration allows a reader/performer to both take on different points of view about justice (and other topics) and also to step back and evaluate these views. Imitation and narration together produce a dual movement from identification with a thinker to removing oneself from that character's views and evaluating them from the "outside."

Why, then, include the Socratic view of censorship here at all, if we cannot equate it with a Platonic vision of best educational practice? For one, Socrates correctly argues that poetry and narrative have tremendous power on the human psyche. There is an educative and moral power to art; poetry is not simply morally neutral. Children especially, but sometimes also adults, can suffer and be misshaped from the wrong kinds of influences, especially if they are not taught how to discern a *huponoia*. Therefore, we cannot separate the question of a just city from the question of what it means to educate its citizens, and poetry is one of the most powerful educators. The philosophical dialogue, however, uses the power of poetic form to increase the audience's capacity to argue about any given topic, while engaging imaginatively in the viewpoints of its characters. Plato accomplishes this in part through the multivocity of different characters within the dialogue and the reader's practice of imitating multiple perspectives as a way of deepening the possibilities of thought. A reader who has encountered and has thought through the objection that injustice may be more beneficial than justice is far *better* prepared to choose justice in challenging circumstances than one who has never considered the temptations of injustice before. Yet she has not done this through experimenting with unjust acts. Her commitment to justice will be deeper after she has considered what motivates unjust people to act as they do, and why they think that justice is better. Monolithic views of heroes may be adequate for children or idealized citizens in perfectly just societies, but encountering objections to one's deepest commitments is necessary for more mature seekers of the good living in more complex societies. Plato's readers have always lived in an imperfect, nonutopian world.[78]

Socrates also states that good rulers should be virtuous men who understand evil, not through firsthand experience but rather through indirect knowledge of bad men. Even if they are not tempted to evil, they will meet and have to rule over others who are. These rulers must be older to be able to have stable and virtuous souls that will not be too affected by bad men around them. They must be both prudent and powerful, and care for the city. But to care (*kēdomai*) for the city, Socrates says, comes out of a capacity to love (*philein*; 412d). Such a love represents the ruler's understanding that what is good for himself is also what is good for the city with which he is friendly. Socrates argues that the happiness of the ruler is found in the happiness of the whole of the city that he rules, on account of this friendship. To be a good friend to the city requires understanding both good and evil, and Platonic dialogue allows for exactly this sort of encounter with both good and evil through diverse characters and the ideas that shaped them.

Within the ideal city and its ideal citizen, Socrates offers another way to reinforce friendship: the noble lie (*gennaion pseudos*). Socrates is hesitant even to introduce such a lie but suggests that this must be told to the rulers, the soldiers, and the rest of the city, that their rearing and education was only a dream, and that the whole city is born from Mother Earth, and all other citizens are their brothers and born of the earth as well. Those who are the rulers have gold mixed into their blood, the auxiliaries (new name for the soldier class that does not rule) have silver, and the craftsmen have iron and bronze (415a).

The noble lie, however, is not a lie that can be perpetually believed by its citizens to be true, even in the most perfectly protected city, for simple reasons of biology. Even the least enlightened adults will surely come to see the impossibility of this story of their origins. Minimally, pregnant women in the city will find themselves to be the actual bearers of children, as will all who encounter them. Clearly, the story can only be understood to be true, at most, by young children, who eventually will outgrow it, soon discovering as adults that they themselves are expectant with children who emerge from their own bodies or from their wives' bodies, not from Mother Earth. Thus, interpretations of the myth by thinkers such as Popper, who saw in the noble lie clear evidence of totalitarian thinking, misread Socrates's intentions.[79]

At the same time, it may yet be the case that the citizens believe the myth, but in a different sense than understanding it to be literally true. Perhaps Socrates has in mind a different way for his citizens to receive this lie, as a story that adults understand to be factually untrue—that is, as not corresponding to the empirical reality of the body—yet that is treated as a grounding myth that expresses some true ideal about the citizens and the meaning of community.[80] Many such myths exist in our own societies. For example, in the United States of America, Thanksgiving celebrates an idealized past in which Native Americans and newly arrived colonial Europeans shared food supplies and ate a meal together. Most citizens are aware that the truth about the colonialists and the native peoples is far more problematic, yet the holiday continues as an expression of an ideal of sharing across cultures and a country founded with respect for multiple ethnic origins. On the one hand, it is crucial that adult citizens become aware of such historical truth, including knowing of the violence between European colonialists and various native peoples; to ignore the complexity of the history for an adult is an abdication of intellectual and social responsibility. On the other hand, one might not choose to report such events to a very young child who cannot yet make sense of them. Eventually, however, the child must outgrow the idealization of the myth itself and recognize the mythologizing of history itself. One may then still choose to believe in elements of the values that the myth represents, while also acknowledging the distance between the ideal and reality—or critique the adequacy of the ideal that has been presented. It is precisely in this act of outgrowing the myth as simple history and taking up inquiry into what it could otherwise mean that such questions can be explored. Mature adults can live creatively in that tension between the ideal and the real in a way that small children cannot.

Socrates's noble lie similarly may be understood as an expression of an ideal to which a just city might aspire: a city unified by a shared heritage with the earth, yet distinguished by three "metals" that also justify differences in types of work undertaken. The myth relies on the value of metals in a way that might be most valuable to moneymakers or artisans who use the material of metals in their crafts. But the myth elevates the role of gold, silver, and bronze to a new symbolic level rather than a material one. The myth attempts to bring together difference and distinctness—such as the differences between social classes or different tasks and skills—with a sense of sameness and belonging.[81] A city of monolithic unity will not be just, nor will one whose pluralism tears it apart into multiple cities at odds with one another.[82] Here, Socrates brings together elements of a Hesiodic myth in which different metals characterize the ages of human beings with the idea of autochthony, or the idea that human beings sprung from the land itself.[83] Howland notes the resonance of this noble lie with the myth of Cadmus, in which men sprung from the earth from the plantings of dragons' teeth.[84] Those men killed one another immediately upon being born, whereas Socrates's myth is intended to preserve the city against the possibility of civil war through the order that the myth of metals imposes.

However, as it is constructed, the myth cannot last into full adulthood.[85] Eventually, the children will grow up, cease to believe that babies are born from the earth, and discover that they are born from other human beings. (Minimally, all mothers will discover this.) A citizen may wonder: if *this* part of the myth was untrue, then what other parts as well?[86] Socrates states the ideal unifying aspects of myth, but as readers we can see that naïve belief in the myth cannot long last.[87] Children who outgrow this myth and who learn that children are not born from the land but from human bodies will inevitably begin to ask questions about its meaning.[88] Then the question will be whether the city can adequately prepare its citizens through education to explore myths philosophically or not. Homeric and Hesiodic myth do not seem to provide the possibility of their own structures being more deeply interrogated.

In contrast, the *Republic* does provide this for its readers. Socrates serves as a model of how to question the traditional poets in his own criticism of their claims and their form. While a poetic work that is believed naïvely to be an exact representation of reality is contrary to the Platonic spirit of philosophy, a mythical account that allows its listeners to grow in understanding of how to understand myth is an artful tale. Its art consists of its capacity to awaken the soul's recognition of how we construct reality and what the limits are of that construction, while also communicating the political and social "truth" that we are intended to live as brothers and sisters, fathers, sons, mothers, and daughter with even those who are not, in fact, our blood relations.

These elements of irony, performance, narration, *mimēsis*, and myth-making are not simply added on elements that enhance the reception of the philosophical ideas in a pedagogical sense. Rather, they are essential to an understanding of Platonic philosophy as such. As subsequent chapters will argue, the arguments of Book One include images both at the level of character and argumentation. Even the most fundamental realities, the forms, can only be known by way of images that present a limited perspective on these realities. While one can grow in understanding of being through multiple images and ideas—and through discarding limited ones that show themselves to be distorted, or too limited—the forms can never be completely exhausted by any given image or proposition. There will always be more to say, and anything that we say will reflect some kind of limit or perspective. For this reason, poetry and narrative have a place not only alongside philosophy but as part of its practice, especially when criticism is built into the form of their expression. Properly used, poetic devices have the capacity to develop the ability to reason well, as this chapter has argued.[89] Thus, Socrates's use of imagery in the dialogue as a whole does not subvert his criticism of poetic education, but rather it is offered as an alternative way of using images in contrast to traditional education. However, in order to use images in this new, philosophical way, Socrates must not only use them. He must also explain how we are to understand their use. Therefore, Socrates not only offers an argument about the nature of justice using imagery, but he also goes on to further reflect on how the nature of images contextualizes them in a larger epistemological framework.

Chapter 2

Visioning and Reenvisioning Justice

This chapter argues that images are central to the arguments of Book One, where Socrates and his companions discuss the nature of justice and its relation to the happy life. Images function as a part of "argumentation" in Book One of the *Republic*. Rather than seeing Book One as the development of three different definitions of justice that are each in turn refuted, I argue that Plato's characters offer a series of *paradigms* of justice. These different paradigmatic images assist in moving toward a better understanding the nature of justice, even though no final picture of justice is arrived at in Book One. Although in later books, Socrates will consider an image or *eikōn* to be at the lowest realm of human understanding, the image has a significant role to play in the furthering of philosophical ideas in the discussion of Book One, as well as later books. In this chapter, I focus on the use of paradigmatic images as part of argumentation with Cephalus and Polemarchus. Chapter 2 then turns to the argument with Thrasymachus and its use of paradigmatic argument, as well as to how the drama of Book One and its characters informs its argument.[1]

Here, I use the term "paradigmatic image" to describe the main way in which each of these interlocutors attempts to communicate their ideas about justice. Each paradigmatic image is an iconic picture that is meant to summarize and show the listener something essential about justice, through a particular verbal representation or exemplar that is emblematic of just living. For example, Cephalus offers the picture of an honest merchant who has been fair in his trade deals and who sleeps well at night because he does not fear punishment after death. His image is particular and gives us a vision in miniature of what the just life looks like, a paradigm or model of what justice is when it is embodied in a particular life.

When using the term "image" here, I have in mind something like the Platonic concept of the *eikōn* as Socrates uses the term in the analogy of the divided line and the myth of the cave. There, the word *eikōn* broadly describes both images in the more contemporary sense of "mental image," and also phenomena as diverse as shadows, echoes off the cave wall, or paintings and other forms of art. In its usage in the *Republic*, the term *eikōn* is not limited to the purely visual. It can include auditory experiences, for example, or even experiences of touch or other senses. Thus one might also name the descriptions of justice that Socrates and his interlocutors give simply as "iconic." However, the term "icon" in English has an even more strongly visual connotation than "image" due to its usage to describe religious iconography and symbols. Another alternative would be to use the term "representation," which could name any internal experience that is quasi-perceptual and would not be limited to the purely visual.[2] However, the language of "representation" has a later philosophical history that might inadvertently emphasize an "internal" mental experience in relation to, and often in contrast to, an exterior object in the physical world, which is not the point here in Book One. Helpfully, Socrates's use of the term *eikōn* retains a conceptual element to it even in the images of the divided line and cave. A shadow is recognized *as* a shadow of a tree, and a painting is seen *as* a painting of a couch. There, an *eikōn* is not simply a quasi-perceptual experience, but already a conceptually interpreted experience.[3] "Paradigmatic image" ought to be understood to include the visual and other faculties of the imagination, just as we can easily say that we can "imagine" the voice of a friend, even though it is an auditory rather than visual experience. However, that being said, Plato himself relies more on visual metaphors to talk about knowledge and its objects, rather than on metaphors derived from other senses.

Socrates's interlocutors offer not so much definitions of justice as paradigmatic images of justice that convey particular, lived sense experiences which become emblematic or iconic of the just life. Their verbal descriptions do not, for the most part, concern the relationship between abstract terms. Cephalus is probably not concerned that his verbal description be sufficient to capture all cases of justice when he first offers it. He is more interested in communicating a picture of what the just life looks like from the perspective of old age. Socrates's friends take up exemplars or paradigms of what it means to be a just person in order to offer a general description of justice. While Socrates will compress those verbal descriptions into shorter formulations, and criticize such formulations for not adequately capturing the nature of justice, his eventual aim is also to offer the right image of justice and what a just life "looks like" when lived.

Cephalus, Polemarchus, Thrasymachus, and Socrates present paradigmatic images of just men in the course of arguing about the nature of a just life.[4] They are less concerned with presenting definitions than they are with offering iconic instances of what the just life looks like. One may ask what difference it makes to understand Book One's argumentation in terms of working with paradigmatic images of justice rather than with definitions. While there are a variety of different approaches to definition in contemporary philosophy (e.g., nominal, descriptive, stipulative, explicative), a philosophical definition is commonly understood in terms of a verbal expression that either is or is not extensionally adequate or inadequate, that is, that does or does not accurately characterize the subject matter being defined, in this case, justice. Such an approach to definition sometimes invites a binary division between a definition that is right or wrong, correct or incorrect, or perhaps more or less extensionally adequate. Of course, Socrates also pursues a more and more adequate verbal description of the nature of justice. However, his approach to what Cephalus and Polemarchus offer is different than what we see in dialogues such as the *Meno*, where Socrates insists that his interlocutor answers a "what is x" question by offering a universal formulation that does not rely too much on specific instances. In the case of Meno, Socrates listens to Meno's different examples of virtue but then insists that he find a way of talking about virtue in a more universal way that can adequately cover all instances, rather than only giving a list of what just actions are for men, women, or slaves.

In Book One of the *Republic*, the process is subtly but significantly different. Socrates still wants to find a general verbal formulation that encompasses what justice ought to include and exclude. However, in his interlocutors' verbal accounts, Socrates seems content to allow verbal images or paradigms of the just person to remain central to those verbal accounts. Socrates's response to his interlocutor's images is not to insist that the other person speak more abstractly, with fewer references to concrete particulars, but rather that he adjust the image or paradigm in response to objections that Socrates raises. In the case of Cephalus and Polemarchus, Socrates will try to widen the *vision* of what the good life includes beyond the bounds of commercial exchange and friendship. In the case of Thrasymachus, Socrates and Thrasymachus offer competing paradigms of the good life and the role of justice in living well.

The language of sight permeates the metaphysical images given in the *Republic*'s middle books, for example, in the analogy of the cave and the image of the form of the good as akin to the sun.[5] There, Socrates develops verbal images of the forms, descriptions that when we hear them ought to paint a rather specific picture in the mind of the listener. Socrates gives instructions about how the line is to be drawn and divided, so that we can "see" it, or of how the persons in the cave are situated relative to other objects in the cave such as the fire and cave wall. Here in Book One, I propose that we see how Socrates and his friends learn about justice through a kind of visioning and reenvisioning of justice through the exchange of images.[6] By attending to imagery in Book One, I hope to show this action of envisioning justice in a way that illuminates Socratic practice differently than an interpretive emphasis on an extensionally adequate definition.

Socrates's discourse with his friends is a practice that helps them to better "see" different aspects of justice. In English, the language of "insight" is also based on a visual model. The interlocutors' particular iconic representations of the just person, and Socrates's responses to them with his own particular counterimages or coun120icons, contribute to new insights on the part of his interlocutors. Together, they experience a kind of ascent within Book One. Socrates's allowance and encouragement of the use of imagery and paradigm constitutes part of his role as teacher, in inviting his interlocutors to make an ascent toward justice with him. Indeed, the contributions of his interlocutors to the content of describing justice are so important that we cannot simply speak of Socrates as leading his interlocutors to a set destination at which he hopes to arrive. The language of Socrates "leading" his interlocutors to a preestablished destination would be *misleading*. We might better describe their discussion as a kind of exchange, a trading in images that each attempt to represent slightly better than the previous one something about the reality of justice. Still, Socrates is especially active in offering criticisms, countering the current paradigm at hand, and pushing the discussion forward.

Andrea Nightingale has helpfully argued that Platonic philosophy relies upon the idea of Greek *theōria*, as something that we see or witness. In her examination of the cave analogy of the *Republic*, Nightingale argues, the *theōros* takes a sacred journey to visit the spectacle of the Forms.[7] As Segal notes, even the *Republic*'s opening language of light and darkness used to describe the torchlight procession for Bendis, a new goddess, is called a spectacle (327a).[8] Gerald Press has argued that understanding Platonic approaches to knowledge as *theōria* rather than as *epistēmē* also helps us as interpreters to avoid two extremes of dogmatism and skepticism.[9] In the world of Platonic dialogue, a philosophical theory is not a set of propositions that one believes has been well defended, but rather a way of envisioning or seeing the world. Socrates's language and images for knowledge in the central books rely on visual imagery and play on the everyday visual element of Greek terms such as *idein* (to know and to see), *idea* and *eidos* (form).

Yet an idea of philosophy as rooted in vision is only a partly adequate description of Platonic philosophical practice. It does not yet account sufficiently for the dialogical and critical elements of Platonic philosophical practice. The language of vision can imply a certain degree of passivity on the part of the one who sees. Sight as a model for knowledge helpfully conveys the sense of having understanding, of possessing "insight," and several Greek terms for knowledge convey this sense of the epistemological receptivity of "seeing" something for one's self. Many Greek authors are aware of these dual aspects of the common terminology for knowing as also seeing. For example, in *Oedipus Rex*, Oedipus uses the term *oida* both in the sense of "I see" and "I know."[10] There, Sophocles emphasizes Oedipus's lack of knowledge and both his metaphorical and later literal blindness through repeatedly playing on these multiple senses of the term.

However, for Plato, even after one sees something of the truth, or *believes* that one has come to an "insight," there is still the further need to test and even to actively try to refute what one thinks one has seen. In the *Protagoras*, Socrates cites a line from Homer to describe philosophical conversation and its relation to discovery: " 'Two go together and one sees it before the other.' For it makes all of us human beings more resourceful in word, deed, and thought. But if he sees it alone, he has to go searching for someone to whom to show it, who will confirm it" (*Prot.* 348d).[11] Sight and insight alike are imperfect and fallible, and so verbal discussion, *dialegesthai*, is necessary to test one's insights.

There are at least two dramatic devices by which Plato asserts the limits of knowing as seeing. The first way is through the use of multiple voices in the dialogue and the disagreements of its characters. To practice philosophy is not simply to "see" something about the subject matter in question. Such a description emphasizes only the "vertical" dimension of learning, or the encounter between subject and object. Philosophy also requires listening to different voices that can challenge, confirm, or otherwise test my own thinking. That is, there is a "horizontal" dimension of verbal interchange between persons who have different insights and ways of seeing the world that can and should break into our own "vertical" relationship to the objects of our knowledge. Socrates says in the *Gorgias*, "What is true is never refuted" (*Gorg.* 473c). Often this has been interpreted simply to mean that

Socrates leads his interlocutors to assert propositions that are inconsistent with other propositions, such that the initial claim must be abandoned and another one taken up, as in the practice of elenchus. Commentators such as Vlastos have argued that while there is no positive and final proof for the truth of a proposition, those ideas that can withstand sufficient testing merit our assent.[12] Clearly, the elenchus has a significant role to play in Socrates's testing of his interlocutors' ideas.

Here, I argue that something a little different is going on in the *Republic*: philosophical discourse includes multiple voices where the ideas of various characters' voices are not simply temporary stopping places so that we can then arrive at a final, correct idea, where the end product is correct and all the prior, rejected conceptions can be dispensed with.[13] Quite often, Socrates's later descriptions of justice in the city or soul retain some of the insights found earlier in conversation. For example, Cephalus's view of justice in Book One, as giving each what is owed, bears strong similarities to Socrates's view that justice is minding one's own business in Book Four. But Socrates's idea of justice is far more expansive in its going beyond mercantile exchange to include a wide range of activities important to the city's flourishing. Cephalus's voice is later echoed in the conversation long after he has departed the gathering.

Moreover, whatever ideas we arrive at by the end of a particular conversation, these ideas are necessarily incomplete and limited because their starting points were not the *only* possible starting points for the problem at hand. My approach here is in decided contrast to those commentators who see Platonic rationalism as exclusively interested in unity over plurality. Segal, for example, argues that the *Republic* seeks to find simplicity over multiplicity, and that its emphasis on unity is an effort to avoid what is multiple and varied.[14] In contrast, I argue that while the forms *themselves* each possess a real unity, Socrates is sufficiently aware of the problematic nature of giving a perfect *account* of such unity. All verbal accounts are provisional since they always begin from the limited starting points and perspectives of living human beings with particular histories that inform their way of seeing. For example, the conversation between Socrates and his friends begins with the ideas of Cephalus, a merchant and metic whose life informs how he understands justice. Socrates's own exploration of justice in Book Two comes specifically out of Glaucon's and Adeimantus's worry that Thrasymachus's claim about the good of the unjust life has not been fully refuted. The dialogical presentation of conflicting voices reminds us that our ideas are arrived at via particular paths that determine their direction, and that different starting points or different turns at various junctures of the argument might have led to either slightly or substantially different pictures of the nature of justice, beauty, love, or whatever is the topic in question.

Cephalus, Polemarchus, and Thrasymachus each present a picture of what the just life looks like. Their descriptions rely on particulars rather than only universal, abstract characteristics, in order to describe the just person. We are asked to imagine what a just life looks like in its concreteness and particularity, and not only what abstract qualities either justice or a just person possesses. Justice is presented as embodied and as enacted, through the development of a verbal picture of the just life. For example, for Cephalus, the just life is largely mercantile, one concerned with the making and fulfillment of contracts, a picture of justice appropriate in many ways to Cephalus's own life as a resident metic and shield-maker. Socrates's objections to Cephalus, and to the others' visions of justice, are intended to enlarge or to reshape, or even to break, these visions of justice so that something new may enter into their vision. The discourse in images is not merely the trading of different images in agonistic fashion, but rather the reshaping of vision through putting images in contrast or opposition to one another. Socrates's objections do not always function successfully for all of these characters—for example, Cephalus leaves the conversation and Thrasymachus remains angry at Socrates. However, even in such cases they may function more successfully for the readers of the Platonic dialogue who themselves witness various visions of justice through the course of the *Republic*.

Understanding the arguments of Book One in terms of paradigmatic images has advantages over understanding them only as definitions. First, such an understanding better captures some of the nuances of the Greek term for what is often translated as definition, as when Bloom translates Socrates saying, "Then this isn't the definition (*horos*) of justice, speaking the truth and giving back what one takes" (331d1). The Greek *horos* most literally means a boundary, a marked limit; for example, it can be used to describe a marker of physical limit such as the edge of a territory, or to name a temporal limit, as in Herodotus's claim that the *horos* of the human life is set at seventy years (*Hist.* 1.32). While the English term "definition" can also capture this sense of being bounded, contemporary philosophical practice often presents definitions as simply capturing the correct "logical" space over which a particular term has domain. Here, I argue, the *horos* of justice also includes whether it adequately captures the *imaginative* space of envisioning a just life for oneself.

In other words, the advantage to using the term "vision" of justice over "definition" of justice to translate *horos* is that it preserves for the English reader how each character's presentation of the ideal just life includes how that life would "look" in its concreteness as a lived life. For it is through imagining the sorts of lives that we wish to live that we as human beings often choose to live them accordingly. Cephalus's vision of justice includes his description of the man who finds "pleasant hope" beside him, like a nurse in his old age (331), and not only Socrates's later reformulation of Cephalus's ideas as "to give to each his due" (331e). The concreteness of Cephalus's idea that he feels as though he is accompanied by a pleasurable hope is not lost, as it might be if we see Socrates's reformulation as a definition that is only tested for the adequacy of its logical extension. Cephalus is painting a picture of the happy life of old age and not especially interested in formulating universals, and Socrates finds that picture to be promising enough to pursue further in conversation. To the extent that I sometimes use the term "definition" to describe the ideas laid out in Book One, I have in mind this enriched sense of definition as a vision or way of looking.

Certainly, Socrates's reformulation of Cephalus's idea of justice as "to give to each his due" plays a significant role in the argumentation, in that it allows Socrates and his friends to see whether the scope of Cephalus's picture about the just life is adequate. But even that reformulation functions by inviting a further set of images to be examined. Socrates will offer the image of the madman who demands his weapons back as a mode of testing whether Cephalus has captured all that he would like to about the nature of justice and the happy life. Socrates offers a new image in exchange for Cephalus's image of the just life, in order to look at what is found within the boundaries of justice, and to seek out where the current boundaries and shaping of justice needs to be reshaped and reimagined.

Second, this way of reading Book One opens up the positive value of each of the characters' contributions to justice and their contribution to the dialectical development of ideas in the larger conversation. Rather than seeing each of the earliest descriptions of justices as a mistake by a philosophically inadequate character whose ideas are then set aside, we as readers of the dialogue can better see how each description moves the dialogue and its argumentation forward, even as they are also revised and reenvisioned. For example, Cephalus's idea of justice is insufficient, but when Polemarchus takes it up again, he expands its scope so that justice includes more than merely mercantile concerns while still retaining certain features of his father's ideas. Their forward, positive, dialectical movement appropriately enlarges the scope of justice without wholly rejecting the legitimate insights that Cephalus brings to their discussion.

The visions of justice in Book One arise from the lived experiences and imaginative resources of its characters.[15] Socrates discusses justice with friends of diverse backgrounds. Glaucon, Thrasymachus, Cephalus, Adeimantus, Polemarchus have different personalities and experiences that influence the way that each sees justice. In helping them to understand the nature of justice and in growing in his own understanding, Socrates is mindful that his audience is not one composed of perfect, unchanging gods, nor even well-formed philosophers, but rather of human beings living in the middle of a political conflict, with all sorts of passions, commitments, and desires, some intellectual and political, and others not. The picture of the soul later introduced in Book Four in which the virtuous soul is the harmonious soul shows that the best soul is one in which all parts—reason, spirit, and appetite—are in "agreement" and coordinated.

However, Socrates's companions are not perfectly virtuous souls with perfectly well-ordered desires. They are not simply "souls." Rather, they are people with souls in need of integration, who are still, at best, en route to becoming people with harmonious souls.[16] They are also people historically situated in the midst of an Athenian war with specific commitments to that particular city. In later books, Socrates's continual use of images as part of his argumentation is an approach that exhibits care for his interlocutor's souls, not only their intellects but also their desires. The attention Socrates gives to images is pedagogically valuable because his friends' imaginative resources are shaped in part by their desires. Glaucon, for example, cannot quite imagine a city without war and honor because he loves honor. That he finds honor to be central to a just and happy life is reflected in the imaginative possibilities that he brings to bear on their conversation. By encouraging his interlocutors to offer images of justice, and then to see the limits of their imagined visions of justice, Socrates offers ways for his interlocutors to think meaningfully about whether there are limits to how they conceive of their own desires.

Images also better capture the particularity and concreteness of matters of justice that human communities face than do abstract definitions. The dramatic significance of the dialogue was more immediately available to an Athenian audience who knew well the histories of its characters. The *Republic* is set in the midst of civic turmoil, in which oligarchs and democrats struggle for power; yet it was written for an audience that already knew the outcome of that struggle in terms that were not idealized. Plato's audience already knew about the unsuccessful war with Sparta that featured betrayals of the city by Alcibiades and others it had formerly held dear and the exile of leading democrats as well as the punishment of oligarchs. An Athenian audience would also recall that Polemarchus was killed by oligarchic supporters under the Thirty Tyrants, not long after the *Republic's* dramatic date.[17] The equivalent today might be an audience reading a play about John F. Kennedy, in which his death is never explicitly mentioned but his assassination can never be too far from an audience's mind. Against the ideals of the *Republic* stands the reality of the historical Athens, whose audience lived in the aftermath of a political idealism that fueled a grim civil war. The force of the civil war's losses to both oligarchs and democrats alike also reminds us that the idea of a harmonious city would have real value to its audience not as an idealistic improvement upon an adequate government, but rather as a response to the suffering and destruction that real civil war had produced.

Polemarchus's notion that justice is often about "helping friends and harming enemies" has some good insights, but his understanding of justice is also entirely compatible with the actions of those who killed him because they perceived him as an enemy and not as a friend, and therefore also problematic from the standpoint of Plato's own contemporaries.[18] The dialogue form continually reminds us that its arguments are spoken by persons with real histories and do not stand completely independently of these histories, while also needing to move past some of the contingencies of those histories. The *Republic* refuses to allow us to rest easy either in the provincial limits of its particular characters, or to flee to an idealized universal vision of justice that omits the fact that such ideals exist not only for the sake of intellectual contemplation itself, but also for the sake of real, living individuals residing in real cities. Justice is neither simply remedying the unjust fate of Polemarchus and his family, nor is it found entirely in the forms, for the world of the forms is not where Athenians lived, nor have any citizens ever lived. Instead, the *Republic* begins with the imaginative possibilities that its own characters can see as a result of their concrete lived experiences, and then asks them to question these categories and frameworks. With such questions, their discussion moves forward, using both the power and limits of the imagination in the pursuit of justice.

The very opening of the *Republic* raises the discomforting question of whether the successful practice of philosophy is even possible in certain political contexts. Socrates has gone down to a festival at the Piraeus with a friend, Glaucon, and he expresses admiration for how the locals made their procession but adds, "no better than the display of the Thracians that marched" (327a). The idea of a spectacle to be seen already dramatically contextualizes their conversation. The Piraeus is a port, a meeting place of what is strange with what is one's own, yet Socrates expresses care for both the alien and the native. He is on his way out of the Piraeus, when Polemarchus's slave boy stops him. The Athenian audience of the *Republic* would know that Polemarchus was pulled off the streets by the Thirty Tyrants and murdered without a trial soon after the dramatic date of this conversation.[19] Even within the relatively peaceful Athens of this dialogue, Polemarchus lacks the ability to participate politically, as his father Cephalus is a resident metic. Cephalus and his family produce the shields that protect Athens from its invaders, and the family actively contributed to the funding of dramatic festivals as well as paying levies during much of their thirty years of residence, according to a later account given by Polemarchus's brother Lysias.[20] Metics were individuals who were permitted residence in the city and had some of the same privileges as citizens but lacked others, for example, certain property and marriage rights. As a metic, Polemarchus is neither fully inside nor outside the polis. His slave boy occupies a similarly ambiguous, but even lower, position in being both present at the conversation but never acknowledged in the dialogue after this brief introduction.[21] The slave boy orders Socrates to wait, and when Polemarchus arrives, the latter says that Socrates must either prove to be stronger than him and his companions, or remain. Socrates suggests that there is a possibility that Polemarchus has overlooked: "our persuading (*peisōmen*) that you that should let us go" (327c). Polemarchus asks whether one can persuade one who does not listen, and Socrates must concede its impossibility.

This opening sequence lays a number of problems about the political value of the discussion about to be held. As Page argues, Polemarchus's pull on Socrates's cloak seems to be playful: eventually he entices Socrates to stay in the Piraeus with mention of the torch race and Socrates is quite engaged in the conversation.[22] Still, there is verbal opposition between persuasion and force, in which Socrates takes the side of persuasion, but verbal argument possesses a certain powerlessness in the face of force—at least until it is given a longer run. As Howland notes, the Battle of Munichia, in which members of the Thirty were killed by democratic forces, took place roughly in the same area, giving these lines an even more urgent tone.[23] There are additional questions about belonging, such as: Who has a voice and who lacks one? Can argument alone persuade Polemarchus of Socrates's desire to leave? Can words take the place of a fight? Can a joke about overpowering one's friend—which is what I take this to be, albeit a joke laden with dramatic irony—bridge the gap between the desires of Socrates and Polemarchus, in order to make the subsequent dialogue of that night possible?[24] Here in these preliminary moments of the conversation, Socrates acknowledges a certain limit of philosophical conversation in cities in which force rather than persuasion rules.[25] At the same time, the location of this conversation in the Piraeus, a planned community, already speaks to the possibility of speech to organize political communities in accordance with rational principles.[26]

Socrates agrees to remain; yet the question of whether the participants in the dialogue are engaged participants does not disappear. In Book One, Cephalus leaves to perform a sacrifice, passing on the arguments as an inheritance to his son (331d)—the only inheritance Polemarchus will ever receive. Another son, Lysias, is present among the listed characters and remains silent for the entirety of the *Republic*, although he was a rhetor whose life was devoted to public speech. Euthydemus, a third brother, also never utters a word. Thrasymachus comes to the argument described as akin to a "wild beast," interested in language to be used as domination, although he also accuses Socrates of the same, perhaps too inclined to see in others what he sees in himself. Later in Book Five, Polemarchus will reenact the cloak grabbing of the slave boy, this time pulling on Adeimantus's cloak, in order to get Socrates to return to the controversial claims that women and children will be held in common (449a–b). In each of these instances, the imagination of the audience is engaged in a way that encourages us to consider that even if a just city is based on persuasion, real cities are often places in which force instead of persuasion rules. Socrates's willingness to work with his interlocutors' images of justice opens up the possibility of persuasion rather than force, for persuasion must take some account of how an interlocutor already imagines the world.

Although commentators tend to be focused on the three major formulations of the notion of justice in Book One, we ought to remember that the discussion of justice begins with a relatively simple and practical question about old age: "Is it a hard part of life, or what have you to proclaim about it?" (328e). Socrates asks a remarkably open-ended question, one that expresses interest in that of which Socrates (so far) has no experience: being old. The nature of old age can only be known and understood by a younger person through the imagination, and that imagination can only be well informed if the imaginative engagement takes place through engagement with real, older people (or their fictionalized counterparts). Socrates alludes to Homer by suggesting that Cephalus is in the time of life called "the threshold of old age" (328c). The passage from which this phrase comes infuses this discussion of justice with seriousness. The same phrase is used to describe Priam in the *Iliad*, in Book Twenty-Two, when Priam asks Hector not to return to battle but to go within the walls of Troy and be protected. His words are as follows: "Have pity on me, the unfortunate, still alive, still sentient, but ill-starred, whom the father, Cronos' son, on the threshold of old age will blast with hard fate, after I have looked upon evils, and seen my sons destroyed and my daughters dragged away captive . . ."[27] The Thirty Tyrants will, in fact, lay waste to Cephalus's fortune and will kill Polemarchus, although Cephalus, of course, cannot anticipate these events. Socrates's phrase is a moment of dramatic irony that points to the commonality between Priam and Cephalus as two men who lived decent lives but nonetheless suffered the loss of fortune and the death of family members late in life as the result of armed conflict. Cephalus is a tragic figure, although he does not yet know it.[28] Thus, just as Socrates cannot know what it means to be old while he is still younger, these images present the Platonic reader with a sense of what it means to be a person like Cephalus or Polemarchus, who has a moderate love of wealth along with a conventional commitment to fairness and decency according to ordinary standards. One does not have to be a merchant or metic oneself in order to gain sympathetic as well as intellectual understanding into why these figures might understand justice as they do. We can both think with and feel with these characters as they take up the discussion precisely because they are characters with histories and not disembodied arguments.

Cephalus responsively gives a long and thoughtful answer. Some commentators criticize him for being too mercantile and self-interested, assuming that Cephalus must be an unjust merchant, as evidenced by his offering of sacrifices when he exits the scene. Others acknowledge that he has lived justly but has been motivated by fear.[29] Their assumption is that the sacrifices must be to atone for wrongs committed, already bringing in some of the critical discussion of the gods and justice in poetry between Socrates and Adeimantus. However, ritual sacrifice served more functions than simply currying favor with the gods for some past wrong or for the sake of future gain. Sacrifice develops relationship between gods and human beings and also strengthens intersocial ties. Moreover, Lysias in "Against Eratosthenes" holds up his family as exemplary in their dealings with the city. Even if he can be assumed to exhibit some bias in painting a good picture of his family, he could not have raised the issue of his family's ties to the city and their generosity in donating money to civic festivals if they had been known as cheating merchants. Last, Socrates also notes that Cephalus is different than many other wealthy people, in that he seems less attached to wealth than most (330b). Plato's portrayal of Cephalus is relatively generous: he is a just merchant, interested in fairness to men and to gods, honest, and more moderate than most in his approach to pleasure. And yet Socrates will still question whether this is enough to be fully just and truly happy.

To Socrates's question, Cephalus gives a rather noble, if conventional, answer: the "wild and savage" passions of youth have calmed, and old age is not too bad if one has a good character. Cephalus articulates a vision of what the good life looks like: if one is of good character, neither old age nor youth are too troublesome, but if one lacks such good character, both are difficult (329a–d). In the course of giving his answer to Socrates, Cephalus cites Pindar: "sweet the heart-fostering nurse of old age that accompanies him: Hope, which most of all steers the ever changing mind of mortals" (331a; Pindar frag. 214). Here, Cephalus refers to Hope (*Elpis*) in a personified way, thus evoking a large poetic tradition that suggests that Hope alone remains when other virtues have fled. For example, in Hesiod's account of Pandora, she held a vessel with spirits (*daimones*) that escaped, except for Elpis who stayed behind to offer care to mortals (*Works and Days* 55). Theognis also remarks, "Elpis is the only good god remaining among mankind; the others have left and gone to Olympos. Pistis (Trust), a mighty god, has gone, Sophrosune (Restraint) has gone from men, and the Kharites, my friend, have abandoned the earth" (Theognis frag. 1.1135).[30] Cephalus adds to this poetic tradition by asserting that when men near the end of life and have anxiety as to whether they have acted unjustly in the course of a lifetime, the one who has always lived in a just way retains hope. He thus links hope as the "last remaining virtue" specifically to justice in a way that neither Hesiod nor Theognis do. Cephalus gives a philosophically unsophisticated version of virtue theory, but a kind of virtue theory nonetheless. Cephalus argues that good character is central to happiness, a theme upon which Socrates and his friends will elaborate in great detail later in the course of their conversation.

Socrates expresses wonder at Cephalus's presentation. In contrast to Polemarchus, who wishes to "pull" another to where he is, Socrates expresses wonder and delight in conversing with Cephalus (329d, 328d). Wonder is an essentially responsive and open stance.[31] In wonder, we are affected by what is outside of ourselves such that we are further opened up to what is different. Wonder requires difference. Unlike experiences of sympathy or friendship in which I primarily identify with what is common between myself and another person, in wonder, the difference between myself and the other is prominent. And yet in wonder, my care ceases to remain within myself. Wonder even approaches the edge of the ecstatic, in which I find myself *within* the world of the other and outside of myself. In wonder, there may be puzzlement, confusion, or even disagreement, but there is also always a receptive element, a sense of the worthiness of what is other or alien to what one already possesses or believes. Wonder creates the opening of receptivity and allows the ideas of others to enter in.

In wonder at Cephalus, Socrates is responsive to him. But his responsiveness is not only a passive responsiveness of acceptance and reception. Rather, Socrates's engagement also brings himself and his own concerns to the conversation. Socrates does not only recede so that Cephalus can occupy the conversational space; rather, he enters into that space along with Cephalus (at least until Cephalus exits!). Socrates has a voice, a voice that invites Cephalus to have voice, too. Philosophical wonder requires this invitation to the voice of another, even as the ground of that wonder is often something that is, as of yet, voiceless. Socrates creates space for Cephalus's experience to enter in, in the very act of asking a question. Wonder, however, does not itself tell us about the value of the object of wonder. As is often the case with the Greek gods, there is also a darker side, an ambiguity in their nature. In Hesiod's *Theogony*, Thaumas (Wonder) is the god that fathers (along with Electra) both Iris and the Harpies, monsters that snatch away evildoers. Wonder thus can be the father of philosophy, as Plato's *Theaetetus* asserts (155d), but it can also be the father of monsters. Thus, wonder alone is not sufficient without a critical evaluation of the object of the experience.[32] The question as to whether Cephalus's vision of the good life is worthy of respect or has serious shortcomings is still open.

Socrates goes on to ask Cephalus a series of questions regarding the metic's attitude toward wealth and what kind of good it is, if it is a good at all. Cephalus introduces the notion of justice to which the rest of the conversation becomes devoted. Cephalus is alien in many ways: literally, he is a resident metic and occupies a social space somewhat in between citizen and *xenos*. Unlike Socrates, Cephalus is wealthy.[33] Unlike Socrates, Cephalus is old. And unlike Socrates, Cephalus interprets the nature of justice through the lens of the exchange of money: fairness in exchange and truth telling are Cephalus's paradigmatic instances of justice. Cephalus's examples and images may also result in the production of images in those who are listening to Cephalus's description: for example, they may evoke for others in the discussion a particular remembrance of a time when Cephalus sold high-quality shields at a fair rate to the Athenians.

Socrates's response to Cephalus is to offer a counterimage to the picture that Cephalus has just developed. Socrates does not simply refute a definition; in fact, the idea often named as Cephalus's definition—"to speak the truth and to give back what one has taken"—is spoken by Socrates *after* Socrates has already given his counterimage of the madman who demands his weapons back from a friend (331d). Although Polemarchus steps in to defend his father's idea (with a phrase borrowed from Simonides), it is Socrates who tries to give shape and limit to the more winding and variegated images of justice in Cephalus's longer description. Socrates's summary and his counterexample both force his interlocutors to look outside of the mercantile realm, while not entirely abandoning the insights offered from within Cephalus's own world of shields, weapons, and merchandise. Socrates's example of the madman and his weapons draws from the materiality of Cephalus's world as a merchant involved in shield-making and exchange.

Socrates provides an objection to Cephalus's definition that at first glance is odd. If justice is giving to each what is owed, then do we owe our crazy friend or family member the return of his weapon if he asks for it? Initially the counterexample appears to be a most exceptional case; not returning weapons to a friend in a case of madness would not seem to refute the idea that in usual cases, the return of property to the owner is just, for normal cases would seemingly include those in which all parties are rational and there are no extenuating circumstances. Understood solely as a counterexample, Socrates's objection seems unfair as a mode of argument.

However, in giving his example, Socrates does something different than merely offer a counterexample to a universal formulation. He introduces the question of a greater good outside of the goods of fair and equal exchange. From Cephalus's point of view, all that had occurred to him to include in the discussion of justice was matters of property ownership and formal obligations surrounding property. With Socrates's counterexample, for the first time, it occurs to Cephalus that the domain of justice is far wider than he had thought.[34] Cephalus's vision is opened up to envision a larger landscape. The borders of justice open up. In the example of the crazed man wanting his weapon, the question of ownership or property is not sufficient to determine the justice of the action; neither is the equality of the two persons sufficient. Honesty alone is not enough to determine justice, for a crazed man is unlikely to listen to reason. A colleague offers to students in his class a contemporary update of this example by asking them whether it would be just to return car keys to a drunk friend. Quickly, they can see that the fair exchange or return of property is not enough to capture the notion of justice in such a scenario.

The example of the madman is valuable because it directly raises the role of reason, which has already been part of the conversation between Socrates and Cephalus. This man seeking the return of his weapons is ruled not by reason, but apparently by passion of some sort. Socrates holds up for us a reminder of the difficulty of establishing justice when not all persons are reasonable, and when passion is a driving force of the human person. The case is most obvious in those overcome by passions such as anger or lust, but the criticism is not limited to them. Contractual models of justice that focus on the rational exchange of goods are insufficient because the human being is not by nature only one who exchanges goods. To more fully understand justice, we must endeavor to understand human desire and its objects better, beyond the mercantile realm.[35] The community that seeks justice must take account of the possibility that at times desires can seem to manage us, to overcome reason, as is the case with the crazed man asking for the return of his weapons. We cannot expect to create a just society that is inattentive to the workings of real human desires. In this way, we can see that although Socrates has refuted the adequacy of Cephalus's verbal formulation of justice, there has nonetheless been progress in understanding something further about justice. Justice appears to Cephalus in a way that is limited, but even this limited perspective when examined dialogically leads the discussion as a whole to learn something new and significant about the nature of justice: namely, that any good account of justice must take account of human passions and how they are to be ruled.

Although Cephalus claimed that he now had a passion for arguments since his physical desires have waned in old age, Cephalus leaves the conversation to attend to his sacrifices (331d), perhaps because his son interrupts in order to defend the idea (331d). Cephalus lacks the *eros* necessary to pursue philosophy.[36] His desires are moderate, but perhaps too moderate with respect to intellectual engagement. Cephalus is no monster, but neither is he much of a philosopher or even to remain as a willing partner in argument. Instead, Polemarchus becomes the "heir" to his father's argument, as he also expects to be to his father's wealth. He cites Simonides as the authority who offers the definition of justice as "giving to each his due" (331e). In antiquity, some stories exist that suggest that Simonides was known for greed. For example, when he was asked to write a poem with payment of only gratitude and not money, he is said to have replied, "I keep two coffers, one for thanks and the other for cash, and when I open them I find the first empty, but the second always full."[37] Understood in the context of Simonides's reputation for greed, then, "giving to each what is owed" retains its economic tones, as was true for Cephalus. Polemarchus's citation of Simonides perhaps even emphasizes the need for economic justice when other kinds of justice are less easily found.

Polemarchus is willing to engage with the objection of the madman that Socrates has offered. He enlarges the scope of justice to include a bigger concept of the good, although his understanding of that "good" is as of yet indeterminate. Polemarchus says, of course, we ought not return weapons to a madman, if he is a friend, for we owe our friends good and nothing bad (332a). He rephrases his father's definition of justice and suggests that justice is "to do good to friends and to harm enemies" (332d). Polemarchus's definition both narrows and enlarges his father's definition. It enlarges upon the economic model by introducing the idea that there is a larger good at which actions aim that must be accounted for in any discussion of justice. Economic exchange is insufficient without a sense of the larger purpose or meaning of such exchanges: some kind of benefit. But Polemarchus also narrows the scope of justice by restricting that we do good only to our friends—something that Cephalus did not assert. This theme of whether the just man does good only to his friends, or whether the just city only attends to the good of its own citizens, will continue throughout the *Republic*, as when Socrates discusses whether war against other Greeks can ever be just. If there is a universal good, then asking that we only seek the good for our "own" is too narrow; if the good is good for all, then justice must be inclusive of all people (or at least all citizens) in its scope.

Socrates objects to Polemarchus's vision of justice as helping friends and harming enemies by asking a series of questions about experts in other *technai* (arts). He asks Polemarchus, who with respect to disease is able to give most help to friends and harm to enemies, and Polemarchus replies, "A doctor" (332d). With respect to the dangers of the sea and sailing, it is a pilot (332e). Socrates then asks Polemarchus, With respect to what work does the just man help his friends and harm his enemies? And Polemarchus asserts that it is "making war and being an ally in battle" (332e).

Here, the *technē* analogy already functions at multiple levels. First, the analogy introduces to the conversation an additional consideration for thinking about the just man: namely, expertise. By drawing an analogy between the practice of justice and the practice of medicine or piloting a ship, Socrates implies that justice must also be a craft or a kind of expertise in specific kinds of action. That is, Socrates brings into the conversation the idea that knowledge is central to justice. Of course, it is not obvious that expert knowledge must be central to just action. In the *Protagoras*, Protagoras's myth exhibits a vision of justice in which all take part by nature, although education shapes how that nature is exhibited. However, some individuals display particular ability in what all can practice to some extent. Here, Socrates injects his own concerns about knowledge and expertise to their discussion of justice, albeit in the form of a question. Not only action, but also knowledge, is central for being a just person.[38]

Second, the *technē* analogy asks Polemarchus to offer a picture of which activities are paradigmatic for the just man. Just as healing is paradigmatic of the doctor's activity, Socrates asks Polemarchus what best exemplifies being a just person. His answer—making war and forming alliances—is reflective of Polemarchus's own concerns. Polemarchus's family makes shields and so materially supports those who make war. His business is more or less useless in times of peace (not that there were many in Polemarchus's lifetime). The Platonic audience knows that Polemarchus will be killed by the Thirty Tyrants. Perhaps their action was purely motivated by greed and not politics, but his murder by them places the family more on the side of the democrats than the oligarchs. After the war, his brother Lysias prosecuted one of the tyrants, Eratosthenes, thus forming an alliance with democratic power once it was restored in Athens. The *technē* analogy allows for a paradigmatic example of activity to enter into the conversation, as well as raising the question of whether justice involves a specific kind of expertise.

Socrates's use of the *technē* analogy here relies on the imagination in at least two ways. First, it connects paradigmatic examples of arts to justice so that we can imagine justice as a matter of expertise, although it does not yet assert with certainty that justice must be a *technē*. Second, the analogy invites Polemarchus to imagine what activity is paradigmatic of the just man, by offering examples of skills where the domain of an expert is limited and specialized. Indeed, a more accurate term to describe Socrates's practice than the more familiar "*technē* analogy" might be "argument from technical paradigms."

Plato offers no theory of paradigms here, but Aristotle's later theory may help to elucidate some of what is happening at the textual level here. In Aristotle's *Rhetoric*, a *paradeigma* functions as part of inductive argument (*epagōgē*). Paradigms are the relation of one particular to another particular through their connection in the universal where a better-known particular is used to help us to understand a different particular that comes under the same genus (*Rhet.* I.2, 1357b).[39] Here, Socrates shows that both doctors and pilots are crafts that require expert knowledge, and then invites comparison of the just person to the paradigms of doctor and pilot, which are more familiar examples of expertise than just persons. According to Aristotle's analysis, this sort of proof is not absolute, but suggests a probable relation (*eikota*), something that *can* be true.[40] A claim about one particular is inferred from arguing to similarities to another particular. However, the universal may not be true in every case. An example Aristotle gives of arguing from paradigms is claiming that since Dionysius has asked for a bodyguard, he must be planning to be a tyrant, based on two other past examples of tyrants who asked for bodyguards. Not everyone who asks for a bodyguard is necessarily a tyrant, but the argument being made is that it is reasonable to think so in this case on the basis of past examples (*Rhet.* 1357b).[41] Like other probabilities, the claim is "not what occurs invariably but only for the most part" and can be argued against through offering counterexamples (*Rhet.* 1402b). As I will argue in the next chapter, offering counterexamples is exactly what Thrasymachus does in his response to Socrates's paradigmatic argument.

Socrates's use of paradigm has a slightly different rhetorical and philosophical value than the use of paradigm in judicial and deliberative contexts, which are the contexts to which Aristotle's *Rhetoric* gives its attention. In a judicial context, the aim is to persuade one's audience to cast a vote in a particular way about an event that has happened in the past (*Rhet.* 1368a29). The argument is future oriented in one sense, in that it seeks to persuade an audience to take a particular course of action, but also past oriented in that it seeks to demonstrate what did or did not happen concerning a particular event or occurrence.[42] In contrast, here Socrates is hoping to discover something about the nature of justice. Their focus is not the meaning of a past event, or what to do in light of some current political decision, but rather to gain insight into some aspect of an ethical and political idea. That is, Socrates adapts the use of paradigm to become a heuristic device for discovering something further about a philosophical question.[43]

This Socratic adaptation requires that he and his interlocutors use their imaginations in order to reenvision justice in more expansive and adequate ways. When Cephalus argues that the just person is the one exemplified by the fair merchant who gives back what he owes and is honest, he offers a paradigmatic image of justice. This initial definition itself requires the use of the imagination to move from particular sensed and lived experiences of mercantile life, to a more abstract conception that captures what he thinks is essential to that life if it is well lived. Cephalus develops a mental schema into which people and their actions can be categorized as just or unjust. Similarly, Polemarchus's idea of justice as helping friends and harming enemies utilizes the imagination in order to organize the material of everyday life. Perhaps from his experience of particular conflicts in the emerging Athenian political conflicts, or particular dealings with friends, he finds the help of friends to be the paradigmatic example of being a just person. He works out of a cognitive schema that organizes and makes sense of a world in which there are many competing values and alliances, in which he is allied to one particular side. His description of justice as helping friends and harming enemies is thus the result of the work of the imagination, insofar as the paradigmatic image functions to bridge the world of abstract verbal discussion with the world of lived, ordinary experience.

In offering his counterexamples, Socrates gives paradigmatic instances that are intentionally disruptive of the cognitive schemas that his interlocutors hold to be true. Cephalus is unable to hold at the same time his narrowly mercantile understanding of justice as fairness and the view that one ought not to return weapons to a manic friend without revising his abstract cognitive schema about justice. Socrates's paradigmatic counterexample challenges Cephalus to reformulate his paradigm so that he can accommodate the added possibility that sometimes the return of what is promised is *not* the right thing to do. Another option would be simply to reject one's own prior paradigm and to experience aporia, as happens with many of Socrates's interlocutors. In such a case, the schema fails because the interlocutor's imagination has failed to be capable of finding a new larger paradigm that can include the new counterimage. Similarly, with Polemarchus, Socrates engages his imagination to ask him to imagine and to consider whether helping a bad person who is nominally one's friend seems like the right thing to do: can he envision helping such a person? When Polemarchus cannot, Socrates shows him that his paradigm of helping friends and harming enemies is not yet sufficient to hold together all the experiences of living justly that he takes to be part of what justice must include.

Eventually, Socrates's use of expert knowledge as paradigmatic for justice enters into the conversation through his use of other expert examples. By introducing the paradigms of doctor and pilot as examples of technical expertise, Socrates also introduces at least two distinct characteristics that justice may share with other *technai*. First, a *technē* has a clearly defined purpose or end, and second, it is a specific rather than a general kind of good. For example, the end of a doctor's art is health and the good of the human body. The doctor does not concern himself with the good in general, but only with the good of the human body, health, which is his art's purpose. Socrates asks whether we can treat justice similarly, when he asks Polemarchus to delineate what specific expertise the just person possesses, that is, when he asks him in what areas the just man's justice is useful.

Whether justice is a specific area of expertise is indeed questionable. For example, one might talk about the just or the unjust doctor, or the just or the unjust cook—imagine a doctor who delighted in poisoning his patients, or a cook who deliberately did the same, as in the plot of a murder mystery. Justice seems to transcend any particular skill or craft, many of which can be used for good or for ill. Socrates makes this point when he asserts that the man who is good at guarding money is also the best suited to steal it (334a). The best boxer in a fair fight will also be the most able to land a blow when one's back is turned. So, Socrates suggests, the just man would appear to be a kind of robber, if justice is about being clever or skilled at guarding wealth (334a). Here, Socrates's own examples seem to suggest that the initial paradigmatic argument that he offered is insufficient when considering justice. In the case of a *technē*, the knowledge that is used to accomplish the goal is separable from the good of the goal itself. A doctor seeks to cure disease and to maintain health in the body of his patients, but does not determine whether his patients are good or bad men, and whether they are fit to live or die. A doctor or nurse who kills his patients is unjust precisely because he seems to take his knowledge of medicine as a license to determine the value of human life, a matter outside of his technical expertise. Justice is not a characteristic needed only by particular technical experts, but by members of a society more generally—as will become clear by Book Four when justice is shown to belong to all, not only some, of the city. If there is to be an art of the good of the community, a *politikē technē*, or political art, the scope of this *technē* must be significantly wider than that of most ordinary *technai*, and larger questions of what is "good" must be brought into the discussion. However, this set of problems is not immediately resolved in the conversation between Polemarchus and Socrates but continues further into the dialectical discourse of the *Republic*.

A second issue that concerns the relation of justice to a larger good is whether justice involves only helping our friends, or only good people, or both good and bad people alike. Polemarchus asserts that justice is "helping friends and harming enemies" (334b). His vision of the world is divided into friends and enemies, where personal relationships guide how people exist in community.[44] However, when Socrates asks whether one can make mistakes about a friend's goodness, Polemarchus must concede that some mistakes in judgment are possible (334c–d). In such cases of mistaking one's friend as good, Polemarchus's understanding of justice would lead to the conclusion that it is just to harm the just. Since this does not seem to be an acceptable conclusion, Socrates tries out a new way of thinking about helping one's friends: perhaps it is not friendship per se that matters, but whether one helps the just. If so, then it may be "just to hinder the unjust and to help the just" (334d). Again, the argument's movement from friendship to just men as the proper recipients of help is not simply the case of rejecting a bad idea, but of revising what the intuition was behind a partially helpful idea through the expansion of an image of justice. Rather than imagining justice as benefiting a friend, the friend is reimagined as a just person. This is a change in perspective insofar as the just person whom I help (if I am just) is no longer only good with respect to his particular relationship to me (as one who benefits me or for whom I have special care). Now he is treated with respect to whether he possesses a particular virtue that makes him worthy of approbation. This is a shift in vision, for the perspective on the recipient of good action is no longer seen in terms of my particular relationship to him, but rather in terms of his identity in the world at large. The focus moves from the relationship of the individual only to myself, to the relationship with the wider community. Again, Socrates relies on the imagination to do the work of expanding the notion of justice, insofar as the imagination is requisite for taking on the perspective of others.

Such a shift is practically important in terms of the political context for the dialogue's characters. The Athens in which they reside is a city divided between factions that support the democracy and those that support an oligarchy. In the context of deep civil and political divisions, justice might well appear to be that which strengthens the well-being of one's own group of friends or political faction. As a metic supported by the democrats, Polemarchus might have understood justice to be helping the democrats in the city, and undermining those who support an oligarchy. But Socrates shows Polemarchus that even these political commitments involve a commitment to a larger sense of the good, one that transcends the private concerns of friendship or even the political interests of one's own group. It is not that the commitment to a larger sense of the good is logically entailed—it is perfectly logically consistent to say that I will only help my own friends and not those who seek to harm me in a civil conflict. Rather, Socrates asks Polemarchus to consider his opinion on what is more significant about the recipient of just actions: belonging to the same group of friends where the goodness of one's friends is irrelevant, or where being good matters.

Polemarchus considers the goodness of his friends to be more important than the particularity of their friendship. Socrates helps them to unfold something further from his original statement about justice as doing good to friends.

Once this is established, Socrates turns to the question of whether it is good to harm those who are bad. Just as it makes a bad horse worse if one harms him, harming human beings makes them even more unjust. But it does not seem right to say that justice can make others more unjust. Socrates concludes that it is "not the work of the just person . . . to harm either a friend or anyone else, but of his opposite, the unjust person" (335d). Polemarchus agrees that what Socrates says is true: justice aims for the good for all. In the course of their discussion, then, Socrates and Polemarchus enlarge justice considerably.[45] They move from a mercantile concern with equality and fairness in contracts and exchange to a vision of justice as that which requires knowledge of some sort and is concerned with the good for all, not only for some, in the city. The movement of reenvisioning justice is both dialectical and paradigmatic. It is dialectical in that Socrates sought to take up what was insightful in Cephalus's and Polemarchus's understandings of justice, while expanding these visions to be more inclusive of other considerations, especially regarding moral goodness and knowledge. It is paradigmatic in the sense that the dialectical movement takes place through arguments from paradigms, paradigms that are imagistic in their content. For example, the paradigm of the just merchant who is pictured as making fair deals is balanced with the paradigm of the friend encountering his madmen desiring weapons. The idea of the just person as one who helps his friends is revised through the use of paradigms of technical expertise. Paradigms here function rhetorically and philosophically: rhetorically insofar as they effectively persuade Polemarchus to revise his ideas, and philosophically insofar as Socrates treats that persuasion as a matter of shared discovery about the *nature* of justice, and not solely winning an argument.[46]

As Howland argues, the interaction between Polemarchus has also established a partnership between Polemarchus and Socrates, for they are now to "share in battle" in the subsequent discussion about justice (335e). This working together in common is already constitutive of a kind of political community and already constitutive of justice being embodied in the manner of argument. Socrates's discussion with his friends relies on the use of paradigmatic images to move forward the argument. As we will see in the argument with Thrasymachus, however, finding common agreement through the use of paradigmatic argument proves to be difficult if the underlying beliefs of the participants are in marked opposition. For what constitutes the most fitting paradigmatic example depends on the initial beliefs of the participants choosing the paradigms. With the argument between Socrates and Thrasymachus, we shall see limits to paradigmatic argument.

Chapter 3

Paradigmatic Argument and Its Limits

B ook One concludes with a heated interchange between Thrasymachus and Socrates over the nature of justice and whether the just life is happier than the unjust life.[1] In the first part of this chapter, my focus will be on how paradigmatic argument functions as part of the argument between Socrates and Thrasymachus. Paradigmatic argument is useful when all parties in a discussion share basic values and beliefs. However, it is inadequate for finding agreement when there are conflicting opinions as to what the best paradigm is for comparison, and when these differences are rooted in deeply different visions of the topic in question. To this extent, imagining justice through paradigmatic argument is limited. This chapter explores differences in vision between Thrasymachus and Socrates, how paradigmatic argument and counterargument function in their discourse, and why a move to a different form of argument in Book Two is necessary. In the second part of the chapter, I step back from the book's arguments to examine the ways in which Plato as author uses the drama of character in the dialogue in order to encourage further philosophical investigation of its ideas by the Platonic audience.[2]

Thrasymachus is a rhetorician. The position that he will stake out is not inconsistent with his practice as a speechmaker, insofar as a rhetorician may well desire to manipulate his audience for his own ends.[3] However, Thrasymachus does not here conceal from Socrates his own views. He willingly speaks about his understanding of justice and injustice and their effects, and offers an ardent defense of his views. To this extent, he acts with a concern for truthful argument and not in order be rhetorical or manipulative. Here I will not spend much time delineating the controversies over what Thrasymachus's position is, as I have already given a more detailed account of this elsewhere.[4] However, I will briefly summarize the broad contours of that argument. There seem to be at least four main claims that Thrasymachus makes about the nature of justice, and it is not clear to readers whether these are internally consistent.[5] Thrasymachus says that justice is the "advantage of the stronger" (338c). This would seem to make justice a beneficial and good pursuit for the strong. However, Socrates forces clarification that leads him to say that justice is the advantage of the ruling body (337a), but it is not necessarily the case that those who rule are innately stronger, strong precisely because they rule, or for some other reason. Thrasymachus then seems to shift to saying that justice is obedience to the laws (339b) and the good of others (343d–e). In this latter part of the discussion, he advocates injustice. Among the many disputes is whether Thrasymachus is a conventionalist or an immoralist.[6] That is, does he see justice as conformity to laws put in place, laws that benefit the ruler? Or does he think that the happy person acts unjustly?

I understand Thrasymachus to be both a conventionalist and immoralist. His picture of "justice" as the "advantage of the stronger" reflects the idea that whatever group or groups are strongest in a particular society determine what is just (conventionalism). It is an empirical and descriptive claim and not so much a normative one at this point.[7] However, knowing *that* the term "justice" is used conventionally also gives an advantage to those who are aware of this fact. Those in power act most advantageously by enacting laws that benefit themselves, while those who lack power act most advantageously when disobeying the just laws, at least in some circumstances (immoralism). Thrasymachus shifts his perspective over the course of the argument, from the point of view of those who rule and name their own advantage as justice (if they are knowledgeable), to the point of view of the ruled over, who recognize an advantage to not obeying if they can see the conventional nature of justice and act for their own good rather than the ruler's good.

Thrasymachus's vision stands in sharp contrast to that which Socrates will later present. While Thrasymachus argues that justice is conventional, Socrates sees it as objective.[8] While Thrasymachus will argue that the well-being of rulers and ruled are often at odds, Socrates will argue that the only just city is one in harmony where the city as a whole is happy and all parts are in harmony.[9] Thrasymachus argues primarily about the external effects of justice, but Socrates emphasizes the internal state of the just person.[10] Thrasymachus accuses Socrates of being naïve while Socrates's narration about him presents him as akin to a "wild animal" (336b). They have quite different visions of one another, although Socrates much later will call Thrasymachus "friend" (498d). However, Thrasymachus's concerns about whether justice makes a person happier continue to drive much of the dialogue even after Socrates has offered an apparent refutation. In Book Two, Glaucon and Adeimantus will ask Socrates to resume the discussion of whether the just life is happier, even if one removes external goods such as reputation or pleasure. They are not yet to be satisfied with Socrates's treatment of Thrasymachus's concerns.

Socrates and Thrasymachus's discussion shares certain parallels with that between Socrates and Polemarchus. Socrates again raises the question of knowledge and whether it is necessary for justice, only this time with respect to rulers, and he will again offer the paradigm of other *technai* in order to address whether just rulers care for their own good or for those whom they rule. However, Thrasymachus's responses are different from those of Polemarchus. He immediately agrees that the strongest rulers are those who possess knowledge, but then offers counterexamples as a kind of counterparadigm to Socrates's claim that the just are the happiest. These counterparadigms further deepen what is at stake in the argument that the just life is the best life. The discussion between Socrates and Thrasymachus relies on paradigms of rulers in order to treat both topics of knowledge and happiness in relation to justice.[11] Here I will focus on these two elements of Socrates's argument.

In order to clarify what Thrasymachus means, Socrates offers the example of Polydamas the pancratiast (an athlete who engaged in a sport that was mix of wrestling and fighting). If Polydamas is stronger than Socrates and Thrasymachus, and beef is advantageous to his body, then the same food must also be advantageous for these two who are weaker. Thrasymachus derides Socrates for offering such an example, for it reduces strength and advantage to physical strength and skill, which are not immediately traits exemplified by most politicians—qua politicians, at least. Moreover, meat is not good for Socrates simply because it is good for an athlete; the example immediately undermines Thrasymachus' argument. On its face, Polydamas the pancratiast is a bad illustration of Thrasymachus's meaning—at least from Thrasymachus's point of view.

This misleading image, however, forces Thrasymachus to clarify what he does mean by "advantage": different forms of government such as tyranny or democracy lay down laws that seek their own advantage, but which they name just for those over whom they rule (338e–39a). It also points out a difficulty with any universal *logos* that speaks about justice in general terms: the specific meaning of each of the terms used in a general definition is also open to question. In this case, the meaning of "stronger" (*kreitton*) and "advantage" (*sumpheron*) is indeterminate. The example of the athlete's meat-eating habits may be annoying, but it forces a clarification of meaning, in that it highlights that "strength" and "advantage" are both terms that may be used to cover a wide range of matters (one could also translate *sumpheron* as what is useful, beneficial, expedient, fitting, profitable, etc.). The example demands clarification of the universals to which it seems to belong.

Socrates asks whether rulers make mistakes or not in seeking their own advantage (339c–d). At this point Cleitophon interrupts. Cleitophon clearly takes a relativistic position and encourages Thrasymachus to do so, when he says that the rulers do what they *believe* to be to their own advantage, rather than what they *know* to be to their own advantage (340b5–7). Thrasymachus decisively rejects Cleitophon's suggestion and says that he means that the rulers *know* what is to their own advantage, rather than just believing what is to their own advantage. A ruler, when he is being a ruler in the precise sense, makes laws that are really to his own advantage (341a2–3). Knowledge defines being a genuine ruler.[12] Thrasymachus's way of arguing for this claim is to do what Socrates did earlier: to offer a paradigmatic argument that rests on comparisons to other *technai*: "Do you call a person making mistakes about the sick a doctor with respect to the mistake that he is making? Or the one who makes mistakes in calculation a calculator, when he is making a mistake, with respect to his mistake?" (340d). He then concludes from these two particular cases from other *technai*, "No craftsman (*demiourgos*), wise person (*sophos*), or ruler (*archōn*) makes mistakes when he is ruling, although everyone would say that the doctor made a mistake and the ruler made a mistake" (340e). Thrasymachus argues paradigmatically from other *technai*, and just as Socrates did earlier with Polemarchus, he offers these paradigms as a way of showing something about the justice, and as a way of working toward a more precise account (*akribei logōi*; 341b).

Socrates then argues against the claim that a precise ruler seeks his own advantage by also using analogies from other arts, including that of doctor, which Thrasymachus just used. Doctors seek the advantage of their patients. Ship's pilots are not pilots because they can sail but rather because of their art (*technē*) and rule (*archē*) over the sailors (341d). Therefore, no knowledge considers the advantage of the stronger, but only of the weaker and what is ruled by it (342d). Again, Socrates relies on two cases from the arts to argue paradigmatically to a universal that then applies back to the particular at hand, the political ruler.[13] Although the argument looks combative and may well feel combative to Thrasymachus at an emotional level—for not too long after, he accuses Socrates of needing a "nurse" (343a)—Socrates's argument is cooperative in that he works with the paradigms that Thrasymachus already used. Socrates wants to see whether the paradigms of these other arts allow us to discover something further about the art of ruling, beyond the feature that all true rulers possess knowledge (a trait upon which Socrates and Thrasymachus agree).

Paradigmatic arguments are not strict proofs of what must be the case, but rather they argue for what is probable based on particulars that are *thought* to share some common feature with the present example. It is therefore entirely appropriate that both Socrates and Thrasymachus further develop the paradigms that they have set forth so far, by filling them in with greater detail. Certain features of particular arts, such as medicine or piloting, may not carry over to all other arts, such as political rule. This is the essence of Thrasymachus's response to Socrates: he brings out the examples of shepherds and cowherds to show that not all craftsmen seek the well-being of those over whom they rule. After all, the shepherd ultimately takes care of the little sheep so that they may be eaten, which is certainly not to the sheep's advantage! Notably, Thrasymachus is returning to the earlier example of meat eating with which Socrates had begun. Thus, we can see that the argument between Socrates and Thrasymachus is highly agonistic, a battle of images over which features of different arts show that his own view of justice is most reasonable.

Eventually, the use of arts as paradigmatic for just rulers is temporarily dropped, and Thrasymachus moves to a more direct argument to show that political rulers constantly seek to benefit themselves: empirical evidence that this is descriptively what all rulers do when offered the chance (343b–44c). He now offers a different kind of inductive argument to show that political rulers seek their own advantage and not the advantage of their subjects by arguing that not only rulers but human beings in general "have more" when they act unjustly than when they act justly.

This shift from looking at the true ruler to the unjust person seems like an abandonment of the original claim that justice is what is advantageous for rulers. A different claim is at work, apparently, that acting unjustly is best.[14] But in fact Thrasymachus is simply changing to a different kind of empirically based, inductive argument to make his claim, which he wishes to defend in this battle with Socrates. In a society in which others rule, acting "justly" (i.e., according to the rulers' benefit) is not usually also to one's own benefit. Acting unjustly in such cases gives one more profit and advantage. The just man "everywhere has less than the unjust man" (343d). He has fewer financial benefits when a partnership is dissolved, pays more taxes on his property, allows his domestic world to deteriorate while he attends to public affairs, and loses the goodwill of his relatives when he refuses to serve their well-being over and against what is just (343d–e). Thrasymachus also offers an account of why justice is praised: because people fear suffering the harmful effects of others' unjust actions, they blame injustice (344c).

At the conclusion of his argument, Thrasymachus attempts to leave, but just as Polemarchus forced Socrates to stay earlier, those present at the discussion now prevent Thrasymachus from leaving. Socrates's narrative account insults Thrasymachus by comparing him to a "bathman" (*balaneus*) who has poured his *logos* over them and then leaves (344d).[15] This verbal image of "pouring over your head" may refer to Aristophanes's *Wasps*, in which the Chorus warns Bdelycleon that a prosecutor may come one day and throw his own words back over his head but in a way that twists and distorts their meaning (483).[16] Despite Socrates's intense disagreement with the conclusions of Thrasymachus's argument, and his emotional aversion to Thrasymachus revealed in his narrative comments, Thrasymachus's argument from paradigms and from other *technai* is no less (and no more) a proof for the relative happiness of the just and unjust men than are Socrates's arguments from paradigm. Both Socrates and Thrasymachus rely on the notion that the features of the *technai* upon which each focuses are the most fitting to describe political rule. The arguments from other arts do not establish anything about justice or injustice in themselves but only rely on the idea that the audience who listens to each argument will "see" the connection between the said feature of the art and justice. The difficulty is that Socrates and Thrasymachus "see" which arts are paradigmatic for justice quite differently. Socrates prefers the model of the doctor and pilot, while Thrasymachus prefers the shepherd. However, there is no judge to rule whether the ruler is most like one of these other practitioners of the arts more than another. All Socrates can say is that he, himself, is not persuaded by Thrasymachus's comparison. He asks that Thrasymachus persuade him, but the latter is at a loss for the means by which he might do so, suggesting that perhaps he has to force the *logos* into Socrates, like a forced feeding (e.g., that a nurse gives an ill baby) (345b).

Socrates then returns to Thrasymachus's favorite analogous *technē* of the shepherd rather than returning to his own preferred paradigms. He argues that the shepherd properly speaking does not care for the sheep for his own benefit and does not intend to kill and eat the sheep. He protects the sheep, which are eventually sold by a moneymaker whose main art is wage-making and not shepherding (345c–d). The shepherd's care is still for that over which he rules. Similarly, the moneymaking art is distinct from that of medicine in that its aim is different from the aim of medicine, since every art has its own distinctive benefit (*opheleia*) (346c). Socrates attempts to move the argument from one of probable comparisons (choosing the right paradigm) to an inductive argument that shows that every *technē*, even one like shepherding, seeks the care for that over which it rules. Socrates implicitly challenges Thrasymachus to find an exception.

However, a problem remains that is characteristic of inductive argument more generally: what if political rule is the lone example of an art that *does* seek its own advantage? Perhaps for this reason, Socrates adds that most who are asked to rule refuse to do so unless they receive additional wages, honor, or avoid a penalty in doing so (347a). According to Socrates's characterization, ruling a city is about as desirable as becoming the departmental chair at a university: somebody has to do it, but the task is seen not as an opportunity for glory and power. It is an activity that must be recompensed for taking the ruler away from his or her usual activities. Socrates and Glaucon add that love of money and glory are not desirable to those who are good, and so only a penalty and necessity will be enough to motivate the good person to rule (347b–c). He adds, "For if a city of good men were to come to be, there would be fighting over not ruling, just as there is now over ruling, so that there it would become clear that the true ruler does not naturally pursue his own benefit but rather that of the ruled" (347d).

Of course, this argument is also based on probabilities, insofar as Socrates, Glaucon, and Adeimantus agree that the desire to rule for money and honor is bad, while the material gains of the unjust man were foundational to Thrasymachus's argument to act unjustly. Thus the judgments as to which comparisons are paradigmatic and which are seen as exceptional rest on the *doxai* that the different characters already hold as to what constitutes a life well lived: money, glory, and power, or something else. Socrates notes the problem himself: if he and Thrasymachus were to go back to this point of argument and again list what the just and the unjust man each have as advantages, there would be no resolution of the argument because there are no judges (*dikastai*) to decide. Instead, they must be both the judges (*dikastai*) and the rhetors at the same time (348b). This can take place if they are able to come to an understanding (*anomologouenoi*). With respect to determining the nature of justice, there is no distinction between those who persuade and those who judge—both roles belong to all who partake in the conversation, and until a common understanding is found, the question of what paradigm is the "right" paradigm, or which image of justice is the most "fitting" image cannot be determined.

Socrates's last argument in Book One against Thrasymachus leads them to verbal agreement, but a rather superficial one. Here is the essence of Socrates's argument: the unjust man attempts to get the better of the just and unjust alike, and the ignorant man attempts to get the better of the wise and ignorant alike, while the just and wise, respectively, only attempt to get the better of those who are unlike them (350a–b). Therefore the just man is like the wise and the good, while the unjust man is like the bad and ignorant (350c). Logically, the argument is not effective.[17] Socrates merely establishes that the relationship between the just and unjust is parallel to the relationship between the wise and the ignorant, but such a parallel in no way establishes that the just are the wise or that the unjust are ignorant. At any rate, Socrates in his narration states that they had arrived at an agreement (*diōmologēsametha*) that justice was wisdom, but even after Thrasymachus blushes, he reasserts that Socrates has not yet convinced him. Although he reluctantly agrees to keep answering Socrates in order to gratify his desire for someone to answer his questions (350d–e, 351c), Thrasymachus is not convinced by the conclusions of those arguments.[18] This is not because Thrasymachus is less rational than Socrates or because he is too ashamed to admit that he really does agree with Socrates but cannot bear the shame of being exposed. Thrasymachus is clear that what Socrates has said does not satisfy him, and he has more to say about why, but he thinks that he will be thought of as merely engaging in demagoguery (350d). Like some of Socrates's other interlocutors (e.g., Protagoras or Callicles), Thrasymachus feels thwarted by Socrates's manner of questioning, unable to express himself fully when locked into the requirements of Socratic question and answer. Here, the reason seems clear: Thrasymachus does not share the beliefs about just rule that Socrates, Glaucon, and Adeimantus hold, and so none of these forms of probabilistic argument are sufficient to persuade him to think differently about just and unjust rulers. (As Howland argues, Thrasymachus's view of politics is not surprising, considering that he was from Chalcedon, a city subjected to the Athenians that narrowly avoided destruction at their hands.)[19] Yet another example of this difference arises: Socrates asks whether a city is unjust that enslaves many other cities unjustly and keeps them enslaved to themselves (351b). Socrates seems to think that such actions would be both unjust and bad. Yet Thrasymachus maintains that the best cities will do precisely this, and within the dramatic context of the dialogue he might find no better exemplar than Athens itself, which during the Peloponnesian War vastly expanded its colonial powers, sometimes killing or enslaving those communities that resisted its expansion. Socrates asks whether strength must be accompanied with justice, and Thrasymachus correctly assesses that they will each give different answers to this question on the basis of their underlying views of justice.[20]

Only Socrates's last image of the "band of thieves" begins to address some of Thrasymachus's deeper concerns. Socrates argues that even a group of unjust men with a common objective cannot accomplish their aims unless they possess some degree of justice and restraint with respect to one another (362b–d). Those who are wholly bad cannot accomplish anything. Still, this argument does not yet show that the wholly just are the happiest; perhaps a minimal amount of justice is sufficient—consider the rules that govern the "family business" in a film such as *The Godfather*, in which cooperation between its own members is mostly present but nonetheless is put to the unjust aims of the family at the expense of those outside of it.

Most significantly, Socrates then adds the further consideration that if the soul has a distinctive sort of work, then it cannot do such work well without the virtue proper to it, just as an eye cannot see well without work proper to its own nature (353b–d). If, then, justice is a virtue of the soul and injustice a vice, then the just man will have a good life that can accomplish its work and the unjust man will not. Thrasymachus only grants this much, however: "It appears so, according to your *logos*" (353e). After all, Socrates has not yet proven that the soul *has* a specific kind of work, or what the soul's activity might be. He has only used paradigmatic examples from other realms of human life—the distinctive function of the pruning knife or of the eye—to argue from analogy.

Socrates admits that he has been like a glutton at a feast who went too quickly to the foods that he desired to taste, without taking a due measure. His conclusion is: "I know nothing" (354c). Socrates must admit that he knows nothing with certainty—although he presumably still holds his opinion that the just life is happiest and best—because of Thrasymachus's determined resistance to shared agreement. In juxtaposing Socrates and Thrasymachus as each argues from a variety of paradigms that attempt to articulate some aspect of justice or injustice that each holds dear, Plato as author attenuates the tension between their different paradigms without immediately capitulating to an easy resolution. In Book Two, Glaucon and

Adeimantus will ask that Socrates truly persuade them rather than only seeming to persuade them, and the argument will resume. Socrates takes up a much subtler discussion of the nature of the human soul in which the proper activities of the soul are laid out more clearly.[21] As Lycos has argued, Socrates considers not the external effects of justice, but the internal effects: how possession of justice as a state of soul leads to a good life.[22] Socrates also needs to shows that certain other desires—such as the desire for knowledge or the desire for harmony—are deeper and provide a more lasting happiness than the desires that Thrasymachus sees as essential to happiness.

At the same time, Thrasymachus as a character is also inconsistent with his own views. Thrasymachus claims that the unjust life is a happy one, but nothing about Thrasymachus as a person conveys a sense of his own happiness. He lashes out at Socrates with his images of forced feedings and wet nurses, suggesting that he feels a need to resort to personal attacks rather than remaining confident in the structure of his argument itself. As Hoesly and Smith have argued, Thrasymachus is not only a bully. He also does not really believe what he says that he believes.[23] He claims that justice is the advantage of the stronger, but when Socrates shows himself to be stronger in argument, Thrasymachus does not praise him. He claims to admire those who master injustice, but when he is at the receiving end of arguments that he considers unfair, he does not express admiration for such injustice. Instead, he wants it to stop, suggesting a deeper commitment to justice than he will admit, perhaps even to himself.

Before moving on to Book Two and its new approach to argument, it will be helpful to step back and to examine what Plato as author accomplishes through his own use of images in Book One. Earlier, I argued for the ways in which Socrates uses paradigmatic images to argue with Thrasymachus, and how this argument displays certain strengths but also some limits to argument of this sort. A parallel phenomenon takes place at the level of the dialogue's drama. Although Socrates's city is a serious attempt to create a city in speech that is just, Plato also builds into the dialogue places where the limits of the paradigm of the just city become apparent. This does not mean that Plato intends completely to undermine the content of Socrates's ideal city. Rather, it suggests that Plato as author is aware that the paradigm of justice being presented through the images of city and soul *is* a paradigm, that is, a limited model of justice. No model, however, can perfectly capture every aspect of justice. While I hope this point will become clearer over the course of many chapters, one place it is visible is in Plato's treatment of resident metics in the dialogue. Cephalus and his family play a central dramatic role in the dialogue, and yet metics are peculiarly absent from the idealized city in speech. The dramatic presence of alien metics who form part of the community of discussion, but who are excluded from any explicit inclusion in the ideal city in speech, serves to caution us as to whether Socrates's later picture of justice is a completely adequate account of justice. Although the question of war with other Greeks is briefly touched upon, for the most part Socrates and his friends only consider the justice of a city for its own citizens and not for those who are outsiders, guests, strangers, or metics. In the very dramatic presence of Cephalus and Polemarchus (and the silent Lysias and Euthydemus), and the slave boy who chases after Socrates at the start, we see the problematic nature of an absolute division between citizen and noncitizen that is assumed in the perfect city in speech in later books.

Especially when one considers Socrates's later rejection of the family as a legitimate part of the ideal city-state, Plato's attentiveness to family bonds in the opening sections of the *Republic* is striking. Socrates's first words report that he went down to the Piraeus "with Glaucon, son of Ariston, to pray to the goddess" (327a). Here Plato draws attention to Glaucon and Adeimantus, Plato's own brothers, through mention of their father. Not much is known of Glaucon, and even his relative age in relation to Plato is controversial, but within the dialogue Socrates reminds his audience that both Glaucon and Adeimantus excelled at the Battle of Megara enough for one of Glaucon's lovers to write a poem noting their distinction: "Sons of Ariston, famous man of godly origin" (368a).[24] Moreover, Socrates makes a point to note that Glaucon is erotic by nature, enjoying the looks of many different young men and never rejecting those who are in the "blossom of their prime" (475a). Thus, Socrates links Glaucon to the polis in three distinctive ways: through his family role, his role as a citizen-soldier, and as other citizens' lover and beloved. Adeimantus is present not only in the *Republic* but also at Socrates's trial in the *Apology*, where Socrates mentions him as being among the many people present who would know him well enough to be witnesses of his supposed corruption of the youth but instead stand ready to aid Socrates (*Apol.* 33d–34a). Both Glaucon and Adeimantus maintain a friendly attitude of philosophical and engaged discourse with Socrates, standing in marked contrast to the angriness of Thrasymachus or the withdrawal of Cephalus. They are interested in challenging Socrates, as when Glaucon insists that Socrates has only seemed to persuade them by the end of the argument with Thrasymachus, when he ought "truly to persuade" them (357a). We find that both family and friendship equally constitute important parts of the constructive dynamic between the trio of

Socrates, Glaucon, and Adeimantus that dominates the dialogue, with Plato's implicit presence as a third son of Ariston in his role as the dialogue's author.

A second set of family relationships is found in the trio of Cephalus and his three sons: Lysias, Polemarchus, and Euthydemus. When Polemarchus interrupts and eagerly takes up the debate between Cephalus and Socrates, Cephalus leaves the discussion of justice to him. Polemarchus jokes to his father that he is "the heir of what belongs to you," and Cephalus laughingly affirms his son before departing (331d). At one level, the exchange between Cephalus and Polemarchus simply expresses a sort of affectionate banter between father and son. Polemarchus's joke that he will someday inherit his father's wealth references the prior discussion that Cephalus is accepting of his eventual death and trusting that his life was well lived and death not fearful. We witness the warmth and affection between a well-regarded but not particularly philosophical metic and his much more philosophical son. However, the narrative of life and death, and Polemarchus's inheritance and coming into his own, is complicated by the fact that Plato's own audience knows that Polemarchus will not inherit his father's great wealth. They know that Polemarchus will be killed by the Thirty Tyrants in 403 BCE, with all his family goods confiscated by the Thirty, his funeral forbidden in any family house, so that even the cloak and pillow for his burial had to be borrowed from neighboring families.[25] The now-silent Lysias will eventually bring one of the Thirty, Eratosthenes, to trial for his brother's murder, arguing that Polemarchus was denied a trial and forced to drink hemlock in violation of the city's most basic laws and mores. In his courtroom speech (later titled "Against Eratosthenes"), Lysias defends himself, his father, and his brother, as significant benefactors to the city, despite their lack of formal citizenship.

While they possessed none of the political rights afforded to citizens, Lysias points out that Cephalus was invited to come to Athens from Syracuse by Pericles and resided as guests for more than thirty years under the democracy, where they offered funds for dramatic performances, special taxes, and even ransomed citizens taken as prisoners by other cities (Lysias, "Against Eratosthenes" 4, 20). When the Thirty Tyrants took over, they found themselves in need of funds and therefore, Lysias argues, came for the wealth of this metic family (7–8). While Lysias was able to escape, Polemarchus was made to drink hemlock without a trial or any kind of defense (17). Lysias emphasizes the lack of respect among the Thirty for his brother's funeral, as the family was apparently not allowed to hold the funeral in any of the family homes, and even pillows and blankets for the body had to be donated by other families (18). While Lysias may be trying to secure a favorable outcome in the trial against Eratosthenes (who seems to have been only loosely associated with the events concerning Polemarchus), his emphasis is on the insatiable greed (*aplēstia*) of the Tyrants (19).

Particularly striking for our purposes is Lysias's analysis of the contrast between the Tyrants as citizens and the family of Cephalus as noncitizens: "Such was their reward to us for behaving as resident aliens far otherwise than they did as citizens!" (20). While Lysias and his brothers were aliens who lacked citizenship in a formal sense, they enacted citizenship. (Here, the Greek has a distinctive verb for acting as a citizen: *politeuō*.) According to Lysias, the Thirty Tyrants formally possessed citizenship but acted contrary to the activity of a true citizen. Here Lysias sets up an implicit identification of the true citizen with him who acts in accordance with the law and who supports the city in its economic, civic, and wartime activities. He does not directly argue that such metics ought to become citizens in law but instead implies that their civic participation shows that they are able to "be political" (*politeuō*), that in a sense they already belonged to the city regardless of their formal status.[26]

Lysias reports his own speech as having been attended not only by Athenians but also many foreigners (12.35) and the speech was in circulation by 403 BCE. Lysias's second career as an orator (from approximately 403 to 380 BCE) was under way well before the composition of the *Republic*. Thus, for an audience of the *Republic*, these political events were quite recent and the trial of Eratosthenes even more so. The lived histories of Cephalus and his three sons in the dialogue stand in ironic opposition with the action and words of the *Republic* in at least two ways. First, the two members of the family who do speak in the *Republic* and offer friendly jokes to one another about the inheritance of wealth and arguments will not inherit them, but instead will face death.[27] Moreover, Lysias will later speak, even becoming an orator and speaking on behalf of justice for his brother, although he is now silent.[28]

Howland has argued that the first two books of the *Republic* stand as a Platonic reply to "Against Eratosthenes," implicitly criticizing Lysias.[29] Howland lays out how Lysias's treatment of the tyrant in that speech closely parallels many of the issues regarding political power raised in the first book of the *Republic*: for example, suggesting that tyrants hide behind a mask of justice while acting unjustly, using private office to secure their private advantage, and being motivated by greed.[30] Polemarchus's definition of justice as "to do good to friends and to harm enemies" (332d) is consonant with Lysias's presentation of justice, especially in Lysias's pursuit to harm

Eratosthenes and the remaining Thirty Tyrants. Yet Socrates criticizes such an approach in arguing that harm of one's enemies in peacetime is not best; instead, peacetime ought to focus on the pursuit of partnerships or "things held in common" (333a). While Lysias sought to inflame anger toward the remaining Tyrants, Plato's Socrates argues that it is not just to harm anyone; only the unjust man behaves in this way (335c–d).[31]

While I am largely in agreement with Howland's argument that Plato's early books in the *Republic* offer an alternative to retributive violence, I would also like to suggest a certain Platonic sympathy for the plight of Polemarchus, Lysias, and Cephalus. I suggest that this sympathy for the family of metics is still present. While Polemarchus's definition of justice in Book One is refuted, his definition reappears later in the *Republic* in new form, recontextualized in light of a larger theoretical vision of justice. Polemarchus is not entirely mistaken to regard justice as helping one's friends; rather, Socrates greatly enlarges the notion of political friendship to include all, rather than only some, in the city. The movement of the argument from Cephalus's definition, to that of Polemarchus, and eventually to Socrates's own definition of justice ought not be seen as definitions that are simply refuted as incorrect but rather shown to be too limited in what the definition captures. Moreover, the dramatic presence of this metic family and allusion to the harm that came to them in the midst of Athenian political turmoil also raises the question of whether they were treated justly, for Socrates's city in speech will largely ignore metics, merchants, and foreigners. Justice is not abstract for them but a lived reality for those who died in the midst of civil war.

The descriptions of justice as "speaking the truth and giving back what one takes" and later as "to do good to friends and to harm enemies" (331d, 332d) locate something important about the injustice that Cephalus's family suffered, even if his definition is somewhat imprecise. Lysias reports that although he was promised safe passage in exchange for money, he feared that the verbal bargain was about to be betrayed, and that he would be killed, and so chose to escape through a back gate (14–16). Polemarchus is killed, despite the city's promise of protection for its metics, through representation by their patrons and subsequent access to the courts. Both sons are betrayed against the promise of a spoken word, and neither one is given "what is due" to him under the city's laws. When Cephalus departs and Polemarchus takes on his part in discussion, the reformulated definition of justice even better captures what happens to Polemarchus at his life's violent end. Polemarchus is harmed because the Tyrants consider him an enemy rather than a friend. For Polemarchus and Lysias, justice might well be understood as "to do good to friends and harm enemies" in a factionalized city where some regard one another as friends or enemies. Such a city stands in stark contrast to Socrates's later understanding of justice as the harmony of all classes in a unified city, but it is Polemarchus's definition that better captures the concrete political reality of the Athens in which he lived and died.[32]

To this extent, while Socrates's objections to Polemarchus's definition are important, the question of how to respond to unjust suffering remains even after Socrates's objections to the definition are made and acknowledged. Perhaps this nagging question of unjust suffering is part of the reason that Glaucon and Adeimantus insist that Socrates take up the case of the just man tortured on the rack and believed to be unjust (361d–62a). Their question as to whether a human being can still be happy if he possesses a just soul but faces unjust treatment is a relevant question to people living in the midst of civil war and injustice.[33] Thus the characters within the dialogue also serve as images of various ways of understanding justice and injustice conceptually. Their presence emphasizes the practical consequences for taking up particular moral and philosophical views of justice.

Chapter 4

Narrative, Poetry, and Analogical Strategies of Argument

Book Two begins with Glaucon's insistence that Socrates's argument against Thrasymachus is unfinished. Glaucon and Adeimantus take Socrates to task, saying that Socrates has only *seemed* to persuade them, rather than persuading them "in truth," that it is better to be just than to be unjust (357a–b). This distinction between a seeming and a truthful persuasion raises the question of the relationship between truth and persuasiveness. Socrates is committed to offering truthful arguments, but unless such arguments are also persuasive, they will have little moral or political effect.[1] In Book One, the use of paradigmatic images from other *technai* did not bridge the visionary gap between Socrates and Thrasymachus. Even if Socrates is assured of the truthfulness that the just life is best—for example, if this opinion has withstood refutation after much testing over the course of his lifetime—this does little good for Thrasymachus, Glaucon, or Adeimantus. Thus, Socrates must find a different argumentative strategy that both uncovers the truth about the nature of justice and persuades at least Glaucon and Adeimantus—and perhaps some of the others who are present. The image of the city and its analogue in an image of the soul is the basis of Socrates's argumentative strategy. The city-soul analogy is intended to assist in the discovery of the nature of justice, in a way that specifically addresses the concerns of Glaucon and Adeimantus. Socrates offers a dialogically informed image, that is, not simply an image that represents his own view of justice, but one that is formed in relation to the specific concerns of the two brothers. As I will argue, the city-soul image is a heuristic device that begins with a partial and incomplete sense of justice and deepens our understanding of those preliminary notions of what is in common between city and soul.

Socrates describes the previous argument from Book One as a mere *prooemium* (opening) in his narration of the evening's conversation (357a).[2] As Ausland has argued, Socrates uses a term that can be used either in forensics (e.g., the opening of a legal argument in the courtroom) or in the opening of a dramatic work, as when an epic opens with a hymn to the gods.[3] The word *prooemium* is rooted in the term *oimē*, or song, used, for example, in Homer's *Odyssey*, when Demodocus opens with his first song (*Od.* 8.74). The arguments of Book One serve as a kind of opening act, summarizing some of the key problems with which an argument for the goodness of justice and the happiness of a just life must concern itself. Like a courtroom speaker who uses the opening to lay down the outlines of a case, Socrates's friends outline some of the everyday concerns about justice that a good philosophical theory must address. A good defense of justice must explain why it makes the just person happier, when many might argue that the unjust person is better off materially and socially. A good defense ought to show how justice goes beyond personal commitments to friends, which can factionalize a city. A good defense of justice ought to show us whether it gives peace at the end life, such that the just person can have some assurance that one's life has been well lived. These practical concerns are still present in the ensuing books of the *Republic*, even if the focus becomes determining a more exacting answering to the question, "What is justice?"

Glaucon and Adeimantus indicate that the argument of Book One is inadequate for them, even though they share Socrates's opinion that the just life is the best life.[4] Glaucon desires more than opinion. He explains: "As for myself, Socrates, while I don't believe in it, I am at a loss when I've been talked deaf by Thrasymachus and many others. But the argument for justice—that it's better than injustice—I've never heard stated as I want. I want to hear it praised by itself (*auto kath' hauto*)" (358c–d).

Glaucon states that there are three kinds of goods: those which we would choose to have for their own sakes, those we choose only for their consequences, and those we choose both for their consequences and as ends in themselves (357b).[5] Glaucon asks, Of which of these three kinds is justice? While these categories are by now familiar in light of the history of philosophy since Plato,[6] Glaucon's movement of the discussion from a "picture" of justice to a "kind" (*eidos*) of good is a significant shift in their approach to the problem at hand.[7] Instead of only describing what the just life looks like through paradigmatic images, as was the approach of Book One, Glaucon places justice into a categorical scheme that defines more precisely the very sense of the term "good" (*agathos*). If we want to say that justice is a good, then we must have in mind some clearer sense of what we mean by "goodness."

Glaucon offers to restore Thrasymachus's argument in a new form and to praise the unjust life and blame the just life, while asking Socrates to praise the just life and to blame the unjust one (358c–d). Glaucon suggests engaging in a form of argument where each of the two parties presents opposing ideas, with Glaucon purposefully taking up a position in which he does not believe for the sake of the argument. This method of exploring an idea bears certain resemblances to the sophistic use of antilogic, that is, arguments in which two opposing *logoi* are offered on two sides of an argument. The roughly contemporary *Dissoi Logoi* is an example of such *dialexis*.[8] The *Dissoi Logoi*'s arguments often concern political matters that would be familiar to readers of Platonic dialogues, such as whether virtue can be taught, or the nature of good rhetoric. However, its treatment of such topics is quite different. For example, the *Dissoi Logoi* opens by asserting that the good is relative, offering examples such as that illness is bad for those who are sick but good for doctors, death bad to those who die but good for grave-diggers and undertakers, and the Spartan victory good for Spartans but bad for Athenians (*Dissoi Logoi* I). While at moments the text seems to indicate both relativistic and objective understandings of the good, its overall emphasis is on the incompleteness of any argument to establish answers to certain questions, such as whether virtue can be taught.[9] Glaucon invites the use of *dialexis* for a quite different purpose: in order to discover more about the nature of justice and to satisfy particular concerns about justice that have been raised in the previous chapter: in particular, whether justice is still good even if its external effects are removed. The *Republic*'s movement from paradigmatic argument to opposing arguments, however, is not a movement from image-based argumentation to image-free argumentation. Rather, the nature of the arguments and counterarguments continues to take place in the form of images.

Socrates answers Glaucon's question about what kind of good justice is by saying that it is the kind of good that is sought both for its own sake and for the sake of its consequences (358a). Glaucon counters that the many would say that it is a form of drudgery, something that must be performed for the sake of the consequences of money and reputation, but which in itself is hard (358a). He then offers an elaboration of that view before inviting for Socrates to give a counterargument. As Ausland has argued, Glaucon follows a traditional epideictic structure in presenting this revival of the Thrasymachean vision.[10] Ausland notes the use of specific

features of *epideixis* such as the description of the generation of the topic
of praise, the action of the person or city being praised, and a comparison
(*sunkrisis*) offered as a means to praise one person or place by placing it in
contrast to another.[11] Glaucon offers an account of the generation of justice
and injustice, describes how the unjust person with opportunity to do so
acts, and then offers a stark comparison between the just and unjust person.

While drawing upon the resources of rhetoric, these arguments are
also philosophical in that they seek to use rhetorical resources in order to
show something further about the truth of the matter at hand, and not only
to produce persuasion. Glaucon, Adeimantus, and Socrates each rely on a
variety of images in order to help their audiences test the truthfulness of
each position. First, Glaucon uses narrative imagery in his narrative account
of Gyges's ancestor in order to invite his audience to consider whether the
motivation to act unjustly when possible is psychologically isomorphic to
his listeners' own souls. Second, Adeimantus uses poetic imagery when he
cites the poetic tradition of Homer, Hesiod, Simonides, and Pindar as a
way to strengthen Glaucon's case. Last, Socrates uses the city-soul analogy
as a heuristic image in order to discover the nature of justice in the soul
and to defend an ideal of justice as a kind of internal harmony.

To begin his restoration of the Thrasymachean position, Glaucon offers
an alternate account of justice, suggesting that doing injustice is good while
suffering it is bad, but that the bad in suffering it exceeds the good in doing
it. He offers a kind of a social contract theory, whereby citizens agree not to
do unjust acts so that they also do not suffer from them (358e–59a).[12] Justice
is a mean between what is best for an individual—doing injustice without
consequences—and suffering it at the hands of others. He adds that even
those who do justice do it unwillingly, out of an inability to do injustice
(359b). To illustrate the claim that those who do justice would act unjustly
if they were given the opportunity (359b), Glaucon retells the story of Gyges
from Herodotus (358d–60b).[13] In shifting to a narrative account, Glaucon
is not simply making an appeal to poetic authority, however. Rather, the
use of the mode of narrative invites Glaucon's audience to situate himself
in the story and to examine whether his motives would align with those
of the shepherd, should he find himself in the possession of such a ring.
It thus encourages the audience of the myth to explore whether the view
that justice is undertaken merely for the good effects such as reputation is
psychologically adequate.

Glaucon adapts elements of the story for his own purposes, not
simply retelling the version found in Herodotus, but changing its central

message so that the question of what the shepherd chooses once he has the ring heightens the psychological dimensions of his choice. To begin, Glaucon tells a story about Gyges's ancestor, and not Gyges himself. Whereas in Herodotus's version, the shortcomings of the king are emphasized, in Glaucon's account, the shepherd's response to finding himself in the midst of power without consequences is the story's center. In Herodotus, Gyges is the bodyguard to the king, Candaules, a king who lacks moderation. Herodotus describes Candaules as a man overly in love with his wife, in excess of passion even for his lawful partner, who persuades Gyges to look at his wife naked because Gyges does not believe him as enthusiastically as King Candaules would like, despite Gyges's insistence that he believes. Gyges is his most trusted bodyguard. Gyges initially does not want to do what he believes to be wicked, but he eventually capitulates to Candaules's wishes. It is the king who contrives a situation where Gyges can hide and see the queen naked, unknown to her. The queen discoverers that she has been seen and tells Gyges that he must either kill the king and take over the throne or die immediately. While Gyges elects to marry the queen, he does so reluctantly, since his choice is either his own death or the king's. His choice, as he sees it, is between his own life and the king's life, and so when the queen places a dagger into his hand, he slays the king. In Herodotus's story, the king's foolishness and queen's power drive the action of the story. While Gyges does actively choose to spy on the queen and to kill the king, those choices are framed within a context of a king and queen who try to "force his hand" toward unjust acts. Herodotus's story is a story about sexual shame and passion. In his version, a servant capitulates to the forces around him: it's the social forces—the king and the queen—that push him to act unjustly, and only when he succumbs to them and does not listen to his internal sense of morality does he become unjust. In Glaucon's version, we find exactly the opposite: the just man becomes unjust when he can escape notice, when *no* social pressure touches him. The queen has no part in Glaucon's version of the plan and she is overcome by the shepherd rather than being the instigator. Even the detail that the shepherd initially robs the corpse of its ring when he falls into the chasm suggests that it is through escaping and being hidden away from the watchful eyes of others that leads the shepherd to act unjustly. Within the gap formed after the earthquake, he is invisible to others.

Several elements of Glaucon's narrative are novel and not found in Herodotus: a ring is discovered deep in a chasm of the earth, and the ring is removed from a corpse inside a horse. This language of descent into the chasm is another instance of the language of ascent and descent that occurs throughout the dialogue. Here we find a quiet foreshadowing of the myth of Er, in which some exceptionally evil souls descend into the earth and do not reascend. Glaucon also changes the main character to a shepherd rather than a bodyguard—perhaps taking up the prior image from Thrasymachus of the shepherd who may choose to care for his sheep ultimately for his own good and not for theirs (343b). Whether the shepherd will only benefit from the use of the ring, or will encounter the punishment of a terrible death like that of the predecessor who used the ring before, is undecided—and in this way, the story perfectly expresses Glaucon's concern that while at times injustice is punished, whether it *always* will be punished is unclear. Glaucon's story has as its main character not Gyges but his ancestor from generations back, pushing the story into a more foundational mythical past.[14]

The presence of details such as lightning and the bronze horse with windows, and the earthquake convey also a sense of mythic power and the possibility of violence in nature. The myth asks, If we could have something that could remove a person from the realm of human society, would we still want to be just? What happens to man when one takes away convention, and descends deeply into his own depths, out of the light of day? Yet in Glaucon's description, there is something strange about even *speaking* about what human beings are like without shame or without social forces to influence their growth, since no such people exist. They are mythical, and so we need, then, a myth to be able to speak of the preconventional, natural man.

In Herodotus's version, an otherwise good man is led into unjust choices by others who seem to have power over him and yet ascends to the throne. Throughout, Gyges is reluctant to choose unjust actions. In Glaucon's retelling of the story, the shepherd lacks shame and self-restraint as soon as he is out of sight. Moreover, the temptation to which Herodotus's bodyguard submits is due to the king's overvaluation of sight as opposed to hearing. Herodotus writes that the king tells his servant: "I see you do not credit what I tell you of my lady's loveliness; but since men's ears are less credulous than their eyes, contrive some means whereby you may see her naked." That is, on Herodotus's account, Candaules finds *logos* to be powerless in conveying the truth of his wife's beauty; instead, a visual experience is needed, to directly convey the reality that Candaules wishes to share. Yet, such an experience is also morally dangerous. Had Gyges simply trusted in the king's words and refused firsthand knowledge by sight in favor of secondhand knowledge, he would not have committed other unjust actions. Thus there is a contrast set up between seeing something for one's self, and hearing about it secondhand.

On the one hand, seeing the truth of something directly allows for greater understanding, but on the other hand, a more mediated form of learning through listening to others also has a place. Seeing for oneself is not always good, depending on the moral context.

In the *Republic* as a whole, there is a frequent movement between sight and hearing as means to understand the nature of justice. On the one hand, Socrates and his friends use a variety of narratives and argumentative strategies in order to discover and to test ideas about justice. To learn about justice, it seems that one must listen to others and offer arguments and counterarguments to test one's own ideas. On the other hand, in the middle books, Socrates offers primacy to sight in his description of the form of the good as the cause of intellectual insight, and in the forms themselves as modeled on a visual metaphor of "shape" or something that can be seen or imaged. This movement between sight as a metaphor for knowledge—especially for the "coming to see" something about justice by an individual inquirer—and *logos*, which in the characters' verbal communication requires hearing, is a dialectical movement within the *Republic*. In order to learn about justice, we need both insight and the verbal testing of ideas by others. Of course, the *Republic*'s critiques of poetry will go on to suggest that the dangers of knowledge as "seeing for oneself" presented by Herodotus are not exclusive to visual approaches to knowing. Hearing the traditional stories of heroes and gods is also powerful; the question of moral corruption is not exclusive to either sight or to hearing.

Narrative of the sort that Glaucon uses combines elements of hearing and sight. It thus draws together the visual to the word. One listens to the narrative, but the narrative includes vivid imagery that encourages the formation of images in the minds of the audience. Moreover, Glaucon's narrative strategy asks the audience to consider his or her own relationship to the character of the shepherd. Listening to a narrative in which a character must make a key choice between just acts and unjust acts invites those who listen to identify or to disidentify with the character. Glaucon's concluding remarks at the end of his mythological account especially encourage such a self-identification.[15] He asserts that the just man and unjust person would act identically if in possession of the ring, having sexual relations with whom he wishes, freeing or slaying those in bonds, and in general, universally stating of all persons, "For every man believes that injustice is much more to his private profit than justice" (360d). Glaucon, in other words, moves from a universal claim about why men act justly (to protect themselves from injustice), to a narrative that provides the possibility of a particular

identification or disidentification with those who act unjustly when they
will not be discovered, back to a universal claim about the nature of human
beings as those who believe injustice is best.

This movement from universal to particular to universal in his argumentation may be mirrored in an audience response. An audience member
may move from listening to Glaucon's story, to assessing whether he would
or would not act similarly if faced with such a choice, and then on to
agree or to disagree with the adequacy of Glaucon's universal claims about
human beings. The listener who critically engages with the story can more
easily make judgments about the adequacy of the general universal claim
about justice when faced with a narrative representation that invites finding
similarity and difference between oneself and the iconic character of the
shepherd. That is, the person who listens to Glaucon (e.g., Socrates or his
friends in Cephalus's house, and also those who read a Platonic text) makes
a mimetic identification or disidentification with the character's choices in
order to assess the argument.[16] A member of Glaucon's audience—or of the
Platonic audience—may say to himself, "I would never use the ring in such
a way," and so actively disidentify (or perhaps identify) with the shepherd.
At the moment of identification or disidentification, the person who does so
might have begun to have better access to *why* he or she would choose as
she thinks that she would. For example, a listener might say that he would
feel ashamed to commit adultery and make an examination of shame and its
motivational and ethical significance. Or a listener might assert that murder
is always wrong and then defend to others (or only to himself) the reasons
why taking the life of another is worse than suffering death, or assert that
he would kill in such a circumstance. We cannot anticipate or force specific
audience responses to any given narrative. But the use of narrative presents
an opportunity for examining any felt psychological isomorphism between
the image of the shepherd with a ring, and that of the soul of the person
listening to the story. Alternatively, a sense of separation of oneself from the
story—as when a reader might say, "But I would never do that, not even
with a ring!"—invites a reader to find *reasons* for that judgment about of a
lack of isomorphism between one's self and the soul in the story. In other
words, Glaucon's use of narrative encourages a philosophical movement
toward self-knowledge.[17] As human beings, we can only recognize who
others are by their actions: a courageous man is known to be courageous
through the courageous acts that he does. We also come to know ourselves
through comparing ourselves to the actions of others, for example, asking

whether I would respond in the same way as another did, if placed in identical circumstances.

If one wishes better to understand how such identification or dis-identification might work, one need look no further than Socrates's own later account of how *mimēsis* affects those who perform in dramatic works. Tragedy and comedy both proceed through the use of *mimēsis* (394c). In the ideal city in speech, the city's guardians should only imitate those who possess the virtues that are necessary to be capable guardians, such as characters who display moderation, courage, and piety (395c). One reason is that one cannot be good at imitating everything. More importantly for our purposes here, such imitations make impressions on the soul that leave lasting effects. Socrates says, "Haven't you perceived that imitations (*mimēseis*), if they are continued from youth onward, become established as habits (*ethē*) and nature in the body, sounds, and thought?" (395d). In mimetic imitation, one may momentarily take on the identity of someone other than who one already is through imitation of another's actions. For example, if I wish to become a more courageous person, I might imitate a person known to have courage, through taking up the particular acts that he does, and refraining from actions from which he refrains: think of a novice firefighter who learns how to judge when entering a fire is courageous and when foolish, from a more experienced one. In observing others from whom we actively wish to learn, we naturally compare our current state to that of others, and form comparisons between their actions and our own. Such comparisons result in greater self-knowledge. Deliberately imitating the skill that I lack over time can produce a capability to undertake actions that I previously did not know how to do, through force of habit. However, imitations of others can also produce negative traits: imitating a man who wails too easily over his misfortune might lead me also to become such a kind of a person (395e). Imitations harm the soul because they lead the imitator to act "as if he were someone else" (393c). Over time, imitations produce habits, changing one's fundamental character.

The guardians are only to use narration when describing others whom they do not wish to be like, such as blacksmiths or those who practice other crafts, women, or slavish or mad men (395e–97b). Socrates says remarkably little about how and why narration saves speakers from the problems inherent in pure *mimēsis*, but we can infer that narration does not demand of the speaker or listener that he choose to be "someone else." Narration does not produce the same immediate habits and impressions on the body and soul as does *mimēsis*. However, narration still allows both the speaker and the listener access to the character being portrayed, but with greater distance, on account of the mediated nature of the narrative. Glaucon's narrative of the shepherd invites the listener to consider whether he is *already* like the shepherd—or would be like him were he to possess a similar power of invisibility.

If we consider Socrates's comments about the power of imitation for producing habits in the person who undertakes the imitation, and the greater advantages of narrative, then we might glean an understanding of how listening to Glaucon's story might work. Glaucon narrates the story of Gyges's ancestor for us and provides a kind of distance from the story—one that would be lacking in simply imitating the shepherd's words and actions—by framing it within the context of exploring the question of justice. Narrative itself provides a kind of critical distance by which the power of *mimēsis* becomes mediated. In effect, rather than passively becoming habituated to act like the shepherd through repeated imitations of his story, a reader is encouraged to consider the very question of whether she would or would not be like the shepherd. Glaucon's narrative framework offers a freedom and openness to compare oneself to the shepherd that *mimēsis* alone would not. Even narration is not completely free of all the qualities of mimetic speech, but rather is a more mediated way of undertaking mimetic comparisons. With narration, one does not already assume the voice of the character being imitated. Rather, one is invited to imagine, to observe, and to assess the character. Glaucon's account, although narrated, is nonetheless imaginatively vivid. But his framing that story within the context of what others say about the value of justice and injustice also asks his audience to situate this image within a larger framework of philosophical judgment and criticism.

We see a similar phenomenon at work with the presentation of characters in the Platonic dialogue. While Socrates describes Thrasymachus as akin to a wild beast (336b), he approves of Glaucon as courageous and as worthy of the poems that were written in his praise (357a, 368a). Elsewhere, Glaucon is presented as highly erotic (368a, 402e, 450a, 468a), and as many commentators have argued, this eros is not limited to sexual desire but extends also to a yearning for better argument.[18] Socrates himself is another example of a just man who had a reputation for injustice, as one brought to court for the corruption of youth. Yet in the *Apology*, he is devoted to justice regardless of consequence.[19] Thus, for the Platonic audience, there is a double set of images at play: the unjust shepherd and beastlike Thrasymachus, on the one hand, and the tortured just man and the just Socrates on the other hand. This "layering" of narrative further invites an audience member to find himself or herself in the dialogue, and even to examine his or her own soul on the basis of a variety of psychological isomorphisms or differences.[20]

Here we can see an interesting element of a Platonic approach to eikastics within the text's argumentation. As I will later argue in my account of the image of the divided line, images continue to play a role in the discovery of truth, when they are properly understood. For example, an image of a line can assist a geometer to understand a geometric principle. A true likeness or image—*eikasia*—is both like and unlike that of which it is an image.[21] In Book Nine of the *Republic*, Socrates will emphasize the dissimilarity of images from that which they imitate, and thus their relative unreality in comparison to the forms. But to the extent that a likeness *is* a likeness, it also bears some similarity to that which it is like; it is, to some extent or another, truthful. This combination of likeness and difference is important for Glaucon's (and Plato's) purposes, insofar as we who listen to or read a dialogue are invited to examine the extent to which the shepherd is like and unlike ourselves or to others whom we know. It hopes to assist us in evaluating the degree of likeness and unlikeness of this *eikasia* of this image of the shepherd to the human being. As Tanner writes of Plato more generally, "the imagination plays a philosophical role: it is analytical because it enables the seeing of differences within identity, and thus enables philosophical inquiry."[22]

The difficulty, of course, is that unlike a painting that can be compared to the *paradeigma* of which it is an image, the very nature of justice is still in dispute. There is no clear mode of access to the paradigmatic "just soul," especially in light of Glaucon's hypothetical claim that all just souls are really only unjust souls who lack power. In fact, in the narrative of the ring, since the just soul is really only a self-interested and unjust soul who chooses to act justly, the *unjust* soul is the paradigmatic "original." Given that immediate access to the soul is unavailable, Glaucon instead offers a narrative account that allows comparison between an image of an unjust soul (the shepherd with the ring) and oneself. Self-knowledge is a means by which the Platonic audience is encouraged to enter into the possibility of making the distinction between a true and a false image with respect to the specific image of the shepherd that Glaucon has presented.

Glaucon next offers a *sunkrisis* (comparison) of the just and unjust man as a means of making the best judgment about them: "As to the judgment (*krisin*) itself about the life of these two about whom we are speaking, if we separate the most just from the most unjust, we'll be able to judge correctly (*krinai orthōs*); if not, then not" (360e). On each side of the comparison is the "perfection" (*teleon*) of each man: that is, the man who is unjust but appears to be perfectly just, and gets all the rewards of justice, and the man who is perfectly just but seems to be perfectly unjust, and is whipped, racked, bound, and has his eyes burned out before finally being crucified (362a). Glaucon challenges Socrates to judge which of the two is happier. Moreover, Glaucon cleverly reincorporates each of the previous visions of justice from the earlier discussion of Book One, by asserting that the unjust man benefits in contracts and partnerships, is better able to help his friends and to harm his enemies, and is better able to make sacrifices to the gods (362b–c). That is, he suggests that the perfectly unjust person accomplishes many of the actions of the just person as presented by Cephalus and Polemarchus, too. He thus caps off his epideictic speech by asserting a kind of verbal triumph over all the previous speeches given about justice insofar as it can also account for many of these earlier points.

Before Socrates can answer, Adeimantus joins in and asserts that Glaucon's argument has not been adequately stated (362d). He thus takes up an agonistic position not only against the Socratic claim that the just person is happier, but also competitively against his brother's skill in speechmaking. Adeimantus argues that the poets also do not sufficiently defend justice and, in fact, their ideas can be reconstrued on behalf of the view that justice is praised only for external goods such as reputation, offices, wealth, and divine rewards (363a–67e).[23] Adeimantus treats the poets of the past as a resource for his own argumentative "case" against justice. They are literally "witnesses" (*marturas*), that is, evidentiary material for Adeimantus as he makes his own case (364c).[24] A defendant or prosecutor in a courtroom is not usually interested in making a point about the witnesses whom he brings to the stand, so much as using those witnesses in order to build up an argument about some other matter. Similarly, Adeimantus here is not primarily attempting to show that the poets *overtly* claim that injustice is preferable to justice. Some poets do, in fact, praise the just man, but their praise of justice is undermined by other instances in which injustice is made to appear worthwhile or even divine. Adeimantus utilizes poetic resources in order to build a kind of forensic argument of his own, alongside the defense of injustice that has been offered by Glaucon. Like Glaucon, however, Adeimantus hopes that Socrates will later be able to tear down these objections with a counterargument as to why justice is intrinsically good.

With respect to the larger movement of the evening's discussion, Adeimantus begins a trajectory of criticizing the poets for whether they are adequate educators, a question that Socrates will later take up and expand even further. Adeimantus uses multiple poets—Hesiod, Homer, Musaeus, Simonides, and Pindar—without making any kind of argument for the consistency of thought among these poets on this point. His purpose is not to offer the best possible critical commentary of any single poet, or of the poetic tradition as a whole, but only to show why the view that "injustice is better" could be concluded even from the traditional education of the day, although it purportedly defends justice. If the poetic tradition wants to defend the goodness of justice—and clearly the passages he cites from Hesiod and Homer suggest that they mostly do want to make such a defense—their education is inadequate, given the kinds of justifications unjust people can find even in the same poems for only *seeming* to be just. Near the end of his discourse, Adeimantus says, "No one has ever, in poetry or in prose, set forth sufficiently the argument that the one [injustice] is the greatest of evils a soul can contain in itself, and justice the greatest good" (366e). Adeimantus's biggest criticism of the poets is that they do not offer sufficient philosophical justification for the claims that they make on *behalf* of justice. Such an argument is what he hopes Socrates will be able to give, however.[25]

Although the poets are criticized, poetry is also a source of philosophical learning in the dialogue, insofar as it forms part of the *antilogos* against the Socratic *logos* that the just life is best. The inclusion of what the poets say is intrinsic to how these three interlocutors—Socrates, Glaucon, and Adeimantus—go about deepening the philosophical questions about justice. While Socrates will go on to criticize certain forms of poetry, its inclusion here in the voice of Adeimantus is an act of Platonic reincorporation of the poetic tradition, not a total rejection of its content as inappropriate for philosophical discussion.[26]

However, Adeimantus's claim that no poet has adequately defended justice seems to be a moment when we can see that the dialogue will attempt to take up the project of defending the goodness of the just life in a more thorough way than any of his poetic predecessors have done. The poets may not always actively corrupt, but even to the extent that they teach that justice and piety are goods, they are unable to answer the kinds of objections that Glaucon and Adeimantus have, as citizens who basically believe in the goodness of justice but want to know *why* it is good. The poets are also insufficient educators insofar as their poetry does not shape the souls of those who listen but have doubts about the goodness of justice. At best, they can only move others who already share in their conviction that justice is good. At worst, the poets suggest that injustice is at times morally acceptable, or practiced by the gods. In other words, the poetic tradition is not sufficient philosophically, psychologically, or pedagogically.[27]

Adeimantus's argument about the poets further supports Glaucon's idea that justice is praised for its rewards. He lists concrete instances of those rewards and also attributes the origin of those rewards to divine sources. Even the gods treat justice in terms of external goods. Adeimantus cites Hesiod, who says that the gods give to the just bees, acorns, and "fleecy sheep laden with soft wool," while Homer attributes productive land and plentiful crops, fish, and herds to lands ruled by a just king (363a–c). Musaeus says that the just receive the divine reward of never-ending drunkenness at an eternal symposium, while others punish the unjust in Hades (363c–d). Hesiod and Homer offer examples of rewards given not to just individuals but rather to whole lands ruled by just kings.[28] The reference to Musaeus's poem brings in a larger cosmic dimension of eternal reward or punishment after death, although Adeimantus does not particularly extol the notion of "eternal drunkenness" as the noblest of all rewards for a just life, either! Still, only the poets can serve as witnesses of the consequences of justice from this larger, divine and cosmic perspective, for the inspired poet's perspective exceeds that of any ordinary person who does not have access to divine motivations and causes.

Adeimantus next moves to instances of poetry and prose that praise injustice as more profitable and as shameful only by "opinion and convention" (364a). Again, Adeimantus gives most of his attention in this analysis to the gods, who sometimes are said to give misfortune to many good men and good things to bad men (364b). Priests and prophets persuade the rich that certain recitations and sacrifices can remedy the injustices that they have committed, or that rites can benefit the dead who may be in need of them (364b–65a). Adeimantus does not himself concur with these claims but rather concludes that those who listen to these poets might reasonably conclude that the advantage of justice lies in appearing just, while being unjust (365b). Although getting away with injustice is difficult, many great things are not easy, and perhaps the poets are incorrect even that there are gods or that they care about human matters (365d–e). Or, if the gods do accept sacrificial and votive offerings as payment for wrongdoing, this ought to lead one to be unjust and then to offer appropriate sacrifice later for the best possible overall outcome (365e).

Adeimantus introduces at least two important elements here: the place of the divine in human happiness—especially whether the gods really reward justice or not—and the place of poetry in education. He identifies a fundamental tension between the Greek understanding of the gods as presented in poetry and the claim that justice is intrinsically good or rewarding. In this way he contextualizes their conversation about the human being's justice or injustice in terms of Greek theology. Moreover, while Glaucon keeps the domain of justice confined to the individual just soul, Adeimantus expands justice to include the interrelationships with others in our own society, and the relation between the human and the divine. Adeimantus asks Socrates not only to prove that justice is best for a human being but also to show how justice affects the person *himself*, when the "wages" of justice are removed. That is, he wants to know what justice and injustice are and what "power" (*dunamis*) each has within the soul. Adeimantus believes that Socrates is best suited to answer this question, since he has spent his "whole life considering nothing other than this" (367e).

These reformulations of the Thrasymachean vision by Glaucon and Adeimantus considerably focus the questions that Socrates must answer. They also give Socrates multiple tasks. First, Glaucon wants Socrates to give better evidence that justice is the kind of good that he said it was, that is, both good for its own sake and good for the consequences. Glaucon removes the good consequences from the just man altogether when he unlinks justice from its effects in his two idealized "statues" of the just and unjust man—presumably because he is most interested in what it means to say that justice can be good for its own sake. Second, Adeimantus suggests that the poetic tradition about religious sacrifice provides a psychological motivation for those who listen to poetry to *choose* the unjust life since it can redeem unjust action. He thus challenges Socrates to describe how justice can be psychologically motivating, in light of Greek poetry and religion. Third, Adeimantus wants to know not only what *kind* of good justice is, but *what* it is in itself, and what power (*dunamis*) it has in the soul. Socrates is thus challenged to give an account of what justice itself is, its effect on the soul, its goodness, its manner of acquisition, and the role of the divine in attention to human justice. It will take until Book Ten to respond to all of these demands.

Socrates expresses both wonder and delight at Glaucon's and Adeimantus's challenges. He briefly praises them, citing a poetic line in their praise for distinguishing themselves in battle at Megara: "Sons of Ariston, divine offspring of a famous man" (368a). His delight lies not only in their capacity to offer a substantial argument on behalf of justice, but also because they are not persuaded that injustice is better than justice even after offering such speeches (368a–b). Here, Socrates notes a certain gap between persuasive argument and belief. It is possible to believe that justice is better than injustice and still to offer a strong argument on behalf of the opposite of this idea. In Aristophanes's *Clouds*, this manner of approaching *logos* is presented as dangerous: to make the weaker argument the stronger destroys tradition and corrupts souls. Here, Plato presents characters who are engaged in strengthening what they believe to be the "weaker" argument, but their basic commitment to justice as a good does not waver. Socrates names this as something "divine" that has happened to them, suggesting that the cause of belief in justice is not restricted to persuasive argumentation alone but has some other source.[29] Indeed, Socrates says of himself that he would distrust (*apisteō*) them on the basis of their argument alone, except that he knows them not to be persuaded (*ou pepeisthai*) that justice is better than injustice, on the basis of their character (*tropos*) (368a–b). Glaucon and Adeimantus take up the challenge to justice not from the standpoint of being unjust men looking for justification for their actions, but as mostly good men seeking to understand better why what they believe to be good, really is good. Their care for goodness guides the approach that Socrates takes in argument. For example, Socrates can take for granted as they build up a picture of a just polis as a model for a just soul that such a polis is desirable to them, and that they will make a good effort to lay out all the elements necessary for a just city.

Socrates's approach is to return to the question of the function or work (*ergon*) of the soul, a line of argument that he had begun with Thrasymachus. A particular difficulty in discovering the soul's function is that the nature of the soul is itself disputable. Unlike physical objects, which can be explored, or even be taken apart and put back together again in order to better understand its function, the soul allows for no such direct access. The soul cannot be seen directly.[30] Furthermore, since human beings undertake many different actions for a variety of ends, the claim that the human person even has a single function is disputable. Thrasymachus, for example, seems to see the human person as a bundle of appetites that, if fulfilled, will make him happy. But this is not to say that there is a "proper" work for the soul, only that at an empirical level, those who have more wealth, power, reputation, and the like are happier.

The analogy of the city to the soul is helpful for making Socrates's case that the soul has a function, insofar as the city in speech and its parts are premised on the idea that human beings need one another. The function of a city is more visible than that of the soul and can be better understood through offering a genealogy of the polis. Socrates does not explain why he thinks that justice in the city is more visible, but we can assume that if justice is some sort of work of the soul, then also in the city's work or function—justice—will become visible. According to the common agreement of Socrates and his interlocutors, the polis exists because human beings are not easily self-sustaining outside of living in an organized city. Adeimantus says that justice comes into being in the city "somewhere in the need these men have of one another" (372a). The parts of the city as presented in their argument arise naturally from the discussion of what they imagine are necessary parts for a city to function for the good of its members. The city as they construct it is meant to address the happiness of the whole as well. Thus, the city in speech displays how structure and function might align in order to produce happiness.

The city is a more visible model of a functioning whole for at least two reasons: first, the city in speech exists only insofar as it is constructed, part by part, by its constructors in the conversation at Cephalus's house, and so its parts can be clearly seen. Real cities, like real souls, are harder to get hold of. For example, in a real city we might have difficulty determining whether its rulers are in fact acting for the good of the whole or only for their own good. In our own contemporary political context, disputes exist as to not only whether particular policies are beneficial or just, but even whether the aim of those in charge is to act for the common good or only for their own good. True motivations are not always visible. Moreover, many particular political questions such as whether an injustice is present, how we ought to measure it, and what specific steps ought to be taken in order to alleviate it, are disputable. In a certain sense, we use indirect measures in order to "see" and to diagnose what ails our own city: for example, in our day, if we want to better understand the injustice of poverty, measuring poverty might be done by surveying the level of unemployment, or average household income, or the number of children who are on reduced school lunch programs. Or citizens of a real city might be ignorant of the existence of poverty, or unskilled in diagnosing its causes.

An ideal city has none of these problems of insight. Not only is it initially constructed as lacking any deficits that face real cities, but it also contains nothing that cannot be seen, insofar as nothing in it exists apart from what its constructors have created it to be. Since the aim of the ideal city is not to address a concrete social problem, or to create an actual city, but rather to learn about the proper function and purpose of the city as such, it can afford—at least in its initial development—to avoid such problems. The city in speech is idealized not because Socrates is a utopian, but rather because an abstract model offers the greatest clarity for the purposes of understanding the nature of justice.

The city-soul image is an analogy. An analogy is a *logos* in which something in an account given about one object of consideration corresponds with and reveals something about another object under consideration. In any analogy, there is both similarity and difference. If the two things being compared are not similar, the analogy has no purpose and cannot be made responsibly. If the two things compared are not different, then there is an identity of the two objects and no analogy at all.

Analogies can function heuristically in order to help one to discover something new about the subject under investigation. They can also function rhetorically, that is, to persuade another that a claim about one topic is true because in a sufficiently similar case, the audience already shares certain beliefs and commitments. For example, if I wanted to make the case that laws to regulate gun ownership were beneficial and should be permitted, even though gun ownership is a constitutional right in the United States, I might give an example of another constitutionally protected right that is also regulated by the law. If my interlocutor thinks that this other regulation is good, I am in a better position to defend my claim that further regulation is desirable and need not entail a violation of rights. In such a case, the analogy highlights only one feature of the issue in question—that there is a precedent for government regulation of constitutional rights—and does not address other considerations, such as whether regulation or nonregulation leads to better protected citizens. Any analogy is therefore always limited, insofar as it only highlights *some* of the shared features between two things. Since these two things are also always different, there will also always be features that are disanalogous. Thus, analogical argument is always incomplete, as the analogy can be open to the objection that something is significantly different between the two objects under consideration, and that this difference has consequences for the outcome of the argument.

Socrates's use of analogical argument is both heuristic and rhetorical.[31] He does not offer an explicit theory of analogy per se. However, he does compare their method to the reading of letters written both large and small, and so offers some insight into who we are to understand the city-soul comparison: "If someone commanded us, who don't see very sharply, to read small letters from afar with not very sharp sight and then someone knew that the same letters were elsewhere, but larger in a larger place, I think it would be a godsend (*hermaion*) to recognize these first and then to look upon the smaller ones, if they do happen to be the same" (368d). Fascinatingly, Socrates uses an analogy to describe what the process of analogical reasoning looks like. Rather than defining analogy abstractly, as I have done earlier, he uses an image to communicate about the process of using one image to interpret another. What can we learn from Socrates's own description of analogy *by* an analogy?

First, Socrates argues that the city-soul analogy allows one to "see" more sharply when our sight is limited. Socrates is explicit that the lack of clear-sightedness includes both himself and his interlocutors, in prefacing the letters analogy with this remark: "Since we're not clever (*deinoi*), in my opinion we should create (*poiēsasthai*) an investigation of it" (368d). Socrates includes himself among those who are not "clever" enough to undertake this question without the assistance of a creative analogy. To this extent, even though Socrates thought his own answer to Thrasymachus was suffi-cient, in light of his interlocutors' doubts he is willing to deepen his own exploration of the nature of the function of soul and acknowledges some limit in knowing the best way to do so. An analogy helps by allowing one to "see" more about the soul than might otherwise be seen.

Second, Socrates tells us that while the larger letters help in reading the smaller letters, both sets of letters must be read and eventually compared. Socrates acknowledges that it may turn out that the two sets of letters do not say identical things after all. Socrates allows for the possibility that this particular analogy may not turn out to be completely adequate, or that there are some important differences between the two entities. That is, justice in the city might not match perfectly justice in the soul. From this, we learn that Socrates is not merely offering this analogy as a rhetorical device by which to explain his own preexisting understanding of justice. Rather, he constructs the city with some prior sense that justice in the soul and city must share in some common feature, if they are both called just, and that the construction of the city in speech will potentially serve as a heuristic device to discover something further about the nature of the soul.[32] The heuristic nature of this device is further emphasized by his use of *poiēsasthai* to name the creation of the investigation through this means, as well as the sense that it would be a godsend if it works—literally, Socrates says it would be like Hermes (*hermaion*), that is, a figure who mediates between the divine and human worlds.

Any analogy between the city and soul is bound to be imperfect. For example, while a soldier might be an excellent representative of what is characteristic of *thumos*—to love what is one's own while fighting against the enemy—any given real soldier has many other traits such as: the skill to hold and use a weapon, a uniform, families at home about whom they care, and any number of features that human beings can have that *thumos* itself does not have. An analogy picks out only certain limited features of the object being used to understand something about the soul, and excludes others. While this might seem to be an obvious if not trivial point, it also has significance when we are evaluating the political adequacy of Socrates's ideal city in speech. The city constructed in order to understand justice in the soul is designed to highlight features that are analogous to those in the soul, and easily overlooks other features of the city and its citizens that might be relevant only to political justice. For example, it might at a practical level be the case that a good army functions best when its soldiers are well paid, have strong social commitments to the city, and receive honor from others according to merit. In Socrates's analogy, however, the soldiers are designed to represent the honor-loving part of the soul, and so legitimate questions about adequate monetary compensation for risking one's life are set aside in the discussion—perhaps since this would muddle the soldiers' love of honor with appetitive concerns, which will belong to the craftsmen for the sake of separating the two parts of the soul later. In other words, insofar as Socrates begins by constructing a city for the purpose of understanding the soul, the direction of that construction will inevitably be shaped and guided by his ultimate goal of reading the "smaller," more difficult to see "letters." Moreover, to the extent that any analogy is also disanalogous, understanding justice in the city will eventually need to involve understanding how it is *unlike* justice in the soul. The limits of analogy might be seen in looking at relations among social classes instead of parts of the soul, or perhaps deeper questions exist as to whether what is good as a model for the soul is good for actual, living cities. Indeed, the isomorphism between the city and soul is assumed and never argued for directly. Socrates's caveat "if they do happen to be the same" (368d) serves as a reminder that this discussion is conditioned on a premise that is assumed but not proven to be the case.[33]

Still, Socrates must see something in common in the just soul and just city, some shared feature, if the analogy is going to work at all. A peculiar feature of the letters analogy is that in order to know that the larger letters will help one to read the smaller letters, one must have some preliminary sense of what the smaller letters say. Otherwise, one might question Socrates with some version of Meno's paradox, and ask: How can one know what letters one is seeking in the larger set unless one already has read the smaller set? And if one has already read the smaller set, what need is there to seek and to read the larger one?

However, as is the case with other instances of seeking what we do not yet fully know, partial understanding is sufficient to consider the analogy a worthwhile one to pursue. Consider this similar case. I can imagine driving down the highway and looking for an exit to an amusement park whose name I cannot quite remember, and if I see a small sign with the outline of a roller coaster on it, I might try to read the words on the sign. Perhaps they are too small to see, or I noticed it too late to read the long title fully. I might look for a second sign that had some larger letters, perhaps looking again for the familiar icon of the roller coaster, or the word "Park" that I was able to make out on the first sign. Socrates suggests that our understanding of justice in the soul is like this: we already have a basic intuition that justice in the city and in the soul share something in common because we already have some "good enough" beliefs about justice in the soul (and the city) that warrant making the comparison in the first place. These "good enough" beliefs are not the final word and might need to be adjusted, but they allow us to make a start. Thus, the letters analogy tells us that analogies such as this one between city and soul are useful when we already have a partial but incomplete access into the nature of justice and can bring those partial insights to bear on our exploration of justice. Book One has already provided Socrates and his interlocutors with some of those insights. Indeed, some of these insights recur in these subsequent books. For example, Polemarchus's idea that justice is helping friends and harming enemies recurs in new form as a virtue of the soldier who, like a philosophical dog, loves friends and hates his city's enemies. Moreover, we can safely assume that Socrates's idea that the soul has a function has some basis prior to his raising the point with Thrasymachus, and so he has some sense of what to look for in exploring the specifics of justice in the soul and in the city.

For this reason, Bernard Williams's well-known critique of the argument can be addressed by approaching the use of analogy differently. Williams argues that the city-soul analogy is one in which an identical quality F is assumed to apply to both city and soul. If one already knows what F is, then the exploration is pointless. If one does know what F is, F applies not only to the whole of the city, but also to its parts. In such a case there is an infinite regress, Williams says. The problem Williams identifies is real, but only if we take F to be a quality that we can know or not know in a binary way. I am arguing instead that justice is something about which the interlocutors already have opinions, but not secure knowledge. They "see" justice imperfectly and unclearly, as the language of the letters analogy states. Through comparing cities and souls analogically multiple times, the philosophical inquirer is invited to deepen his understanding of justice. Many images of the city exist in the *Republic*, not only one: the city of sows, the feverish city, the purified city, the somewhat comic city of the three waves, and the degenerate cities, among others. Many images of the soul are also presented: souls that are compared to ideal cities but also souls compared to a beast (as Socrates calls Thrasymachus); dogs, which are used as an image for the best soul of a guardian; an image of a man who is part man, lion, and beast; and the many degenerate forms of soul found in Books Eight and Nine. Although the tripartite city and tripartite soul is the central image, these other secondary images also contribute to our understanding of the just and unjust soul and city.

Analogical reasoning here functions as a heuristic device insofar as different analogies bring different features of the topic being examined into relief. For example, if one compares the structure of the soul to three kinds of animals (as Socrates does in Book Nine), that analogy highlights ways in which human beings are both similar and dissimilar from other animals. Comparing desires to a many-headed beast emphasizes the unending nature of satisfying those desires and also draws a relationship between the parts of the soul to the whole (if reason is not strong enough, the whole soul is in trouble). The analogy of parts of the soul to animals brings out this dimension of the appetites in a way that the analogy of the soul to the city does not. Not only the similarities, but also the differences, between the two objects being compared via analogical reasoning are important in the exploration of justice. For example, one may notice that the analogy of city to soul fails to take account of exactly *how* the craftsmen in the perfect city will be just souls, if they do not have the kind of rational autonomy developed through a philosophical education that the rulers have.[34] The same feature is true of some of the similes that Socrates uses in his narrative description of the days' events: Thrasymachus is *like* a beast (336b), but he is *not* a beast, and as at least one commentator has argued, Socrates seems able to tame him.[35] Through imagining different images of the soul and images of the city, Socrates and his friends increasingly come to "see" more of what justice is.[36]

In Book Two, Socrates makes one additional claim about the relationship between city and soul. He says that by investigating what justice is like in the city, they will be able to consider "the likeness of the greater in the *idea* of the less" (369a). Although Socrates does not yet explore the concept of the forms in Book Two, we can already see the informal way in which he points to it here, well before the middle books' discussions of the forms and ontology. The reason that justice in the city and soul share something in common is that the form is apparent in both. Given that the Greek words for the forms (*eidos* and *idea*) can also simply and nontechnically describe the "look" or appearance of a thing, we can also understand its mention here nontechnically as something that we "see" in common between the city and soul.[37]

To sum up, we can see several significant features in how Socrates's development of the city-soul analogy relies on the imagination. The city as constructed in speech is imaginary and not real, but it is in the simplicity of the clear structure of an imaginary city that the model becomes most useful to understand the soul. Real cities lack such conceptual clarity and are "messy" in their realities. The ideal city can serve as an analogical component to the soul precisely because its formal structure is clear and precise. The imagination contributes to Socrates's and his friends' deeper understanding by idealizing the city and highlighting only certain features that are relevant to the discussion of the soul, while leaving aside other practical and concrete concerns not relevant to the analogy.[38] The city-soul image also allows Glaucon and Adeimantus to imagine what it would mean to discover the form of justice even before they have, in fact, discovered it. The model of the letters gives a familiar example of reading sets of letters, one clearer than the other, in order to communicate the idea of a shared "idea" or "look" in ordinary and everyday language. Even if Glaucon and Adeimantus have no sense whatsoever of what a common *idea* or form is, and even if they lack clarity about what justice is, they can still understand what it *would be like* to arrive at an adequate account of the idea of justice. Namely, it should somehow look similar in both the city and in the soul. Thus, the letters analogy also gives us a nontechnical and accessible model for what a "common form" is, as well as providing a specific route to explore justice in the soul. Last, Socrates's caveat that the letters analogy only holds up if the letters are alike in both cases cautions that the imagination is limited. An analogy is only an analogy, and not a detailed and precise topology.

The city-soul analogy may also have its limits, limits that stem from its constructed nature as an image. Later, Polemarchus and others will begin to explore some of those limits in their insistence that Socrates offer a better defense of the political proposals he names. For the moment, however, Socrates is most interested in the city as a model for the soul.

Here in the analogy between the city and the soul, Socrates uses a way of arguing that is different from paradigmatic argument and much more like what Aristotle describes as argument from similarity in the *Topics* (especially I.17–18). In argument from similarity, the universal under which the particular cases fall is not secure (*Top.* 156b).[39] Instead, the approach is to look to see if there is a similar attribute shared between the two things being compared, for example, "a man, a horse, and a dog; for insofar as they have any shared attribute, they are alike" (*Top.* 108a). This kind of analogical reasoning is preferable to arguing from a paradigm in the current situation, because arguing from paradigms led to an impasse. Socrates and Thrasymachus did not share an identical understanding of justice, and they did not even agree on the matter of whether the aim of ruling is to care for one's self alone or for those people or things over which one rules. Because the differences between their visions of justice were so great, the argument from paradigm was not persuasive to either of them or to those who listened. Here, Socrates tried something different, in order to see if there is a common attribute that justice in the city and justice in the soul share, such that if it is visible in the city, it may be more easily seen in the soul.[40] Socrates assumes that as they explore the nature of the just city, some quality or property that they describe will become clear that will help them to understand why we can call both souls and cities "just."[41] The nature of the similarity is unknown but is assumed on the basis of the shared language that is used to describe both souls and cities.[42]

On Aristotle's account, a good analogical argument is one that can show a number of similarities between the things being compared, and even better if it can also show underlying common causes.[43] Such a turn toward causation begins with the origin of the city in speech in Book Two. As Glaucon, Adeimantus, and Socrates build up a picture of the just city and what is required, an underlying assumption is that the city exists in order to care for the citizens' needs. That is, Socrates's argument about the just city is premised on a claim about its origin that Thrasymachus might well dispute: the aim of the city is to take care of the citizens who inhabit it and does not exist for the good of the ruler. One reason for giving the genesis of the city is that providing its genetic roots helps to demonstrate that the very *cause* of the city is the good of the citizens. By providing a narrative account of why and how people live together in cities, Socrates offers a logic for why the citizens' needs are central to its functioning. Socrates is not giving a historical account of how cities actually came to be; instead, he describes the reasons why people live together rather than live apart. To this extent, his account is like those of Hobbes, Rousseau, and early modern social contract theorists whose descriptions of the state of nature exist as philosophical idealizations that reveal something important about why cities and social life exist as they do. But unlike social contract theorists, Socrates assumes that human beings are always social and live in community from the beginning. Socrates builds up a city in part to show that human beings need community. While his genetic account does not decisively prove that the city must exist for the advantage of those who live within it—clearly, tyrannies can and do exist—by grounding the city in human *need* rather than *desire*, Socrates gives a reason why the good of the citizens is central: the polis was designed with just this purpose in mind.

Socrates begins his discussion of the city by saying that a city comes into being because each of us is not self-sufficient but in much need. Socrates's idea bears a close relationship to some ideas from Book One. The importance of human dependency already arose in the discussion of Thrasymachus's argument in asking whether perfect injustice is possible, since even a band of thieves cannot accomplish anything if they are unjust toward one another. They depend upon others even in order to commit a crime (351c). Moreover, Polemarchus's definition of justice, although limited, contains within it the idea that friendship is central to human life and that one's interactions with others have repercussions for one's own happiness.

In examining the founding reasons for a city, Socrates focuses on the *cause* of the city's coming to be and grounds it in human nature (*physis*) and not only the conventions (*nomoi*) of justice. If Socrates is to reply to Thrasymachus's claim that the unjust man has "more" than the just one, or to Glaucon's worry that justice is only a social compromise between the best and worst ways of living, he must get to a more essential layer of what constitutes justice: the origin of human community itself and why we need one another at all. The fundamental fact about human nature upon which Socrates relies is the reality of human need. The city exists as a means of mutual giving and mutual receiving (*metadidōsin* and *metalambanei*; 369c). Human beings by nature are needy people and not, for example, the autonomous agents in much modern social contract theory, for example, in Rousseau's state of nature, where "natural man" moves blissfully from stream to tree to field, eating acorns and satisfied with brief, chance interpersonal encounters. Socrates's basic city focuses on material needs: providing for the needs of food, housing, clothing, and so on. When Socrates asks whether each person in the city will undertake only his own care, by getting his own food, making his own housing, clothing, and shoes, or specialize, Adeimantus suggests that specialization is "easier" (370a). Socrates adds an even stronger claim that will later become central to the ideal city in speech: each person differs in aptitude for different tasks and varies in talent by nature (370a–b). Moreover, the person who practices one art produces a finer product, and some forms of technical production require attention to and acting in the right moment (*kairos*; 370b–c). Thus the city makes life not only easier but also qualitatively better for its citizens. Socrates names particular kinds of craftsmen that are needed: farmer, toolmakers, shoemakers, herdsmen, weavers, cobblers, and merchants. These examples illustrate a second level of mutual need in the city. Not only will a craftsman be unable to be attentive to his craft if he does not specialize, but he may not be able to perform it at all if he does not have the right tools. Farmers need plows, and shepherds need someone to turn the sheep's wool into material that is useful for the weaver. The crafts themselves turn out not to be self-sufficient practices but rather practices that are dependent on other crafts. In other words, even technical arts are not the work of only one or more specialists but the result of the cooperation of multiple kinds of specialists who mutually benefit one another. Socrates even gives attention to the need for the simplest city to trade with other cities who have items not available in one's own city and so introduces merchants, traders, and salespeople (370c–71d). One city alone cannot exist in a self-sufficient way. Even the well-founded city still depends upon other cities.

These simple but compelling examples demonstrate through ordinary empirical evidence that human self-sufficiency is an illusion. Thrasymachus's claim that most human beings care only for themselves and their own advantage is not a very good description of what most people actually do in ordinary life. Most craftsmen engage in trade and commerce of mutual benefit that is grounded on mutual human need. Socrates also gives attention to the relational needs of people: couples who enjoy "sweet intercourse," the love of parents for children, singing, and love of the gods. We have need not only of one another's technical skills but also of others as persons in relationship. Justice is found "in some need that they have of one another" (372a).

Glaucon rejects this first, simple city. But it is worth pausing to consider, suppose that Glaucon were satisfied with the city as described. What then might this analogy of city to soul have shown Socrates and the others about justice in the soul? Would it have been successful in showing what a just soul looks like and whether such a just soul is happy?

Socrates never has the opportunity to apply back the city-soul analogy to the soul in light of this first, "healthy" city because Glaucon objects to its sufficiency so quickly. The images of the city and soul are dialogically developed images in which Glaucon's input matters to the outcome. However, we might speculate briefly about what could have been learned, for this very process of speculation can also teach us something further about how this kind of an analogy works to help us better understand justice. (Thus, it is less important whether my speculative interpretation is right than what it might show us about the process of connecting city and soul by an analogy.)

If the simple city were held up as a model of the soul, then justice in the soul could be understood as cooperation of all of its parts, but without any clear hierarchy to those parts. After all, the simple city consists of cooperation between different persons whose differences consist mainly in their occupation. In Socrates's healthy city the cooperative exchanges between different craftsmen are grounded in need: if the farmer needs a plow to prepare his ground for planting, he goes to the plow-maker, but he does not seek a plow unless there is a need for its use. Justice in this city might well look somewhat like the vision of justice that Cephalus first offered up: honesty and fairness in trade, and giving each person what is owed. Perhaps we would also see elements of Polemarchus's final insight, that justice includes a kind of friendship between good people, for in the simple city, its members are friendly and peaceable. By analogy, a just soul might be one in which each human need is attended to and fulfilled, but only on the basis of need and not beyond need. Such a soul would be psychologically whole and unified, not battling internal conflicts between different parts as the tripartite soul does struggle with conflicts between reason, spirit, and appetite.[44] A just soul might be one in which all of the needs of the individual are attended to in a balanced way: hunger, thirst, desire for safe shelter, sexual appetite, desire for companionship and conversation are all fulfilled. To this extent, justice would be nearly identical to moderation, insofar as each soul would seek the fulfillment of its own needs but not to excess and happily provide for the needs of others in accordance with the demands of moderation. Justice and moderation would be nearly indistinguishable.

However, we cannot be entirely certain of what kinds of conclusions that Socrates would have drawn from a comparison to the simple city, since analogies are not completely determinative of which similarities or differences are to be highlighted by the analogy-maker. That is, any claim that the just city is similar to the just soul in a specific way requires *recognition* of some common feature. We must be able to pick out a particular similarity between soul and city in order to make the analogy work, but such capacity to pick out the feature requires imaginatively connecting the common feature across the differences of city and soul.[45] To illustrate using my preceding speculations about an isomorphism between the simpler just city and a simple just soul: to say that the fulfillment of each craftsman's needs is analogous to the fulfillment of hunger, thirst, and other appetites requires an act of imagination. By attending to something that seems obvious about just trade (that it is just to give both craftsmen what is due), and connecting it to something not so obvious (that it is "just" to give both hunger and thirst their due), something new about the human soul and the relations of its different internal desires is opened up. The image of the city does not itself dictate how it is to be connected back to the soul, before the connection is made, but rather offers new imaginative possibilities for how to think about the soul.

In other words, an analogical approach allows us to consider something difficult to grasp—the nature of the human soul—according to novel categories or relations of categories that open up our capacity to "see" something about the soul that had previously escaped our attention. Analogical thinking invites a reimagining of the self and the soul but does not determine exactly how that reimagining will take place. There remains a kind of openness and indeterminacy as to how the analogy will be applied back to the soul. Filling in the details of this analogy requires an act of the imagination—indeed, many imaginative acts.[46]

The same is also true when Socrates applies the city-soul analogy to the soul in Book Four after developing a tripartite class structure for the city. How that structure is applied back to the soul is somewhat indeterminate due to the differences that remain between these two similar but not identical complex structures. Someone other than Socrates might well have seen something different in common between the soul and the city, on the basis of the city-soul analogy. For example, a non-Greek speaker whose vocabulary about soul does not include the terminology of *thumos* is unlikely to see the connection between soldiers and *thumos* and will have to find some other term to name what is soldierly about the human being. The image of the city alone does not determine in a precise way what can be better seen in the soul as a result of arguing from analogy. Here, analogical argument is not a proof but rather a heuristic device, one that helps us to see something new about the nature of justice. If we also include Glaucon and Adeimantus's approaches as species of philosophical argument, then Plato's understanding of argument is not reducible to proofs or even to finding the right propositional claims to make. Neither can we say that these kinds of argument are merely rhetorical, since the process of discovering the nature of justice—and not just persuading others of one's own conclusions—takes place through such argument. Plato includes a wide variety of approaches to argument that are more varied in approach than some contemporary approaches to what counts as "philosophical argument."

Images are central to the discovery of justice. Socrates assumes that we have the capacity to see justice, even if only partially and obscurely. Through the process of drawing an idealized model of the city, he can attempt to give greater structure to something that initially seems as amorphous as the soul. By attending to the greater clarity with which one can discover the function of a city, the function of the soul may more easily become visible. Here, we can see the centrality of image-making to philosophical discovery in Socrates's approach to articulating the nature of justice in the city and soul.

Chapter 5

Images of Justice

The *Republic* contains not just one image, but three images, of the just city: the first simple city, the "feverish" city, and the tripartite city that forms the model for justice in the soul in Book Four. Even this last city, however, is developed further over the course of the dialogue, so to the extent that its details are further filled in, the image of the city continues to change. In Book Eight, Socrates will also describe a series of degenerative cities and souls, offering us still further images to help us conceive of ourselves in our current, imperfect condition. This multiplicity of images is worth exploring, for we can learn about justice from the cities that are set aside, or that reflect justice imperfectly. Even the tyrannical state helps us to understand the value of justice, insofar as Plato's reader can see the deep unhappiness of the tyrant himself and why tyranny is bad not only for the ones who are being ruled, but for the tyrannical ruler himself.

The first city in speech is one commonly called the "city of sows" for Glaucon's own naming of it in a disparaging way (372d). As argued in the last chapter, how it would be applied back to the soul as a model of justice in the soul remains indeterminate, so long as the analogy is not further fleshed out. While one can make conjectures about how such a model might be useful, such ideas must remain speculative. However, we can also learn something further about why the later city is developed as it is from the reasons that Glaucon rejects it. Glaucon rejects the first city, even though Socrates seems quite happy with it, but Socrates is willing to go along with Glaucon's rejection. To this extent, the city that results later in the *Republic* is a joint exercise between the two of them. One way to read this development is to think that Socrates also agrees with Glaucon's objections and so realizes that the first city is incomplete. On this reading, the one, correct model for the city has not yet been found, and so an incorrect one must be rejected. However, an alternative way to read the rejection of the model is to say that Socrates willingly incorporates Glaucon's concerns about the city not because Socrates needs for the first city to be different, but rather because he thinks the philosophical development of the ideal city must take into account the concerns of his interlocutors. These concerns may be not only intellectual but also personal, for example, concerns rooted in desire. Here, the shared agreement about the nature of the city is already a political act, to the extent that Socrates is flexible about giving Glaucon what Glaucon—and others like him—desire from a city. Even if Socrates's own desires are simpler, he is not the only type of person who must be able to live in the best city. Glaucon's input into the conversation suggests a need for a city that can accommodate more kinds of desires than Socrates himself may possess. The fact that Socrates allows for the needs and desires of his interlocutor to form the city shows a spirit of cooperative development of the image.

On this reading, Plato presents us with the development and rejection of the first city in order to show us that the ideal image of the city is dependent on the interlocutors who developed it. This does not mean that Plato is merely being ironic about the city that forms the main basis of discussion of justice. However, it suggests that Plato is showing us how the model is developed so that we as readers can understand that it is a model, and not a perfect account of justice itself. Its creators are imperfect human interlocutors whose ideas at times stand in tension with one another, as will also be the case in the discussion of the "three waves" the city must withstand. Later in Book Nine, Socrates will be clear that images such as paintings fall short of the perfect reality of the objects that they image and are even further short of the ideal form. I suggest that Plato is quite aware that the dialogue's own models of justice also are imperfect. In principle, they could be further revised or even rejected on the basis of further argument. No model can perfectly capture justice itself.[1]

Glaucon's language shows how and why his desires inform the rejection of the simple city. The first city in speech fails to please Glaucon, because Glaucon possesses other sorts of desires that the city fails to take into account. Glaucon rejects this city as a "city of sows" (369d–71d). As interpreters, we might take for granted that in its animality, "sow" simply stands for this city's being not yet fully human.[2] Indeed, Glaucon rejects Socrates's city for its simplicity. However, Glaucon rejects this city not because it is a city of animals rather than one composed of sophisticated human beings. Socrates's inclusion of singing, religious worship, technical crafts, care for the family and especially children, and verbal discussion already point to uniquely human dimensions to this first city. Instead, I suggest that Glaucon rejects the city because it is built upon feminine practice; it is a city that lacks the masculinity of politics, war, and the honors that accompany war.

There are suggestive gendered dimensions of Glaucon's evaluation of the first primitive city as the "city of sows." Socrates's use of the imagery of the "sow" evokes elements of the religious celebration of the Thesmophoria, a festival celebrated exclusively by married women. Socrates's description of this simple city includes many elements similar to practices found in the Thesmophoria.

The Thesmophoria was a gynocentric festival at the heart of the cult of Demeter: Athenian women, normally confined to the home and excluded from the public sphere, gathered together overnight in the sanctuary without men or children present.[3] The festival centered around the loss of Persephone (Kore), Demeter's daughter, to Hades and preceded the autumn sowing of crops. The festival began with an ascending procession up the hill to the Thesmophorian on the hill of the Pnyx and so bore the name "Road up (*Anhodos*)."[4] The center of the festival involved the sacrifice of a pig or piglets in the evening, with the remains of the sacrifice being thrown into the snake-filled "chasms of Demeter and Kore," or *megara*.[5] Symbols of fertility were also present, such as dough models of male and female genitalia, snakes, and other "sacred things."[6] On the second day, women fasted and abstained from sex, sleeping on simple mats. Such a period of fasting was followed by the retrieval of the remainder of the unconsumed remains of the sacrifice, which was brought up from the chasm and placed on an altar. This remainder (the *thesmos*) was thought to guarantee fertile crops when mixed with the seeds scattered for the new harvest. The celebration also focused on the women's hope of bearing beautiful and healthy children.[7] Fasting was replaced with feasting and destruction with a hope that what remained would lead to new plenty at harvest time. As Burkert notes, there is a pattern of descent into the underworld and death, coupled with signs of fertility and renewal.[8]

Nearly every particular in Socrates's description of the first city resembles some of the features of the Thesmophoria. In Socrates's city, its citizens build small houses for themselves but feast while sitting on rushes covered with myrtle and yew (372a–b). At the Thesmophoria, women erected small temporary tents to serve as simple shelters and slept on mats. Socrates's first city evokes the primitivism retained in the celebrations of the Thesmophoria, one of the few Greek festivals to retain the ancient practice of sleeping on mats.[9] No beds or furniture were allowed in the religious festival; instead, women slept on the ground on the leaves of plants (such as a willowlike tree called the *lugos*) said to dull the libido.[10] Socrates's city likewise features its couples sleeping on beds of yew and myrtle (371b). Socrates's city centrally features cakes of wheat and barley, just as the Thesmophoria featured wheat and barley cakes in the shape of the female pudenda, and dough creations in the shape of phalluses.[11] Socrates describes the city's wheat and barley cakes, as *gennaias*, suggesting a kind of nobility to their function (372b).[12] The Thesmophoria featured fasting preceding a large banquet meal honoring Kalligenia, the goddess of beautiful births. At this banquet, women indulged in *aischrologia* (shameful speech), offering mocking poems, dirty jokes, and trading barbs at one another.[13] Socrates, too, speaks of a city in which those lying on the mats enjoy food, hymns to the gods, and taking pleasure in being with one another (*hēdeōs sunontes allēlois*) (372b). Socrates's city in speech evokes many features that are central to the Thesmophoria. Even if he does not have this festival explicitly in mind, their parallel reminds us that these activities are associated with women and also take place outside of the context of political life, from which women were barred.

Glaucon's angry dismissal of Socrates's first city as akin to a "city of sows" implies that he rejects this city because it is too feminine. The term *hus* is not only a term for "sow" but also a Greek slang term for female genitalia. Henderson in *The Maculate Muse* shows that both the terms *delphax*, pig, and *hus*, sow, can refer to the female genitalia of a mature woman.[14] Jokes centering around the double entendre of the term sows or pigs abound in Greek comedy, for example, in the Megarian scene of the *Acharnians* (e.g., 729–817) and at several points in the *Lysistrata*.[15] Thus, Glaucon's dismissal of the "city of sows" could even be translated more aggressively: "If you were providing for a city of cunts, Socrates, on what else would you fatten them than this?" (372d).

The sacrifice of the pig at the Thesmophoria served as a reminder of the rape of Kore by Hades and her descent into the underworld, as accounts of the rape suggest that pigs of the shepherd Eubuleus were pulled into the earth along with Demeter.[16] Such signification carries over into the concept of the grain of wheat that must go beneath earth before rising again in the form of new plants and sustenance.[17] This reference to the cycle of death and rebirth is also connected to the physical dependencies of human beings, insofar as human life itself depends on the sacrifice and eating of other life forms, whether grain or animal. The sacrifice of a pregnant sow and her fetuses in particular was connected to the fecundity of women as well as crops.[18] Although life inevitably ends in death, death is also the condition for the generation of new life. The sacrifice of the pig and its use toward new crops serves as a symbol of cycles of birth, death, and new birth.

Of course, a significant difference in Socrates's city is the presence of men, women, and children. While the Thesmophoria was the sole province of women alone—and only adult married female citizens were permitted to participate in the Thesmophoria—Socrates's city includes both.[19] Yet although men and women form Socrates's first, simple city, Glaucon's objection seems to be in its placing feminine *practices* at the heart of civic practice. While many commentators focus more narrowly on Glaucon's desire for more material luxury—and this motivation cannot entirely be excluded—Glaucon's language in referring to "a city of sows" offers us clues into the deeper nature of his objection as one that is defined by the female and not the male.

Indeed, arguably, the Thesmophoria-like city proposed by Socrates is unrecognizable as a Greek city. The Athens in which Glaucon, Adeimantus, and Socrates reside is defined by war, honor, and a political assembly that centered not on the cycle of birth and death or the generative capacity of womb and soil but rather on economic, judicial, and interpolitical matters. Even the language of Glaucon's exclamation—"No relishes for the men (*andras*) you say are feasting!"—uses the gender-specific *anēr* rather than gender inclusive *anthrōpos* (372c). Glaucon's objection is that this city is not fit for men, as men. It is a city of women and their practices. Glaucon cannot imagine the first moderate city as a city that fully takes into account masculine desire.[20] Indeed, he seems unable to imagine it as political at all.

Socrates takes these objections seriously, allowing for a revision of the city that can accommodate those objections. But that this objection is Glaucon's and not Socrates's is clear from the contrast in Socrates's and Glaucon's attitudes to the city of sows. Socrates describes the first city as both "healthy" and "true" (371e–72e), while Glaucon objects vigorously. In this first and feminine city, home and the state are not separate entities, nor is there a strong social division between men and women, or even one of social class akin to the later tripartite division of the city. The *oikos* and the polis are one. This first city reflects something of Socrates's own priorities and values. Socrates's own political practice as one who questions others in Athens also subverts this public and private distinction: he names his own private cross-examination of others as a political gift to the city, despite others' charge that he is "useless" because he appears to be apolitical (*Apol.*

30e). He acts as midwife to the ideas of others, preferring to participate in the social practice of philosophy rather than the development of a written doctrine or a famous name. Socrates suggests that his most important legacy lies in passing along the practice of philosophy and care of the soul to a subsequent generation (*Apol.* 29d–30b). It is not Socrates, but Glaucon, who resists the first city.

We know from other sections of the *Republic* of Glaucon's great love of honor. Socrates especially highlights the poetry that was written by a lover to extol Glaucon's courage in the Battle of Megara: "Sons of Ariston, divine offspring of a famous man" (368a). Glaucon agrees with Socrates's criticism of poetry as removed from the truth with reference to the claim that it would be better to leave behind many deeds worthy of honor when one dies, and not mere imitations (599b). Moreover, Socrates calls Glaucon an erotic man, loving young men of all sorts of dispositions and appearances: "You praise the boy with a snub nose by calling him 'cute'; the hook-nose of another you say is 'kingly'; and the boy between these two is 'well-proportioned'; the dark look 'manly' and the white are 'children of gods'" (474d–e). When Socrates suggests that in the best city, the bravest men might kiss others upon their return from war, Glaucon adds: "And I add to the law that as long as they are on campaign no one whom he wants to kiss be permitted to refuse, so that if a man happens to love someone, either male or female, he would be more eager to win the rewards of valor" (468c). Thus we see that Glaucon is not only an erotic and thumotic man, but one whose *thumos* and *eros* are directed toward other men and masculine enterprises, especially deeds of honor performed in war.

In contrast, Socrates's first city is not feverish, but it is fecund. In his city, men and women alike enjoy the fruits of labor and intercourse with one another; their lives of simplicity are hardly lives of privation. The *eros* of this city still remains directed at objects that are largely concerned with the body: food, feasts, sex, sleep, protection from the elements. Some of the activities of this first, simple city are also goods of the soul: the enjoyment of one's children, the talk during feasts, and perhaps even the practice of natural philosophy or ethical concerns that arise in such a society. However, the "city of sows" lacks *eros* directed at the honor of the exceptional man, whether we understand him to exist in contrast to the vulgar person or as the city later develops him as the philosopher in contrast to the nonphilosopher. If a philosopher can even exist in the first city, she or he is not a product of specialized training in mathematics, science, or study of the forms, but one who philosophizes from ordinary human experience. Such a city would hold little appeal to Glaucon, who is focused on war-centered honor as well as *eros* directed at men and masculine enterprises. The most developed city in speech of the *Republic* incorporates these values.

The first city in speech and its rejection displays the intimate relationship between the political imaginations of Glaucon and Socrates and each of their desires. The desires of these characters with their lived histories, cultural practices, and other particular elements of their lives inform the development of the city in speech. Thus, the imaginative activity that gives rise to the city in speech is not one based on pure reason alone. It is a model that arises in part from the interaction of reason and desire. Here, the imagination acts to integrate reason and desire. On the one hand, Glaucon wants certain goods and activities in the city that are lacking in the city of sows. Desires inform how the city comes to be. On the other hand, Socrates insists that rationality must moderate and control how these desires are expressed even in creating the idealized model. Thus, a system of arranged marriages and rigorous class divisions becomes necessary as a response to immoderate desires that are allowed into the city. Through imagining different models of the city, reason and desire are integrated in ways that are perhaps novel and not already part of the current Athenian political structure.

Thus, the act of imagining the city is explicitly an attempt to harmonize desire with reason. It is not only the just soul or just city as end products of the process of imagining that must harmonize reason and desire. It is in the very *process of imagining an ideal city* that we can recognize the need for cities and souls in which both desire and reason have a place. This Platonic display of political imagination requires that we be attentive, as Glaucon and Socrates both are, to the nature of human desire and the response of reason to problems that arise from desire.

The second model of city in speech is feverish, and Socrates insists that its feverishness must be considered. Socrates says that the "true" city is the simpler city but that "nothing stands in the way" of exploring the feverish and luxurious one further. Indeed, it is only through exploring the problematic, feverish city that Glaucon will come to understand the problems entailed by luxury. This grappling with such problems of desire also allows for the purification of the city, and the development of a third city that dialectically develops out of the first two cities. Nonetheless, much is learned from considering the model of the feverish city.

The more luxurious city will have furniture, perfume, relishes, cakes, courtesans, and decorative arts such as embroidery and painting. Poets and rhapsodes, actors and performers, teachers, nurses, those who cook and prepare delicacies, and many others will be necessary in order to produce these goods or provide services (373a–c). Socrates's concern is less with the direct effect of these practices on the souls of the citizens, and more on the indirect effect their presence will have. In order to sustain such a lifestyle, the citizens will need more land, which they will want to take from their neighbors, and their neighbors will want to take land from them as well (373d). Socrates anticipates war and a need for an army. Glaucon agrees and seems untroubled by this prospect. If this war is to be accomplished well, then specialists in war must also exist. With the luxurious city, guardians come to be, and the beginnings of a class system. Even when the city is purified, it never reverts to a classless structure but rather retains features of the class divisions made as a result of this luxury. To this extent, their imaginary city has a kind of "history" that is not literal but rather a genealogical display of how appetitive desires can form the body politic, and how they might be subdued. The moderation of such desires cannot easily take place by a return to simplicity in a real polis, and neither is this suggested in the purification of the feverish city. Some incorporation of real human desires is necessary even in the development of the ideal city. Thus, even the ideal city is not ideal in the sense that it is absolutely perfect. Even the ideal city takes account of problematic aspects of human nature. It attends to real human desires. The ideally just city does not completely abstract from desire. Rather, the model is ideal in the sense that it is an abstract paradigm. No actual city may embody its features perfectly, but because it exists in thought and not materially, its structure can be developed and criticized without many of the usual political concerns that accompany the critique of real, living cities. To criticize the Athenian democracy or the Thirty Tyrants is one thing, and to intellectually critique an abstract model of a city is another.

The soldiers require particular personal virtues that may not be shared by all persons, and for the first time Socrates suggests that some people are better suited than others for particular work. If seeking justice in the soul requires seeking the *ergon* (work) of the human being as such, seeking justice in the city requires looking to how more specific kinds of work can be best undertaken in a city that has a plurality of different sorts of people in it. The good guardian will be spirited (*thumoeidēs*) and friendly to his fellow citizens but cruel to enemies. While these traits of friendship and enmity seem to be contraries at first that cannot be found in one person, eventually Socrates settles on the dog as an image that can reconcile such contraries. Dogs can be warm and friendly with those whom they know, and hostile to those they do not know (376a). Socrates's image allows for him to reconcile these contrary traits not by giving an exact account of how they can be simultaneously present in the soul, but rather with an image that simply shows *that* it is possible for them to coexist.

With the image of the dog, Socrates returns to Polemarchus's earlier definition of justice as helping friends and harming enemies, but with an important change. Ultimately, the guardians must be philosophical: that is, they must love learning and wisdom, just as a dog loves those whom he "knows" (375b–c). With this reformulation, Socrates changes the Polemarchean idea of love of one's own into something that is far more than love of the "in-group": the love of wisdom supplants the love of like-minded friends. Socrates offers no logical justification for this leap here in Book Two, but if one recalls the argument from Book One against Thrasymachus, the reason is clearer. Loving one's friends does not guarantee that one loves what is good or true. Loving wisdom, however, at least orients the philosopher to love what is genuinely truthful and good. The guardians—who so far have not been split off from soldiers as a distinct third class—do not simply love the city because it is their own city, like a loyal family dog. They love beyond civic loyalty, which may be contingent, and extend their love to truth itself. Already Socrates implicitly begins a purification of the city from selfish desires, in his extension of guardian love to a more universal love of wisdom itself.

In order to have such guardians, however, they must receive a special education, in both gymnastics and music. This leads Socrates and his companions into a discussion of poetry and its value. Their discussion of poetry also helps to deepen an understanding of a philosophical role for the imagination. Although Socrates is highly critical of traditional education and poetry, and wishes to replace it with an education that includes extensive training in mathematics, the discussion of poetry does more than only banish imagery from the city. Rather, as argued earlier, Plato's own poetic practice attempts to address and overcome some of the problems with traditional poetic education.

In Book Four, Socrates finally arrives at an account of justice and other key virtues that more comprehensively addresses the claim that he had made in Book One that justice is the "work" of the soul. Here, we learn what the work of the soul is, both in its parts and as a coordinated whole. The models of soul and of city are sufficiently parallel to one another to be useful for discussing both personal and political justice. However, as I will argue, even these models of justice are still only models, and no model is a complete account of justice. Were these models to be sufficient, there would be no need to continue on to the middle books and their images of the forms in order to answer Glaucon and Adeimantus's challenge, but the *Republic* continues on well past Book Four. The models of just city and soul are each what Socrates calls an *eidolōn* of justice. These images of city and soul help us to see justice as it is instantiated in the soul and city.

The evidence for such an approach to language and imagery is three-fold. First, while these accounts of justice in the soul and in the city are helpful accounts that help us to learn something more of justice, the models of the city and soul are only that: models rather than perfect descriptions. Socrates acknowledges that the picture of the soul that he develops may not be precise, and his language makes clear that he sees these images of the city and soul *as* images. Second, justice in the city is an effective model for developing a picture of justice in the soul, but the mapping of political justice onto personal justice is imperfect, thus suggesting that the model has limits and is not intended to reflect a perfect isomorphism of just city and just soul. Treating these images *as images* helps to address some of the noteworthy problems that commentators have noticed. Third, by understanding Book Four's descriptions of justice in the city and soul as models of justice, greater coherency can be found between Book Four and the more metaphysical middle books of the *Republic*, in which the forms are explored. In the middle books, the idea that justice itself exceeds any particular images of it is developed through the analogies of the sun, divided line, and cave. Socrates's images of justice are meant to inspire real insights into justice itself, but ones that are partial and perspectival. More-over, to the extent that the notion of a harmonious soul may itself hold some psychological appeal, this image of the just soul may also encourage Socrates's listeners to want to be just, and not only to understand the nature of justice abstractly.

Socrates's model tells us that justice concerns the harmonious relation-ship and work of a hierarchical, inner structure of soul or city. The model of the ideal city consists of guardian-rulers, soldiers, and craftsmen. The model soul consists of reason, spirit, and appetites. Justice exists in both the city and soul when each part "does its own work" (443b). In the case of the city, this means concretely that rulers rule, craftsmen undertake their craft specialties, and soldiers train for war or fight. No class attempts to undertake the work of other classes. In the case of the individual soul, the just person rules himself and "harmonizes the three parts, exactly like three notes in a

harmonic scale, lowest, highest, and middle" (443d). "Doing one's own work"
is given as a succinct description of the nature of justice. Commentators
often take this to be Plato's definition of justice, that is, and many accept
the "tripartite structure" of the soul as a precise description of its nature.

One difficulty, however, is that Socrates does not claim that the soul
is exactly tripartite in structure. As I will argue later, Socrates is clear in
Book Four that he is developing one *model* of the soul, but there may be
more parts to the soul, and his language indicates that "parts" ought not
be taken too precisely as a description of the nature of reason, spirit, or
appetites.[21] The language of parts is useful, but to an extent it is a metaphorical way of dealing with the grounds of action in the soul. Even the
individual descriptions of each of the three aspects of soul are given at first
only a preliminary view and are later developed further. For example, Socrates in Book Four emphasizes how reason rules over the rest of the soul,
but later reason is expanded to include its desire to know the forms, which
are outside of the soul.[22] Later in Book Nine, the image of the tyrant's soul
will also have three elements, ones that mostly line up with the triune of
reason, spirit, and appetite, but which also evoke other associations. The
many-headed Hydra, for example, seems to represent the appetitive part of
the tyrant's soul, but the analogy of a beast that keeps on growing further
as its heads are cut off would not apply back particularly well to the just
and well-ordered soul. The tyrant's soul seems to have appetites that have
become qualitatively different through the lack of the rule of reason, so a
different image is needed to describe his soul more precisely. Similarly, the
image of the lion to represent the spirited part of the soul suggests something far more ferocious than the earlier and gentler images of the dog and
soldier who are friendly to friends and only aggressive with enemies. Were
one to branch out further to other dialogues, one could also compare and
contrast images such as the *Phaedrus*'s image of soul, in which charioteer,
chariot, and the two horses are not quite a perfect match for reason, spirit,
and appetite. There, the white horse and black horse are yoked together
to serve the purposes of *eros*, including love's ascent to the forms, but the
Republic does not give the *eros* of the lower parts of the soul any part to
play as a driving force toward the forms.[23] Rather, it is *reason* that "desires"
to know the forms in the context of the *Republic*'s model of soul, although
the desiring nature of reason is not more fully developed until after Book
Four. Thus we see within the *Republic* and between different dialogues a
variety of images of soul that seem to be contextually constructed in order
to address specific questions at hand.

The *Republic* has already shown that a different model of a just city as an analogue for the soul can exist—the earlier, simpler city of sows. This city had only one social class although multiple craft specializations, and yet Socrates initially thought that it, too, might have served as a model of justice. Yet, once we see that the later model allows for internal conflict and harmonization of the soul, it becomes clear that such a simple model would only work in reference to a unified soul without conflict, and not the sort of soul that is both subject to erotic and honor-based concerns, yet also intellectually curious—that is, a soul like Glaucon's. Instead, we can see the model of justice in the city of three classes as one that helps us to better understand justice than any of the previous models or images in the dialogue so far, but one that remains a model that may still have limits. This model arose from the particular contingencies of this conversation and was influenced, for example, by Glaucon's desire that the city provide more honors and relishes than the overly feminized city of sows. It also arose from the development of a city that required only three classes, and not one that made further differentiations or added other functional civic necessities.

There is overwhelming textual evidence for the idea that this philosophical model of the soul is one that Socrates himself *sees as an image*. Socrates's language about his own imagery is clear about its more limited and imagistic nature. Immediately after arriving at accounts of moderation, courage, and wisdom as features of the just soul, Socrates says to Glaucon, "Then our dream (*enupnion*) has come to perfect fulfillment (*teleon*), as we said that we suspected that right from the beginning of the founding of the city, through some god, we dare to get to an origin (*archē*) and model (*tupos*) of justice" (443b–c). Socrates then adds that the perfect city where each person does only his task is only an image of justice: "And it was indeed, which is why it helps, Glaucon, an image (*eidōlon*) of justice, that the shoemaker by nature correctly practices shoemaking and does not do anything else, and the carpenter does carpentry, and so on for the others" (443c). In other words, the model of justice in the city as found in each person sticking to his own assigned work is useful to discover something about the soul, but it is a model that does not transfer perfectly over to the soul. For justice in the soul is an internal characteristic, unlike vulgar conceptions of justice that focus on external actions alone.[24] To this extent, the political action of "doing one's own work" within the city does not yet get at justice as an *internal* trait of the soul, since the city focuses on what its members do for others, that is, their external actions. Still, that analogue is useful for helping them to access the nature of true justice, insofar as it allows us to imagine a soul where each part undertakes its own function properly.

In this passage, Socrates describes their philosophical process as the language of a dream (*enupnion*) that has reached its goal. He also evokes the language of a divinity that has somehow assisted their inquiry in chancing to find the origin of justice in the founding of the city. This language of their activity is not the language of a precise philosophical technique that inevitably produces the only possible correct outcome; instead, Socrates uses the language of divine inspiration and dreaming. But he does not use such language in order to undermine their conclusions. Rather, he points to the way that their model is the result of a creative enterprise in which many ideas have arisen spontaneously, as if inspired, in a way that has borne fruit for discovering the nature of justice. Their development of the ideal city has been an act of the imagination. They have had to bring a city into being by imagining what a good one might need, and then critically examining what each version that they have so far created lacks—for example, more luxury, purification from its "feverishness," or the need to separate guardians into a soldier and ruler class. The model has been worked and reworked, through a mixture of creative images and rational assessment of what has been imaged. The result of these imaginative acts that led to a model city is to have arrived at an *archē* (first principle), but also a *tupos* (model) or *eidōlon* (image). Together, these three terms that Socrates uses suggest that their philosophical discussion has produced a useful image of justice or a model. On the one hand, the model helps us to get to the primary *archē* of justice, to an underlying cause or its fundamental sense. On the other hand, although they have hit upon the fundamentals of justice in the city, what they have named and described is named as only an image or model.[25] In the middle books, Socrates will clarify that an image is not identical to the form that it images and reflect further on what it means for something to be an image of a form. But even here, before the notion of such metaphysical entities or their relationship to images is introduced, Socrates is quite careful not to overstate the nature of his claims: the perfectly just city makes for a good *tupos* or *eidōlon* for justice in the soul, but a model is still only a model.

Socrates's language about the three harmonious musical notes to describe the just soul gives a second image of justice in the soul: it "harmonizes (*xunhamosanta*) the three things, exactly like three notes in a harmonic scale, at the low, high, and middle" (443d).[26] *Harmonia* in the classical Greek context does not mean a simultaneous harmony of three notes as in the contemporary sense, as music was not polyphonic; rather, it refers to three sequential notes. This musical analogy thus suggests that each note in the scale or melody has its part to play in making the final set of sounds. But Socrates adds a brief remark that cautions us against thinking that *only* these three "notes" of the soul are definitively the soul's own nature. He adds, immediately after the three-note comparison, "And all the others that may be between them, he binds them together and becomes wholly one out of many, moderate and harmonized" (443e). Thus, Socrates says that *even if* there are other parts to the soul—or other musical notes in the melody, so to speak—justice would still be a harmony between all of the parts. In other words, justice would remain a harmonious state of soul where all "notes" worked together, but this vision of justice could accommodate other specific pictures of the soul. For example, were one to argue that some passions or emotions do not neatly fit into the categories of appetite, spirit, or reason, and that a fourth element of the soul needed to be added, one could adjust the model of soul so as to say that justice exists when all the parts work together in common harmony and purpose.[27] What *would* carry across a variety of images of the soul is the claim that in a just one, these parts are harmonious, well ordered, and coordinated in their actions *because* each part does its own work in the whole and reason rules. That view of justice does not stand or fall on whether the soul is tripartite per se.

This view of the soul as harmonious, and the comparison to musical notes, also has a psychological appeal that makes justice attractive. Musical harmonies are naturally pleasant, while dissonances are unpleasant. The use of a term that not only signifies unification and a sense of wholeness—themselves appealing notions—but also the pleasantness of musical harmony that makes the notion of a soul ruled by reason appealing. Moreover, Socrates's examples of people whose souls are in conflict are not particularly appealing examples. Few people relish the idea of being at war with oneself, and examples such as that of Leontius looking at corpses are equally unpleasant (439e–40a). Not only does the picture of the soul as harmonious help Socrates's interlocutors to see more of the nature of justice itself, but it also acts to attract his listeners to the just soul as an appealing sort of soul to possess.

When Socrates first develops the picture of the soul, he cautions the others about the difficulty of capturing the nature of the soul accurately. It seems that the soul, like the city, has an aspect that learns, one that is spirited, and one that desires pleasures of nourishment and generation (436a–b). The justification for naming reason (*to logistikon*), spirit (*to thumoëides*), and desire (*to epithumētikon*) as separable is because each can be opposed to one another in concrete instances of human motivation. A person's reason can help him to hold off on strong appetitive desires for unhealthy food in order to remain healthy, for example. But at other times appetite might rule over reason and lead the person to, say, eat cakes instead of healthy fare, and a struggle between these parts of the self may ensue. Thus reason and the appetites must be separable if they are capable of opposing one another. Spirit can at times be an ally of speech and of reason against the appetites, as when one reproaches oneself for wrongdoing, but spirit can act contrary to the appetites, as in cases of inappropriately expressed anger. Thus, the reason to claim that the soul is composed of different kinds of things is that internal conflict is possible.

To defend the separation of the soul into three elements, Socrates states that the same thing "will not do or undergo opposites in the same way, with respect to the same thing at the same time" (436b). In other words, if one both wants x and does not want x at the same time, this cannot be the same part of the self that is both wanting it and not wanting it. This principle of opposites is presented not only as a feature of psychology, but even more generally as characterizing any object: even a spinning top that appears to be both still and in motion can be explained if we properly characterize the parts that are in movement and their relation to the whole.[28] Socrates thus offers a reason for why there must be *something* beneath the experience that indicates a separateness or division in the self, even though the claim is partially based on an attentiveness and reflectiveness on the first-person point of view of the subject.

But what are these differences within the soul? It is clear that each of these "somethings" has a motivating force. Indeed, as Kahn has argued, Socrates treats reason, spirit, and the appetites as each being a particular form of desire.[29] Rather than assuming that all of these faculties are separate "things" that possess the property of desiring x or y object, Socrates treats them *as* different sorts of desires.[30] As Kahn argues, Socrates moves comfortably between the language of *to logistikon* (reason) and *to philomathes* (love of learning) to describe the rational aspect of the soul.[31] But to say that the rational part is a loving part indicates that reason is not only a calculator but by its very nature is desirous of the objects of rational activity. That both spirit and appetites are also "desires" is even clearer, insofar as the appetites desire food, drink, sleep, sex, and so on, and spirit (also later named *to philonikon*) loves to dominate, win, and receive honor (581a–b).[32]

Socrates is not concerned with *all* possible kinds of conflict, and does not think that every difference in desire shows a corresponding division in the soul, such as whether to vacation in the Bahamas or Hawaii. Rather, only some conflicts that concern different *kinds* of motivations lead to a sense of internal division, as if there is more than one "self" present within. If I want to eat a cupcake, but I also rationally know this is not healthy and I want to be healthy, I am aware of more that is happening in my *psuchē* than that I both want and don't want the cupcake. I also feel subjectively as if different "parts" of myself are at odds with one another. This is not the case when I am conflicted about where to vacation—unless perhaps my interest in one locale or another were about a conflict between, say, whether to satisfy appetitive desires or to increase my intellectual understanding. In the case of choosing a vacation destination, the focus is on two different kinds of objects that appeal to the "same" kind of desire. Moreover, both seem good to the same parts of the soul—it is simply not possible to have both simultaneously as a practical matter. But in an experience of true soul conflict, more is at work than only my desire about the object itself. A conflict of the kind that Leontius experiences concerns a sense of "who I am," that is, a felt sense of myself in which one might say, "Part of me wants not to look at the roadside accident, but a part of me really wants to see what is happening." I am faced with a choice as to how to resolve this multiplicity of "selves," and that sense is generally uncomfortable—a feature that will figure in Book Nine's argument for the unhappiness of the tyrannical soul. In one way, the language of parts or kinds helps to name that experience of conflicting desires that coalesce around a sense of self. Yet in another way, the language of parts of the soul is *not* applicable in the same way as, say, naming the parts of a table, or other physical objects. Unlike most physical objects, where the part-whole structure remains stable and visible, the division in the soul is manifest in a way that is temporary from the point of view of first-person experience. Indeed, my sense of myself as divided or unified waxes and wanes over time in the course of hours or even minutes. For example, once I decide to turn away from a cupcake, my appetitive desire may wane and I may experience a sense of reunification as a single self.

The image of the city is especially helpful to describe this rather amorphous experience of internal division in the soul, because we can think of cities in the midst of civil conflict and the injustices that can ensue when a lack of harmony overcomes unity—as in the very situation of the dialogue's drama that was to lead to the death of Polemarchus. This image helps us to make sense of an apparently similar internal conflict in the soul. Indeed, Socrates sometimes also uses the military language of "factions" to describe the divided soul, as though it were experiencing a kind of civil war within (440e). The image of the city provides a graspable picture of what is at work in the rather amorphous experience of internal conflict. However, this image of the internal conflict of the soul is a way to give form or shape to the soul, when in reality the soul is not visible in the same ways that ordinary objects are.

Indeed, as several commentators have noted, Socrates does not rely very much on the language of part (*meros*), a term that only arises relatively far into the description of soul conflict at 442b and is hardly used at all overall in the description of the soul.[33] Neither does he consistently use any other term in a consistent and technical way. Instead, he begins with subjective, first-person experience to talk about divisions in the soul, without delving deeply into the nature of what these different aspects are. In addition to *meros*, he also uses the terminology of *eidos*, *ēthos*, and *genos* to describe reason, spirit, and appetite, and at times he uses only indirect verbal for-mulations (see also, e.g., 436a, which reads *tôi autôi touthtô hekasta*, or see 436d, 439c, 441e for other formulations).[34] Thus, sometimes Socrates treats each aspect of the soul as a part (*meros*; 442b), sometimes as a *genos* (441c), sometimes as a disposition (*ēthos*; 435e), and quite often as a form (*eidos*; 435c, 435e, 437c).[35] By Book Nine, he uses the language of *eidos* again to described the soul's three-ness (580d). Whatever Socrates's aim, it is not to develop as a precise account of what it means for a soul to have a part, that is, to determine whether the language of shape, look, sort, or part is more accurate—as frustrating as this might be for modern commentators with our own philosophical concerns.[36] Rather, his primary aim is to understand the nature of justice in the individual soul and to show that the just soul is *happier* than the unjust soul, even apart from external rewards that the just person might receive. Demonstrating that the unified and harmonious soul where each aspect of the soul does its own work is necessary for showing that this soul is happier. Whether the soul has three aspects or potentially more, and whether these are best named as parts, forms, kinds, aspects, or given some other name is less central for Socrates's own purposes than to further disclose the nature of justice. The language of parts, kinds, shapes, and so on remains metaphorical, even though it describes a real underlying reality. Socrates deliberately moves between different terms for these aspects of the soul precisely because they are hard to grasp.

At the same time, without *some* kind of division in the soul that at least generally follows the image of the city and its class divisions, the discovery that a just soul is one where each aspect of the soul does its own work could not exist. Thus the metaphor also must reflect a kind of underlying reality about the soul as possessing different kinds of faculties. If there are no differences at all, then there is nothing to bring together into a harmony that can be stated in terms of a unity. As Book Nine will make clear, part of the unhappiness of the tyrant is his experience of always being divided, and by implication the just person's happiness exists in the sense of both his own unity and even humanity (as becomes even clearer with the image where the rational part of the soul is a stronger rather than a weaker "little man"). Perhaps already-perfect souls would always experience themselves as a unity, but in reality justice emerges from the unification of a soul that often experiences itself as divided.

Socrates says that we know from the point of view of our own psychological experience that we can feel conflicted, or feel like a "divided self." Socrates's approach here is, broadly speaking, phenomenological and focused on first-person experience as its starting point. However, the image at which he arrives models the soul *as if* we can see it from the outside, like an ordinary object. That is, the starting point for saying that the soul is divided is to look at the subjective experience of being overcome by an aspect of the self, or divided in our desires. But the *naming* of this experience of division and labeling them in terms of three parts or kinds within the soul is for the sake of being able to look at the soul as though it were an ordinary object in the world, that is, one that has parts yet forms a unity: something like a city in miniature. Socrates's approach suggests that our own experiences of internal conflict are difficult to grasp at an intellectual level. If part of the difficulty in naming justice in the soul is a difficulty in grasping even what the *psuchē* itself is, then we need to have a way to *look* at the soul and to name its activity.

The difficulty is that, depending on our psychic state at the moment, our souls *look* different at different times, even to ourselves.[37] When I experience a harmony of desires and internal peace, I may have no sense at all of myself as divisible. Unity and a sense of wholeness predominate. When I am torn between, say, seeking the honor and affirmation of others and doing what reason tells me is right to do, however, the differences in my own potential motivations are apparent. In ordinary language, we may say things like, "Part of me wants to be respectful to him, but part of me continues to feel angry at past harm and to continue to resent him." Thus, first-person experience alone will not do to address the larger question of justice and its nature, because experiences of unity and difference fluctuate considerably. The subjective sense of the self is not stable. In order to "look at" justice, it seems that we must move from the subjective experience of being unified, or divided, and develop a way of describing the soul that gets to the causal root of these experiences, which presumably is more stable than the feelings, actions, or subjective sensibilities that arise from them.

Many ordinary objects in the world have parts while remaining a unified whole: for example, a unified city is such a kind of an object. So, too, are artifacts such as tables that are composed of legs and a flat surface. Organic, living bodies are still more complex reconciliations of part and whole, in which the parts are even more integral to the functioning of the whole than in some artifacts. Thus, the external perspective of looking at the soul gives us a way to grasp a process that subjectively feels more fluid. Part-whole language helps, albeit in an imperfect way, to make sense of the soul and how it can be both a single unity and the sort of being that appears to fluctuate between wholeness and division.[38] But we can notice that even this is a sort of image of the soul that does not perfectly map onto how we experience our own souls: try as we might, deciding whether we have one, two, or eight "kinds" of things in the soul is not the same as looking at a table to see how many legs it possesses. Instead, we have to examine our desires and feelings of conflict or harmony, make inferences about what is occurring, and decide how we might image the soul as a result. The quest to understand justice gives rise to the necessity of imaging what the soul is like in light of our own subjective experiences of a changing soul, one whose structure is not immediately visible in the way that the structures of other ordinary objects are. By asserting that the soul is threefold—reason, spirit, and appetite—Socrates can give a nameable structure and *logos* to the soul that articulates a structure of human experience. The use of terms such as *eidos*, *meros*, or *genos* to describe these parts also encourages us to think about "what the soul looks like," while the even more frequent indirect verbal constructions emphasize that whatever is happening in cases of internal conflict, the "same something" is not involved in two different desires or motivations.

Socrates's use of a paradigmatic image of the soul is not weakness on his part, but rather strength.[39] A paradigmatic image of the soul is stronger than a mere metaphor, insofar as it is a structured model that claims to disclose something significant and true about the soul. However, it is also weaker than claims to have disclosed the exact nature of an object whose true nature is complex and elusive. Giving an overly precise account of the soul, when we simply do not have access to its nature with the same ease as with chairs, tables, or even more complex observable objects external to us, would not give us the truth of the matter. Instead, Plato's strategy over the course of different dialogues is to offer multiple images of the soul. These images often do share something in common, while also offering new insights from a slightly different angle. For example, in the *Phaedrus*, the soul is also named in terms of three aspect, but both horses are said to be capable of experiencing shame or reverence, suggesting that honor is not the motivator of one part alone. Socrates's aim here in the *Republic* is to find a way to give a logical structure and account of first-person subjective experiences of feeling motivationally torn or harmonious, in order that a distinction can be made between the just and unjust soul. Then, a decision is made as to which is happier.[40] The just soul is harmonious, and the just person happier because he is not at odds with himself.

Let us examine more carefully how Socrates applies back the image of the just city to the just soul. Socrates begins with the other virtues of wisdom, courage, and moderation. In his treatment of wisdom, Socrates engages with the Homeric tradition while differentiating their ideas about the virtues from it. Socrates says that this city must be wise, since it has good counsel (*euboulia*) in its leaders (428b). Knowledge guides the city, from craftsmen and their technical specialties to the soldiers' and rulers' different kinds of knowledge. The rulers' knowledge is most important because it is the guide for all the rest of the city's activity and oversees it. The guardians will be fewest in number but will have the most important knowledge that makes the whole city run well, even if they lack the specific knowledge of the shoemaker, or how to win wars. One might wonder, however, at whether this account of wisdom as *euboulia* is a sufficient account of wisdom.

This same term *euboulia* is used in the *Iliad* to describe the notion of a good leader. As Schofield has stated, the term *euboulia* appears only three times in all of the Platonic corpus: as a descriptor of what Protagoras teaches to young men in the *Protagoras* (*Prot.* 318e–319a), in Thrasymachus's description of the practice of injustice in the *Republic* (348d), and here again in the *Republic* in the description of the city's wisdom (428b).[41] *Euboulia* does not recur again, although knowledge and wisdom remain central topics of the *Republic*. Schofield attributes its use at 428b to the fact that the guardians in the city in speech have little need for any kind of wisdom beyond something akin to administrative skills, the skills to know "how to keep class structure intact," how to educate the city well, and how to keep the breeding system going.[42] He offers an account of *euboulia* in the *Iliad* as the use of, at the most literal level, good councils and assemblies that occur throughout the *Iliad* and that are central to its action and to the heroism of its leaders. Excellence in counsel in a leader is understood to be a heroic virtue, as much as excellence in fighting skillfully in battle in the *Iliad*. Excellence in counsel also requires the right use of not only reason but also attention to the emotions, since to persuade others requires attentiveness to emotion.[43] Schofield correctly notes the general lack of a Platonic interest in *euboulia* as opposed to other forms of wisdom, as evidenced by its rare mention. Still, we might note a strong connection between the ideal Homeric chieftain who combines excellence in mental counsel and physical strength and the ideal guardians who are both strong in body and well balanced in soul as a result of their gymnastic and musical education. Eventually, however, these two excellences of the soul are split in the splitting of the guardians into the two classes of soldier/guardian and educator/ leader/guardian. Socrates's city, then, like the Homeric hero who is both a heroic warrior and a person of good counsel, requires such unity in light of the danger that these two values can become opposed to one another. A city that is moderate and just, in which all of its parties remain solely within their own domains of "minding their own business" and letting the rulers rule, is crucial to its success. If we cannot have an absolute unity of courageous willingness to sacrifice oneself for the city, and a more restrained sense of good counsel and wisdom that knows when to act or not to act, at least these different temperaments can be divided between the different classes of the city. Socrates seems, at least, to take up this approach in the divisions that he creates in the city. Similarly, in the city, only the guardians must have an advanced education that prepares them to rule. Others need only obey the guardians in order to be obedient to reason.

Socrates also redefines courage to be more in line with following good counsel and not as seeking glory or heroism. While Achilles can seek glory through a highly thumotic and even mad seeking out of his enemy, in the *Republic*, the picture of courage is redefined as a characteristic of the soldiers to *know* what to fear and what not to fear, when to fight and when not to engage in battle, and they are taught this by the guardians. Courage is "the preservation of the opinion produced by law (*nomou*) through education concerning fearful things" (429c). Courage in the city then, comes under the domain of the guardian/rulers not the guardian/soldiers: while the city will only be courageous if the auxiliaries fight well, with the proper opinion as to what is terrible and not terrible, it is the guardians who have the task of educating and training the soldiers so that they know what to fear and what not to fear. For example, they should fear throwing down their shields and leaving their posts in battle, but not fear their own deaths.

Socrates uses the image of dyed wool that is colorfast under many adverse conditions to explain the concept of the courageous soul. Once again, Socrates uses an image in order to make sense of a psychological phenomenon to which we do not have direct access. Courage is not an element that is directly visible in the soul; at most, we can see courageous actions, but the trait in the soul is not fully visible in the same way. Rather, we learn about the soul by applying a series of images that help us to "see" it. Here, the image of dyed wool helps us to understand the psychological phenomenon of those who are able to withstand pleasures and pains and maintain their opinion of what is truly terrible or not terrible, and those who are not. Those who easily change their opinion when faced with adverse circumstances are like wool whose colors fade in the sun, or fade after the first wash. This image allows Socrates also to incorporate the view that the soldiers may not know the reasons why something is to be fearful or not but so long as the opinion "sticks" it is good enough. But expressing philosophically exactly *how* an opinion that does not reach the level of knowledge is "fixable" in the soul is a difficult philosophical problem, insofar as opinion lacks the security and thus fixity of knowledge. Socrates sidesteps this thorny issue. He instead uses an image from ordinary life to show how it is possible for one who lacks knowledge to nevertheless remain steadfast in an opinion, under even great duress.

Moderation is a kind of order and mastery of certain pleasures and desires (430e). In order to find out what moderation in the city is, Socrates first has to turn to ordinary intuitions and ideas about what moderation is in the soul. The soul becomes an image for moderation in the city, and then the city is reapplied back to the soul as an image of itself. Socrates notices that in ordinary language, we often say that a moderate person is "stronger than himself." In saying this, we imply that one part of us is stronger, and another part of us is weaker, in other words, that there is a hierarchy to the self. We must assume that one part of us really is "better" than another part and deserves to rule (431a). But Socrates observes that few people ever reach this moderation of the soul, and most need to be controlled by others: not only children and women, but also some free citizens (431c). Moderation is most likely in those with the best natures and best educations combined. What would moderation in the city be, then? Shared opinion among the different parts as to who ought to rule. That is, in a moderate city, the craftsmen and auxiliaries both agree that the guardians should rule, as well as the guardians themselves. Unlike courage and wisdom, which resided in just part of the city, moderation extends through the whole city: it doesn't work if only the guardians agree among themselves that they should rule. Socrates again uses musical language: moderation "extends throughout the whole scale, making the weaker, the stronger, and those in the middle sing the same song together" (432a). Like a chorus that comes together to produce a single, unified sound, moderation is a characteristic of the whole soul in harmony, a concord to the city constituted by a whole that becomes larger than the sum of its parts. Moderation in the city is not merely the additive summation of all the individual citizens but a relational modality that characterizes the whole, since the work of different citizens is different.

Finally, justice remains as the last of the four virtues that Socrates undertakes to explain. He relies on what at first looks like a rather weak argument: once the other virtues have been named, justice will be whatever is left over (433e).[44] Here he gives no argument that there are only four virtues, and not five (as in the *Protagoras*) or many more (as in Aristotle). Moreover, looking for justice is clearly not at all like looking for the name of the last of four objects where three have already been picked up and named: rather it requires an act of *recognition* of where justice is in this whole and part structure. Individual justice ought to come to be *evident* in the structure of the soul, as they seek for what else is needed if the soul is to function well in a way that is somehow analogous to what the city also requires for its smooth functioning.[45] The "work" (*ergon*) of the human being was said to be hard to find, as Thrasymachus had implied when he challenged Socrates to state it more directly at the end of Book One. However, since this function has now been found in the city, the city as an analogue allows for the creative reimagination of the soul as akin to a "little city" where its function can also emerge.

In other words, rather than saying that the soul has three parts with a set structure, that must be perfectly isomorphic to the structure of the city, Socrates offers an analogy. As Ferrari argues, the nature of the connection between the city and soul is analogical and metaphorical rather than being a case either of complete isomorphism or of causal connection.[46] The image of the city, with its well-developed picture of justice as "doing one's own work," is creatively connected to the more amorphous and hard-to-grasp soul in a way that allows the sight of justice to emerge in the soul, in which Socrates said it was hard to see justice. Less important than the precision of the city-soul isomorphism is the way that the analogy brings to light how individual justice concerns *the soul's relation to itself*—how it recognizes, treats, and responds to a variety of impulses and desires and *not* simply whether it tells the truth, gives back what is owed, sacrifices to the gods, helps friends, refrains from stealing, or performs the many externally oriented actions that the other interlocutors had assumed captured the nature of justice. Socrates is not trying to get his interlocutors to understand a precise psychology, or what it means for a soul to have parts. Rather, he is trying to show his friends that justice is not primarily about what they have always thought it was about: how one acts toward others. Rather, justice is primarily a characteristic of the soul and its own actions. As Annas argues, Socrates's account is agent centered, and not action centered.[47] What was easier to see in the city might now, finally, help us to see how justice can be the "work" (*ergon*) of the soul.[48] When we can see justice visible in the city or the soul, we can also see something of what justice looks like.

If justice in the city is "having and doing one's own and what belongs to oneself" (434a), Socrates says that they will see whether this allowed them to attempt to "catch sight of" (*theasasthai*) what justice is (434d). Socrates uses the term *theaomai*, to gaze at or to behold, emphasizing the visual metaphor. He next evokes the imagery of light and flame—images that will be used to even greater effect in the middle books' images of sun and cave—in order to describe this process of "seeing" justice in the soul: "What came to light (*ephanē*) for us there, we must apply back to that one, and if the two are in agreement, all is well. But if something different is exhibited in the one [person], we will return to the city and examine it. And perhaps beholding them side by side and rubbing them together like firesticks, we would make justice flash forth (*eklampsai*), and once it's become apparent (*phaneran*), confirm it for ourselves" (434e–35a).

Socrates's language here is not what we ordinarily think of when describing analogical reasoning, in which some common element between two things under comparison confirms some larger set of similarities between the two systems. Indeed, the tripartite nature of the soul and city as such a shared feature by itself would not be particularly strong evidence for drawing an analogy between the two of them. Many objects have three parts, and yet many presumably would not be suitable models for discovering justice in the soul. As part of the larger arc of the argument, Socrates relies partly on the fact that we use the same language—justice, courage, moderation, and wisdom—to describe both souls and cities, and therefore that there must be something common to the fundamental reality that these words are attempting to describe. This is evident in his readiness to move back and forth between soul and city when initially developing definitions of the virtues in the ideal city. However, Socrates seems to think the image functions differently. In this passage, his images of light and the flashing forth of a flame suggest something more like "insight" is at work when the two models of soul and city are set side by side. Socrates hopes that if one *looks at* justice in the city and inquires into what justice is in the soul in proximity to the inquiry into justice, that the nature of justice will in some way show or present itself, suddenly.

The city to soul comparison is meant to produce some sort of sudden "catching sight" of justice itself. If this happens, then the models have done their work. If it fails to happen, then the models might need to be revised, so that justice might "come to light." In other words, the models are presented as functional for the sake of producing a set of insights into justice. They are neither precise descriptions of justice, nor are they merely rhetorical, unless by rhetorical we mean that the images persuade through promoting insight.[49] Later, Socrates even says rather directly that a precise grasp on the subject matter of their inquiry would require a "longer and harder way," but that this procedure will suffice for now (435d). The model here is described as a kind of catalyst for insight rather than as a perfect description of justice. The just city and just soul must both be "like" the form of "justice itself" (434b), but to be *like* the form does not mean that the likeness is perfect. The middle books will clarify why the image is inadequate to the reality.

Socrates says that the way to decide whether the model of the city is correct is to examine it: ". . . get yourself a sufficient light somewhere, look yourself, and call your brother, Polemarchus, and the others—whether we can discover where justice might be and where injustice, how they are different from one another, and which of the two one must have in order to be happy" (427d). Using the imagery of light and vision that the sun and cave images will later develop even further, Socrates suggests that the model must be held up and examined. To examine it means to see whether justice has become visible in it. Even the form of justice is an *idea*, or a "look," so it makes sense that a model made of such a form is also subject to being "looked" upon. Yet in this looking, which might appear to be an individualistic action between inquirer and object of inquiry, Socrates also states the need for community. Glaucon, Polemarchus, Socrates, and the others must assist Adeimantus in taking a look, and their joint enterprise of examining it inevitably will involve conversation about what they see (or do not see) in the model. Thus we find two kinds of inquiry are at work simultaneously: a kind of "vertical" mode of a subject who feels inspired, "sees" and incorporates something about the nature of justice into a model or type, and a "horizontal" modality by which, through interpersonal discourse and reasoning, this model is tested. Socrates describes this "vertical" mode mostly in visual terms: he asks them to consider if they can "see" justice in the model of the city. His earlier language of inspiration and dreaming also seems to point to this sort of activity. However, the notion of "insight" is almost by definition not philosophically precise. Like the poet's inspiration, the experience of "seeing" something about justice is not easily described. Neither is it publicly accessible in the way that a verbal formulation or shared picture or model is. To this extent, it would be a mistake to characterize Socrates's technique as simply hoping that his model leads to a moment of recognition on the part of his interlocutors, at which point one could claim that they possessed knowledge. After all, many ideas that we take to be correct turn out not to be well founded when subject to rational argument. The concepts of the poets that Adeimantus raised with Socrates were cases in point. Therefore, the ideas that arose as a result of applying the city structure and its virtues to the structure of the soul must be further examined to see if it can withstand argument. For example, while the model of the city is supposed to have given rise to an insight of the nature of the soul, the principle of opposition "tests" whether this structural application of the model is helpful or not.[50]

This critical testing of the model goes beyond individual insight or understanding to a discursive set of ideas expressed in language, in which disagreement and criticism are an integral part of their evaluation. The back and forth dialogical character of Socrates and his friends shows this social and logic-centered mode of evaluating ideas. Together, both insights into what a good model would require, and the testing of various aspects of the model through conversation, leads to the development of this particular model of justice. Socrates moves between using images in ways that seem to give rise to an insight into justice or other related concepts, and then testing these insights to see whether there are limits or warranted objections that make the model untenable.

For example, Mitchell Miller has argued for a fundamental kind of limit in the city and soul analogy. While in the city, it seems self-evident that the rulers should rule and so "do their own work," in the soul, the fact that the calculative aspect of the soul thinks does not yet seem to be sufficient justification for its ruling over the rest of the soul. There needs to be some independent reason to suppose that the rational faculty is best suited to being in charge of the soul as a whole.[51] My point here is to argue that when the model of the city is applied to the soul, the possibility that reason is a good guardian of the other faculties is raised through the very claim that the relationship is analogous. It still remains for Socrates and his friends to consider whether this similarity really applies: perhaps guardians are well suited to rule in a just city, but reason is not well suited to rule in the soul or, as a thinker like Hume will argue, reason is only a slave to the appetites. However, Glaucon and the others seem readily to accept that reason is suited to rule. This suggests that they have some insight into how and why, when reason rules the rest of the soul in harmony, the resulting harmony is a good. The imagery in favor of this point is even further developed in Book Nine, when the image of the tyrannical soul as akin to a weakened man, lion, and many-headed monster further suggests that a person whose reason does not rule is unhappy and out of control. The point is that the imagery lends itself to a new way of framing, or seeing, what the human soul is like, despite considerable lack of clarity when one naïvely tries to examine "the soul" without such clarifying images.

To the extent that Socrates does see part of their process as suddenly "seeing" justice as a result of the models, Socrates and his friends are engaged in a kind of *poiēsis*, or creation. These models of the city and soul are constructions, ones that do not correspond directly to any real entity—there are no perfect and ideal cities or souls. Indeed, the very development of the city as akin to a body does not predate the *Republic*, as Ferrari has shown, and develops along with the metaphors of bodily health and disease.[52] Socrates also creates a medical metaphor that runs through the *Republic* in order to describe the justice and injustice of the polis in terms of health and sickness. Early on in Book Two, Glaucon named health as an example of a kind of good desirable both for its own sake and for its effects (357c), and this metaphor is also carried through the course of the *Republic* to refer to the city. We find it, for example, in the comparison of the ruler to the doctor who prescribes medication for his patient (459c),[53] in the radical claim that the city is best when it is like a "single body" in which the part feels the pain as a whole and suffers along with the suffering of any of its parts (462d), and in the view that in the tyrannical city, the tyrant purges the best and leaves the worst, like the doctor's opposite (567c). While we might be tempted to find a "tripartite structure to the soul" that is non-metaphorical and argue that this kind of an account is different in kind from the medical metaphor, in fact both are metaphorical. Plato does not present philosophical thought as opposed to metaphorical thought by saying that philosophy ought to be image free, or by asserting that literary images are somehow less precise than nonliterary ones. We ought not confuse the criticisms of Homeric poetry with their emphasis on bad ideas passively received with the literary form as such. Plato—whether through the voice of Socrates or the other characters—frequently uses metaphor and literary modes of describing fundamental realities.

Plato's imagistic analogies such as the city-soul analogy are synthetic as well as analytic. That is, not only do they break down wholes (such as the soul) into parts (such as different desires or kinds of forces in the soul), but such analogies also give us a way of seeing the whole. Of course, propositions also function in this way, but a visual (or auditory) image such as a city or series of musical notes presents a familiar experience from ordinary life in which part and whole are integrated. This sense of integration is particularly helpful when it comes to developing a picture of the just soul because Socrates wishes to show *what it is like* for a city or soul to be integrated, that is, to exist as both a single unity and as a divisible being in which the oneness and the plurality of the city or soul is reconciled. The just soul is *like* a healthy body, or *like* a well-ordered city, and this experience of likeness not only gives us insight into the nature of justice at a purely abstract and intellectual level, but also at an experiential one. In this sense, the images are both philosophical and rhetorical—philosophical because they are intended to give insight into the nature of the being of that which they describe, and rhetorical because they wish to help the person who listens to the description integrate that information into his soul in a way that makes sense of his experience.

Still, Socrates's philosophical *poiēsis* is quite unlike the *poiēsis* of Homer and the traditional poets, who prefer the passive reception of the model as a necessary part of education. In Homeric performance, a picture of justice is presented and simply absorbed by its audience. Socrates's practice with his own interlocutors is to develop a picture of justice that subjects supposed moments of insight and inspiration to rational testing. Indeed, Polemarchus and the others will take Socrates up on his offer, and demand that he give an account of novelties such as the equality of men and women, and the abolition of the family, that form part of this particular image. Thus, the model is a middle point between the mere reflexive holding of untested opinions and claims to secure and perfect knowledge. Indeed, in the middle books, it becomes clear that some kinds of images do have a positive place in developing human understanding—even though the image is not yet the reality of the form itself that it seeks to describe.[54] In those books, Socrates will offer a model in which some images do have an epistemological value, if they are properly understood.

If we understand Socrates's application of an image of the city to the soul, in order to give rise to an insight about what it means for a soul to be just, we can also make better sense of some textual problems. For example, although Socrates is using the model of justice in the city in order to discover justice in the soul, he sometimes refers to virtues in the individual in order to discover and name their political equivalents. This might be seen as illegitimate if the discovery of soul virtues were supposed to only arise from seeing them in the city first. For example, to know that courage belongs to the soldier class implicitly requires first knowing what kind of an individual person is courageous. Socrates thinks it is easy to "see" that the soldier who defends the city is the place to look (429b). Yet to know that the ideal soldier is courageous requires *some* preliminary insight into courage in the individual, however imprecise, even to be able to apply it back to the class of the city as a whole—for it is normally a solider and not only a social class that we name as courageous. Likewise, Socrates relies on temperance in the individual to help us to discern where it might be in the city. Such an approach might appear to be circular, if the *only* source for knowing a virtue of the soul depends on first knowing the corresponding political virtue.

But this is not Socrates's way of developing these models at all. Just as the image of the larger and smaller letters had proposed, Socrates thinks they must know enough about even the little letters to know *that* there is a correspondence to the larger ones in the first place. Their opinions are taken to be reasonably good starting points because they do have some insights, however unclear, into what courage or these other virtues entail. In a way that is compatible with the *Meno*'s theory that all knowledge is recollection, Socrates assumes that recognition of the commonality is possible because of some "prior" sense of what one is looking for—though we need not assume that recollection per se is at work here. We have had a glimpse of the big and small letters, so to speak, enough so to think that looking at one is easier than looking at the other, but where there may be some movement back and forth. The nature of courage is in some way, accessible to us, in a way that helps us to locate it in the city and also to locate it in the soul. Identifying the soldier as courageous helps us to "locate" political courage in the right social class, and to name it as having the right opinion about what to fear and what not to fear. And then this notion can be applied back again to the soul and its more amorphous nature in order to say that it belongs to an identifiable part, or kind, or experience of fearing and responding to that fear rationally. Thus, Socrates moves freely between the model of the city and the model of the individual soul because the assumption is that both models offer insight into justice, courage, and so on. His process is not merely circular, but rather genuinely dialectical.

One might make the following objection to this line of argument: If the claim is that the vulgar conception of justice gets it wrong by focusing too much on external action, then how can it be argued that these models help us to catch sight of something that, at some level, is familiar enough to be recognizable as justice? Socrates's claim that justice is internal and not external is a major shift from both tradition and from some of the assumptions of the others present in the dialogue. The answer needs to be grounded in the characters of this dialogue itself. Socrates has been working with Glaucon and Adeimantus, who in Book Two clearly asserted that they do believe that justice is the sort of thing that makes one happy both for its own sake and usually because of its rewards. Socrates has reasonable grounds to say that at least these two interlocutors do, at least intuitively, think that justice is some sort of trait that is good for the just man apart from the rewards that he gets. They will recognize in greater detail in the model of the just soul something of the more general intuition that they already held about justice as intrinsically good. In addition, Socrates's model of justice in the individual soul has resonances with the earlier ideas of characters from Book One, too. His definition of justice, as having and doing what is one's own, revisits Cephalus's first definition of justice, which had emphasized giving back what one owes, and keeping only what is properly one's own things. In fact, all three of the definitions of Book One are revisited here in some way or another, but revised significantly. Whereas Cephalus seems to have thought of justice in material terms—that is, giving back money or items that one owes to others—the perfect city is just if each member of the city does the right activity appropriate to his or her nature. Socrates locates true happiness in doing the sorts of activities that fulfill our particular natures, and what is most important to the selves of the city in speech is not what they own, but rather what they do.

Polemarchus's definition was already found in new form in the philosophical nature of the guardians who, like the good dog, are friendly toward friends and harsh with enemies. Courage, however, becomes further expanded beyond the Polemarchean ideal. Courage now includes *knowledge* of what is terrible or not terrible. Thus wisdom plays a stronger role in the Socratic understanding of courage than in the Polemarchean notion of justice. Moreover, by establishing the ideal city in speech as moderate, Socrates also addresses a deficiency in Polemarchus's vision of the city as composed of some friends and some enemies. In the ideal city, not only do all perform their own tasks, but also: each person desires to do so and agrees that this is the best way to run the city. While contemporary readers might find this hard to agree with, Socrates's model is again a model of what justice *would* look like: if a city is to be just, it must also be moderate, which means not only that the rulers serve the city with wisdom and care, but also that those who are ruled want for such rule to take place. Whether such a city can arise as an empirical reality or not, Socrates's claim is that justice and moderation are intertwined in ways that would prevent the problems inherent in the Polemarchean vision of a divided city, or a Thrasymachean world where the advantage of the ruler and not the ruled drives the city's leadership. Socrates's view of justice includes some intuitions about justice held by others in the dialogue, but developed and incorporated in a new and more comprehensive model. Among these intuitions is that justice must include a kind of friendship but also acknowledge the reality that, in the real world, there are friends and enemies, and even rulers who care for the good of themselves more than the good of those over whom they rule.

This inclusion of moderation in Socrates's model gives us reason to say that the perfect city in speech is not intended to be totalitarian, as some commentators such as Popper have thought, due to the sense of friendship that each person is supposed to have for the others in the city.[55] The guardians rule not for their own goods, but for the rule of the whole city. The soldiers defend the city not only out of a sense of personal loyalty, but with steadfast opinions about what is good and bad to support their actions. The craftsmen make what they make not only out of skill or personal pleasure, but also for the sake of the city. Totalitarianism is the result of a city built on power, but Socrates advocates a city built upon friendship. This friendship recognizes real differences between people within the city who possess differences in their natures, but still sees each part, whether at the top or the bottom of the hierarchy, as integral to the whole. Whether such friendship is realistic to human nature has led to considerable skepticism in response to this ideal, but the aim is less about the rulers' exertion of power than about the care for the city by all, but exhibited in different ways. While the city does exhibit authoritarian and paternalistic elements, as Taylor has argued,[56] this mutual care of all persons for all other persons in the ideal city also moderates the meaning of the hierarchical differences.

Still, model of the soul as given here does not sufficiently treat the nature of desire. As Roochnik has argued, the account of the soul develops

further over the course of the *Republic* and moves away from a more calculative dimension to an erotic one, in which the desire to know becomes
more prominent.[57] In Book Five, Socrates will assert of the philosopher
that he "desires (*epithumētai*) all of wisdom" (475b). Reason is not value
neutral. Instead, the philosopher is the sort of person whose reason seeks
out the forms, and the desire to know becomes a more significant desire
than the desires of spirit or appetitive desires. While in a just soul, all three
sorts of desires are fulfilled, the larger description of reason that we get
over the course of the dialogue is not a reason that simply enjoys ruling
over other parts of the soul, or that likes to determine and order its own
ends. Rather, the person whose reason is most developed seeks the forms
and wishes to know and to imitate them.[58] This is particularly clear in the
image of the cave, in which the enlightened soul *desires* to know the truth
about reality—although even here, Socrates complicates his picture of desire
insofar as initially the inquirer must be dragged up the cave. The soul is
shown to be erotic, as desiring the good for its own sake, at least once the
soul has experienced a certain kind of awakening.[59] (This interpretation also
makes the Socratic position here more compatible with the picture of the
philosopher as a lover of the forms in the *Symposium* and *Phaedrus*.) While
I will save details of the analysis of the cave image until a later chapter, for
our purposes here it is clear that Socrates has much more to say about the
nature of the soul in later books, especially Books Seven and Nine.

Moreover, there is a significant lack of a parallel between justice in the
city and in the soul. A perfectly just soul exercises all of its parts—reason,
spirit, and appetite—perfectly. No part fails to receive what is due to it.
This means more than that reason can successfully *suppress* the immoderate
aspects of appetite or spirit, for these parts of the soul must also have their
needs met. A person who fails to eat sufficiently and causes herself ill health
would not be just. As spirit inspired proper patriotism and care for fellow
citizens, a person who lacked appropriate care for friends and fellow citizens
would also not be a perfectly just soul, any more than one whose appetites
or spirit were excessive and unchecked by reason.[60] Moreover, the just soul
has developed its reason so that all parts of the soul can have their due.
Eventually, on the Socratic picture of the soul, this will be a soul that not
only can calculate how the rest of the soul is to act, but an enriched vision
of the soul that seeks and learns more and more of the forms and of the
good. If justice is giving the soul its full due, then a soul that is fully just
must seek and learn, that is, it must be philosophical.

However, as Williams has argued, there is a problem with the just city. A just city ought to be just if and only if all of it citizens are just. But in the just city, since the craftsmen must be ruled over by the guardians due to the lack of rational rule in their own souls, not all of its citizens are just, at least as justice is defined in the model of the just soul.[61] Williams also notes a problem with applying the city image to the soul isomorphically. If the guardians are composed of many people who each possess reason, spirit, and appetite within, then each part of the soul, when this structure is applied back to the soul, is also tripartite, ad infinitum.[62]

Moreover, as both Williams and Roochnik have argued, most people in the perfectly just city will not meet the requirements for possessing a just soul. The just soul has to be wise, courageous, and moderate. Yet the craftsmen in the city are none of these things: they are not wise, because wisdom requires the possession of knowledge. They are not really courageous, because this belongs to the spirited part obeying reason's commands as to what is to be feared and not feared; but the craftsmen do not have the knowledge of what is terrible and what is not. They are not even moderate, since moderation consists of all three parts of the soul agreeing that reason should rule, but the craftsmen would have to be wise in order fully to know this. And they certainly are not wise as this trait belongs only to the guardians, and yet Socrates requires that the just soul is wise and possesses knowledge. So it seems that the city is just and moderate and yet does not possess many just individuals.[63]

To this we can add that the craftsmen and soldiers do not fully develop their rational faculties such that the highest part of the soul is completely fulfilled—part of the argument for the happiness of the just soul. The virtues of the soul that in a just soul are unified—courage, wisdom, and moderation—are divided up in the just city. If the longer-term argument is that the just soul is happier not only because it avoids enslavement by appetite, but also because it seeks, loves, and knows the forms, then only the guardians in the city are happy, for only philosophers receive the education that allows for such development and fulfillment.[64] Indeed, given that the philosophers might also be forced to rule, one might argue that no class of people is fully happy, while paradoxically claiming that only the city as a whole is happy. Early on Adeimantus notices this problem: "What would your defense be, Socrates, if someone were to object that you're not making these men happy . . . ?" (419a). Socrates's reply is that it is the whole of the city and not its parts that they are looking for (420b). Since the very

goal of the original challenges posed by Glaucon and Adeimantus is to prove
that the just soul is happy in a way that the unjust soul is not, Socrates
must show that the just soul as a whole is happy. The soul is the whole
with which he is most concerned. But Adeimantus wants to know how
the different classes of the city are to be happy, if they lack certain goods.
While his focus is on material goods that the guardians lack, he notices a
real difficulty, and Socrates's answer does not yet sufficiently address it: the
whole of the city may be happy but it is conceivable that the good of the
whole may be achieved only by the expense of the happiness of some within
it. As Rosen notes, this marks a curious turn in the argument, insofar as the
question at hand had been to show how and why the just soul is happier,
but now it turns out that in the just city, some individuals may have to
be unhappy.[65] One wonders how persuasive this view of justice can be to
someone like Thrasymachus, who argues for getting away with injustice if
it makes one happier.

There are a few potential ways out of these difficulties. One is to say
that Plato does not really intend to propose the city of the *Republic* as the
most just city and instead wants to show a more complex thesis. Rosen,
for example, argues that it would be just for philosophers to rule, but the
exercise of such rule inevitably leads to injustice.[66] He finds it difficult to
call this just city happy at all since it seems only to restrict desires for its
citizens. However, if we understand moderation not to be the enforcement
of *rule* by the guardians, but a genuine belief that one's own work is more
fulfilling (for oneself) than doing the work belonging to other individuals
within the city, then this need not be felt as oppressive. Neither will the
rulers mind relatively little in the way of wealth if they are satisfied with the
work of running the city, have their material needs met adequately, and can
seek and know the forms. Socrates does not propose total impoverishment
for the guardians, only the lack of wealth and property.[67] Moreover, if the
root of the communal spirit is a kind of friendship and a harmonious desire
to contribute to the common good, then things look different. What is
difficult for us as moderns to believe is that such a focus on the common
good can really be aligned with one's own desires in a way that does not feel
like oppression, or that guardians exist who could be capable of identifying
who is best at a particular line of work, or that doing what one is best at
is also the most enjoyable work. And indeed, Socrates sometimes speaks as
if this harmony about who rules is agreeable to all in the friendliness of a
just city, and sometimes as though the craftsmen need to be kept in line.[68]

Another solution to the difficulty would be to say that the model of the city is solely intended as a model to help us to understand justice in the soul, such that individual people within the city do not have to be happy or possess all the virtues. On this reading, the city is not intended to be a political plan but only an image useful for discovering justice in the soul.[69] What matters is that we have a *model* for how parts can coordinate to make the whole happy, and so can ignore the details of the political model in order to focus on justice in the individual.[70] Such a view has some textual support in Socrates's emphasis on the development of the pattern of justice in Book Five. There, Socrates repeatedly uses the term *paradeigma* (pattern or paradigm) to describe his activity: "For the sake of a pattern (*paradeigmatos*), I said, we were seeking what justice by itself is, and for the perfectly just man if he were to come into being, and what he would be like; and likewise for injustice and the unjust man" (472c). Socrates adds that he was never seeking to prove whether this city really could come into being. Williams's and Roochnik's problems with isomorphism are solvable if the soul analogy is *not* applied back to the city, such that all of its citizens must have souls that are identical to the just souls that are modeled on the city.[71] If, in the perfect city, only rulers are wise, and only soldiers are courageous, and the craftsmen simply stick to doing their own work and agreeing not to rule, the city can still be said to be just. The problem arises only when we expect the citizens of the ideal city to have the sorts of ideal souls that Socrates describes as just, wise, courageous, and moderate, that is, unified in all of the virtues.[72] By seeing the ideal city solely as a model of the just soul, these problems disappear.

However, any interpretation of the text that emphasizes the question of individual virtue with total neglect of political questions would have to contend with the large quantity of specific political proposals, especially in Book Five's examinations of sex and gender, family, treatment of other Greeks and non-Greeks, and so on.[73] The dialogue does not move directly from the city and soul analogy in Book Four to why the tyrant's soul is unhappy in Book Nine, which might suffice to answer Thrasymachus's claim that the unjust soul is the happiest. Instead, a long foray into politics ensues beginning in Book Five. To the extent that Plato's voice is more than Socrates's alone, the voices of these other politically minded characters are also a significant Platonic presence.

Another way to solve the political difficulty of how and whether the souls of the ideal city can be happy if they do not have all the virtues is to say that since the craftsmen and soldiers are ruled by the reason of the guardians, they are in fact happy enough, since their souls are still well ordered. Indeed, Socrates early on says that in the ideal city, each group will be given its "share" of happiness by "nature" (*phusis*) (421c). In other words, not all classes of people will be equally happy, but they will be as happy as their nature allows for them to be.

However, implicit in this approach that the craftsmen will be "happy enough" if ruled by others' reason is the idea that such souls are happy because their spirit and appetites are kept under control and yet given a degree of fulfillment, rather than that the exercise of reason per se contributes to the soul's happiness. There, the source of the happiness would be not to be overrun by the difficulties of unrestrained appetite or spirit while still enjoying a degree of pleasure associated with each. But Socrates later suggests that the reason that the just and philosophical soul is happy is at least in part because the rational part of the soul gets what is due to it. The tyrant is unhappy in part because of the excesses of his appetites, as later books clarify, but the philosopher's happiness is not merely found in the sort of moderation of appetites that Cephalus advocates as being a benefit of old age and waning interest. Moderation indicates a kind of contentment that all three parts of the soul possess with their proper order and place in the soul—yet not only a lack of conflict, rather an active fulfillment of each faculty. By Book Nine, it becomes clear that reason seeks to know and when its desire to know is fulfilled, a greater happiness ensues than would be possible if it were not to fulfill such desires. There, all aspects of the soul are described with reference to their different kinds of desire (580d–81c). No one can be fully happy without pursuing a philosophical desire to know.

An objection to this claim might be found in the fact that Socrates does not think that everyone has the necessary personality traits to be a philosophical guardian. Not everyone loves every kind of learning, whereas the philosophers have a particularly insatiable desire to learn no matter what the topic (475c). Philosophers are set apart from lovers of sight and sound, lovers of art, and practical people (476a). Socrates seems to identify a particular sort of love of truth that sets the philosopher apart from others. By implication, doing philosophy will only make the lovers of the truth happy, not other kinds of people. Moreover, true philosophers also possess a good memory, are courageous in the face of death, have little attachment to money, and are measured (485b–86e). Socrates does not seem to think that everyone is, or should be, a philosopher. So, to some extent we must concede that even in a just world, not everyone is as happy as they might otherwise be. Even the happy guardians must rule the city when they might prefer to contemplate the forms.

However, there are difficulties with concluding from the claim that only some people are, in fact, philosophical in any given city that the rational part of the soul need not seek knowledge in order for a person to be both just and happy. One can concede that a soul ruled by reason externally—one that follows the commands of the guardians and yet does not itself seek or know the forms—reaches a sort of minimal threshold for happiness, since at least his or her appetites are not out of control. However, Socrates does not differentiate the intellectual and moral virtues or separate reason into two parts, one that seeks to know and another that simply calculates what the rest of the soul needs, as in ethical theories such as Aristotle. Instead, he treats reason as a whole, but with different sorts of *objects* that are loved by different sorts of people: sights, sounds, art, mathematical objects, or forms. One might even argue that the lovers of art do exercise their rationality along with their sensibility, and so utilize their rational capacity to know, but differently than the philosopher. However, most of Socrates's treatment of the philosopher focuses on the ways in which a philosophical approach to knowledge, to what is unchanging and beyond sight and sound, brings the deepest sort of fulfillment—at least to the philosopher. The philosopher "delights in" these objects. Those who love sight and sound have missed something fundamental in not looking at sights and sounds as a way to see through to the forms, such as the form of beauty.

In addition, while a longer analysis of the cave image will need to be given in a later chapter, for the moment we can briefly note that *everyone* in the cave is initially enslaved, and *anyone* who reaches the outside of the cave and sees the forms is transformed—not only people already designated as philosophical by nature or as possessing a particular set of character traits. There, it is the act of experiencing knowledge, rather than a "special" kind of reason that the philosopher alone possesses, that leads to a love of the forms. Moreover, any person who lacks knowledge and is fixed to the cave's bench is described as enslaved and to be "pitied." If a native lack of reason were to require that most souls listen to only rhetoric and persuasion and remain with their eyes fixed on the cave wall, for Socrates this is not a very admirable situation in which to find oneself—even more so in an imperfect city where shadow casters and puppeteers may in fact be the ones in charge.[74] However, such a permanent state of soul is not what is found in the image of the cave. What will matter there will be the "turning around" of the soul more than its initial character. Education can be transformative for anyone, according to this image.[75]

Thus, not only do we find multiple models of just cities, or multiple images of the soul. We also find that the model of the self varies. In the myth of the metals, nature and subsequently a person's happiness is determined by a fixed nature or "metals" in the soul that must be educated differently. In the cave image, human beings are treated as relatively alike and transformed by education into being a different sort of person. There are not three classes of people in the cave, only free and unfree people. The cave image leaves aside this tripartite structure of the city and focuses on nurture and not nature. It, too, however, is a model of the city, or aspects of civic life and the relationship of philosophy to civic life. Thus, it is clear that Socrates feels free to create and to set aside different images of the city depending on what his purposes are in creating the image. The image of the city was a heuristic device for catching sight of justice in the soul. But neither the model of the just city nor the model of the just soul as found in Book Four is a perfect model of justice itself. Socrates has not yet articulated the importance of seeing an image *as an image*, but soon, he will. As he does, the reader is then invited to consider the images of justice that have so far been offered and to see them in a new light.

A final indicator that the political model of justice is to be understood as a model is to be found in a Socratic engagement with criticisms of the city in ways that emphasize the possibility of its limits. In Book Five, Socrates will defend his claims that in the just city, women and men will be equals and children will be held in common. Although examining these arguments is beyond the scope of this work, it is notable that Polemarchus and Adeimantus find this city to be objectionable. They demand further argument. Clearly, this line of argument is a detour for Socrates, whose focus is on the individual just soul. However, the voices of these other interlocutors are also Plato's voice and indicate a deeper set of concerns about Socratic political ideals about how such a model of city would look in practice. Even the same model, then, can be understood and used differently. Its meaning is not entirely contained in its initial use to make sense of justice in the soul but rather has the potential for being taken up and expanded in new ways for different kinds of purposes. Perhaps for this reason, among others, the middle books offer a clarification of the nature of images and their place in a larger picture of the pursuit of philosophical truth.

Chapter 6

Image, Argument, and Comedy in the Ideal City

In Book Five, Polemarchus interrupts Socrates in order to press him for a further defense of the ideal city thus far. While Socrates had seemed interested in moving on to apply their conclusions back to the question of why the just man is happier than the tyrant, his interlocutors stop him. They have political as well as moral interests. As is often the case in any conversation involving a group of people, the voices of others in the conversation—not only Glaucon, Adeimantus, and Socrates—take their conversation in a different direction before the initial line of argument is resumed. While the detour may seem to introduce some discontinuity in the dialogue, it is only because of the further political arguments that the metaphysical images of the middle book are introduced. Socrates describes "three waves" that the city in speech must survive if it is going to stand, and the last of these is the rule of philosophers. If philosophers rule, however, they must also be educated to learn about the forms. Thus, what looked like a set of practical questions about marriage, family life, and gender equality leads to a more deeply theoretical account of the nature of the good and the forms. A more robust account of the nature of reality is needed, beyond particular arguments for the equality of women and men, or the abolition of the family structure.

In this chapter, I argue that in the presentation of the political proposals of Book Five, Plato as author presents Socratic utopianism against the backdrop of Aristophanes's *Assemblywomen*, which challenged similar ideas in a comic manner. While the *Republic* as a whole is not a comedy, Plato writes in a way that borrows particular features from comedy in his treatment of this idea.[1] Socrates is both a philosopher who argues for a perfect ideal of justice, and a kind of comic hero within the Platonic dialogue. On my reading, Plato's reading is not ironic. Rather, I argue that Plato as author appropriates comedy in a way that takes up a key feature of the genre: in a comic performance, a comic hero may criticize key elements of Greek society—particularly its leading elite politicians or intellectuals.[2] Yet the comic hero who offers such criticism is often also painted as ridiculous, and these alternative solutions may be shown to be just as problematic as the order that they seek to criticize.[3] I argue that a similar dynamic of political criticism is at work in Book Five's political proposals. But Plato also adds something new to the mix. Plato's presentation of Socrates's proposals asks us to examine Socrates's utopian proposals with a "double consciousness." We are asked to question not only whether these utopian principles have value, but also *why* we find the ridiculous to be ridiculous. The *Republic* asks us to imagine different ways of living as a means into greater insight into the relative justice or injustice of our own current social and political arrangements.

Socrates's proposals in the *Republic* closely resemble those of Praxagora in the *Assemblywomen*. Indeed, Plato even alludes to the comic nature of this section when Socrates says it is time to turn to the "female drama" (451c). On the one hand, Socrates offers philosophical arguments for the reform of Athenian gender roles, family arrangements, and political rule by offering radical, utopian proposals to replace the current arrangements. As is often also the case in comedy, he takes up a case for the political or social inclusion of groups that are otherwise marginalized in Greek society—in this case, women.[4] On the other hand, Socrates' arguments also contain funny, comic images.[5] As Saxonhouse has shown, Socrates's arguments are frequently referred to as "laughable" in the *Republic* (e.g., 392d, 398c, 432d, 445a, 499c).[6] Socratic idealism may seem to be ridiculous, and Socrates acknowledges as much. Yet in inviting further exploration of what is perceived as ridiculous, Socrates also invites those who listen to him to deeper self-knowledge.

Here, I hope to develop a "third way" between two common ways of reading the political proposals of Book Five.[7] Many commentators take Socrates to be offering serious proposals that directly reveal Plato's views as to what real cities ought to do.[8] These authors often overlook the difference between Plato as author and Socrates as character, or ignore the comedic elements of Socrates's speech.[9] An implicit assumption seems to be, if Plato were comic, then his claims would lack seriousness, and since Socrates offers arguments for his views, this cannot be the case. But such an approach ignores the prominent place of comedy in Greek social criticism and its serious political role. Other interpreters of the *Republic* have understood the proposals to be ironic and suggest that Plato is trying to show why these proposals cannot become reality, and that it is even unjust to implement them.[10] Although these interpretations have the strength of noticing difficulties with utopianism that are clearly present in the text, commentators sometimes insufficiently emphasize the force of Socrates's criticisms of his own Athenian society and its social and political norms.

On my reading, Plato is not being ironic in order to argue directly against these ideals. Neither, though, are we to take these proposals as a blueprint for how political justice ought to be implemented in the city. Instead, Socrates's arguments are comic in giving attention *both* to social problems and utopian solutions of them, as some comic works also do. Socrates, however, goes a step further than comedy. Socrates draws our attention to the "laughable" nature of these arguments and asserts that we need to question not only accepted social structures, but also to question the causes of our own laughter: what we find to be ridiculous, and why. Thus imagining other alternative possibilities, even ones that may not be easily implemented, increases our self-knowledge as a community.

As interpreters and readers, we all come to the text with our own biases: for example, today the equal treatment of men and women may seem rational, while the rearing of children in a group pen irrational or even heartless. Philosopher-kings may bring to mind a picture of tweedy academics moving their offices from the ivory tower to the White House. Yet in Plato's own cultural context, all of these proposals have quite different meanings, not only because of his own difference in social location, but also because these ideas are additionally situated in a comic tradition to which the text is responding—one that no longer forms part of our own cultural context. However, when one considers the ways in which Plato's presentation of these ideas picks up on similar images and themes in comedy, while departing in other ways, it can help us better understand Plato's approach to political criticism and idealism.

As Jeffrey Henderson argues, comic poets were among the most significant intellectuals of the city in the fifth century. Only in the late nineteenth century did commentators cease to understand these comic poets as offering genuine insight into social and political life.[11] Henderson argues that the role of the comic hero is to embody the voice of the *demos* against the political elite. In particular, comic heroes often take on the voices of those who were politically marginalized in some way, for example, championing the views of women, metics, and foreigners, or a minority view within the democracy.[12] Sometimes these championed ideals are utopian in nature. At the same time, the voice of the *demos* is affirmed despite the criticisms. Aristophanes does not advocate the overthrow of democracy but typically allies himself with its basic values.[13] The most ordinary Athenian in an Aristophanic comedy is often shown to possess virtues that an elite might falsely wish to claim only for themselves. In this way, Henderson argues, comedy reaffirms the unity of the city and the good of democracy against the political elite.[14] Plato himself indicates awareness of this function of comedy: in the *Philebus*, Socrates describes the ridiculous as that which exposes false conceit, which we find laughable in comedy (*Phil.* 49a–50b).[15] In this chapter, I use the term "comic" both to indicate a Platonic reliance on the genre of comedy, and to refer to the laughable or ridiculous that forms a central feature of the comic genre.[16]

The comic poet is not an antirational enemy of philosophy, but rather also attempts to promote an audience's insight into human politics, and to increase self-knowledge in those who watch the spectacle. Comedy can simply be a release, and while this function of comedy should not be undermined, it can also have a philosophical purpose if it encourages its audience to see and imaginatively to encounter aspects of themselves and their larger social or cultural groups that normally remain hidden. Just as actors might arrive on stage cloaked but later uncloak themselves to reveal costumes beneath, as in frequent uses of "stage naked" outfits, comedy seeks to bring into visibility elements of human nature that are hidden, often because polite society does not allow for their discussion.[17] Aristophanic comedy is neither uncritical nor antirational but rather seeks to reveal the irrational so that it becomes visible. It seeks to affirm democracy by bringing all down to a common level. Leading politicians or intellectuals might be openly mocked on stage.[18] Comic plays did not merely mock political leaders but rather played a more sophisticated role in providing political critique of social structures that might be assumed to be natural. Thus the term "comic" should not here be understood as opposed to that which is serious, if by "serious" one means worthy of consideration and consequence.

Before looking at the *Assemblywomen*, it will be helpful to examine first how Socrates frames his own argument and his treatment of ideals and their concrete instantiation. The inclusion of this frame of the political issues directly draws our attention as readers to the question of utopian ideals and whether they can be brought into reality. I will then explore how a similar set of utopian questions is at work in Greek comedy, especially in the *Assemblywomen*, before going on to examine Socrates's more specific claims.

Socrates is highly idealistic in his presentation of the nature of justice. He is not only utopian in positing a perfect city but also consistently more concerned with the reality of the idea as such than with its implementation or practicality. However, Polemarchus and others in the discussion do have concrete political concerns. As discussed earlier, as a historical matter, Polemarchus himself dies as a result of the conflict between the oligarchs and democrats. In the context of this dialogue, these characters actively seek to understand whether Socrates's ideas are serious and whether they might be made into a concrete and lived reality. But Socrates cares far less about the implementation of justice in the city. When pressed by Polemarchus to examine the political feasibility of his scheme, Socrates is clear about the locus of his concerns: "It's not easy, my dear, to go through. For it has many doubts [*apistias*] even more than what we went through before. For, it could be doubted whether what is said is possible; and, even if one conceded the possibility, there will be doubts whether they would be best" (450c).

While commentators have widely noted the cautionary nature of Socrates's words, the philosophical role of doubt has been less widely explored. Doubt is an epistemological concept: if a person holds an idea to be true that has not yet reached the level of knowledge, that is, where there is as of yet insufficient evidence to be secure in one's knowledge claims, then he ought to doubt its veracity. Socrates directly asserts that this part of the argument is "fearsome and slippery" (451a). He himself worries about whether his ideas are best. But in Socrates's reflections, the notion of doubt concerns not only one's epistemic status, but also an appropriate emotional reaction to that epistemic status. His word for doubtful things, *apistias*, more literally means things that are not trustworthy, or not believable. Here there is not only a logical but also a psychological question being raised. Socrates says that the idea might not be credible. But to be credible in the city would mean two things, for Socrates: not only to know that the idea itself is best, with more security than the slipperiness of opinion, but also to be psychologically credible to the city as a whole. Socrates's suggestion that the marriages will have to be rigged or that many devices will have to be found to disguise children from their birth mothers suggests that the city would lack a psychological credibility even to most of the citizens who participate in it. In this sense, it may be "unbelievable." Thus, Socrates acknowledges that even if the argument logically seems to support an ideal of justice, not all ideals can or should be implemented. The notions that these ideas are "best" and that they are "possible" are both in question, but possible does not automatically follow from best. Reading the Platonic text as a straightforward political blueprint for a city ignores this element of Socrates's own preface to his defense of the ideas. These remarks suggest that we ought to hold these ideas lightly even as we explore the issues that they raise.

One might assume that if a particular ideal is good, its implementation is always also desirable. However, this is not necessary the case for a variety of reasons. It is possible that one ideal might be in conflict with another, equally important principle. For example, we might decide that although censorship of a particular poetic work would be desirable in an ideal world, the implementation of general laws that impose censorship upon an entire people might limit the availability of other, desirable poetic works. Or consider Socrates's own proposal that the ideal city would require casting out all members who are over the age of ten before beginning anew. Certainly the cost of broken families, the likelihood of war between the new city and those who formerly belonged and held resentment, the problem of how children are going to farm or be competent craftsmen, and so on, are all numerous practical problems that might well be reason not to implement the ideal city at all. Socrates's proposals need not be considered ironic in the sense that he does not really think that the ideal is amiss, nor should we assume that they are unjust. Rather, it might simply be the case that the costs of moving from utopian ideal to reality are too high to make such a move desirable.

Indeed, as I will argue, Aristophanic comedy cautions against precisely this sort of naïve implementation of an ideal in ways that overlook the psychological contingencies of being human. Political critique was widely practiced as part of Aristophanic comedy.[19] Comedies such as the *Assemblywomen* and *Lysistrata* provide deep, significant critiques of Athenian social structure and practices. Old comedy is not meant simply to make its audience laugh; it also has a serious purpose. While not all comedies were utopian, the proposal of utopian ideals is a frequent theme.[20] In these cases, highly idealistic solutions are offered to address what ails the city, and yet the comedy also mocks the very solutions that its own dramatic action offers. For example, *Lysistrata* provides provocative criticism of Athenian warmongering, but it does not seriously suggest that a women's strike of refusing to participate in sexual relations is an answer to peace. Socrates sitting in a basket in order to be nearer to the heavens in the *Clouds* suggests a potential irrelevance to philosophy in the midst of an educational civic crisis, but burning down the *phrontestirion* is not intended to be a practical solution. While the sophists are the objects of ridicule, Strepsiades is hardly a model of the best alternative to the sophists. He is a buffoon. While the "weaker argument" criticizes the insufficiencies of the "stronger argument" and its traditionalism, the traditional values of the day are also presented as antiquated and out of touch with contemporary needs. They are no solution to the educational quandaries of the city.

However, this does not mean that comedy was seen only as parody or a source of emotional release. Significant challenges to the political establishment were raised, not only for the value of entertainment but even for the sake of enacting better laws. In at least one case, the Athenians implemented a specific political proposal from a comedy. Aristophanes's *Frogs* called for the chance for the oligarchs who had supported the Four Hundred to make amends, and indeed, a few months afterward, the disenfranchisement of some oligarchic supporters was rescinded, followed by a decree in praise of Aristophanes's *Frogs* and a call for a repeat performance.[21] The documentation of this case of movement from comedic proposal to law suggests a close tie between comic performance and serious self-reflection and deliberation on the part of Athenian citizens who attended.

Socrates's political proposals in the *Republic* stand in continuity with this Greek comic tradition of providing social criticism.[22] Indeed, the dialogue has strong parallel proposals raised by Aristophanes's *Assemblywomen*, which also argued for men and women to be held in common and for the political equality of women.[23] A question may be raised, however, about the very notion of reading a Platonic text with the lens of another author's prior work. To utilize intertextual interpretation in order to fully understand the Platonic text here requires a brief defense. After all, if an author does not explicitly name an earlier author as an influence, one might ask how we can know that the influence is at work in his or her writing, much less that he expected his own text to be interpreted in light of another artistic performance?

Whether it seems for better or for worse to a modern interpreter, Plato's text is already explicitly intertextual at many points. As discussed earlier, Plato alludes to Homer almost one hundred times in the course of the book, and not only in his discussion of poetry but throughout the course of the dialogue.[24] Plato also makes explicit reference to other poets such as Simonides, Hesiod, Aeschylus, and Pindar. He engages with Damon's musical theory. His own myths and fables draw directly on elements of earlier authors, as already argued in the case with the story of the shepherd's ring and its reworking of the original tale in Herodotus. Moreover, intertextuality was a common feature of many Greek works, both written and performed, and as Nightingale has demonstrated, the dialogue form itself both relies upon and reshapes other literary and dramatic genres.[25] The longer Greek literary tradition preceding Plato was comfortable with taking up parts of prior Greek dramatic works and mythology and reworking them for the author's own purposes. For example, aside from Sophocles's *Philoctetes*, we know from Dio Chrysostom that Aeschylus and Euripides also wrote plays about Philoctetes, but with significant shifts in the characters and their portrayal.[26] This intertextual practice was not limited only to comic or tragic performances, but also infused the writing of many intellectuals. Gorgias's "On Non-Being" takes up an Eleatic style in a parodic form, just as Plato's *Phaedrus* parodies Lysias's speeches. Gorgias takes up the treatment of Helen—a popular topic of Greek drama—in his *Encomium of Helen*,[27] while Plato's *Gorgias* then takes up the analogy of rhetoric as medicinal from the *Encomium* and replaces it with the analogy of philosophy as true medicine.[28] In many cases, while the text can be partially understood apart from the other sources, knowing something of the other related texts significantly deepens our understanding of them.

One might like to think that Plato's *Republic* was the target of Aristophanic parody in the *Assemblywomen*, rather than to see Plato's work as responding to the comedy. This would fit better with a presupposition that Plato must hold the serious view, and Aristophanes must be mocking it, thus separating philosophy from comedy. However, the *Assemblywomen* was performed in Athens in 391 BCE, and Plato did not start to write any of his dialogues until after Socrates's trial and death in 399 BCE at the earliest but probably much later.[29] Moreover, Aristophanes does not name Plato in the *Assemblywomen*, whereas he is quite happy to name Socrates in other contexts such as the *Clouds* and the *Frogs*, when relevant. The absence of his name when there would have been plenty of opportunity suggests that Plato was not Aristophanes's target. The best evidence suggests that Plato's work came after Aristophanes's play, even if we cannot precisely date the *Republic*.[30]

While some have suggested that an undiscovered sophistic source may be the origin of the utopian ideals of both works,[31] or that such ideas were being considered among leading intellectuals of the day,[32] the most straightforward claim is to say Aristophanes himself was the first to create a dramatic work, in the absence of any extant source that says otherwise.[33] If we grant Aristophanes full credit for the ideas in a comedy like *Lysistrata*, or what becomes an enacted political idea in the *Frogs*, why not grant that at least the shaping of many of the ideas in the *Assemblywomen* is likewise original to Aristophanes? As Ruffell notes, of the many sorts of ideas that Aristophanes sets forth in his comedies, the ideas of the *Assemblywomen* are among the most plausible to enact.[34] If the main reason for saying that Aristophanes is not the origin of these ideas is that he is a comic poet, this alone is not a very good reason. Moreover, Sparta already had a system of partially communist social arrangements in which boys left their private homes by age seven and lived in groups with other boys, and men slept away from their private homes with other men well into their teens and twenties. Meals were shared, as well as some goods such as horses and dogs.[35] With men absent, women had considerably more independence than in Athens and received education and gymnastic training. It would not be at all surprising if Athenians looked at Spartan life and wondered whether any of its elements were preferable to those of their own city.

In any case, the *Republic* includes such ideas in a cultural context in which it was already known as a subject of comic consideration.[36] Aristophanes's treatment of the idea would have been well known both to Plato and to his audience, especially keeping in mind that comic plays were widely attended by average Athenians. Unlike our contemporary theatrical scene, often frequented by a relatively small proportion of middle- and upper-class individuals who can afford them, comic performances enjoyed wide civic participation, including poor citizens and perhaps women.[37] In a relatively small city, moreover, a good number of citizens may have seen or known of the Aristophanic play, Plato included.

Let us look at the general contours of *Assemblywomen* and its treatment of embodiment and gender. The comedy takes up the charge that not all men are especially well suited to politics through the conceit that women instead will rule. Although radical democracy might seem to be the best form of rule, in reality, neither men nor women are perfect in how this rule is exercised. Women mock the inefficiencies of men in the democratic process, and yet their proposals, too, are ridiculous. In the midst of its exploration of an alternative cosmos of rule by assemblywomen, the play also takes up matters of sexual expression and the contingencies of erotic attraction, both within and outside of marriage. Much of the comedic action itself concerns concealing and revealing, of both actual bodies and political plans sprung on the body politic.

The *Assemblywomen* opens with a group of women meeting secretly against the wishes of their husbands, plotting to take over political control of the assembly. The women have stolen their husbands' clothing so that they can walk around the city unnoticed and act manly in other ways. One of the women announces that she has not recently shaved: "I've grown an absolute forest under my armpits, as per instructions" (*Ass.* 60–64).[38] In secret, she has rubbed herself with oil and lay naked in the sun in order to become tan. A second woman emphasizes that she has become so hairy that she does "not look like a woman at all" (*Ass.* 65–66). Their leader Praxagora and her friends don false beards, and they travel to the assembly together disguised as men. Here, Aristophanic comedy plays upon the absurdity of a disguise that fundamentally alters the body but remains secret. Hair may be temporarily cloaked, but a tan fundamentally alters the body. The first woman's suggestion that she has tanned in secret or can convincingly portray her husband by wearing his cloak and a false beard is comedic because the body is not so convincingly disguised. Thus, Praxagora emphasizes to the women: "Don't you realize we mustn't let anyone see any part of our bodies?" (*Ass.* 94).

Minimally, the comic effect intended from such cross-dressing requires its incompleteness or failure to convince. In a Greek theatrical enactment, male actors would have played the women, who were pretending to be men; thus there is an additional level of reversal in the gender disguising and enactment of "other" genders going on here. As the *Assemblywomen* goes on, the men must wear their wives' clothing, since their wives have taken their cloaks. Much of the humor of cross-dressing lies in the inability of the dress fully to cover the gendered particularities of the body despite all efforts to minimize one's body and what that body's gendered signs—unshaven skin, shape, voice pitch, gait, and so on—signify. No doubt male actors would have deliberately exaggerated these juxtapositions of masculine and feminine features for the greatest comic effect.[39]

The women easily convince the men to hand over rule of the assembly to them, on the grounds that it is the only new thing that Athens has not tried yet (*Ass.* 456). Thus Aristophanes pokes fun at the democratic process and its penchant for novely for its own sake. The men initialy object to the women's proposal for reasons connected to the fulfillment of their lowest appetites, complaining that their wives might require them to have sex with them, or else deprive them of their dinners (*Ass.* 465–69). But the women have something different in mind. Praxagora argues that all property will be held in common. No one will be either rich or poor, and everyone will have "an equal share in everything" (*Ass.* 590–600). What begins as a serious-sounding political proposal, however, eventually develops into equality in other matters as well. Praxagora proclaims, "I'm making girls common property too. Any man who wants to can sleep with them and have children with them" (*Ass.* 614–15). When her husband, quite pleased by this proposal, says that he intends to sleep with the prettiest women in Athens, Praxagora says that first the plain women will lay down next to the beautiful ones, and in order to sleep with the beautiful women, the men will have to sleep with the plain and unattractive woman next to her first, by law (*Ass.* 618). Children will not know their fathers or fathers their children, but each person will think of others as like father and son, and there will be no more lawsuits (*Ass.* 633, 657).

Praxagora's proposals in the *Assemblywomen* closely parallel those outlined in the *Republic*: women rule in the assembly, formerly reserved only for men; men and women belong to one another in common; parents and children do not know one another; property is shared; and all will think of one another as parents and children, or brothers and sisters, rather than as members of distinct families.[40] She claims that, in this way, happiness itself will also be distributed evenly. But the play also presents the body and the contingencies of bodily desire as impossible to regulate and to control. In part, Aristophanes's humor arises from its reversal of expectations, and from moving quickly from the high activity of politics to the lowest activities of the body. For example, when the women state that they will both rule and do the housework, the men happily reply that they will spend their newfound time farting, suddenly bringing the audience's focus to the most banal aspects of the body (*Ass.* 464). The men are delighted at the possibility of greater sexual expression. Women are not presented as chaste, either: in one scene between Praxagora and her old husband, Blepyrus, he assumes she has been out to see a lover, or maybe several, and her comment that there is no perfume in her hair defends her immediate actions but also acknowledges previous infidelities (*Ass.* 520–26). Once the law is implemented, one scene features an old hag who demands her right to sleep with a young man. This man prefers the young woman he had intended to visit, and he is uninterested in the old woman, who nonetheless demands her right. The law, while claiming to enforce equality and work for the happiness of all, cannot direct *eros* accordingly. Rather, erotic attachments are shown not to be subject to lawfulness, fairness, or standards of equal happiness.

The *Assemblywomen* does not mock the ideals of equality of men and women or female political participation per se, so much as it examines the human capacity to live all of life according to rigorous lawful regulations that impose equality—especially in matters of love. Yet it also acknowledges that the political structure that Praxagora rejects is not at all ideal, especially in its treatment of men and women. Praxagora and her friends are relatively competent, and she especially is neither ugly nor hideous and is rather well spoken and persuasive. The *Assemblywomen* questions the status quo of political arrangements, giving voice to women where it is usually absent, while also questioning the notion that these high ideals can ever fully rule the human condition as it really exists. Political utopianism ignores other dimensions of the human person, including appetitive desires that are beyond legal regulation. The play unveils these limits while also knocking down a political idealism that too highly elevates human beings and their capacities for regulated behavior. The *Assemblywomen* should not be read either purely as a critique of male domination nor only as intending to show the problems of communism.[41]

Socrates's proposal that men and women should be equals, with children held in common, also has comic features, although Plato's treatment cannot be equated with traditional comedy. As Nightingale has argued, Plato is doing something new in his dialogue form, but borrows from multiple genres, including comedy.[42] Socrates is a far more sensible and moderate person than any comic figure. He seems to possess the virtues of which he speaks, while comic heroes mostly do not. Socrates both criticizes outbursts of laughter and makes ridiculous claims that he knows will provoke it.[43] Plato's treatment of laughter and comedy is complex. Glaucon laughs in the dialogue (451b), although laughter is also seen as potentially problematic.[44] Yet not *all* laughter is considered bad: in Book Ten, laughter that strengthens the lower part of the soul is said to be harmful (606c); however, in the case of laughing with Socrates, his concern that we reflect on the nature of what we find to be ridiculous seems to strengthen the rational part of the soul.[45]

Socrates argues that men and women are equals and should be treated as such, although he qualifies the conclusion with the claim that most men are, on the whole, stronger than most women.[46] He and Glaucon first agree that if men and women are to share in the same tasks, they must receive the same educations. Second, they agree it is fitting to prescribe for each thing work according to its nature (*phusis*) (453a). Women and men differ in their natures, and are opposites. However, they are only opposite with respect to their place in childbearing (454e–56d). Just as we would not say that because the longhaired and the bald are opposites, we should make one class a carpenter but forbid the other class from doing so, men and women need not perform different tasks in the city just because the one "mounts" and the other "bears" (454e).[47] We should only pay attention to the forms of otherness and likeness that are relevant to the activity in question itself (for example, if men and women were opposites with respect to skill with a javelin). Socrates says that if we find women who have the same natures, that is, the same propensity to learn certain skills that men do, then we ought to allow them to perform these same tasks as well. Socrates argues that if two individuals are opposed with respect to two characteristics in one area, this need not mean that their natures are any different in a separate domain. Indeed, the emphasis on the outer appearance of the longhaired and the bald also emphasizes that external physical traits such as hair length are clearly unrelated to other capacities, and so biological sex might also be unrelated to talents to perform particular kinds of tasks.

These are all well-argued points. However, what is often overlooked is the comedic ring of Socrates's examples. Socrates's specific example of shoemaking could even be an allusion to the *Assemblywomen*, insofar as Praxagora and her friends pretend to be shoemakers since they are untanned and so fail to appear sufficiently masculine (385). Part of the comedy there seems to rely on a stereotype of shoemakers as rather pale and unattractive sorts of men: if, in Aristophanes, the shoemaker is not the paradigm of the ideal male citizen, but already a bit of a joke, then Socrates's example is not nearly as strong an argument for equality as one might think. To say that hair length is unrelated to skill in shoemaking is not to elevate all to a high social standing, but rather to present both the bald and longhaired alike as banausic. Moreover, long hair was associated with aristocracy (see, e.g., *Knights* 579), while balding with old age. As Roselli argues, long hair is frequently portrayed in comedy not only as aristocratic, but also as anti-democratic (see *Lys.* 561–64 or *Wasps* 463–70).[48] In offering this specific example, then, of the longhaired and bald, Socrates asks his audience to imagine a noble class of citizens who ordinarily would never perform the banausic manual work of shoemaking, alongside old, bald men doing the same. The joke is easily lost on us since we lack the social signifier of long hair—though perhaps not baldness. One might imagine today an example in which those who wear Versace and those who wear coveralls are equally capable of doing the plumbing. The image of a person in designer clothing doing manual labor is funny and mocks the wealthy person, and no less so with the image of a longhaired aristocrat making shoes. These are humorous images that play with constructs of social class and disrupt convention, as did Greek comedy. As Halliwell has argued, comic laughter can be hostile or playful. Here there is Platonic playfulness rather than hostility, but play-fulness with a purpose, namely, to remind his own audience of the utopian nature of Socrates's proposals.

Socrates's discussion also compares people to dogs, for a second time since his earlier mention of the ideal guardian who is like a dog. Again, we find a comedic note along with a serious claim. He argues that among hunting dogs, females as well as males guard and hunt, rather than staying indoors all day. Socrates says that if we do not leave dogs inside, just because they are female, and a bit physically weaker than the male dogs, we ought to have women also being taught and doing the same things as men. Socrates's comparison of human beings is a serious challenge to Athenian social norms. In Athens, the women not only lacked the rights of political participation given to male citizens, but they lived nearly entirely indoors, in their own households, and even slept in bedrooms on a separate floor from the men. Each woman had a guardian (*kurios*), generally her husband or closest male relative. This guardian regulated nearly every decision about her life. Parents made decisions about their daughters' marriages on their behalf, often when they were as young as fifteen.[49] Women and men socialized separately and women were confined to the domestic sphere.[50] Socrates's claim that women and men ought to undertake the same activities is striking in going against ordinary Athenian convention. Yet, as Foley has argued, Greek comedy also purposefully and playfully distorts gender in ways that question conventional sexual distinctions and encourages its audience to consider the extent to which gender distinctions are natural or merely conventional.[51] Plato's dialogue is not novel in this regard. To this extent, Socrates engages with a comic theme for similar purposes of upsetting the conventional social order. Yet his argument also offers logical support to this idea: if biological sex is not determinative for other creatures, is there sufficient evidence to show that it warrants the extreme kinds of divisions in activity as found in Athens? If not, the grounds for this particular organization of social life are not warranted.

Socrates's claims have appealed to some contemporary thinkers, especially in his minimization of natural differences between men and women and an emphasis on individual ability as the mark of suitability for a task, ideas that are more familiar to our own cultural sensibilities than the traditional way of Athenian life. Gregory Vlastos names Plato as an early "feminist" for this reason.[52] However, as Annas has argued, Socrates's primary concern is not to offer a treatise on the rights of women to choose their own work, for no individual in the city is offered the kind of freedom to choose work envisioned by contemporary liberal and democratic societies.[53] Instead, Socrates's city in speech includes both men and women who perform the necessary for the flourishing of the city, for the sake of the community, and not primarily for the sake of the individuals who may or may not desire to do these particular tasks. Neither men nor women are guided by a principle of free preference as the ground of choice.[54] In fact, because the female guardians are forbidden from doing any tasks other than those that the male guardians do, they are not actively involved in the mothering and care of their own children—even if an individual woman might prefer to do so.

The second "wave" claims that all the children will be raised in a group "pen" and not be known to their own mothers or father as they grow (457d). The second wave is necessary if the first wave is to exist as Socrates has articulated it. The first limits one job, one task to each person, according to ability, for both men and women. But if women are to devote themselves wholeheartedly to the work of guardian, shoemaker, or soldier, then they cannot also be devoting themselves to the work of parenting, which by its nature removes one from full commitment to the city and instead becomes a private commitment. Children, however, also depend on others and require care of a specialized nature for their survival, so a "pen" with specialists in child care who completely supplant the place of the parents becomes necessary. With the first wave, the second wave becomes an important logical step in planning how the first wave is to come into being, as well as articulating a way of encouraging broader social bonds between its members.

Socrates presents a series of arguments in favor of relationships between men and women, and parents and children, which are regulated according to logical necessity. Socrates builds his city according to a model of human beings in which each person possesses a relatively stable nature that is not deeply affected by the contingencies of either *eros* or particular familial bonds. Rather, it is skill at performing tasks that is most central to the nature of each person, whether man or woman, and education in the virtues that allows for a stable social order overall. But as Ludwig argues, it is not *eros* per se that is dangerous to justice according to Socrates, but rather the possessiveness that comes with erotic attachments.[55] Likewise, family life is not problematic because small groups of biologically related people reside together, but rather because parents give preferential treatment to their own children over others' children, and the shared activities between people who call one another family deepen social attachments that can replace or at least be favored over broader political attachments. Socrates locates real difficulties inherent in familial preference and erotic attachment that can threaten the model of justice in which like is treated alike. A father may, for example, place his son into high political office even if the son is not especially competent.

But Socrates's treatment of men and women as akin to dogs and children, as beings that need to be put into the "pen" like animals, are also comic comparisons. Socrates treats the city's individuals as though they are merely animals to be bred. When he compares human sexuality to the mating of dogs, in which the only relevant difference is that the male "mounts" and the female "bears" (454d–e), he reduces sexual activity to the vivid image of one dog mounting another—using a term for mating that is ordinarily used only for animals and not people.[56] These images of comparison to dogs and herd animals are clearly meant to be comic, that is, resonant with the genre of comedy and funny. Even the term dog (*kuōn*) itself can comically refer either to a phallus or to a woman's genitalia.[57] The comparison of children to animals in need of herding in a group pen may seem aversive if considered as a real political proposal, but at the purely imaginative level, may also amuse as it captures the unruliness of children and parental exasperation at trying to control behavior. These kinds of comparisons to animals both emphasize the animality of the human being and what is shared with dogs, pigs, and other creatures. But in another way, such comparison emphasizes our humanity and non-animality even more. To the extent that the comparison of human beings to breeding animals provokes laughter, it is because the metaphor seems to have been stretched too far. The reduction of the body and reproduction to its mere animality thus also draws our attention to what is problematic about Socrates's proposals.

Indeed, Socrates frequently excludes the body as such from having much place in the city, except for the purposes of reproduction or for undertaking the necessary tasks of the city (e.g., crafts of shoemaking and medicine, or acts of waging war). In the *Republic*'s ideal city, Socrates excludes public acts of crying during the process of grieving (itself partly a bodily experience) from poetry (387d), prohibits particularized expression of sexual desire from naked people exercising together in the gym (458e), and seeks to exert control over the body in arranged marriages for the purposes of controlling reproduction (458e–60b). Not only the family but also the body and its particularized expressions of feelings are disrupted in the *Republic*'s proposals that women and men be treated alike. While ordinarily *eros* is directed at particular others, often in ways that are unpredictable and highly particularized, the city in speech proposes to treat bodily *eros* as though it were a universal, homogenous force that can be satisfied through being offered any "appropriate" object in Socrates's scheme of arranged marriages.[58] However, audience members will know this is not true, not only from having seen

Aristophanes's humorous treatment of the same, but also simply because they are human.[59]

The comic element of the Platonic text relies upon a degree of opposition between the purely logical and argumentative, on the one hand, and the imaginative with all of its affective elements, on the other. While Socrates's arguments about the equality of men and women and holding all women and children in common are logical, it is precisely when we are asked to *imagine* the reality of these rational political principles in concrete form that the proposals have an added layer of complexity. For example, a mother who fully understands the reasons why family life interferes with public goods might still wish to know and to love her particular child differently from others, even after accepting the Socratic argument. As she imagines sending her child to the "pen" where she will not know which child is hers any longer, she may have a quite different response to such imagery than to the argument that equality of affective ties is necessary for perfect justice. Likewise, regulating erotic love is likely to fall prey to the same difficulties that Aristophanes portrays in his comedy. In many utopian comedies, a character simply refuses to participate in the new system, unconvinced by the goodness of the ideal or simply unwilling to adhere to it.[60] There is no reason to think that the composition of many different sorts of people in the nonideal world in which Socrates and his interlocutors reside and converse would be different.

If the task of justice is partly a task of psychic integration, of creating wholeness out of potentially disparate parts of the soul, then any concrete political proposal for a real city with imperfect people must take account of whether total integration is possible. One legitimate response to the comic nature of Socrates's ideas is to assert that the problem lies with the ways in which his logical principles fail to take full account of human desires, such as the desire to fall in love with a person spontaneously, or the desire to rear one's own children. If Praxagora is excessive in her desire to regulate that men sleep with the "ugly" women before the "beautiful" ones, then is Socrates any less naïve in thinking that love and family life are capable of such legal regulation? Like Praxagora, Socrates works from an idealistic standpoint that does not take into consideration the contingencies of human desire and the difficulties of exerting rational control over love, whether romantic or familial.

Socrates shares some traits with the comic hero. On Henderson's reading, a comic hero questions cultural values of the day by giving voice to those who are normally systematically excluded from the *demos*.[61] As

Ralph Rosen shows, the views of the comic hero often have more obvious overlap with the voice of the author than other characters do. They can also be intensely self-assertive.[62] Yet, at times, the views of the hero are highly idealistic or even utopian, and part of the humor comes from this very idealism. Here, we see something in common between Socrates and comic heroes such as Praxagora, who is neither grotesque nor arrogant but rather quite sure of herself and the good of her political and social reforms. At times, that philosophical idealism overlooks the whole of human nature in favor of only its rational part. Just as Praxagora and her companions attempt to set up an idealistic world in which their own embodiment and gender do not matter, and both men and women will be sexually fulfilled while also simultaneously practicing a perfect equality between all people, so too does Socrates fall prey to a similar foible. Praxagora raises a series of significant critiques about the rule of democracy as it is practiced before the women take over. But her solution is also not perfect; it is funny and subject to critique.

Socrates's proposals are both more inclusive and more exclusive than the Athenian democratic practices of his day. On the one hand, Socrates's imaginative vision not only allows women a place in all social activities but also abolishes the family in order to completely democratize familial ties. Everyone is "family" in the ideal city. On the other hand, Socrates develops a class structure in which hierarchical differences between philosopher-kings and queens and the rest of society eliminates the shared rule by all that is central to Athenian democratic society.[63] As much as a modern reader might understand "philosopher-rulers" in terms of the rule of an academic elite, we should keep in mind that when Socrates proposes this idea, it is assumed to be objectionable not because philosophers are among the academic and class elites, but rather because they are held in such low esteem as to be worthless. Socrates is not talking about the modern academic, but rather an intellectual seeker of truth who normally stays well outside of politics and pursues what to the rest of the world looks like "pointless" activities. Socrates describes this third wave as a "paradoxical" one, that is, literally one that goes against received opinion (472a), and the paradox is that those who are least a part of the rule of a city in a democracy are now to be made its rulers. This third wave, Socrates says, will lead him to be "washed away in a wave of laughter and poor opinion" (473c), again emphasizing the ridiculousness of his claims. To this extent, Socrates's establishment of the rule of philosopher-kings is more like Praxagora's proposal that women should rule in the place of men: a comic idea that rejects the conventions of the current democracy not in order to return to a traditional form of elitism, but rather to give voice to an otherwise invisible group.

Plato is far more modest in what he writes than Aristophanes. There are no phalluses, jokes about flatulence or masturbation, compromising sexual positions for the characters, or other elements that are the stuff of Greek comedy.[64] Moreover, Socrates is critical of the sorts of jokes made in comedic presentation that would otherwise be shameful to express. In Book Ten, he remarks to Glaucon that witnessing comedic imitations or listening to jokes awakens the part of the human soul that is normally restrained: "the laughable" (*geloiou*) (606c). While a person might be ashamed to make a particular joke himself, when he hears it made by another, his demurral to participate in the content of the joke is removed: "For while by argument (*logos*) you kept down that in you which wants to make laughter, out of fear of the reputation of being a coarse joker, making it youthfully headstrong (*neianikon*), you often let go inside (*oikeiois*), and unawares you become a comic poet" (606c). Socrates's remarks here on the effect of witnessing a comedy are fascinating, and ought not be too quickly digested merely as critical of *all* comic laughter. Here, the rational part of the soul and the thumotic alike are said to cooperate in normal restraint over making ridiculous comments or bawdy jokes. It is not only an argument but also fear of a bad reputation that leads someone like Glaucon to be self-restrained. However, when one witnesses another make the same joke that is unbecoming to speak for oneself, a remarkable thing happens. Socrates says that the listener first releases into laughter, much like a teenager who is impetuous, but this change primarily takes place internally—Socrates's use of *oikeiois* in this context probably does not literally mean "at home" (since no one waits to laugh after he has left the theater), but rather "in his own space," that is, inside himself. There is now a split between the public self who is seen as being self-restrained and would *never* make jokes of *that* sort, and the private self who laughs and returns to a state of youthfulness with all its pleasures and foibles.

Socrates then adds that the person who listens to the comic poet "becomes" one himself. Of course, by this he cannot mean that he writes or performs comic poetry, but rather that his mimetic identification with the joke is so strong that he becomes the creator of his own comic state. Here Socrates does not emphasize a mimetic identification with the character in the comedy. Indeed, when witnessing a comic character that is being ridiculed, we rarely take on a strong sympathetic identification with him: we usually laugh *at* him, and not *with* him—although Plato's *Laws* will later distinguish between hostile and playful laughter along these same lines and argue that the best education allows for the playful but not hostile sort (*Laws* 816e–17a, 936a).[65] Rather, Socrates says that we become more like the comic poet. Socrates does not explain this comparison, but he seems to mean that despite a denial of being a crude buffoon, when we laugh at a crude joke we really are like the one who tells it. Not only does the poet ridicule others, but the person laughing along with the comedy also participates in the creation of the ridiculous, in that he holds a certain responsibility for the creation of the response of laughter in himself. Socrates worries that comic poetry can shape the soul badly. Comedy makes us at least temporarily creatures of passion and emotion rather than of reason, and it "waters" the parts of the soul that are often in need of more restraint, not more encouragement (606d). Perhaps for these sorts of reasons, Platonic dialogue leaves behind many of the bawdier elements of Greek comedy. Along with the adaptation of certain features of comedy, there is also some significant distancing.

Still, Socrates's very reference to comic laughter in the midst of this discussion brings to our attention as readers the fact that his ideas might strike us as funny and make us laugh. For example, when Socrates says with a straight face that men and women will have no difficulty exercising together in the gymnasium since the women will be clothed in virtue instead of robes (457a), many readers may find this funny.[66] Whether Socrates thinks it is funny is not the only point: it also matters whether those who are *listening*—for instance, Polemarchus, or the reader of the dialogue—find what he says to be amusing. Socrates's notion that the "clothes of virtue" make a good enough cover-up for the stark naked is witty and emphasizes even further the highly idealistic nature of the proposal.

Socrates himself takes up this question of whether his "three waves" are comic or not. Socrates admits that the equal treatment of women and men would be "ridiculous" (*geloios*) in the eyes of some and that many jokes could be made about it (452b–c). However, he asserts that what is ridiculous "disappears" when arguments reveal what is the best (452d), and so implies that this first wave will not seem too funny once a good argument has been given on its behalf.[67] Socrates reminds us that it was once seen as ridiculous and shameful to see men naked but then became normalized (452c–d). Thus, what seems comic at one time may not be comic in another context. As a case in point, the first of Socrates's controversial proposals—that men and women be treated as equals and both participate fully in human life—no longer has the same comic effect that it once did in ancient Athens.

Especially when coupled with Socrates's statements about the need to examine laughter, Platonic comedy differs from ordinary comedy in that Plato draws his audience's attention to the nature of the comic itself. Rather than passively receiving comedy, or simply experiencing the ridiculous, Socrates's words engender reflection upon *why* we respond to what is perceived as ridiculous as we do, why we laugh when we laugh, and whether at times there can be a lack of symmetry between what we in fact laugh at and what is truly "laughable." As Nightingale writes, we are given "instructions" on how to handle the ridiculous.[68] Socrates's reflections on comedy and its limits do not lead to a Platonic prohibition of everything comic from his own philosophical mode of discourse. After all, Plato includes them in his dramatic work. In Plato's *Laws*, the city allows for comedy because the serious cannot be learned without the ridiculous (816d–e).[69] Here in the *Republic*, comic moments are also tempered with reflection on why we find the comic to be comic, and so to follow up on any immediate emotional experience with further rational reflection.

A parallel can be found in the experience of comic actors. As Hughes discusses, comic actors, including ancient Greek comic actors, experienced a kind of "double consciousness" in acting out a comedic part.[70] On the one hand, the actor needs to sufficiently identify with the experiences and emotions of the character that he plays to effectively convey those emotions to the audience. Hughes notes many instances of comic actors who reported great emotional effect in portraying such a character—for example, Parmeno reportedly suffered great thirst from the emotional intensity that he put into his comic performances.[71] On the other hand, comic actors must also always be sufficiently detached from their own characters so as to pay attention to matters of deliberately posing a certain way, following the choreographed blocking on stage, entering and exiting at the right moment, speaking prescribed lines, and so on. The comic actor thus only partially identifies with his character, and ordinarily his identification ends when the play ends.[72]

Similarly, to the extent that Socrates is comic in the proposals of the three waves, the reader who reads the part can also approach the material with a "double consciousness." On the one hand, we are asked to partially identify with the Socratic argument. This may lead to laughter, and Socrates has already warned his own audience that laughter may lead us to ignore a serious matter and to write it off entirely and without justification—the possibility of the equality of men and women or of different childcare arrangements is not to be merely ridiculed. At the same time, when and if we do laugh at Socrates or his proposals, the invitation is to examine the *cause* of the laughter, to learn how and why what we find to be ridiculous is experienced in this way. Why is the notion of men and women exercising naked together so funny after all? And does our laughter reveal a kind of truth about the objection, or a mistake about the limits of our own opinions? Thus, in the treatment of the three waves, we have two responses that are encouraged in those who listen: first, attention to arguments with both comic and argumentative features that may produce persuasion or may produce laughter in those who listen, and second, attention to the cause of one's own laughter, and to the reasons that the ridiculous is found to be so.

To this extent, Plato utilizes *some* of the elements of comedy while remaining philosophical and adding an additional layer of argumentative analysis and self-analysis. He does so not only by including arguments, but also by coupling potentially laughable arguments with a critique of laughter. The comedic imagination functions in Plato through the work of this kind of double consciousness, in which we can both experience the imaginative utopia that Socrates sets out on the stage of our mind's eye and also critically evaluate this imagined world and our own responses to the views that he sets forth.

In the third wave, Socrates builds on the groundwork undertaken in the second wave. The second wave allows for the first wave to come into being, insofar as the common rearing of children frees up women to participate fully in civic life, and the number of children is limited for the sake of the health of the city overall. The second wave also supports the third wave, however, insofar as the shared rearing of all the children also leads the city to regard all as brother or sister, or father and mother (463c). The city will see itself as "one body" rather than as disparate individual or family interests in competition with one another (462c–d). Socrates's proposal of philosopher-rulers is built on this sense of shared friendship that is so deep as to be an extension of the familial. If the city is peaceful and not in a state of faction, then the guardians will also be happy, since so many evils will have been removed from the city, and a desire to live the life of a craftsman will seem like a "foolish adolescent opinion" (466c).

Socrates asserts that the rule of philosophers is the *only* way in which the other ideas would become realized in an actual city. It is at this point that Socrates reminds them that what they have been discussing so far was for the sake of a "pattern in speech of a good city" (472e), and that it is not important that the ideal be realizable, any more than a painting of a person would need to have a concrete counterpart that looked like the painting

(472d). Yet if they were interested in making the ideal real, the only way in which it would be possible were if philosophers were to rule. Political rule and philosophical practice must come together in the same place, or else there will be no rest from what ails the city (472d). Here, Socrates not only says what he thinks it would take for his ideals to become reality, but he also provides a diagnosis of the city's ills. Without philosophy informing political decisions, the city will suffer.

This proposal seems ridiculous to Glaucon. Again, there is a comic moment when Glaucon says that the response of anyone who hears this will be to strip their clothing, grab a weapon, and assault Socrates to do "dreadful deeds" (474a). This image itself is funny, even more so than the image of the philosopher-rulers themselves. This time, Plato paints a picture of the *objector* to the Socratic ideal as laughable. Like Strepsiades who is both critical of the city's intellectual elite in the *Clouds*, this anti-intellectual is also ridiculous. Comic actors often wore two layers of clothing: an outer garment and a layer of flesh-colored underclothing in which the buttocks were padded, nipples visible, and an oversized leather phallus attached. A comic undergarment was a standard part of all comic actors' costumes beginning at least as early as 430 BCE and continuing for at least a century.[73] Therefore, the action of removing one's outer garment to reveal nakedness underneath is an action that is specifically found on stage in comedy. Once again, we see Plato offer a comic structure in which both the ridiculousness of the idea and some mocking of the one offering the critique takes place.[74] Such laughter opens up critical space for us to consider both the object of the critique and ourselves: maybe the idea of philosophers as rulers is hilarious. But maybe we ourselves are funny in our inability to conceive of such a notion.

Socrates states that it is not what we find atypical that ought to determine whether we laugh or not, but rather that the standard of the beautiful ought to be the good (452e). If the idea of exercising naked together with members of the opposite sex seems laughable, we must consider *why* what we find ridiculous *appears* ridiculous and examine our own reactions. Perhaps the difficulty is not in the nakedness per se, but in the cultural shaping that has led us to find it to be laughable. If the reduction of complex gender dynamics to bald and longhaired shoemakers strikes one as laughable, a philosophical response to our own laughter requires still more than mere expression of what we already find to be ridiculous. The next move is to consider the reasons for one's own reactions, as well as the proposal's merits and limits. Socrates encourages us to laugh with him, but then to consider why we find what is laughable to be so funny. Here, we see a way in which philosophy could inform the political practice of the city without having philosopher-rulers in exclusive charge. If Plato's audience examines the source of what they find to be ridiculous, and they subject it to further argument, while also keeping in mind the limits of utopianism, they will be more capable of making prudential political judgments.

As for Socrates, his main aim is not to implement the city in speech into a real city. Instead, he most desires to find a *pattern* of justice: "It was, therefore, for the sake of a pattern [*paradeigmatos*], I said, that we were seeking both for what justice itself is like, and for the perfectly just man, if he should come into being, and what he would be like once come into being; and in their turns, for injustice and the most unjust man. . . . We were not seeking them for the sake of proving that it's possible for these things to come into being" (472c–d).

What good is a *paradeigma* that may or may not be realizable, or where might its imposition be as problematic as in comedic utopias? Polemarchus, like many action-minded people, seems to wonder about the practicality. Socrates's paradigm remains important for the practice of politics even if it is never realized in its ideal form. For example, his idealistic treatment of a city with no family may cause other problems if implemented—one can imagine the protest and grief of mothers and fathers who do not desire to be permanently separated from their children immediately after birth. Even if such a policy serves the ideal of justice, there are other considerations of human nature at work.[75] Still, Socrates's ideal reveals deep and real problems with the favorable preference family members show to one another over and against the more universal call of justice to treat alike who are alike. A reader who lives in an ordinary and nonideal city can still learn from this ideal pattern something about his own city and its limits. In seeing what the just ideal *would* look like, Plato's audience is challenged to imaginatively compare his own city to the paradigm of justice, and to learn where and how it falls short. Socrates's alternative paradigm allows those who listen to it to imagine their own cities differently, through a process of contrast between the city in which they reside and an idealized city in speech that challenges norms and values.

Thus, as we consider Socrates's ideas, it is important to keep in mind that the existence of an ideal paradigm does not mean that it must be implemented precisely in order for the paradigm to have value. One reason is that the ideal itself may not be correct, and Socrates is cautionary against the move from the ideal to the concrete. A second reason is that even if the ideal is good, it may not be better to implement it exactly as it is. For example, an ideal may be in conflict with other realities of human nature, because human nature itself involves contingencies that are not completely subject to the normative rule of ideals implemented as political laws.

Socrates is clear that there is some doubt about whether his plan is best and whether it is attainable. Book Eight will suggest that even if the ideal is attainable, it is liable to decay as all cities and regimes do. But even if utopian claims cannot be perfectly attained, this does not mean that they lack all political value for concrete life.[76] For example, it may be that the current practices need to be reformed but through other means than political imposition. Plato's Academy seems to have had women students, a decision that is not imposed on the citizenship through an act of law, but nonetheless a political decision. Or laws against nepotism and favoring one's own family for political offices may benefit the city even if the abolition of the family as such is thought to be too extreme.[77]

Part of the value of the human imagination is our capacity to imagine ourselves other than how we already are. Whereas most other animals, presumably, do not imagine alternative forms of life for themselves, no matter how intelligent, human beings can imagine cities that are arranged with entirely different structures than those that exist in their current cities or states. Unlike honeybees, which must arrange their social lives in a particular way, and have no possibility to act otherwise, human beings' living arrangements are far more flexible. As such, they allow for the possibility of greater or lesser happiness, and more or less justice. Socrates's exercise of the imagination allows us to consider these alternative ways of living without actually immediately undertaking the corresponding political actions. Through imagining ourselves in a different kind of social arrangement, we can go through the process of enacting these ideas and test them out in certain respects in advance. Of course, our imaginations can be deeply flawed: we might imagine that eliminating or raising taxes will produce a social utopia, and in either case we are likely to be deluded if we propose simple solutions to complex problems. But through the mediation of the imagination, we can consider possibilities that heretofore have not yet been tried. In the realm of comedy and tragedy alike, we might see something of our own society more clearly when it is mediated sufficiently to give us some distance from it. The distance afforded to us in the act of spectatorship paradoxically grants us the ability to see ourselves more clearly. Socrates's proposals invite his audience to consider what may be problematic in Athenian practices of the treatment of women, the favoring of the family at the expense of the larger body politic, and a source of rule that is not grounded in any kind of love of wisdom. This is distinct from creating a political plan or policy. It is an effort to affect our imaginations so that we might have the capacity, before acting, simply to be able to look and to see what has so far been absent from our sight. Comedy asks us to reconfigure our own social and political identities, if only for a moment. The ridiculous is initially acknowledged in the other, in whom it is made literally visible in performance. Only then can what is limited in oneself also become visible.

The final discussion of Book Five looks at what it means to be philosophical, in a way that is harmonious with this view of comic purpose. Socrates delineates a number of character traits that a philosopher-ruler must have. He must be a lover of all of wisdom, not only of one part but all (475b). He is insatiable with regard to this desire and willing to "taste" many new ideas (475c)—perhaps much like the ones that Socrates and his friends have laid out. He also has a specific set of metaphysical commitments and believes in the existence of "beauty itself" (476c), understands that beautiful things participates in beauty itself, and is able to "catch sight" of both it and what participates in it (476d). Suddenly, Socrates introduces a series of claims about the philosopher-rulers that are far removed from the earlier claims about what is necessary in the guardians. The guardians are now said to be able to distinguish between knowledge of what is and opinion, which merely regards what is in between being and nonbeing (478a–80a). Nothing so far in what has been said of the guardians in earlier books would seem to require a belief in beauty itself or to distinguish between love of the ordinary and of the ideal (476c–76d). The philosopher-rulers are said to love the objects of knowledge—what will soon be described as the forms—unlike the lovers of sights and sounds who do not recognize a higher reality in which lower objects participate.

This sudden move to metaphysics and epistemology might seem unwarranted, although it provides a transition to the material of Books Six and Seven. However, these claims about the difference between loving the ideal and loving sights and sounds are closely connected to the preceding comic material. Here, Socrates reiterates a separation between the ideal and the concrete that his interlocutors so far have failed to see. Polemarchus and Glaucon alike push for *how* this city is to come into being, while Socrates frequently resists their rush to implementation of the ideal of justice. Instead, he grants a kind of reality to the ideal paradigm and pattern that is worthy of greater love than its practical implementation. Socrates is not so much an idealist in the sense of being a utopian in how he wants to practice politics. He is instead an idealist in the philosophical sense of the term, in asserting that the ideas are the greatest objects of love—more lovable than concrete human political realities.

This is quite a remarkable claim to make in a book on politics. However, the images that Socrates offers in the next books move between the world of the ideas and the world of politics. The images of the sun and divided line speak about the greater reality of the world of ideas. But the image of the cave, and subsequent images of degenerate souls and cities, moves us back into the realm of real-world politics again. Socrates asks for his listeners to ascend out of the cave with him for a while, but a descent also takes place in which a return is made to a nonideal world. Eventually, Socrates shows that the just person is happier than the tyrant even in the imperfect world. Comedy may show that philosophical idealism is difficult to implement, but Socrates will also offer reasons to think that the pursuit of philosophy in the nonideal world is also a good, and a cause of greater happiness than any other way of living.

Chapter 7

The Image of the Sun

The central descriptions of the forms in the *Republic* are images rather than exacting descriptions of the forms. Yet relatively little commentary exists on how and why images are used to describe the forms, rather than some other mode of expression.[1] This question is particularly pressing in light of the criticisms of imagery that will come in Book Ten. In this chapter, I explore the use of imagery to describe the forms in the comparison of the form of the good to the sun and in the image of the divided line, while the next chapter will undertake to examine the image of the cave. Here, my task is not so much to provide an account of Plato's metaphysics as to examine how and why Plato uses imagery to describe the forms, and why they are best described through images rather than through some sort of image-free language.

Language is a human reality and we cannot automatically suppose that language and reality immediately exist in a perfect, one-to-one correspondence. Plato's contemporaries and recent predecessors were well aware of this fact. For example, this possibility was already countenanced by Gorgias in his essay "On Non-Being," in which he playfully argues for a separation between language, thought, and being, such that rhetoric is free to say whatever the rhetorician likes without any necessary commitment to the truth. When Plato takes up this topic, he does so not with a naïve assumption at play that language and reality must correspond. Rather, he writes in a cultural milieu in which the sophists sought wisdom but, in many cases, detached wisdom from truth-seeking, where truth is understood to be intelligible and beyond one's own power or creativity. For example, in Plato's *Protagoras*, Protagoras describes wisdom as *euboulia*, something like the capacity to make prudential practical judgments that young men in the city will need to possess in order to be successful at politics (*Prot.* 318e–19a). Protagoras's idea that "the human being is the measure of all things" sums up his relativistic perspective on knowledge. In the *Theaetetus*, Socrates presents Protagorean relativism as a form of epistemology in which knowledge is reducible to perception (*Theaet.* 151e–79b). While the *Theaetetus* rejects this view, it is also clear that the view is appealing to consider, insofar as it attends to the fact that all truth-seeking begins, and must begin, with the experience of the subject.

Although Socrates gives an account of the forms, his caveats about how he can speak about them and his expressions of his own ignorance suggest that he is not a naïve rationalist. Instead, the middle books make clear that he shows awareness of a possible gap between how we see the world and the nature of being itself. The divided line image presents a view of reality in which the world of sensible experience taken at face value is not a reliable place in which to find knowledge. The forms are the true objects of knowledge. But neither does Socrates suggest that the forms are easy to know, or that language can adequately capture them. Indeed, Socrates gives no direct argument for their existence. Instead, he gives an account of what it means to seek the forms and to possess beliefs or knowledge of them. The *Republic* does not possess as robust a "theory of forms" as one might like if one wanted to develop a detailed theory of metaphysics. But Socrates's aim seems to be less to present a full-fledged metaphysics than to examine our relation to the real, and to paint a picture of education in which learning is a kind of difficult and slow ascent to the forms. Of course, to talk about such an ascent requires some description of what the forms are, but these are mostly described through metaphor or analogy.

These images are central to teaching us about what this process of coming-to-know looks like. One reason is that the images Socrates chooses of sun, divided line, and cave allow one to speak about some unfamiliar and difficult concepts through familiar, everyday comparisons. Instead of receiving an education in mathematics, like the guardians of the ideal city, Socrates thinks that images are a helpful way to describe the forms to Glaucon and Adeimantus, who are not themselves guardians in the ideal city. But as I will argue, the role of images is not limited to its pedagogical value. Images are also an appropriate way to describe the forms because our access to them is often given only perspectivally, that is, partially and from the point of view of a particular model or paradigm.[2] Visual images convey this sense of partial insight and a nonbinary understanding of coming to know.[3] Socrates's model for knowledge does not concern propositions, although many commentators attempt to describe the forms in these terms. Instead, his model is that of sight, but of an intellectual kind of seeing.[4] On the one hand, philosophy is about the seeking of a truth outside of ourselves, not merely created by us. As Nightingale says, the visual metaphors emphasize that formal reality is not something that can be touched, changed, or fundamentally affected.[5] The forms are the objects of the philosopher's love, and he is willing to reject his own inadequate opinions for the sake of coming to know these realities. On the other hand, as a being who sees, hears, and generally senses, the sensible world is also the means by which he seeks what he desires to know.[6] Even abstract activities such as the pursuit of mathematical truths often depend on visual guides such as lines and figures to provide insight into the nature of that abstract truth. Moral and political truths are even more tied to the visible and sensible world, insofar as we come to learn about justice through experience. Socrates assumes as much when he asks Cephalus, with genuine curiosity, what old age is like and then explores what Cephalus takes to be justice. Socrates presumes that conversation with imperfect human beings, who reside in real, imperfect, and visible cities, somehow can assist us in seeking the truth about forms such as justice. Thus, the very process by which Socrates and his friends have made discoveries about the form of justice, through models of the city and soul, assumes that the visible world has something to offer the philosopher in terms of access to the intelligible one.

As this book has argued in previous chapters, Socrates and the other interlocutors have already presented *images* and *paradigms* of justice as the best way that they can describe the form of justice. In Book Four, Socrates uses an image of a just city to describe justice in the soul. So it might be tempting to say that a form *is* a paradigm, that is, an idealized model of justice. However, the central books seem to indicate something different. Socrates presents the forms as beyond any particular images or models of them, and yet as accessible in part *through* images, if those images are correctly understood. An image of justice is not identical to the being of the form of justice itself. The analogies and images of sun, divided line, and cave assert a relation between image and form in which the form is above and beyond any image of it. Yet Socrates himself gives us images of the sun, divided line, and cave to indicate what the forms are and what our relation is to them. Thus, Socrates has confidence that an image can point beyond itself to an intelligible reality, if rightly understood.

The term "form" (*idea* or *eidos*) has an ordinary Greek meaning of "look" or "shape." In its nontechnical use, it is the visible form of something.[7]

Since Socrates uses a series of visual metaphors in the central images of the sun, divided line, and cave, it is helpful to bear in mind that Socrates's decision to use the ordinary Greek term *idea* in a more technical way is already a visual metaphor. On the one hand, its being a "look" emphasizes that the highest realities are things that appear to us in a certain way. They can be accessed; reality is not so irrational as to be completely inaccessible. On the other hand, Socrates does not want to reduce these highest realities to either human perception—as in Protagorean relativism—or to human language where we assume that our way of speaking creates the structure of reality—as sophists such as Gorgias implied.[8] Instead, reality is both separable from perceptual and language-based reality and yet also accessed through it.[9] We can be certain that Socrates thinks that the forms are not only creations of human language or perception, since the form of the good is said to be the *cause* of the *being* of all the other forms. Moreover, the sensible world participates in the forms in a way that is clearly dependent on them. Both the form of the good and the other forms are not caused by us but instead are prior to our perceptions, judgments, and accounts of them.

The Greek term *paradeigma* can mean both a pattern or model, or an example. While some paradigms are human constructions (such as instructions for how to build a birdhouse), a paradigm can also express the idea of a "model" that expresses the essence of what it is to be a certain kind of thing. For example, a model of a human skeleton may allow a medical student to see and understand how the bones of the body ideally fit together.[10] But Socrates has a still stronger sense of what a form is than a model of justice or beauty: a form is not only a verbal description or image of the essence of a sensible thing, the way a model of a human skeleton is, but the ontologically rich cause of the being of the things that partake of the form. As Rosen has argued, in the *Republic* we find a hierarchy: at the top are the forms themselves; then verbal models or paradigms of the forms of the sort that Socrates offers in the dialogue; and individual, historical just cities or souls—for example, Socrates, who is a just person.[11] Thus, in the case of justice, we have the form/idea of justice, models or paradigms of the form, and particular instances in the ordinary world.[12] If we do not distinguish Socrates's models of justice from justice itself, we lose both the causal agency of the form of justice on the one hand, and the constructed and developed nature of Socrates's arguments on the other. But all three sorts of things—the form, the models, and individual just persons or cities—have the "look" of justice to some extent, since all are related back to the form of justice that is the ultimate cause of anything being just. To the extent that a paradigm does help us to see the form, a good paradigm must have something of the "look" of the forms.

For Socrates, the mathematical model is central to helping the guardians of the ideal city to understand the existence of such forms: the geometrician, as Socrates understands him, uses visual drawings not in order to construct a mathematical theory but rather to make discoveries about mathematical objects, for example, the relations between proportions in quadrilinear or triangular figures. These objects may exist nowhere perfectly in the ordinary world, but through abstraction one can gain access to such objects. A visual model of a mathematical object can help us to understand not only what a perfect circle might "look" like, even if our drawn one is imperfect, but also what the intelligible relationship between different mathematical objects is, for instance, proportional relations. Forms such as justice and beauty show that the concept of the forms is not limited to mathematics but extends to what contemporary philosophy would name as moral and aesthetic concepts. Higher still is the form of the good, a form that exists "beyond being" (509b). This form is the cause of all other being, since it is the cause of even the forms themselves. Socrates seems to mean this in a quite strong, ontological sense, since he compares it to the sun, which allows for the genesis of living things.[13] He means more than only a logical relation. To this extent, the forms also share something in common with how Socrates described the gods earlier: a god never changes "form" (379a–b, 380d).[14] While Socrates never reconnects the gods to the forms in the middle books, we can see that this view, that the highest goods must be unchanging and not depend only on our constructions of them, has already been given an abbreviated argument in Book Two: what is best can never become either better or worse, and therefore never changes.[15] Similarly, the form of the good and other forms are not dependent on our constructions of them for their being. And yet, because we are human, how we are to describe these highest realities depends on the mode through which we can see, know, and talk about them. Socrates thinks that images are a promising way to talk about the forms, so long as the image is not mistaken for the reality itself.

To say that a form has a "shape," or a "look," also suggests that it is *not* a construction of ours. Rather, metaphorically speaking, it already has a determinate "form" or content, and then we look at it in order to gain understanding of what it is. As I will argue, however, Socrates's metaphors about the forms suggest that no single image is ever a complete image of the forms. That is, the forms are not exhausted by any single or any limited set of words or images that can be given about them.[16] Socrates says that he is only giving an image of the form of the good here. One might hope that somewhere else, we would be given a nonimagistic description. However, in no other dialogue do we get another account of the form of the good that claims to present it in an image-free way. If Plato did, it might be possible to hypothesize that the form of the good is only given in image form for the sake of Glaucon or Adeimantus, or for Plato's not yet philosophical reader.[17] However, the absence of any nonimagistic account elsewhere suggests that it is also possible that no image or account suffices to capture fully its nature.[18] Indeed, as Rosen has argued, language itself only always offers models of that which it describes.[19] And yet, because we do have some access to the forms, and have a capacity to know them, we can also say something about what they are and test our perceptions of what we believe them to be through conversation with others. The problem is that many people think that their images do describe reality accurately. They do not understand an image of justice *as an image*.

As Hart has argued, the contrast between the lovers of sight and sound and the true philosopher centers around how each understands images. The lovers of sight and sound take an image to be reality, and so remain like those who are asleep and only dreaming. The philosopher, in contrast, understands an image as an image.[20] As I will argue later, Socrates uses images in order to talk meaningfully about the forms. However, he also emphasizes through these images themselves that the image is not already the fullness of the formal reality that it describes, but rather only an image. Nonetheless, an intelligible image is still useful for understanding what it describes, so long as it is understood as an image, and not as the form itself. Through elaborating on visual metaphors, Socrates develops a place for intellectual insight as a mode of coming to know, while also maintaining a picture of relative human limit. The philosopher can come to know more about what she loves, but the philosopher is also a lover of wisdom rather than perfectly wise.

When Socrates offers images of the forms, he simultaneously uses images that show us *that* these images are only images. In other words, Socrates's images of sun, divided line, and cave do two things at once: first, they give us a way of imaging the forms and their relation to the ordinary world from an omniscient point of view, even though our actual access to the forms may be partial. Second, the images that he uses also help us to understand *that* an image is only an image, and that the forms are beyond any images that we have of them. This is even true of images that describe what the forms are. Socrates uses three images to describe the forms rather than one, so that we can see the same entities in three slightly different ways. Socrates offers three different perspectives on the nature of the forms. As I will also argue, this approach to Socrates's descriptions of the forms also helps to avoid a problem when the idea of "two worlds" is taken too far, in which the forms are knowable while ordinary reality is unknowable.[21] The forms are knowable, in a way, through images. But these images do not capture the forms completely and so knowledge is, as Gerald Press puts it, only "partial and perspectival."[22] On this reading, beliefs about forms are possible. One need not have perfect knowledge for the forms to be accessible.[23] Moreover, to the extent that sensible reality does reflect the forms, in imaging them, these images allow the sensible world also to be knowable, in a way. For example, while no painting is perfectly beautiful, to the extent that I know beauty through the painting, I am knowing the painting, too, and not just the form apart from it. A helpful metaphor here might be the difference between looking through a piece of clear glass to see an object, where the glass is not paid attention to at all, and admiring a photograph of a beloved person where the likeness reminds one of the real person. The photograph may also be cherished, and not a mere instrument of reminding one of the original, and yet what is lovable about the photograph stems from its relationship to the original. Socrates seems to have more of the latter approach to images and the sensible world in mind, insofar as he uses images to help his interlocutors to discover forms. At the same time, vision as a metaphor for knowledge also reminds us that vision can also lead us astray. Just as we can have perceptual errors in what we see, how we understand reality and conceptualize it through models can lead us into relative ignorance. Thus, it is not enough to say images can lead us closer to the forms; they can also lead us away from them and into ignorance.

Accordingly, Socrates distinguishes between knowledge (*epistēmē*) and opinion (*doxa*) by stating that each is a different kind of power (*dunamis*) (477b). Knowledge is not about propositions, but rather about different capacities of the inquirer.[24] One power is different from another if it has a different object at which it is aimed and if there is a different result. Knowledge has as its object "what is" whereas opinion is of what both "is" and "is not." Socrates adds that knowledge is secure, whereas opinion is insecure. As a result, some have taken this to mean that knowledge only concerns forms, whereas belief concerns the sensible world, which can never be fully known. If this is the case, one possible consequence might be to deny that one can even have beliefs about the forms.[25] In that case, one could not move even in principle from beliefs to knowledge, without abandoning all opinion-based inquiry and perhaps even by abandoning the sensible world altogether.

Such a view leads to a serious textual difficulty, because Socrates is clear that he has opinions about the forms, but not knowledge.[26] For example, he says, "Is it your opinion that it's just to speak about things one doesn't know as if one knew them?" (506c). If knowledge is always of forms and belief always of sensible reality, then how can one describe a form and yet not have knowledge of it? Moreover, even when Socrates built up a model of the city and applied it to the soul, Socrates did not claim epistemic security but rather asked his interlocutors to look at it and tell him whether it really looked like justice or not (427d, 435a). And yet, clearly, Socrates thinks that his model offers a better view of justice than any of the other accounts that have been given so far. Thus, it seems that it *is* possible to be able to say something meaningful and true about the forms—or at least to offer a better model than other possible models—and yet not to have perfect and secure knowledge.

At the same time, Socrates's contrast between the philosophers and the lovers of sight and sound emphasizes a gap between those who understand images as images and those who do not. A beautiful painting always falls short of Beauty itself. One way to understand this notion is to say that not only does even a masterfully beautiful painting have small blemishes and imperfections, but also that it does not, and cannot, capture the whole of what it means to be beautiful. For example, a beautiful piece of music captures a different aspect of the beautiful than does a beautiful painting; indeed, many different pieces of music may exhibit beauty, but none exhaust beauty itself. The form of beauty possesses the attribute of beauty in an unqualified way, while particular beautiful things always do so in limited and imperfect ways.[27] Thus, the lovers of sights and sounds are not necessarily incorrect in finding their images or sounds to be beautiful, but they do not make the move of loving beauty itself. Philosophers seek the whole of beauty.[28]

Socrates, though, does not say that he knows the form of the good comprehensively. Yet he offers to Glaucon to speak about beautiful things: "Do you want to contemplate (*theasasthai*) ugly things, blind and crooked, when it's possible to hear from others ones that are bright (*phana*) and beautiful (*kala*)?" (506c–d). How then, can we understand his serious presentation of images of the good while not reading his claim that he possesses only opinion about the good ironically? One way to read the distinction between knowledge and opinion can help to make Socrates's view internally consistent. Much depends on how we interpret the idea that knowledge is of "what is," while opinion is both of "what is" and "what is not." I take Socrates here to mean "is" in an existential sense: the forms *are* in a strong sense, in that they are eternal and unchanging, much like the gods of Book Two, although they are not personal.[29] But the objects of opinion both are and are not, insofar as they come to be and pass away, literally in the sense that they come to be and decay again. Sensible objects, like plants, animals, and artifacts, come to be and pass away. They both are and are not. What "is not" absolutely, of course, does not exist. While it may seem absurd to talk about nonbeing, Socrates's including it at one pole (nonbeing), and locating the stable and permanent being of the forms at the other polarity, makes it possible to locate opinion conceptually as in between perfect knowledge and total ignorance. (Socrates does something similar in naming Eros as the child of Poverty and Plenty in the *Symposium*, albeit in mythological language, at 203b–4a.)

On this reading, Socrates may simply be saying something quite simple about the nature of knowledge and belief: to the extent that our images of justice do describe the form of justice well, then our knowledge of it will be stable. Since the form is stable and unchanging, what we have accurately said of it also will not change to the extent that we know. If our beliefs shift and change as a result of philosophical discussion, however, we can then recognize that they are at least partly false, though they may also be partly true—as was the case with some of the earlier ideas about justice in Book One, where Cephalus and Polemarchus captured some aspects of justice but missed others. In this case, we can judge that what we said was only a case of belief, because it concerns what both is and is not. It is mixed, neither complete knowledge nor total ignorance. If we were to know and grasp a form completely, our image and words about it would cease to change. But as will be clear in the discussion of the image of the sun later, it is possible to see something of a form and yet not to see all of it. Our more usual state is to have beliefs about matter such as the nature of justice, or even what a form is. To the extent that those beliefs *do* shift, rather than remain stable and unchanging, we can tell that they have not yet captured the forms adequately.

Knowledge and opinion are two powers in the soul, but we are not always aware of when we are using one or when we are using the other, until we test our models through conversation. After all, distinction between using our capacities to know and to believe is not experienced in the way that we clearly distinguish between two capacities for sense experience, such as the power of sight and the power of hearing. I always know when I am hearing rather than seeing. But this is not the case with knowledge and opinion. I don't know whether what I think I know about justice really is knowledge or is only opinion, at least not in advance. Indeed, if paradigms and models are central to how I come increasingly to know matters such as the nature of justice, then I also must be aware of the potential limits of each model and how any given model might also lead to ignorance, or at least be an incomplete account. Only when I test it to see whether it is unchanging after much discussion—of the sort that we see in the development of the dialogue's main moral theory—can I have a reasonable sense of whether it might be knowledge. But because in principle, I cannot know whether my belief might someday change when faced with a new series of questions or considerations, I can never be completely certain that what I now "know" or "see" about justice is knowledge. I can only say that what I think I have seen has so far been examined and discussed in a way that justice seems really to have "come to light," as Socrates said of his own model of justice. Thus, Socrates seems to think it safer to say that his own view of the forms is only one of opinion, and not absolute knowledge—not because he is completely ignorant of everything about the forms, but rather because his opinions do not reach the very high standard of being completely stable and unchanging.

The forms are not only known for their own sake, although this is what the philosopher loves most of all. Once they are known, they also can become the basis for the intelligibility of the ordinary, sensible world. We can see how this might apply back to the earlier sections of the dialogue. For example, the discussion of the form of justice was not only for the sake of understanding the nature of justice better, but presumably also to help Socrates and his friends better understand the nature of just and unjust cities and people in the ordinary world. While it need not be the case that Socrates is developing a blueprint for the city, there is good reason to think that in learning more about the form of justice, the justice of any given city, or any given soul, will be easier to discern. As Miller writes, the conversion of the soul to be oriented toward the forms is not only for the sake of pure understanding, but also for the sake of making a "return."[30]

Socrates's discussion of the forms arises within the context of the education of the guardians. Not only do the guardians of the city need to study geometry, astronomy, and other subjects that encourage abstraction, but they must also study the idea of the good so that they can rule over the city well. Socrates offers a practical benefit for studying this seemingly impractical idea: "The idea of the good is the greatest lesson, and by it just things and all the rest become useful and beneficial" (505a). One way to understand Socrates's words here is to say that in any decision that a guardian might make, some set of beliefs of the good always at least implicitly informs that decision. To take a few contemporary examples: whether one raises or lowers taxes, or encourages or discourages immigration into one's own country already relies implicitly on some notion of the good. The converse is not true: not every discussion of the good always involves discussing the merits of taxation. Socrates makes a claim about human action: "The good is what every soul chases and on account of which it does everything" (505d–e). He seems to take a teleological approach much like the one found at the start of Aristotle's *Nicomachean Ethics*.[31] Each person acts for the sake of a goal and that these smaller goals may be subordinated to some larger goal and perhaps a single, unified largest goal of all. Socrates names this ultimate end, for the sake of which we pursue everything else, the good.[32] However, unlike Aristotle who defines the good for human beings in terms of the greatest human desire (happiness in accord with one's human capacities), Socrates reverses the picture. The form of the good is the cause of all other forms and is needed for any knowledge whatsoever. As will become clear in the subsequent discussion, I take this to mean that the good is prior to our desire for it, and our acting for its sake secondary to its existence and its "pull" on us.

Socrates uses the sun as an image of the form of the good. The image of the form of the good clearly has pedagogical value, and so it might be tempting to explain it only as a rhetorical or as a teaching device.[33] Moreover, his argument is oriented toward the lovers of sight, and so he might choose visual metaphors in order to address them.[34] One of the limits of the lovers of sight and sound is that they do not recognize an image as an image.[35] However, there are at least two reasons to reject a purely pedagogical view of his imagery. First, Socrates says that he must use images *not* only because Glaucon or the others would not be able to follow him, but also because Socrates *himself* is ignorant, and potentially like a blind man leading them along the way (506c–d).[36] And second, if this image were meant to bring perfect clarity to us as to the nature of the form of the good, then Plato seems to have failed. The image does not accomplish even close to all that we might want for it to teach philosophically, for example, to give an account as to *how* the form of the good is a cause of other forms, or exactly *in what way* it illuminates the act of knowing. In other words, whatever the image of the form of the good is doing here, it is not attempting to provide a detailed epistemology or a precise ontology. Rather, we must look to other explanations of the reasons behind Socrates's use of this image.

I suggest that his use of images communicates a peculiar epistemological relationship between human beings as they undertake their moral and political deliberations and the good. Socrates says that with respect to the idea of the good, the human being lives in a paradoxical situation. Although the soul chases after the good and does everything for its sake, it "divines its being, but is at a loss (*aporousa*) and unable sufficiently to grasp (*labein*) just what it is, or to declare stable trust in it like the others" (505e–6a).[37] Socrates says that we all pursue the good in whatever we do. We seek the good not only with respect to cognitive acts, but also with respect to actions that are part of everyday, ordinary lived experience. Human beings seem to act for the sake of a good in every action that they undertake. We seem to have some intuition of what it is; Socrates uses the language of divination to describe this pre-knowing. At the same time, we do not know the good nor even have trust in what we think it to be. As a consequence, our knowledge of the good does not reach the same level as our desire for it. Our desire always exceeds our capacity to know that which we seek.[38]

However, Socrates does not simply say that the result is either a state of total knowledge or total ignorance about the good, or that we fall on the side of ignorance yet must act. Rather, he says that the soul "divines its being (*apomanteuomenē ti einai*)," that is, we have a kind of inspiration or intuition about its nature. However, this intuition also leads to an experience of being at a loss: "*aporousa de kai ouk echousa labein ikanôs ti pot' estin oude pistei chrēsasthai monimô hoia kai peri talla*" (505e). Despite having some sense of the good, we also find ourselves at a loss, in an aporetic state, unable fully to grasp what it is, or to trust in our intuitions in the way that we can trust in other things. Socrates borrows from religious language, using terms often used to describe oracular pronouncements: *apomanteuomenē* is the participle form of *apomanteuomai* or "to divine by instinct, to presage."[39] Its root word is the verb *manteuomai* or "prophesy." Similarly, when Socrates says *oude pistei chrēsasthai*, he uses the middle aorist infinitive form of *chraô*, proclaim, which in its middle form means to consult an oracle. Of course, Socrates does not mean that one literally consults an oracle to know what the good is, but rather he uses this religious language metaphorically to describe the human experience of drawing upon our intuitions of the good.

Why this sort of language? Socrates offers no further explanation of his language here.[40] I suggest that we interpret Socrates's oracular language as a kind of metaphor that gives an account of what it is like to search for the good philosophically. When searching for the good, a person may find himself experiencing a moment of insight, a sense that he intuitively knows what it means to say that something is good. We do have access to the good in a way that is prior to language, when we have the sense of having arrived at an idea but have not yet expressed it discursively.[41] This felt sense of having an insight, however, must be expressed in language, and yet the movement from insight into defensible definitions is often problematic. Expressing claims about the form of the good is particularly problematic, even more so than, for example, expressing claims about justice. For example, imagine if someone were to ask us why the equal treatment of a particular marginalized group is good and ought to be pursued, we might appeal to concepts of justice and equality, and say that equal beings should be treated equally. But when we are asked why the good is *good*, there is little left to say. The good is the final category toward which all other more particular or partial goods are linked. There is no further category to which to appeal. One can only say about the goodness of the good, that it is good because . . . it is good.[42]

Socrates thus uses the imagery of divination in order to express what it is like to seek the form of the good. As Socrates presents it, the good itself is foundational and prior to the definition of any other more particular good that can be defined. It is a real objective unity, rather than a set of many different goods that all are given the same terminology.[43] Socrates's language about our relationship to the good relies on the image of the reception of an oracular pronouncement to convey something of how we seek it. The process of consulting the oracle at Delphi was multifaceted: one would ask the oracle a question, wait to receive a response, and then have to go to interpret it. Socrates's interpretation in the *Apology* of the oracle at Delphi that "no one is wiser" than Socrates is a case in point: Chaerephon asks his question, but even after receiving an answer, this answer still must be made sense of, and Socrates's own answer that all are ignorant turns out to be quite different than Chaerephon's initial adulation of Socrates as positively wise. While the English language does not utilize this language of oracular inquiry and proclamation to describe the imagination, Socrates uses the term *apomanteuomai*, or to pre-divine, in order to highlight a particular feature of inquiry into the good (505e). As human actors, we ask what is good; receive what we feel to be a kind of prelogical, not yet articulated intuition that something is good; and then we use language to try to articulate in words *that* it is good and *why* it is good. This is the sort of approach we see in

Book One, when he asked Cephalus and Polemarchus to tell him something about the nature of justice. Cephalus has a sense of what is good about the just life, but there is a movement from a general sense that justice is a good that he has sought, to being able to express verbally the nature of his intuitions about it. Of course, Socrates does not argue that we are in fact always *correct* when we seek to describe what is good. In Thrasymachus, we can see an example of someone who believes that to act unjustly is good. Socrates does not give any role to a god or anyone else as a guarantor of correct intuitive insight. Rather than being a literal description of human access to the good, then, I suggest that Socrates uses this language of divination as a metaphorical image of what it is like to live as a seeker of the good. We are *like* those who go to oracles and await a response when we seek the good in the course of ordinary living. But even an oracle demands interpretation. Socrates, for example, goes around speaking to others after the oracle declares that "no one is wiser than Socrates" to Chaerephon. Thus we ought not take Socrates's borrowed language from oracles to mean that insights are infallible. Instead, insights require further investigation. Just as oracular pronouncements require a philosophical hermeneutic, insight is primary for beginning a discussion of the good or any other form but always requires testing and rational evaluation.[44] Moreover, it is language itself that gives stability to an insight, which may be experienced far more indeterminately and fluidly. There must be a movement between the "vertical" dimension, that is, the soul's relation to the intelligible forms, and the "horizontal," or human-to-human dimension of speech whereby we test out our ideas in conversation with others.

Socrates, however, does not retreat from the task of trying to talk about the good, or reject the idea of a good itself, simply because the fullness of understanding its nature eludes us. Indeed, it must be talked about because Socrates says it is the object of philosophical love (475b). Instead, Socrates develops an image that allows us to say something *about* the good without exhaustively determining its nature. The image of the sun does this work. Socrates says that just as the sun gives light and heat and is the cause of the growth of plants, animals, and other forms of life that depend on its light and heat, so also the form of the good is a cause of the other forms. Just as the sun's light illuminates the eye's capacity to see objects in the world of sense perception, so too does the form of the good allow the intellect to have access to the forms as the objects of knowledge. Here, Socrates's images are integrative, as Patterson has argued.[45] The image of the sun and its relationship to both that which it has created, and that which perceives it, brings together many disparate elements into a whole. Thus it provides a synthetic overview of the relationship between knower, known, and the conditions of knowledge.

Socrates says that he cannot speak directly of the good but only of the sun as the "offspring" (*ekgonos*) of the good (506e), that is, of something that is the result of the good as its cause. Since the sun is also the cause of the generation of living things, then the good is also the greatest cause of all. One way to read this image is teleologically.[46] The good seems to be that upon which all of our other moral and political questions already depend. But in naming the sun as the offspring of the good, Socrates seems to be saying something much stronger than that the good is that at which all things aim, as does Aristotle. Instead, he seems to be stating that the form is the cause of all that is, but a kind of cause that is accessible to us through its effects or offspring, rather than directly.[47] This can help to explain Socrates's ignorance. Socrates does not claim to *know* the good in the same sense that he might, for example, claim to know that it is better to suffer harm than to commit it. Socrates seems to know of claims of the latter sort through repeated testing of his intuition. But the good itself cannot be tested in the same way that a particular claim about what is good can be tested, because the good is the ultimate category from which all other claims get their bearings. The image of the sun as the form of the good, then, attempts to do something different than to give us the full *content* of the good. This would be impossible, because the good as the cause of every other form must exceed them in being. To be able to see the good fully, one would have to be able to see what is good about justice, beauty, piety, and every other form. From a finite point of view, the good is not capable of being exhaustively known. But here, Socrates is not trying to explain what is good *about* specific forms, or good *about* beings that participate in the forms. Instead, Socrates uses the image of the sun in order to state something about our relationship to the good, and what kind of a thing it must be in order for the relationship that we already have to it—in ordinary life as well as in philosophical inquiry—to exist in the way that it does.

An image or analogy is especially useful in these circumstances because it does not pretend that what the image describes is exactly like the image. No one thinks for a moment that the form of the good *is* the sun itself, that is, the actual object seen in the sky that shines upon and warms the earth. The sun has many features that the form of the good lacks, and vice versa. To this extent, an image does not claim too much for Socrates in light of Socrates's claim that he does not know securely. Perhaps it is especially important, then, that along with this imagery of the forms of the central books Plato also includes a critique *of images* in Book Ten, in which the distance between images and the reality of the forms is articulated. Plato himself has written numerous images of the forms into the text of the *Republic* and so, by the dialogue's end, must offer a meta-theoretical account of what he is doing and what he is not doing with those images. (This critique will be treated in the final chapter.)

The language of *idea/eidos* is itself imagistic, and so the language of the sun is especially helpful for suggesting how the form of the good helps our intellects to "see" the forms. Moreover, Greek, like English and many other languages, often relies on the language of sight to describe knowledge and related terms. Thus, we can say "I see" in order to mean "I know," and *oida* plays a similar role in Greek. In English, we might say that we have had an "insight" to describe a moment of coming to understand. To the extent that ordinary language does provide us with useful terms to express philosophical meaning, it may be because ordinary language itself already connects something about the act of knowing to the act of seeing for good reason.

Socrates's image of the form of the good as akin to the sun offers us some information not only about what the form of the good is, but also why visual language is a helpful metaphor for human beings to use when seeking to understand the good. First, Socrates draws a *causal* relationship between the form of the good and other forms. The form of the good is the cause of the other forms in a way that parallels the light and heat of the sun as nourishment for plants and animals. The other forms depend upon the form of the good for their being. Without the form of the good, the other forms would not exist. Much is left unsaid in Socrates's account, but our purpose here is only to understand the point of the imagery and why it might be useful to a person like Glaucon, or a reader of the dialogue, to hear. In this way the image of the sun is quite clever. The dependency of plants and animals upon the sun for their existence is a readily available fact known to more or less everyone: we all know that a plant that does not receive enough light does not grow, or will not fruit or flower. An animal that is too cold will eventually die. The causal dependency is clear. But one does not have to know anything at all about the nature of the sun, or at a mechanistic level, how photosynthesis works, or how animal metabolic systems are affected by heat or cold, in order to understand the causal dependency. Still, the general fact of a causal dependency is clear and arises from observation of many particular instances from which one can infer the universal importance of the sun as a cause of being.

Socrates's metaphor likewise does not require that we know the essence of the form of the good directly in order to be able to say *that* it is the cause of all the other forms.[48] We do not even have to develop a theory of causation of forms to be able to say so, either. Rather, all one would have to do would be to know *that* other forms depend on the form of the good for their being. And Socrates has already given us a kind of inductive argument as to why the form of the good is the cause of all the other forms: when human beings seek to do anything at all, they seem always to be making an implicit claim that they are also seeking the good in this same action. Of course, such an argument might not satisfy everyone: Aristotle objected to the need for such a form to explain the teleological nature of human activity. Still, the argument is broadly speaking inductive—without giving a detailed account of what it means for the form of a good to be a cause, or precisely what this form itself is. To this extent, the metaphor of the sun accomplishes a significant task: Socrates can claim *something* about what the relation of the form of the good is to other forms, and its logical priority to other forms, without being able to say everything about the content of the good or its essence. He can make a reasonable claim about their relation, even if he truly does not "know" the form of the good fully and is partially "blind" and "ignorant," as he claims to be.

Still, we might be able to make some speculative claims about the nature of the form of the good from Socrates's claim that it is the cause of all the other forms and his earlier claim that all human beings pursue it. Mitchell Miller has argued that the form of the good is perfection itself, insofar as the idea of the perfect grounds and orients, for example, a geometer's understanding of the perfect triangle in distinction from an imperfect, visible one.[49] If the form of the good is perfection, then this would allow for it to be the source of truth or knowability of the forms, insofar as the geometers only start to understand what is intelligible when the geometrical forms such as triangle are understood as perfect triangles rather than as imperfect and sensible ones. Miller's hypothesis also explains the singular causal origin of the forms, insofar as only a perfect being could be a lone cause of the multiple forms and their variable ideal natures, although it leaves open the question of whether the form of the good is both oneness and perfection and a series of other questions not addressed in the *Republic*.[50]

However, Socrates never says that the form of the good is perfection itself, nor does he define it according to any other term. The term "good" remains fundamental, irreducible to any other term. There are some good reasons for leaving "goodness" as an irreducible, foundational term. First, if we were to define the good according to multiple terms, then it would lack the unity that Socrates wants to give to it as the sole cause of all other forms. These other terms would be that which explains the good, but the good itself is the final end and cause of all. Moreover, the form of the good as the origin of all the forms would also have to be the origin of both aesthetic and moral perfections in order to be the source of forms such as beauty, justice, courage, and the like. Thus, if the form of the good is perfection, it cannot be only a bare, abstract concept of perfection, as in mathematical perfection, but rather an ontologically rich "fullness" of perfection, a plenitude of perfection that can be a positive ontological source of all forms, even those with moral or political qualities, for instance, the form of justice itself.[51] Socrates does not develop this notion here but it is a requirement of the form of the good that its being is rich enough to supply the being of all the other forms.[52] It exceeds the *being* of all beings, not just by virtue of being a form but by being the ultimate form, the form beyond all forms. However, if one were to describe the form of the good by defining it according to some other category—like naming it the concept of perfection—then the good would be subsumed under that category: goodness would follow from perfection rather than being its cause. Perfection would be the cause of goodness, and goodness would no longer be the ultimate form. But the form of the good is responsible for the very existence of all the other forms, their being.[53] Indeed, since these forms are also the cause of all the things that participate in them, the form of the good is ultimately the cause of all being. To this extent, the form of the good is more akin to God than to any other concept—in fact, Socrates calls this form a god (508a).[54] As McPherran has demonstrated, language associated with divinity occurs not only in Book Two but also in the descriptions of the good: Socrates uses the terms *dēmiourgos* (507c) and *basileus* (509b–d).[55] Like God, who is not *a* being but rather the source and ground *of* being in many religious traditions—some of which understand God in this way in part due to the influence of Plato—the form of the good is beyond being and therefore not *a* being at all.[56] Unlike God, however, the form of the good is not personal. The forms exhibit no care and concern for the human person. Although the philosopher seeks the good in all that he does, the good does not seek him back. Yet for Socrates, the notion of the "good" captures best this idea of that which all seek, and which is the cause of all other forms and the condition of all knowledge.[57]

The metaphor of the sun is useful in its offering an account of the claim that the good illuminates noetic understanding, without already giving a full account either of the nature of *nous* or of the form of the good. Just as the eye depends on the sun's light in order to see a tree, or a flower, or a human being, the intellect can only grasp its objects in the presence of the form of the good. Here we have an analogy, in which some features of seeing have corresponding analogues in intellectual understanding. In order to see, the objects of sight must exist and have a power to be known. Likewise, there must be a capacity to see that exists on the side of the knower. Something must exist in common between these existences in order for the knowing to take place; light plays this function. Socrates does not give an account of how the good connects the knower and the one known. But it is not necessary to know the essence of what the sun is in order to recognize that one cannot see in the dark, or that dusk and shadows tend to make seeing an object more difficult. Indeed, the sun itself cannot be looked at directly. The light is simply too bright. Furthermore, with the unaided eye, one can learn more about the sun by *not* looking at it directly, but rather by observing its indirect effects. One can know *that* light is essential to vision without understanding much about either the eye or the sun, or even the specific object in question. Thus, the metaphor of the form of the good, also, describes *a set of relations between* intellect, form, and form of the good without having to defend detailed claims about what any of these individual components themselves are. Socrates can explain *that* the form of the good is needed for noetic insight to take place at all, and can make reasonable claims about this relationship, without having to possess perfect knowledge of the form of the good, *nous*, or the other forms.

Socrates's description of the power of sight might help us to better understand why Socrates thinks that he is able to describe the relationship between intellect, form, and form of the good, without being able to claim that he knows the form of the good completely. Socrates states that the eye is the "most sunlike of all organs" and that the power of sight arises from "a sort of overflow from the sun's treasury" (508b). He also refers to the soul as an *augē*, or a beam of sunlight (540a).[58] Here, Socrates seems to be pointing to, without fully developing, an emissions theory of sight along the lines of the one found in the *Timaeus* (45b–47e).[59] According to the *Timaeus*, sight can only take place because there is some congruence between the light that makes seeing an object possible and the eye itself. There must be a relationship of "like to like" for sight to take place at all. Today, we understand sight in terms of energy: the eye receives light that passes through vitreous gel onto a retina that then transmits electrical impulses to the brain—light as a form of energy affects cells whose own distinctive form of energy is then passed on to other cells. In an emissions theory of sight, however, the eye sends *out* rays of light that then coalesce with sunlight in the world. In the *Timaeus*, the eye gives off a "mild" (*hēmeron*) light akin to the light of day (*hēmeras*) (45b)—Plato even puns on the two words.[60] This stream of light, when it contacts a body outside of it, is affected by a motion, which then reverberates back onto the eye and so produces the sense experience of sight. Thus, in an emissions theory of sight, there is an actually continuous physical connection between what is happening outside and inside the human eye. Any object that is seen "shapes" the flow of light only according to the shape of the side of the object that is seen, such that how one sees the object is always perspectival. There is no universal vision of the entirety of an object, for the effect that is sent back to the eye depends on what shape or form the flow of light takes as it molds itself on the portion of the object that is directly in line with the eye. In the *Republic*, Socrates gives a shorter but similar enough account. As is also noted in the *Timaeus*, when there is light out, this process can take place, but in the dark, the absence of a like fire in the air to correspond with the fire of the eyes prevents the eye from connecting with its object.

Socrates then draws the analogy and suggests a similar process in the soul. He reminds his interlocutors that when the "lusters of night" extend over visual objects, they are dimmed and the eyes seem to be almost like blind eyes (508c). However, "when they look to what the sun illuminates, they see clearly, and vision appears to be in those same eyes" (508d). He then explains: "When it [the soul] fixes itself on that which is illumined by truth and that which is, it intellects (*enoēsen*), knows (*egnō*), and appears to possess intelligence (*noun echein phainetai*). But when it fixes itself on that which is mixed with darkness, on coming into being and passing away, it opines and is dimmed, changing opinions up and down, and seems at such times not to possess intelligence" (508d).

We can now return to the way in which knowledge and belief are two different powers (477a). Given that Socrates later places the forms at the very top of the divided line, in the realm of intellectual rather than the sensible, we might want to assume that *any* contact that takes place between *nous* and the forms is an instance of secure and complete knowledge, whereas the realm of sense experience is the realm of opinion. However, if what we mean in our contemporary usage of the terms "knowledge" and "opinion" is a clear-cut distinction between justified and unjustified opinion, the image of the form of the good does not support this line of thinking.

Neither are the powers described as two different faculties.[61] Instead, this image suggests that the world of the forms and the world of the senses are different in their being, but *both* are experienced along a continuum of illumination and darkness.[62]

If we apply the understanding of sight back to its analogical counterparts, then Socrates seems to be saying at least two things: first, our intellects already have something in common with the form of the good, even before we seek to know any particular intellectual object. The form of the good provides for the very possibility of intellectual experience, not only because it shines on the forms but also because there is already some sort of commonality or "fit" between our intellects and the form of the good. Socrates says nothing detailed about this, so it is difficult to offer more detail where none is given. However, the image affirms that even if one does not know the form of the good directly or completely, we can still say that we have indirect access to it since there must be something that allows our minds to know forms in general, that is, something that exists *in common* between us and them. The emissions theory of sight grounds the commonality in the eye's sharing of light that it emits with the light surrounding an object. Analogously, the forms to be knowable at all must be surrounded by something that is shared in common with the intellect, in order to be known at all. Since every act of seeking knowledge, like every other human action, is always also seeking the good, the good seems to be a reasonable candidate for being this "something."

Second, the image offers a model of encountering the forms in a way that is perspectival. While knowledge is free from error (477e), one's intellect can still encounter the forms and yet possess something less than this complete knowledge.[63] My argument here rests on a particular interpretation of what Socrates says that might be translated literally, if inelegantly, as: "Wherever truth and being shine and it [the soul] settles into this, it knows, recognizes, and seems to possess *nous*. But when [it goes] to that which is with darkness, that of becoming and destruction, it opines and is weak-sighted without *nous*, and shifts its opinions, and again does not possess *nous*" (508d). This passage lends itself to at least two possible interpretations. On one reading, the forms are always fully illuminated and the place of darkness, becoming, and destruction is the sensible world. Opinion describes the soul's action when it interacts with the sensible world, while knowledge describes a relationship to the intelligible one. In such a case, whenever one is in the realm of the forms, the mind is illuminated, but when one turns toward sensible things, the mind of the eye is darkened.

However, there are substantial difficulties with making such an interpretation of 508d consistent with the rest of Socrates's statements. Socrates
has also already said that every human being seeks the good in the most
ordinary human actions. Ordinary people who are living out their lives, even
nonphilosophers, already seek the good, though they do not understand it
as a form. For the good to be sought, however well or badly in practice, it
must be present in at least some minimal way to those who seek it. Thus,
he implies that even those people who are mostly living in the day-to-day
of the ordinary world have some minimal sense of the good, even though
they are not contemplative philosophers.

Moreover, Socrates uses the language of opinion to describe *both* his
own and Glaucon's relationship to understanding the form of the good,
which is higher than even the pursuit of stable knowledge. Socrates says to
Glaucon: "As fair as these two are—knowledge and truth—if you believe
that it [the idea of the good] is still fairer than they are, you will believe
rightly" (508e). Clearly, in referring to belief, Socrates is not referring to
an experience of the sensible world, but rather to a belief about the beauty
of the good. Socrates also tells Glaucon, "It is your fault for forcing me to
tell my opinions (*dokounta*) about it" (509c). Again, opinion here refers to
claims about the form of the good and does not refer to sensible things.
Therefore, it is clear that the forms are things about which one can have
opinions, and not only knowledge.

Socrates has not yet offered the divided line image, so we cannot
read that image back into this metaphor for its interpretation; his claims
about opinion ought to make sense within image of the sun alone, even if
incompletely so. However, even in the image of the divided line Socrates
names the faculty that relates to ordinary sensible things *pistis* or trust, and
not *doxa* or opinion, while Glaucon uses the term *doxa* (511d–e).[64] *Pistis* is
closely related to the Greek verb "to persuade," *peithô*. To trust in ordinary
objects is then either to take them at face value, not inquiring at all, or
to be persuaded that things are in a particular way, that is, to accept what
others have said about them. Thus the human response to the ordinary
sensible world can include both passive acceptance of what our senses tell us
about objects and passive acceptance of arguments. This point becomes still
clearer in the image of the cave, in which those chained to the benches take
what they see and hear alike to be truthful even when it is lacking in truth.

Socrates never refers to sensible being or two realms in the passage at
508d about being in darkness and light. He only says that when the soul
opines, it is looking at something that has darkness, genesis, and destruc-

tion in it. Given that no object other than the forms has been introduced within this single analogy, Socrates must still be describing the soul who is looking at the forms but encounters some sort of darkness and change.[65] The forms themselves are stable and unchanging, and cannot be the source of change. But the reference to "becoming and destruction" could refer to changes in the soul's own perceptions, which are ever changing because its view of the forms that it seeks is obscured by darkness. To draw out the analogy further, even though the sun always shines, our eyes can at times exist in relative darkness or light when clouds obscure the sun. The sun is unchanging in its brilliance. But our visual perceptions change as a result of the kinds of conditions that our eyes need to see. Similarly, the form of the good is always illuminating, but this does not mean that our noetic faculty has no limits that allow us to remain in its light all of the time. It is our limit that allows us to remain in relative darkness or light.[66]

On this reading, it is possible to explain why Socrates and Glaucon can be said to have an opinion about the forms and not only about sensible things. Coming to know the forms would mean having greater clarity of sight about the forms, with the consequence that one's vision of any given form, such as the form of justice, is more comprehensive and remains relatively stable. Having an opinion could still mean seeing *something* of the forms, but with great obscurity and instability. As Schindler argues, the being of the forms is intelligible precisely because the good doesn't simply exist; it exists "for others."[67] To the extent that the good gives rise to the existence of the other forms and to their intelligibility, those who seek to know the forms have partial access to them precisely because the form of the good has provided a kind of potential unity between the seeker of knowledge and the known object. Much like the eye can see its objects because light connects them, the form of the good provides for the possibility of intelligibility—but also for the possibility of only partially seeing that which is.[68]

Such a reading of the form of the good analogy also helps to connect this image back to the practice of Socratic questioning in this dialogue and others: while some of his interlocutors' ideas may need to be completely rejected, others may possess some insight into the truth. Socrates here gives a theory for how it is possible to understand opinion as in between knowledge (*epistēmē*) and ignorance, in a way where opinion still has a valuable role for pursuing the truth.

In other words, it is possible for certain kinds of opinion to be of the forms: for example, the opinions of those who seek to know what something like justice really is, but who do not yet (fully) know. Knowledge names a state that is fully illuminated, while opinion names a state that is only partially so, and therefore apt to change as further inquiry takes place. Socrates's reference to "becoming and destruction" in the preceding passage would then refer not to the changeability of sensible *objects* in contrast to the eternal forms, but rather to the changing light of an inquirer's partially obstructed *vision*. Not all knowledge is partial, for Socrates's examples of mathematics suggest that there are some forms that can be known and related to one another. But the point is that opinion need not be only of sensible reality of becoming and can also name a partial access to being.

Here, Socrates seems not to mean the mere expression of unthinking opinions by nonphilosophers, or those who do not seek the truth at all and only express untested beliefs. (The image of the cave will take up as its topic such persons.) Rather, he is distinguishing between the ideal condition of complete knowledge and the more realistic condition of the philosopher who seeks knowledge but so far has not completely achieved it, that is, a person like Socrates himself. Socrates knows far more about justice than his interlocutors do. To this extent, his view of the forms is better and more illuminated by the good. But we could still fairly assert that he does not know everything about them. For example, Socrates sets aside the question of what justice is like between Greeks and non-Greeks and questions such as under what conditions, if any, war would be just. Their model so far does not give a clear way in which to address this particular question. Further exploration of these kinds of questions about justice would, indeed, help us to better understand the form of justice, which so far has only been explored in terms of the internal relations between parts of a soul or parts of a unified city. Even in Book One, Socrates's interlocutors do see *some* aspects of justice, but inadequately. Their views are better characterized as opinion rather than knowledge, because of the partial nature of their visions and the consequent ways in which questioning leads to the shifting and movement of their views.

At the same time, Socrates clearly wishes to distinguish himself from relativists such as Protagoras who refuse to separate knowledge and opinion at all, such that knowledge is merely perception.[69] The image of the sun suggests that the good's illumination of the form that the intellect is attempting to grasp is present *both* when knowledge is present and when the person only reaches a state of partially correct opinion. In offering this interpretation, it is essential to note that Socrates's model of knowledge here is not centered on propositions. That is, he does not consider knowledge to be a case of having the correct propositional claims about a state of affairs. Rather, knowledge is compared to clarity of vision and a kind of wholeness of vision rather than partiality. (The image of larger and smaller letters also follows this metaphor.) According to this analogy, knowledge is both gradable and perspectival: gradable, because one can see more or less of the object in question, and perspectival because depending on what one's angle is at looking at the nature of justice, different aspects of the nature of justice may be understood.

On this reading, the process of coming to know is one of seeing relatively more or less of the forms, rather than as a single epistemic act in which one either grasps a form in its totality or does not, or as giving a single verbal definition that adequately describes a state of affairs. One eventually does need to give a verbal account of what one sees, but saying that one must give verbal expression to an insight in order for it to be tested is different than saying that the forms are themselves verbal descriptions or properties. The forms are not identical to our language about justice, beauty, courage, and so on. Yet it is through speech that not only others but we ourselves come to be able to make sense of what we have seen.[70] Only in *naming* what is seen, where something is named as *x* in distinction from something else that is named as *y*, are we able to move from how something "looks" to speech, which tells us what it is.[71] Moreover, only when we have named the forms can the structure of the ordinary world, which participates in the forms, become intelligible. After all, Socrates's goal in all of this is not simply for us to know a form, but to make the world intelligible as a result of knowing the forms.[72] Thus, there is a movement between thought, which is not merely verbal, to the articulation of what is thought about in verbal form, since such verbal expression allows such experience to be shared and examined.

Of course, as human beings we can also share in experiences of many sorts that are not verbally expressed and yet are still experienced in common: for example, looking at a sunset with another person, or listening to an orchestra together. To the extent that the contemplation of art or music is not reducible to the verbal account given of it, but can still be called a form of thought, it is clear that not all thinking is verbal. But to the extent that we desire to make political decisions about how to live together, as when we desire to live in a more just city, then our thinking must be verbally articulated, shared, discussed, and tested. It is precisely in this verbal discussion that one can come to know that one's perceptions are limited and not the whole of what can be known about the reality of the object of discussion. Indeed, over time, the person who frequently undertakes philosophical discussion will learn that his own perceptions of matters such as justice are not already knowledge and thus have a different view of his own epistemic state than those who fail to distinguish even in principle between their own perceptions and the nature of being.

This reading is consistent with my earlier chapters' readings of Book One, in which Cephalus, Polemarchus, and even Thrasymachus have some insight into the nature of justice, but their ideas are incomplete.[73] Cephalus is right to think that justice includes fairness, but there is *more* to justice than fair trade. Polemarchus's picture of justice is found in new form in Socrates's claim that the good auxiliary is friendly to his own in the city, but aggressive with the enemy. Thrasymachus mistakes justice as the advantage of the stronger, and mistakes what it means to be "strong," but Socrates also says that what is truly strongest in our humanity (the rational faculty of the soul) should rule over what is weaker (spirit and the appetites). Each of these opinions about justice arises from a partial insight but one that is incomplete. We need not treat knowledge as binary, that is, as either present or absent, on the visual model that Socrates offers. Moreover, a large variety of ways of speaking might be helpful to describe one's insight: for example, the longer images and myths that Socrates uses to describe justice are as significant as the brief definition of "doing one's own work." Plato himself gives us different models of the soul across the dialogues, as in the variety of imagery used in the *Phaedrus*, *Phaedo*, and *Republic* to describe the soul's nature and activity. The adequacy of vision, rather than the correctness or incorrectness of propositions, is central to Socrates's epistemology here, and different images can enhance our vision as we move from greater obscurity to greater clarity.[74] Poetic images as such are not the problem. The difficulty is that most of the time, poets do not acknowledge that their images are only images, or test their supposed insights to see whether they are really instances of knowledge or not.

The analogy also tells us something significant about ourselves as inquirers: we are erotic creatures with respect to knowledge.[75] This approach would be consistent with Socrates's description of the philosophical souls who follow the circuit of Zeus to get only a "glimpse" of the forms in the *Phaedrus*, but who continue to seek and to grow in knowledge as erotic beings. Similarly, the *Meno* presents the theory of recollection as an example of moving from opinion to knowledge. As the slave looks at Socrates's geometric drawings and listens to his questions, he does not move from sensible things to nonsensible things but rather is always discussing intelligible matters (through the facilitation of drawings), both when his opinions are incorrect and when he understands the correct solution to the problem. Moreover, Socrates's procedure with his interlocutors throughout the *Republic* has been to use images of sensible objects in order to try to get closer to the form of justice, but these inquiries have resulted in differing degrees of success. Their inquiry is marked both by instances of relative obscurity, for example, Cephalus's vision of justice, and of relative clarity, for example, Socrates's portrayal of justice as giving each part of a multipart soul or city its due in Book Four. But the shift from Cephalus to Socrates is not effected by leaving behind models and images from the sensible world altogether. Rather, the nature of justice seems to be better known by choosing the right kinds of paradigms and images.

If vision is the primary metaphor for knowledge, then images can be useful in the pursuit of knowledge. This may seem to be a surprising thing to say, given Socrates's clear rejection of art as inadequate in Book Nine and the criticisms of poetry in Books Two and Three. But the grasp of intellectual objects can take place through images, if Socrates does not mean sensible images, but intelligible images. Jacob Klein helpfully uses the term "intelligible image," drawing upon Plato's use of the term *eikasia* to describe not mere fantasy (which would better be represented by the term *phantasia*) but images that do help us to have access to the forms so long as these images are understood *as images* and not mistaken for originals.[76] Insofar as the forms are patterns for all of the rest of reality, then to this extent, anything that is patterned after the forms bears some of the image of the original. Ordinary things can reveal to us something about the fundamental reality of the forms, and even "mere" images of those ordinary objects, shadows and the like, however imperfectly, do still point back to the forms *if properly used*. This does not mean that the form itself is an image,[77] but rather that the form is accessible to us *by way of* images, because of who we, as human beings are: that is, the sorts of creatures who "see" reality intelligibly in a manner that is analogous to vision or sight in the everyday word. Intelligible images, such as the analogy to the sun or the divided line image, can offer us real insight into the forms precisely because the forms are paradigms, that is, they are models after which all of the rest of reality is patterned, and to the extent that our intelligible images imitate these patterns, then the philosophical imagination grasps something of their being through these images.[78] Intelligible images can lead us toward the higher forms of thinking; as Smith says of the divided line, such philosophical images can draw us "up" the line.[79] The difficulty, of course, is that the average person does not look at the ordinary world in order to better "see" the forms and their more fundamental reality; instead, she takes everyday objects to be what is most real and does not see an image *as an image*. This is precisely the problem with the lovers of sight and sound, who take beautiful works of art to be beauty itself. On this reading, they fail to distinguish between the image of beauty as a way in which to better see beauty itself, limiting themselves to the pleasure of beauty in a particular beautiful work of art.

In describing intelligible images, it is important to note that such acts of the imagination for Socrates need not simply be understood in terms of the repetition or re-presentation of sensible experiences to the mind. When an image such as the form of the good is compared to the sun, of course, our minds do re-present prior sensory experiences that we have had of the physical sun, in the course of considering this analogy. But our minds are also engaged in many nonsensory matters as well. For example, the act of drawing a comparison between the triadic relations of the form of the good, the intellect, and another form, and the sun, the eye, and a physical object, is not a sensory act but rather an intellectual act. Grasping the relationship between two triadic relations (form, *nous*, form of the good and sensible object, eye, sun) is not itself a sensible experience or the re-presentation of a sensible experience. In this way also, Socrates's image of the form of the good is an intelligible image.

It is perhaps especially helpful to keep in mind that for the Greeks, mathematics itself was not propositional but essentially based on geometry, a visual way of doing mathematics. Doing a geometrical proof by drawing it, as Socrates does in the *Meno*, gives us another instance of image-making that allows our intellects to grasp something intelligible. In both the cases of a drawn line and the spoken image of the sun, the imagery exists in order to draw the intellect toward an understanding of nonvisible reality. This does not mean that the image is left behind; quite to the contrary, the image is the means by which the nonvisible becomes visible to us. At the same time, as Miller has argued, some of the mathematics in which the guardians are to be educated purify the guardians of their dependency on spatial and visual imagery; thus, Socrates points to a further education beyond images as part of the "longer way" of dialectic.[80]

In this image and its exposition, Socrates is not offering any *criteria* for knowledge along the lines of Descartes's call for an idea that is clear and distinct in which ideas that are clear and distinct are cases of knowledge and others are not. He is not giving a criterion for *how to evaluate* any particular idea to find out whether it is or is not an instance of knowledge. Nowhere in the image does Socrates give us a principle or rule of thumb by which to evaluate our ideas. Instead, Socrates offers a picture of ourselves as knowers, one that helps us to understand how it is possible to assert that we are *both* the kinds of beings that can know, that is, beings for whom there is a kind of a "fit" between our intellects and the forms, *and* beings who in practice often fail to fully understand the truth. He claims the intelligible world is accessible to our intellects, instead of asserting skepticism or a complete gap between our cognition and being. At the same time, he acknowledges a partial divide between being and knowing by using the familiar model of sight, in which the experience of partial sight or unclear vision can be understood as both a seeing and a not seeing at the same time.

For Plato, images are an especially appropriate way to speak about fundamental realities to which we do not have complete or direct access. Some matters can be grasped through intellectual inquiry; for example, the solution to the geometrical problem of how to double the size of the square that Socrates presents to Meno's slave in the *Meno* has a correct answer. However, we do not have any similar access to the higher, meta-level that would allow us to precisely describe the meeting of the human person and the world from an outside perspective. The *Republic* uses an image of knowledge and of the intellect's relation to the forms because there is no superhuman point of view that sees the form of the good, the other forms, and the intellect whole. However, we know what it means to seek knowledge of the good only from a perspective that begins with human experience: that is, Socrates posits a form of the good because we human beings seek it in all that we do, and it seems to be the end of every action. The forms seem to be necessary to account for the distinction between claims like "these two sticks are equal" and understanding "equality" itself: they are not the same kinds of claims. Yet when Socrates and his friends seek to understand justice, they also do so from the inside out: they begin with ordinary claims from lived experiences and seek to clarify, refine, and enlarge these visions of justice in the hope that the ideas at which they arrive grasp more, rather than less, of justice itself.

Philosophical language, then, must be appropriate to the sort of reality that we aim to explain and to the nature of the human being who is engaged in trying to understand that reality. Often, for Socrates, it is a question of finding the right kind of image. In undertaking a mathematical problem, for Socrates the geometrical image is most fitting. In seeking to understand justice, images of cities, soul, or particular just actions—such as the return of what is owed to another—help his interlocutors to see the form of justice better. In attempting to describe our very process of coming to know, it is to images from sensory experience that Socrates turns. However, lest we forget that an image is only an image, Socrates also offers the images of the divided line and of the cave, which also remind us of our limits as image-makers. At least in the *Republic*, there is no completely image-free language that one can use to describe justice, but we can see something about justice and also see *that* the very way in which we see is a mix of seeing and not seeing well. Socrates uses images, but unlike the poets who lack sophistication about their own enterprise, Socrates also makes images that remind us what it means to make an image, and the limits of such practices and of ourselves.

Chapter 8

The Divided Line and the Cave

Socrates next offers a more comprehensive view of our process of experiencing the world in the images of the divided line and cave. These images are complementary. The divided line articulates a reconciliation of the one and the many at both the epistemological and ontological levels. The divided line is both a singular whole and divided.[1] As such, the unity of the line models the unity of different modalities of the real and how we can know or opine the real. At the same time, the line is divided, emphasizing discontinuity and hierarchy in reality. Knowledge and opinion are distinguished, and the objects of each mode of experience are likewise divided. In this chapter, I argue that the imagery of the line is crucial to its proper interpretation.[2] The divided line is no less an image than the images of the sun and cave. Perhaps because of our own cultural tendency to "read" mathematical images as instances of knowledge and to separate mathematics and poetry, the imagery of the divided line may seem to disappear for the contemporary commentator. Nonetheless, it is an analogical image that describes not only different parts of reality, but also the relationships between those aspects. While there is some similarity between an analogy and what it describes, every analogy is disanalogous insofar as there is not a relationship of exact identity between the image and the reality described by the image.[3] When one examines the divided line's particular elements, this makes sense: after all, mathematical objects are not the highest entities on the divided line but are rather secondary to the forms themselves. To this extent, as will be further explained in this chapter, the image of the divided line exemplifies what it intends to explain: that is, it itself exhibits both the continuities between different parts of the divided line and its discontinuities.[4]

The image of the cave functions quite differently, in part because its intention is to reveal the effect of proper education on the *theōria*, or way of envisioning reality, of the person who is undergoing education.[5] In order to emphasize the transformative nature of education, and the illusoriness of an existence that lacks such an education, the image of the cave emphasizes discontinuity at the expense of continuity. While images in the divided line are the "lowest" aspect of reality, they are also related to, and caused by, realities higher on the line. To this extent, even images at the lowest section remain in a kind of ontological contact with the forms and with ordinary things, which image the forms. While images are at some remove from the forms, they nevertheless do contain traces of that which they image and so even images can be quite useful for understanding higher realities. In the image of the cave, however, the cave dwellers are presented as enslaved, and listening to mere echoes while gazing at shifting shadows. They do not recognize their own condition and must be freed from it. Whereas it is in principle possible for Socrates's observer of the divided line to see an image *as an image* from the point of view of the whole of the divided line, the enslaved person of the cave does not possess an omniscient vantage point. Thus, it is clear that the function of the cave image is not to present a detached vision of being. Rather, its imagery takes on a vision of the whole, but also various perspectives that different kinds of persons may have within this whole, where persons are positioned differently, both epistemically and politically. The cave image emphasizes the lack of freedom of the person within the cave and his need to become free. Later, the cave image also presents the "compulsion" of the freed person who must return again to the world of the cave, offering another opportunity for reflection on the nature of philosophical knowledge and its relation to political action. Even the perspective of the freed prisoner is not from a standpoint of absolute omniscience. His point of view changes depending on whether he is enslaved, outside the cave, immediately reentering the ordinary world and allowing his sight to readjust, or fully adjusted to life within the cave. At the same time, the person who listens to the Socratic myth does get a view of the whole journey of ascent and descent, a sense of how each part of education fits into a larger narrative of growth. The cave image displays a kind of heroic journey, one that shifts our perspective as we accompany the freed prisoner.

These two viewpoints—that of the divided line's relatively omniscient, detached supra-ontological standpoint, and that of the changing perspective of the heroic journey—complement one another. On the one hand, being itself is presented as a total unity. Every aspect of being has the potential, when rightly understood, to be of philosophical value. Even images have a place in the process of coming to know. On the other hand, our point of view within that cosmic whole is a specifically human one. We are not, in fact, gods with omniscient views of the whole, but rather human persons who learn and develop our understanding of our relation to the world over time. While the image of the divided line is static, the poetic imagery of the cave is temporal and includes overtly social and political dimensions. Political relationships can distort as well as free, and so Socrates shows that education is crucial if we are to live out the full potential for human growth and experience. Moreover, the descent back into the cave by the freed prisoner also suggests a sense of care for the polis that is entirely missing from the image of the divided line. As such, the image of the cave does not only describe epistemology but also embodies a politics of care.

Thus the two images function together to assert a philosophical-poetic vision of the world that attempts to offer the perspective of the human person, and of a cosmic whole that transcends the partial insights of any singular perspective. The divided line places images at the lowest part of reality, but because images also have a relation to the highest parts of reality, they can be useful for talking about the forms and hypotheticals. What is important is that an image be recognized *as an image* and as a way to see the forms. The cave image describes the education of the person enslaved to images *without* recognizing such a distinction. Because it is an image that relies on familiar objects, it can describe what it is like to make the ascent to someone who has not yet made this ascent. To this extent, the cave image functions to allow us to imagine a way of existing beyond the current state of our own knowledge. One may not yet know the forms after listening to the cave image but can understand the concept of a world that exceeds what one takes to be fundamental to one's own reality. This itself is preparatory for the pursuit of philosophy even if it is not yet an image by which philosophical truths can be known about specific forms.

Socrates's account of the divided line divides up reality into four unequal parts, in which the two middle sections are equal in length. While Socrates does not state whether the divided line is horizontal or vertical, one wonders whether the question was insignificant in an age before books, chalkboards, and most permanent media, in which student and teacher might sit in a circle to look at a geometry problem, or sit facing different directions. One person's vertical is another's horizontal in such cases. (For purposes of clarity in this chapter, I will use the terms "higher" and "lower" to refer to the different sections of the divided line, with the highest being the realms of greater clarity and the lowest being the least clear.) More important for Socrates are the different sizes of the divisions in the line. Socrates notes that the visible and intelligible dimensions of reality are represented by different lengths. Likewise, within each of the visible and intelligible dimensions, a cut of the same proportions is to be made within in each part. The intelligible realm is composed of forms and hypotheses, known by way of *noēsis* and *dianoia*, respectively, while the visible realm is composed of things and images, accessed by trust (*pistis*) and imagination (*eikasia*). Even from antiquity commentators have disagreed as to which segments are shorter and which longer.[6] Plutarch argues that the objects that are more obscure ought to be given the greater length of line, in order to represent the great obscurity and multitudinous nature of these objects. This idea seems right, but perhaps even more important is the point that we as readers of the dialogues ourselves must reconstruct the line and move from word to image. Thus, the very task as readers of moving from verbal *logos* into visual image itself serves as a reminder of a potential gap between the world of words and visual models. Words can describe images, and images can be ways of representing verbal ideas, but they are not identical and may not perfectly map onto one another.[7]

At the "bottom" of the divided line we find the visible world. While the visible world is not the ultimate intelligible reality, the divided line image makes it more intelligible even just by situating ordinary things within an organized hierarchy. Visible reality has a place in the larger order to which it belongs. Moreover, the kinds of being that exist on the lowest half of the line—things and images—exhibit a rational set of relations to one another. Socrates does not simply present ordinary reality as chaotic. Rather, images bear resemblance to the ordinary things that cast these shadows, reflections, and so on. Shadows and reflections, if taken as all of reality, would remain confusing and unintelligible. However, once a shadow is related back to the object that casts it, the shadow becomes something that can be better understood. For example, if as I walk in the woods, I mistake the movement of a shadow by way of my peripheral vision and take it to be an animal, once I realize that it is in fact the shadow of my companion who has fallen behind and I can relate it back to its true cause, the shadow is more properly understood than before. Its greater intelligibility rests precisely in my grasping my friend's shape as the cause and the true reality of the shadow's existence. Likewise, visible things have an analogous relation to the forms: the forms serve as patterns for the things that participate in them. Socrates's examples of things that belong at the second lowest portion of the line are animals, plant life, and artifacts.

The images on the lowest portion of the divided line correspond to originals, in that shadows are images of the things that cast the shadows, and reflections in lakes and streams have a corresponding thing whose likeness is reflected in the water. But, of course, both are part of our physical reality and both are experienced in the same sensory acts of vision, hearing, taste, and our other senses. A shadow or reflection is no less part of the material world than is the original that made it. Moreover, although such reflections can be deceptive, they also *do* reflect aspects of the original. For example, a reflection of waterside trees at the peak of autumn foliage reflects some of the visual appearance of the trees themselves. It may even *enhance* our experience of the oranges, reds, and yellows of the trees, at the same time as distorting the shapes of the individual leaves or the height of the trees. However, the image may fail to capture some element that is essential to the tree, such as having a trunk, if the image only reflects a wash of color but not much in the way of a distinctive shape. Similarly, insofar as ordinary objects in this world reflect the forms, they give us partial access to the forms that they reflect, if they are understood in terms of their causal origin. A horse, if understood as an instance of the form of a horse, is not merely a brute thing. Its essential being is found in its horse-ness, but not in contingent factors such as whether it is gray or brown, fast or slow, young or old. In this way, the divided line image emphasizes equally both a need for seeing continuity and difference between the forms and ordinary things, and between things and images. Again, the divided line works particularly well for emphasizing this feature of being, for it is both a single continuous whole and one that is separated by distinctive demarcations.[8] It is both discrete and continuous, holding together in itself what verbally sounds like a paradox, but one that *as an image* can contain opposites together into a single visible and intelligible reality.

While Socrates compares the division between the visible and intelligible world to the distinction between opinion and knowledge, he never says that there is no possible knowledge of sensibles or that all encounters with the intelligible world are instances of knowledge. Instead, Socrates only asks Glaucon whether he agrees "that with respect to truth or its lack, just as the opinable (*doxaston*) is distinguishable from the knowable (*gnōston*), so the likeness is distinguished from that of which it is the likeness" (510a–b). In other words, Socrates says only that if one is willing to say that opinion is not at the same level as knowledge, and merely imitates it, so too, a likeness is distinguished from that which it imitates. Socrates does not claim that everything in the sensible world can only be opined about, while every encounter with the intelligible world is an instance of knowledge.[9] If the earlier interpretation of the image of the sun is correct, then understanding the intelligible world can take place in ways in which knowledge is gradable and perspectival. Moreover, Socrates himself says that he has only opinion of the good, and in the cave analogy, says that the philosophers' knowledge of the outside world will help them to be better rulers within the cave. There can be degrees of knowledge, opinions about forms, and knowledge useful for living in the sensible world.

It seems that sensible things can become intelligible if the person who looks at them understands the form, or something about the form, of which the sensible thing is a likeness. Given that the forms serve as patterns for these ordinary sensible things, items such as couches, flowers, and horses become intelligible when the form of the same is understood. Indeed, Socrates and his friends have discussed justice beginning with the world of sensible reality and working their way through that reality into a model of justice that represents the nature of the form of justice. Socrates and Cephalus began the conversation by discussing the trade of goods and weapons, while the dramatic events that take place in Athens, such as allusions to the civil war, are all elements of the visible world. Socrates has an interest in the ordinary experience of old age. Insofar as these kinds of everyday concerns first motivate the discussion of justice, it is helpful also to notice that according to the divided line, events such as the handing over of weapons, or the bodily process of aging remain unintelligible without an interpretation. While the divided line can be used to explain simple objects, such as tables or horses, as an image it becomes even more powerful when describing the "messier" affairs of the moral and political world than when we restrict it only to artifacts or natural objects, precisely because moral and political realities require a movement between the sensible and intelligible reality. Taken apart from any claims about justice, the events within a city are hard to make sense of with respect to the multitudinous nature of all of its social and political events. Much happens as a series of bare events, and without a framework for organizing these events into meaningful categories, the concrete and ordinary city as such would not even be intelligible. We would simply see a dying body here, a ship sailing there, exchange of goods there, and so on. However, when the city is related to a model of justice or injustice, or other conceptual categories, these same events can now be grasped philosophically: we see the same event in terms of an unjust death in a civil war, a just sailing for battle, or a fair exchange of goods. Even a terribly unjust city becomes more intelligible, insofar as it is compared with the form of justice, and the degree to which its structures and events are at variance from the pattern of justice. Thus, the visible, sensible world is *not* completely unintelligible according to Socrates's way of treating such realities either in the image of the divided line, or in course of the dialogue as a whole.

What makes sensible reality more intelligible is when it is understood in relation to the categories on the upper part of the line (forms and hypotheses). Such an understanding of ordinary things in terms of their forms is possible because of proportionality between the two line segments. The proportional relation between intelligible reality and the everyday objects of experience reflects the notion that the world of the senses can be philosophically meaningful. In an everyday experience of objects, we merely trust in what we see and take them for granted as they are presented to us—thus, the faculty that describes the ordinary world is *pistis*, translated as belief or trust. In evaluating these same realities against a model of the form of justice, we understand them by way of our intellects and not only through a trusting acceptance. This is not to say that the ordinary world is unintelligible, but rather the opposite—if approached in terms of its relation to the forms. Indeed, Book Eight will take up a whole series of degenerate souls and cities in precisely this way, comparing them to the ideal models of just city and just soul. This combination of continuity and discontinuity in the divided line image nicely expresses the sameness/difference of the world of ordinary objects from the world of the forms. It ought to emphasize for us that even if the forms are in a different "world" than what we know through sensibility, the philosopher is not "other worldly" but rather also interested in understanding *this* world—as well as the world of the forms— through models of justice.

The upper half of the divided line is difficult to interpret, especially in light of the identity of proportions between the second and third highest portions of the line (i.e., that which is known through *dianoia* and through *pistis*). While the forms are the objects of *noēsis*, *dianoia* interprets hypotheses. Socrates says that, in one section, "by using as images the things that were imitated before, the soul is compelled to search from hypotheses, not making its way to a beginning (*archēn*) but to an end (*teleutēn*); while in the other part it makes its way to an unconditioned beginning (*archēn anupotheton*); starting from hypotheses and without the images from the other part, by forms themselves it makes its pursuit (*methodos*) through them" (510b). In response to Glaucon's subsequent confusion, Socrates illustrates what he has in mind with an example from mathematics: mathematicians do not explore the nature of odd and even, kinds of angles, or natures of particular shapes. They work with them as starting points and proceed from these notions that are taken for granted in order to make other claims. Socrates asserts that they use "visible forms" (*horōmenois eidesi*) (510d) in order to make their arguments. They also make models or draw physically what they are talking about but for the sake of thinking through (*dianoia*) the matters about which they are speaking. As Klein and Howland have argued, "intelligible images" are part of the practice of these mathematicians.[10] Socrates is clear that mathematicians make physical drawings, but these drawings do not "exist" only in the world of the senses, insofar as the mathematician uses an image of a triangle or square to talk about an ideal triangle or square. The physical triangle is, in a sense, looked "through" in order to see the ideal one, through a process of abstracting from, say, the wax tablet or the imperfection in the straightness of a line. Klein names this seeing through an image to the intelligible reality a "double seeing."[11] As Smith has argued, the same sorts of objects exist in the second and third highest portions of the divided line, for example, a line drawn for a geometry problem. What is different is *how these objects are viewed*: as only a visual line or as an image that represents an ideal mathematical line. In the second highest portion of the divided line, what is visible is still present, but it is taken or interpreted as an image.[12]

Here we find an act of the imagination in the work of the mathematician: she does not look at the visible line merely as a physical object, but rather as an image of a further reality. The mathematician uses an image of a rectangle in order to get to an ideal rectangle. She creates an image in order to better understand the nature of an ideal object. Yet objects at this level need not be literally visibly present, for example, if a teacher describes an image of an isosceles triangle and hopes that her student can imagine it. An image may be visible or it may be mental, but what matters for our purposes is that the image is understood to be an image, rather than only be taken at face value. A good mathematician knows that the real object of thought is not either on the paper or blackboard, or even in his imagination: the triangle is beyond it. Yet this image is needed to do the work of geometry in developing a proof. Thus while *eikasia* is located at the bottom of the line, in making sense of shadows and reflections, and relating these reflections back to the original trees, animals, or other figures that cast the reflections, in the divided line, we have more than one kind of eikastics. In order for the mathematician's visual aids to be about ideal objects at all, when she draws them she must already have in mind the ideal object. Thus the ideal object or formal object serves as a basis for the image, which the image will always imitate imperfectly. However, a student looking at the same object, and learning about the relation of two angles for the first time, begins with the image but does not take it for mere image, as she proceeds to understand something ideal *through* the image. So even though the movement from a hypothetical starting point to the conclusion of a mathematical argument is "downward," the individual's relation to the image moves both ways: in looking at a visible image of a mathematical shape, we move "up" to the intelligible image, and in drawing an image of an abstract mathematical object, we move "down" to the concrete and particular image. Thus a person ordinarily moves between the sensible and the intelligible world in doing mathematics, though the sensible world is used for seeing and discussing the intelligible one. The imagination here has an *integrative* function, a faculty that brings together intelligible object and visual object. It is precisely the imagination that allows us to move between the sensible and intelligible aspects of the world.

Although Socrates restricts himself to a discussion of mathematics, the term "hypothetical" is far more wide-ranging than math. The root of the Greek term *hupotithēmi* lies in the Greek verb *tithēmi*, which just means to lay down, or to set forth something. The term *tithēmi* is often used in the *Republic* to talk about setting forth an idea as part of an argument: for example, when Socrates asks whether we should set down (*tithēmi*) the claim that the possession of money is useful (331a). As Robinson has argued, the word *tithēmi* is used primarily in the *Republic* to describe a person who posits an idea; when we put forth an idea, we say for the moment that it "stands," that it is part of the argument that one is going to pursue.[13] In the future it may or may not be refuted, but at the moment that we set it forth, it is the starting point of the argument. What is set forth is done provisionally, and not because it has been proven to be true. The term *hupotithēmi* or to hypothesize, seems to mean to posit something as a preliminary to something else. In ordinary Greek, *hupotithēmi* simply means to place under and can be even used to describe physical objects. As an instance, one can place kindling at the bottom of a fire. In the context of the divided line, the meaning seems to be more specific. When one hypothesizes, one is not just setting forth a thesis, but a thesis for the sake of figuring out *something else*. A hypothesis is not the matter under direct investigation, but rather something that one needs in order to investigate something else. So, for example, in a geometric theorem, one might have to hypothesize that a line is the shortest distance between two points, but one need not prove it, if the real question concerns the relation of angles where lines intersect. At times, Aristotle treats hypothesis in this way, in terms of what a teacher offers but does not prove to a student, who assumes the hypothesis and accepts it (*An. Post.* I.10). At other times, Aristotle treats it as a basic *archē* of a particular science; but in either case, the hypothesis is not under investigation.[14]

The term *tithēmi* and its cognates can also be used to talk about moves made in a game of draughts.[15] *Tithēmi* can mean to make a move, while *anatithēmi* is to take back a move in a game of draughts. *Metatithēmi* means to change one's position, for example, on a game board. Indeed, this image of a game of checkers is used directly in the *Republic* in order to describe the "moves" that Socrates and his interlocutors make. Adeimantus likens Socrates's arguments as akin to a game of checkers (draughts): "And just as those who are not clever at playing checkers are finally shut in by those who are and don't know where to move, so they too are finally checked and have their mouths stopped by this other game of checkers, played not with counters but words" (487b–c). While Adeimantus is challenging the content of Socrates's speeches, he identifies that the course of the argument is one in which the next step is not necessarily predetermined by the previous steps, but rather, choices are made at various junctures to pursue one line of reasoning rather than another one that is potentially open to them.

Indeed, the flow of the argument in the *Republic* as a whole is somewhat like a game of chess, in that it relies upon particular starting points set out by Glaucon and Adeimantus. The future of each part of a chess game is determined by the past moves of the game; there is, however, no single correct game of chess, even though there are good and bad moves, and wise and unwise claims to make in any given circumstance—in this case, directions that might lead them closer to understanding the nature of justice, or decisions that might lead them astray. Indeed, we see in other dialogues that Socrates and his companions try out different approaches to similar problems: for example, while the *Republic* focuses on the nature of justice in the ideal city, the *Euthyphro* examines whether a decision to take one's own father to court—a particular matter of justice—is right from the point of view of piety. To this extent, we might see Socrates's reasoning about justice through the course of the dialogue as a form of hypothetical argument, one that uses images and models of justice in order to get closer to understanding intelligible realities. While Socrates takes mathematical objects to be the primary instances of hypotheticals, it is possible to include other sorts of arguments in the realm of the hypothetical—for example, Socrates's own arguments about the nature of justice in the city as they proceed from certain assumptions about what cities need and why they are formed.

Robinson notes five major characteristics of Platonic hypothetical method.[16] First, a hypothesis is deliberately and clearly set forth. That is, Plato helps his own audience to see the ways in which he is being explicit about as many of the argument's assumptions as possible, rather than bringing in his ideas in a hidden way. This way the audience can make a clearer determination as to whether the hypothesis is warranted or not; we are always free to assent or to dissent with the arguments offered to us. Second, the method of hypothesis is deductive. Socrates often explores the implications of an idea set forth, but these implications may be practical and not only logical implications, as we see from how Socrates actually argues. For example, if a city is going to have luxuries, then it must have guardians to protect it against war, which will practically follow from the possession of such luxuries, even though it is not logically contained within the idea of luxury per se. Third, in using the hypothetical method, one tries to avoid contradiction. The ideas set forth after have to be consistent with one another. Fourth, hypothesized opinions are held provisionally, rather than dogmatically. We have to be willing to reconsider, in the light of future argument, our hypotheses as well as conclusions that come from them, if we find new reasons to do so. Last, Robinson explains that the method of hypothesis is what he calls a "method of approximation," by which he means that since our ideas here are always hypothetical, they might be further revised.[17] The result that we have is never final; it can be closer to or farther from the truth, compared to other approximations, but because it never proves its fundamental ideas beyond a doubt, it is never a perfect vision of the truth, but only an approximate one. Again, we see this revision of the model of the ideal city in the continual revision of the city from a simple city with no luxuries, to the feverish city, to the purified city, to the ideal one in Book Four and its three classes. The model of the soul is revised for even longer, insofar as the nature of the rational part of the soul is further developed in images such as these central images of divided line, cave, and sun/eye, and the later image of the tripartite soul in the discussion of tyranny in Book Nine.

The practice of mathematics is more rigorous than hypothetical reasoning about politics, and the ideal nature of its ideal objects is more readily seen than in the case of Socrates's arguments about the nature of justice itself. All the conclusions of a geometrical proof logically follow from the starting points. Socrates's arguments in the dialogue begin with far less certain premises, and many of these arise from intuitions gained from practical life: for example, that a city is based on the need that its members have of one another, or that the specialization of crafts is better for the city than a city in which each person is a generalist. Moreover, Socrates often faced particular decisions that needed to be made that did not necessarily stem from the original premises about the requirements of a city at all—as when Glaucon's erotic desires informed the shaping of the luxurious city. Thus, the fit between Socrates's arguments and the way that Socrates describes hypotheticals in the divided line is not completely clear. But if we allow for a less rigorous form of reasoning than mathematics to belong to the second highest section of the divided line, then Socrates's way of proceeding in the dialogue also shows how visible images can be made use of and become intelligible ones. After all, the arguments about justice in the *Republic* cannot be said to belong to the visible world alone. In discussing the ideal city or state, one does not simply trust in ordinary objects of sense experience or look at shadows. Neither, though, are the arguments perfect descriptions of the form of justice itself, and so part of the highest section of the divided line, for these models continue to develop over the course of the dialogue and to be revised. Socrates's description of hypothetical reasoning as "downward" movement from hypotheses best characterizes the practice that Socrates undertakes with his interlocutors in the dialogue. Thus, Socrates's own interest is perhaps not to distinguish mathematics from other enterprises, but rather to show that there are types of reasoning that exist, to use Glaucon's words, "between opinion and intelligence" (511d). Not all are deductive in the sense that geometrical proofs are. The arguments that give us models of justice in soul and in city within the *Republic* seem to be examples of discursive reasoning, or *dianoia*.[18]

What, then, lies at the top of the divided line? The top segment of the divided line concerns the intelligible part, "which *logos* itself grasps with the power of dialectic (*dialegesthai*), making the hypotheses not beginnings but really hypotheses—that is, stepping-stones and springboards—in order to reach the unhypothesized at the beginning (*archē*) of the whole. Having grasped this, following back what follows from it, it descends (*katabainē*) again to an end, making no such use of anything of sense, but using forms themselves, going through forms to forms, it ends in forms" (511b–c).

Socrates's description is notoriously less detailed an explanation of dialectic than one would like, especially insofar as it describes its action and objects primarily through negative language, that is, through what it is not.[19] Dialectical thought does not use the senses. Dialectic does not use hypotheses as beginnings to move "downward." It does not remain in the realm of "if-then" argumentation. Somehow, dialectic grasps an unhypothesized beginning, and then moves from one form to another. Unlike the image of the sun where the eye of the intellect simply sees the form in a single act, Socrates describes *movement* as part of noetic thought, but a movement in which hypotheses lead one "upward" to an *archē*, rather than "downward."

If we recall that the primary Greek meaning of *hupotithēmi* is to place something underneath something else, as support, Socrates's words are somewhat clearer, however. The hypotheses serve as support structures for moving upward to the forms, the way that a stepping-stone supports the body of a person who crosses a stream so that he does not fall down into the water, or the way a springboard allows an athlete to jump higher than he might rise on his own strength, to elaborate on Socrates's own images. The hypotheses themselves are not the forms, nor are ideas deduced from them in order to find the forms. They lie beneath the upward movement that is to take place. We can understand the models of the perfect city and perfect soul in this way, not *only* as images that are arrived at through the downward argumentation of hypothetical reasoning, but also as models that potentially allow the inquirer to come to have a better glimpse of the form of justice itself.

Socrates does not describe what the process of dialectic and upward movement might look like in detail. Instead, he points to a "longer way." While the dialogue may point to something that is preliminary to that longer path, it is clear that Socrates thinks they are taking the shorter way.[20] The nature of dialectic is not fully explicated within the *Republic*.[21] Nonetheless, as has been argued in previous chapters, Socrates has already described the process of coming to know at times in terms of moments of insight that can arise from looking at models or paradigms. *Noēsis*, the faculty that corresponds to forms on the highest part of the divided line, describes a synthetic rather than analytic approach, a way of knowing the forms through an intellectual act that Socrates describes primarily through analogies of seeing and grasping, rather than through analyzing or through the discursiveness of language.[22] Such a grasp should lead one to be able to say something about what one has seen, but the visual metaphor suggests a parallel to sense experience, in which one might see a sensible object and be capable of describing it as a result, but the sight of the object is not itself reducible to the verbal account given afterward. The image of form of the good as akin to the sun already provided an analogy to vision that suggested that while *noēsis* may be partial and perspectival, it is nonetheless a real insight into the being of any given form. Socrates also said of his own model of the perfectly just city that they might "catch sight" of the nature of justice (434e–35a). The image of the form of the sun as a causal good of all the forms, including justice, offers yet further information about the form of justice, namely, its transcendent nature and its being caused by the good (as opposed to, for example, being invented by human beings as a contingent outcome of their particular political arrangements). But these verbally articulated models are not yet themselves the forms. Rather, in the exercise of *noēsis*, one is no longer fundamentally oriented to particular just cities or souls, or their imperfect and unjust counterparts, nor even to the models themselves as developed through hypothetical reasoning. Instead, *noēsis* catches sight of the forms in a nondiscursive moment of insight and apprehension of the form in a form of intellectual seeing.[23] The Seventh Letter similarly describes the process of coming to know as akin to "like light that flashes forth in the kindling of a fire" (341c–d).[24] To many in contemporary philosophy, the notion that the highest kind of knowledge is nondiscursive may seem counterintuitive, when proofs made about propositions are central to knowledge. But Socrates does not speak of knowledge in terms of proofs, but rather in terms of sight.[25] What he seems to have in mind here is something like understanding what a form is, that is, being capable of speaking about its nature directly rather than only indirectly as a starting point for hypothetical reasoning.[26]

Thus, this intuitive grasp of the form does not mean that knowledge is ineffable, inexpressible, or private. Indeed, what the subject "sees" *can* be given shape or definition in a way that makes it describable and expressible in language, at times through models or paradigmatic images. But this is not the same as saying that the verbal expression itself is already knowledge.[27] The language of "sight" is itself a metaphor for talking about the experience of knowledge. Even when in ordinary sense experience, we see something—for example, a garden full of foliage and flowers—the experience is *not* reducible to the words that we can give about the garden. The qualitative experience always surpasses the words that we might use to describe it. Yet it is only in giving the experience words that the experience is given a shape: whether we try to label its items (fern, peony, green grass), name it qualitatively (as "beautiful" or "peaceful"), or give a narrative structure to the experience ("As I walked through the garden, I was overcome with a sense of beauty when the scent of the rose . . "). What is grasped in the experience of the garden is more primary than the words that can be offered about it. Socrates's movement between the language of sight and the language of models parallel this kind of an experience of sensible reality, but on the intellectual plane. Justice and beauty themselves may be encountered, and yet when we do encounter them, it is through verbal models and paradigms that their nature is given a shape. Again, Socrates's use of the term *eidos/idea* itself has this dual connotation of both something with a "form" or shape that can be seen, but also an "idea" that can be known.

Here, Socrates is not especially concerned to show that such knowledge is certain, or beyond doubt. It is possible to *think* that one has "seen" and yet not to possess knowledge in an infallible way. Yet greater understanding of a subject over time ought to be more comprehensive and less partial.[28] Therefore, this upward movement to the forms and insight is always brought back to verbal discussion of what one has seen, there is again a "downward" movement that Socrates describes to discussion with others and argument.[29] Indeed, we can even see some of the ordinary practices of discussion in the course of the *Republic* as reflecting this movement between insight and *logos*, even as early as Cephalus and Polemarchus's descriptions of how they see justice. Likewise, Socrates is able to say something about the forms, even if only by creating models of city and soul by which to know them. Thus, in looking at *dianoia* and *noēsis* together, we can say that verbal discussion and the development of models through conversation allow one not only to draw out the logical consequences of particular starting points about justice, but also to ascend and possibly to have insight into the nature of justice. But this seeing can then itself be brought back into discussion, indeed, ought to be brought back into discussion, since one may think that one has seen clearly but may have seen only partially or incompletely, as the image of the sun indicates is possible. In this sense, even if there is another kind of dialectic to which the *Republic* alludes, we have already within the *Republic* Socrates's practice of *dialegesthai* as a demonstration of another way of coming to know. But while this kind of dialectician can give a *logos* of that which he knows (534b), it does not mean that knowledge is reducible to that *logos* itself.[30] This line of interpretation makes sense of how Socrates's description of *noēsis* uses hypotheses as springboards: hypotheses are not left behind altogether but move one toward a different mode of seeing than discursive reasoning. After one has moved to the forms, however, the philosopher does not just rest forever in his own insight but rather discusses these insights with others, as Socrates himself seems to bring his own insights into the nature of justice and the virtues into the discussion with his friends.

Such insights need not be instances of godly omniscience of the whole: Socrates's caveat that he lacks secure knowledge of the good suggests that even the quintessentially devoted ideal philosopher does not cease to learn and to grow in what insights he gains.[31] As the image of the sun made clear, one can see the forms with greater or lesser clarity. Moreover, he says that even in the best-case scenario, one can only barely see the good (517c). But that Socrates can speak about the forms *at all* suggests that he has had *some* glimpse of them and uses imagery to convey an experience of the nature of their being—so far as he thinks he understands it—in a way that allows those who have not yet had such experiences to have an image that is comparable to, but not identical to, the noetic intuition of the forms that someone like Socrates has had.

One final note about the divided line: the image itself potentially spans all four sections of the divisions within it. If we imagine Socrates drawing a physical representation of the image of the divided line, then his drawing exists in the physical world as well as the intellectual world. As an image presented in a Platonic dialogue, we do not actually see any physical line, but only hear about an imitative image in the dialogue's drama: the reader is given an imitation of a physical line. The divided line is also a mathematical object that can be used as an assumed starting point for hypothetical reasoning: if knowable reality is modeled on a divided line with both its continuities and its discontinuities, then what else might be the case? The image also attempts to point toward the forms, without fully describing them, through its imagery: if reflections and shadows have a source in ordinary things that are their "real" origin, then things in this world might also have a source that is ontologically prior to them. One need not understand the forms fully in order to grasp the idea *that* a cause of this sort exists. Thus the image of the divided line is meant to lead us from a dramatically mediated image of a physical line, into hypothetical thinking about the relationship between intelligible reality and sensible reality, and upward toward forms. To this extent, the divided line is itself something that participates in all levels, from mere sensible object, to mathematical reality, to something that points toward the forms themselves.

In using the image of the cave, Socrates explores the question of how we as humans can come to know reality in its different aspects, this time by focusing on education. Socrates's fundamental claim is that educating

is not like putting sight into blind eyes (518b–c). Rather, the power to
know is within the soul, which "must be turned around from that which
is coming into being together with the whole soul until it is able to endure
looking at that which is and the brightest part of that which is [the good]"
(518c–d). Rather than understanding education in terms of content or
the gaining of a skill, Socrates treats education in terms of a fundamental
reorientation of sight, in which the soul turns toward different objects, and
then over time gains the capacity to see the good. Education is a kind of
conversion of the soul, not from one set of beliefs to another, but rather it
is a fundamental kind of turning around to care about one kind of thing
(the forms, especially the good) rather than another (the shadows and echoes
of conventional politics). Indeed, as I will argue, there is also a second kind
of conversion for the philosopher who has left the cave, or perhaps more
precisely a second movement in the progression of his conversion, which
is to return to the world of politics and to seek to integrate the encounter
with the forms into the everyday world and its concerns. The structure of
the cave image suggests that the philosopher who returns to the cave is
also the one who frees those who remain enslaved within it. Thus, Socrates
expands upon the earlier notion of a philosopher-king or queen to include
the philosopher as educator, but as a kind of educator who seeks to turn
around the souls of those whom she educates so that they may undertake
a similar philosophical journey.

    The cave image is peculiar in that it seems to be about the education
of the guardians to rule the ideal city, and yet does not fit very neatly into
the picture of the ideal city's education in its treatment of the world inside
the cave.[32] In the image of the cave, Socrates does not include any reference
to different natures who may be suited to be freed or to remain enslaved.
He includes nothing about alternative educations for craftsmen or soldiers.
To a surprising extent, the class divisions and notion of three natures that
exist in the model of the just city is completely abandoned in the image
of the cave. Instead, the cave image even seems to favor the view that it
is simply undesirable to remain enslaved, and desirable to be freed. There
is no indication that the person who is freed from among those who are
chained together looking at the cave wall is chosen because of his philosophical nature, and that others of a nonphilosophical nature deserve to stay in
chains, or are somehow better off that way. In the image of the cave, not
only distortions of the truth, shadows, and blindness but also manipulations
of those shadows are part of the citizens' political experience. There exists
a class of persons inside the cave that deliberately cast images on the walls

for the enslaved to see. This is not the activity of the philosophers who return, but of some other group of persons.

In this image, human beings are from childhood relegated to being chained in such a way that they can only see a wall straight in front of them and cannot turn their heads freely (514a–b). Behind them, a fire and human beings carrying various sorts of artifacts cast shadows on the wall, and some utter sounds that are echoed back for the prisoners to hear (514c–15a). Because of their position, these prisoners cannot see either themselves or others, not even the others who are on the bench next to them (515a). They take the shadows of artifacts to be ultimate reality (515c). The freedom of such a person from such a view to become a philosopher is not a very close match to the picture of education through play beginning even from childhood that Socrates set forth for philosophical natures in his ideal city. It describes much better what it is like to become philosophical after previously living an unphilosophical life.

Thus, I suggest that the cave image bridges the *Republic*'s movement from the discussion of the ideal city to its eventual treatment of degenerate regimes, unjust types of souls, and problems with images and image-making that end the dialogue. The cave image can speak to what it is like to be a philosopher-ruler who must return to rule the just city. But the image is even more useful for those who listen to it as an image of what it means to be a freed and philosophical person in an imperfect city. Here Socrates is already beginning to embark on an analysis of living in the imperfect world, rather than the ideal one, a theme that will continue from now until the end of the dialogue.

Before we analyze the journey of the prisoner, it is worth noting some peculiar features of the initial condition of imprisonment. First, the prisoners are not self-aware of their condition because they lack knowledge of the entire whole of which their own experience forms only one part. Such experiences of having one's vision limited by a partiality of experience are a familiar part of ordinary human life and growth. For example, parents often can see the wider context in which a child or adolescent's disappointment over some perceived difficulty or loss will be understood differently by the child when he grows up. These prisoners are enslaved in part due to their lack of movement and lack of changing perspective: with even their necks bound in chains, their view is unchanging except insofar as the shadows and echoes themselves change. That is, their own activity does not contribute to a change in perspective, as would movement, or looking at the cave, others, or oneself from a different angle. They remain passive.

One curious feature of this initial situation is that there exist persons
who are freed from the bench and are mobile, but who are apparently not
on the journey to leave the cave as will the freed philosopher. Thus, there is
a question as to how, if all those on the bench are there from birth, there
can be a second class of people who walk around and concern themselves
with artifacts. While the artifacts are images of elements of reality outside
the cave, these persons seem to take the objects to be reality, rather than
shadows on the wall. They are the shadow casters and creators of the echoes
that others hear. They possess a more active role, without being wholly freed.
Socrates presents these individuals as though they are partway through a
journey that will never come to completion. They have made a kind of
partial ascent, insofar as they are further "up" the cave than those on the
bench. However, they do not seek freedom outside the cave. To this extent,
they fail to have been completely turned around to the forms and the good.
Their orientation remains wholly with human things but not with the
origins of these human things. Socrates does not identify these individuals
but we might reasonably see them as sophists, poets, or other individuals
who perform and enact educational approaches without the context of the
forms to guide their performances.[33] In Book Six, Socrates presents the
sophists as corruptors of the soul who educate others with the beliefs of
the many (492a, 493a–b). The sophists remain in the realm of opinion,
as represented by the cave, and do not ascend to the level of knowledge.
They take their bearings from the human world and not from the forms.
These descriptions of the sophist fit especially well with the image of those
who are not themselves the passive audience as are the prisoners, who create
images rather than receive them, and yet who are in a way also not fully
free, insofar as they remain in the darkness of the cave. Picking up on the
earlier imagery of light to describe the conditions for the intellect's capacity
to see the forms, Socrates suggests that the fire that casts shadows within
the cave is a secondary and derivative sort of light. But these shadow casters lack any sense that these human creations are secondary to the forms.
Socrates uses the term *thaumetopoein* to describe the activity of the shadow
casters. The term means "to work wonders" and can be used to describe
not only orators but also entertainers such as jugglers. So, these individuals
may be, more inclusively, any educator whether identified as a sophist or a
poet, who seeks to shape the perceptions of those who receive their performances, and who do so in a self-conscious way. The wonder workers have
a larger context than do the prisoners, for they must be aware of those to
whom they are casting the shadows, having been born in this condition

themselves. Yet in another way, they lack self-knowledge, since they are only partially free, unaware of the still larger space of the world outside of the cave. While the prisoners cannot see even themselves due to the fixity of their necks, the freely moving shadow casters cannot see themselves as knowers, that is, as beings capable of coming to know the forms. Perhaps they falsely see themselves as capable educators above the common rabble, when in fact they lack a sense of the larger, cosmic whole.

To this extent, Socrates takes the divided line's purely epistemological and ontological concerns and shows that there are political consequences for not understanding who one is, or who others are, in the larger whole of being. Socrates's myth fundamentally names the person who is enslaved as potentially a free being, that is, one who if compelled to take the difficult path of a proper education can come to know. Unlike in the myth of the metals, there is no testing to see whose nature is well qualified for the ascent. Instead, the *experience* of education trumps any particular natural abilities and differences. However, most people do not fundamentally see themselves as potential knowers of the forms. They therefore do not even seek them. The reason is that such an experience of knowledge is only possible for one who has already left the cave, and is not available to those who still remain within it. The world of the cave, whose being is derived from and dependent upon the outside world of true being, can be understood from the context of the experience of being a free person outside of it. However, the reverse is not the case. Seeing for oneself is necessary for the knowledge of the forms to make sense. Thus education can only prepare another for the act of seeing, but cannot put sight into blind eyes.

Socrates states that a prisoner comes to be released by another individual. Yet because the path out of the cave is rough and steep, the released prisoner must be dragged up it. Such a person's experience of education is one of irritation and distress (515e). Moreover, even the initial sight of the world outside the cave is insufficient to relieve such distress initially, until the eyes of the seeker adjust to it. Socrates describes the path of education as essentially one of discomfort. This approach to education is in keeping with the manner in which Socrates treats his interlocutors throughout the dialogues, refusing to flatter them and often creating confusion and anger in those whom he questions. In the *Apology*, Socrates attributes such questioning to be the true cause of his being brought to court, but he understands his questioning to be an act of caring for the soul, although others do not receive it in this way. One way to explain the presence of sophists, poets, or others in the cave is to understand them as those who are only partly freed by someone like Socrates, but who cannot withstand the discomfort of education. Earlier, Socrates describes the democratic assembly as an especially volatile context in which "true" sophistry is found, when gifted young people cannot withstand the blame, praise, applause, and uproar of the social setting, which acts like a "flood" upon the human soul (492b–c). An example of such a person is Alcibiades, who reports in the *Symposium* that he desired to change his entire way of life when in the presence of Socrates, but could never seem to overcome his desire to be loved and admired, desires that stood in the way of deeper philosophical desires. The person who ascends out of the cave undertakes a journey that, like the hero's journey, includes at least substantial discomfort if not suffering and trial.

As Kastely writes, in this image Socrates engages in an "imaginative act of translation that employs images to allow this audience to glimpse better what it cannot understand fully."[34] That is, Socrates gives an account of the philosophical journey that tells of the rewards of the ascent to those who have not yet made the journey themselves. By presenting the ascent in terms of a heroic journey, Socrates adapts an epic trope in which hardship is endured but followed by reward, much like the journeys of Odysseus or Heracles. The actual content of the encounter with the forms cannot be explained adequately to one who has not personally seen them, but by offering images that are accessible to an ordinary listener, Socrates tells the nonphilosopher *what it is like* to pursue philosophical education to its end. Socrates gives analogues from everyday experience—going from the inside world to the outside world, from darkness into light, climbing an arduous path—that give context for the whole in a way to those who have not yet seen the forms. Thus, he speaks to the nonphilosopher who is still "on the way" or perhaps even hesitating at whether the life of philosophy is essentially good or not, and he seeks to inspire a care for the goods of the soul in lieu of the distractions with which many citizens occupy themselves.

Socrates says that once outside of the cave, the person who emerges will only be able to see reality by graded stages: first shadows, then things themselves, finally heavenly bodies and the sun both in itself and as a cause of other things (516a). Socrates's ordering of the nature of discovery is not an exact mapping of the divided line onto the cave, for on the one hand, the interior of the cave is supposed to correspond to the visible world and the exterior to the intelligible world, but on the other hand, there are now gradations of things known outside of the cave, too. The social and political world of the interior of the cave is entirely absent from the divided line. Moreover, the shadows on the wall of the cave cannot correspond directly to the level of mere images on the divided line, since presumably no human being literally lives without exposure to any human artifacts and only sees images. Rather, the outside-inside of the cave seems to correspond to the intelligible-visible world difference more broadly. The divided line also omits specific mention of the form of the good, which the sun here represents. Thus, the imagery of the cave is not a simple retelling of the divided line and its ontology. The cave is less precise in its descriptions of the nature of objects in the ascent, instead focusing on the psychological experience of coming to know. This does not make it somehow less philosophical than the more precise divided line image, however. In some ways, the cave image more accurately depicts the experience of coming to know from a subjective perspective. It includes the temporal element of changing in knowledge over time, rather than only a static universe that exists outside of the first-person subjective perspective. But, of course, there is no extra subjective, omniscient view of the whole available to actual human beings. Instead, Socrates describes what it means to relinquish insufficient modes of understanding—for example, passively accepting political opinions—and the psychological experience of relatively greater illumination.

One might argue that once the person outside of the cave has seen the heavenly bodies of moon, stars, and finally sun, he has seen the whole and so can provide an omniscient perspective. However, Socrates says that the freed person must again make a descent into the world of the cave. Anyone who has seen the outside world will not want to return and will think the world of the cave to be comparable to Hades in comparison to the realm of the forms (516d–e). Yet the journeyer must be compelled to make a return. Socrates frequently uses the term "compulsion" (*ananke*) to describe the motive for both the ascent and descent of the philosopher. He is even compelled to look at the light of the sun outside the cave itself (515e). Why should such compulsion be necessary for the philosopher, especially given the emphasis on the philosopher's natural inclination to love all kinds of knowledge from earlier books? Why must one be compelled to look at that which one already loves? Ellen Wagner argues for a more developmentalist view: the philosophers in training who are not yet fully educated must be compelled to look at the form of the good because she is not yet fully ruled by her reasoning part, and may not follow reason if her spirit objects.[35] Perhaps the *thumoeides* of the still-developing philosopher fears failure and so must be pushed to complete her education. Moreover, the encounter with the form of the good is initially overwhelming, and so there is a problem of circularity to be overcome. Unless one has seen the good, one will not commit to turning toward it, but unless one turns toward it, one will never see it. Thus outside intervention is necessary.

The question of why the philosopher must be compelled to return to the world of politics inside the cave is also a thorny one.[36] Strauss interpreted the movement of the philosopher outside the cave back into the cave to be an essentially negative movement that suggests a kind of incompatibility of philosophy and politics; on his view, the compulsion needed to return to the cave shows that the just city is impossible.[37] At the opposite end of the spectrum, Irwin argues that the philosopher-ruler would want to express the knowledge of the forms in his actions.[38] Others suggest that the ordinary, mortal world is not lovable to the contemplative philosopher but that Socrates demands the return as a matter of justice but not desire.[39]

This question of desire is fundamental. Does the philosopher see the world as having value, and would the knowledge of the forms or of the good itself teach that the world still holds value? The brief answer to the latter question is: no, not initially. While the forms are lovable in themselves once known, and the freed prisoner now loves them and finds pleasure in their contemplation, his experience of them is not yet integrated with the ordinary political world from which he came. On the ascent up the path of the cave to the outside world, the journeyer appears to be rather bewildered. On the descent back, this experience of being out of sorts is duplicated in new form: now he looks "graceless" and seems "ridiculous" (517d). But Socrates adds that if a person has intelligence (*nous*) he will recall *both* kinds of disturbances of the eyes, in moving from dark to light or light to dark, and understand a corresponding set of movements in the soul (518a). This wiser person will be able to make sense of what is happening to both kinds of souls, and will have two sorts of responses: he will deem the one who has moved out of and back into the darkness happy (*eudaimoniseien*), while the other who is still emerging into the light he will pity (*eleēseien*) (518b). While the verb *eleeō* can mean to pity, it also potentially has connotations of mercy and even compassion. Socrates seems to be saying that the person who has already made the full journey out of the cave and back again has a larger context for understanding the psychological experiences of a philosophical education both upward toward the forms *and* downward in the return to politics. He understands the difficulty of moving toward the forms, having himself also taken such a journey toward greater understanding. But he also can see that the person who is seen as merely ridiculous from the perspective of those within the cave who have never made such a journey will eventually be happy, despite his initial difficulty with integrating his experience outside of the cave with the life inside of the cave.[40]

Socrates's coupling of two seemingly opposite ideas—that the philosopher-ruler must be compelled to return and that he is happy even inside the cave—suggests that it may take time for the philosopher to adjust to his political role and to see the merits of the world inside of the cave. Socrates does not say that the philosopher must be *continually* compelled to continue in his role as a ruler. Rather, he says only that he must be compelled to return. This leaves open the possibility that he may again readjust to the world inside the cave, as in the metaphor of the readjustment of the philosopher's eyes such that the world of contemplation and the world of politics becomes more fully integrated. That is, the philosopher can potentially see that justice can still be seen and known in a more limited way in the human world, and that it is desirable that the city as a whole embodies justice, which it will not do if there is not a philosopher to rule and to educate it. The alternative would be a quite counterintuitive claim: one would have to then say that the person who loved justice as a form was not at all bothered by the existence or potential existence of injustice in the city to which he belongs. It seems implausible to argue that one could love the form of justice and take pleasure in seeing it, and yet not find it painful to see injustice in one's own city. If we read the cave image in this way, there is also a parallel between the ascent outside the cave, which must also initially be compelled but then later becomes intrinsically desirable, and the descent back into the cave, which must also be compelled but might well also have its own merits over time.[41]

Socrates adds later in Book Seven that the philosophers who are finally compelled to see the good at age fifty will then each in turn be compelled to use the good as a paradigm for ordering the city. Though this is drudgery for most, Socrates adds, "For the most part, each one passes time in philosophy, but when his turn comes, he toils in politics and rules for the sake of the polis, not as though doing something fine, but rather necessary (*anankaion*)" (540b). In other words, Socrates does not envision guardians who, once they complete their courses in philosophy, then rule for the rest of their lives. Instead, he seems to treat the work of rule as more like a necessary job in which the philosophers take turns—more like academics who reluctantly accept the task of being departmental chair than those who are career politicians. The philosopher-rulers are contemplative philosophers first and rulers second. However, there is more yet to say about the role of the practical life for the contemplative philosopher.

In this earlier passage in which Socrates describes the person who returns to the cave, he does not call this "ridiculous" person pitiable. Rather, the one who is the object of pity is the one who is still ascending and has not yet fully emerged into the light and seen the good adequately. The one who returns to the cave looks ridiculous, but is said to be fundamentally "happy" (518b). Moreover, he can still see more clearly than those who have not yet seen anything of the forms at all. While Socrates does not claim to know the forms, he is much like this person, who will also be "compelled in courts or elsewhere to contest the shadows of the just" (517d) but who basically lives a happy and good life despite others who see his life as ridiculous (e.g., Callicles, Meno, and other interlocutors who question the value of the life of the philosopher).

Why is the return to the cave nonetheless a happy experience? The answer to this question can help us to better understand why the return to the cave is good for not only those who are ruled or educated by the philosopher, but for the philosopher herself. Socrates does not elaborate, but here are a few suggestions. First, if indeed Socrates thinks that the visible world is modeled on the intelligible world in which it participates, and has the "look" of the ideas after which it is patterned, then by virtue of its similarity to the forms, the visible world becomes lovable as well insofar as it displays the goodness, justice, beauty, and so on of the forms. Despite Socrates's claim that the contemplator of the forms will not want to return to the cave, there is some evidence in Book Six to suggest that Socrates holds such a view. Socrates says that the philosopher wishes to act like a kind of a painter, who looks to the just, beautiful, and moderate and mixes together these forms to produce a human image (501a–c). The philosopher desires to be a painter of regimes, where the ordinary world of politics begins to look more and more like the divine pattern. Even if the rule of the city is not the philosopher's favorite activity, the capacity to help the city embody justice is desirable. If one recalls the distinction between the lovers of sights and sounds and the philosopher, the former loves the objects of sight and sound for their own sakes, but the philosopher does not hate the ordinary world. Rather, she loves what she experiences in the sensible world insofar as such experiences continue to provide insight into the forms. A beautiful painting still allows one to see something about beauty itself even if it is not the whole of beauty. Similarly, there might be a kind of pleasure in seeing justice in the ordinary world if one loves justice itself. Surely the lover of justice will want to see his fellow citizens be just and act in morally virtuous ways, rather than in bad ones. Not only the sight of the forms, but their embodiment in real persons could be a source of pleasure, while witnessing the injustice that would result from bad rule would be a potential source of pain.

Second, since Socrates goes on to say that the philosopher-guardian does not spend *all* of his time ruling, but rather takes turns with others, there is no reason to suppose that the philosopher cannot move freely in and out of the cave. Socrates never forbids that ascent never take place again, only that the initial movement down must be compelled, just as was the case in the initial ascent. In fact, to the extent that Socrates specifies that they "take turns" ruling, he implies that there is still time for philosophical contemplation. The philosopher may therefore appear ridiculous to those who do not know of life outside of the cave, but his happiness stems not from honor or dishonor, but rather from the continued fulfillment of his reason in acts of contemplation as well as political rule.

Third, insofar as the guardians are the educators, it seems clear that the figure who comes to free the enslaved prisoner must be none other than a philosopher herself.[42] The philosopher as educator may find a kind of deep satisfaction in freeing those who are enslaved and assisting them in making an ascent. Indeed, Socrates himself is in the depths of the Piraeus and ready to ascend back to Athens proper when he is stopped by Pole-marchus and his friends. He remains in order to educate, and then makes the return. At first he is compelled to stop, but later stays on willingly. Socrates himself is a model of the philosopher who not only experiences his own freedom, but acts to free others. He is not a politician, but his actions are nonetheless political insofar as they are intended in part to help defend a notion of justice that can have political effects even in the imperfect city. For example, if Socrates is persuasive that his understanding of the just life as the happy life and that Thrasymachus's ideal leads to unhappiness, he may thereby prevent an injustice from taking place in their real, ordinary city. If Socrates can show even some who are present that the seeking of the forms in a life of philosophy is desirable, then he has at least begun to free that person. Socrates may not possess comprehensive understanding of the good, but insofar as he seems to have had a glimpse of the forms, enough to posit that they are, and that they are lovable, he is like the one who descends back into the cave. The "necessity" in Socrates's case, however, is not one of external necessity but an internal one. While in the *Apology*

Socrates says that the god gave him his mission and that his life is about following that mission, this external command becomes internalized. To care for the souls of others is an activity central to *who Socrates is*. To this extent, we can say that the person who ascends out of the cave but has no desire to pass along the benefits of philosophy to another is not yet fully converted to the most just life and still needs a degree of compulsion to descend. A soul-like Socrates, however, seeks the good not only for himself, but also for others, such that his own philosophical experience goes on to have political value, insofar as he cares for the souls of others.

In conclusion, the images of the divided line and cave serve complementary functions. The divided line emphasizes both the continuities and discontinuities between the visible world and the world of the forms. It presents a view of ontology "from above," an almost divine perspective on being as a whole. The image of the cave takes on the first-person perspective of the experience of education, its temporal movement, and the affective challenges that accompany such growth. Both of these vantage points are necessary for the one who has not yet traversed the difficult path of ascent to the forms, for they offer a vision of the rewards of making such an ascent, and provide explanation of the difficulties encountered. By placing one's own experience within the larger context of a greater whole, the particular difficulties of philosophical ascent are given meaning even to the one who has not yet completed the journey. In this way, Socrates provides a rhetorical model that encourages and exhorts, but one that is also philosophical in seeking to reveal some of what is being sought as the object of philosophical love.

Chapter 9

Images of Imperfection

The central images of the *Republic* are the dialogue's peak, the completion of an upward ascent to describe the forms through images. The image of the cave serves as a bridge between the ideal world of the just city and soul and the imperfect world of politics. For the remainder of the dialogue, Socrates's focus is on the nonideal city. In Socrates's own world, the philosopher must reside in the ordinary city and not in the ideal one. The remainder of the dialogue takes up, largely through image and myth, a way to make discerning judgments about how to live in this ordinary world.[1] Books Eight and Nine offer images of imperfect regimes and souls. Socrates develops the image of the tyrannical soul as a response to the final argument against Thrasymachus's claim that the unjust life is the happiest. But this argument about relative happiness is not only for people who already reside in a perfect regime. Rather, it is for those who are discerning whether to live a just life in an ordinary, perhaps even flawed and corrupt city—that is, people like Glaucon, Adeimantus, and Thrasymachus. Socrates argues that even in an unjust city, the just life is a happier life than the unjust one. This need not be understood as an argument for political quietism, but rather as an encouragement to care for justice even in the absence of ideal conditions. First and foremost, the just person has a locus of control over the good of his own soul. Even if the world does not recognize the good of justice, he himself can live happily, or at least more happily than other kinds of souls.

In Book Ten, Socrates also offers a substantive criticism of imagery and art in a return to the discussion of poetry and *mimēsis*. As I will argue, the placement of this material at the end of the dialogue gives a context for how to understand the imagery that has preceded the critique, that is, the imagery in the *Republic* as a whole. Last, the dialogue ends with a cosmic myth about death and choices of life in light of death as a human reality. Taken together, these final sections serve not only to finalize Socrates's argument that the just life is the happiest life but also as a discussion of what it means to live and to participate a world in which the ideal of justice is not fully embodied.

Surprisingly, nowhere—not even in these final books—does Socrates offer us a concrete politics of how to make discerning political judgments or how a government ought to balance competing interests in a nonideal world. Rather, his concern is overwhelmingly ethical and moral.[2] He focuses on how the individual person can live philosophically even in a just, or relatively unjust, world along with the contemplative existence of which he might also partake. Socrates's answer to the problem of an injustice that is not remedied with philosophical rule has very little to do with partaking of political organizations and is instead centered around the choice to live justly, even if the world around onself is terribly unjust.

Book Seven ends rather ominously with the claim that if the ideal city were to come into being it would be necessary to cast out all citizens over the age of ten (540e–41a). Aside from practical questions as to how that could work—for example, how a world of children citizens unskilled in craft or war could even survive—such a radical break in the city's social bonds would itself seem unjust to many. Socrates's point, though, is not so much to argue that Athens itself ought to raze its own political or familial foundations, but rather to display how radical a break the ideally just city *would* be, given the moral and educational claims that parents make on their children. Book Eight takes up this topic, arguing that even ideal souls or regimes can give rise to increasingly degenerate ones. Socrates offers nothing in the way of advice as to how to prevent such a decline. Again, his aim is not to give political or even educational advice at this juncture of the discussion. Rather, he provides an intellectual set of models for how to make sense of different sorts of souls that exist in the city. That is, Socrates develops a kind of typology of souls or a psychological framework that allows the philosopher to find order within the often seemingly irrational disorder of politics. By understanding what general types of souls exist, a person is in a better position to discern how to make good judgments about the best way to live, and perhaps also to discern how to respond to the shortcomings and failings of the particular regime in which he resides.[3]

Socrates's models of the souls of the timocratic, oligarchic, democratic, and tyrannical persons are based on deviation from the aristocratic ideal that has been set out in previous books. That is, the way in which Socrates chooses to conceive of the wide variety of kinds of people who form a city and participate in political life is framed in reference to an ideal that may not exist in any concrete city. Even in unjust cities, it is possible for just persons to exist. Socrates earlier had remarked that while the philosopher who survives the praise and blame of the Athenian assembly is rare, at least a few philosophical souls *do* survive even in deeply distorted regimes (496a–e). There, Socrates states that a philosophical soul can continue to live well even in a bad regime, but he "remains quiet and minds his own business," like a person who huddles behind a wall during a storm (496d). Of course, Socrates himself both fits and does not fit this image of a quietist philosopher. On the one hand, he does avoid conventional politics and insists at his trial that he has never been involved with the law courts before (*Apol.* 17d). On the other hand, Socrates's contentious argument with others, and his very pratice of political philosophy such as that found in this dialogue are overtly political acts. Socrates understands himself to be a gadfly to Athens (*Apol.* 30e), and as Baracchi notes, cannot be identified as the sort of person who simply huddles under a wall to practice justice privately.[4] Indeed, in order to lead others effectively toward philosophy, Socrates must understand the souls of those with whom he speaks. In both the cases of the Socratic gadfly and the private practitioner of justice, understanding the souls of others is essential. Thus, Socrates's descriptions in Books Eight and Nine give a way to model the souls of others into five rough categories (including the aristocratic). These categories only fully make sense from the point of view of the philosopher, however, who accepts a general picture of the just soul that Socrates has already set out.

If the model of the just and moderate soul is one in which reason, spirit, and appetites all work in harmony, the models of the unjust soul are to be understood in terms of various distortions of this ideal. As Brill has argued, Socrates uses the language of medical pathology to describe these degenerations of soul.[5] The degenerations are described as diseases, for example (e.g., 552c). These distortions culminate in the picture of the tyrannical soul as one in which the most human element of the soul cowers before the Hydralike appetites that seek to dominate both it and the spirited lion. While in the just soul the rational part rules, in the tyrant's what is meant to be a subdued part of the soul becomes monstrous. In a certain sense, the soul becomes alien to itself, insofar as the lowest elements of the soul terrify the most human parts of the soul into submission. Whereas in the just soul, every part of the human being gets what it is due, in the unjust soul, none do: not even the appetites, which in their Hydralike nature continue to grow new heads and remain insatiable.

With these two polarities of ideally just artistocratic soul and tyrannical soul in mind, it becomes clear that Socrates's model of all these souls is based around varying conceptions of human desire. By desire, I mean here not only appetitive desires, but also different ways in which the soul wants something for itself that is beyond itself. As argued in previous chapters, even the rational part of the soul is a kind of desire—a desire to know the forms—and also a secondary desire that the ordinary world at least partly embody and show something of these forms. Spirited and appetitive desires have their appropriate needs that are to be fulfilled as well in the just soul, but relative to a process of discernmenet guided by reason. The varying "forms of human character" are explicitly set next to the just person in order to be in a better position to judge the relative happiness of each kind of character (544d, 545a). Indeed, Socrates specifies that he offers these models in order to better persuade whether he or Thrasymachus is correct about the relative happiness of the just and unjust lives (545a–b). That is, Socrates's explicit concern in offering all of the models, not only the tyrannical soul, is to make an argument for the greatest happiness of the just soul. Although the just soul is the happiest, Socrates nonetheless allows for relative *degrees* of alignment with the model of the perfectly just soul. Thus, rather than treating justice as a condition that is either present or absent in the soul in a binary way, Socrates offers a hiearchy of those souls that look *more* like or less like the just soul. There are four degenerate regimes that are degenerations of the ideal regime, or aristocracy, that is, rule of the best. The regimes, in descending order of goodness, are timocracy, oligarchy, democracy, and tyranny. Similarly, there is one best form of soul and four degenerate kinds with names that correspond to these regimes. Even a perfect city cannot last forever. Socrates states that the best regime cannot last indefinitely for the reason that its complex mathematical calculations regulating reproduction will eventually fail, and the citizens will give birth to children when they ought not do so (546b). As commentators have noted, Socrates seems to admit a lack in the capacity of mathematics completely to regulate *eros*.[6]

In offering models of city and corresponding models of soul, Socrates is clear that not all of the souls within a given city type will be of the sort of soul that corresponds to the model. For example, Socrates says that the timocratic youth is sometimes (but not always) the son of a good father who lives in a bad regime, but who flees the trappings of the bad city (548c). Socrates here clearly asserts that it is possible to be a different kind of soul than the regime in which one lives.[7] Thus, we see a potential value to identifying both a range of types of cities and range of soul types: if one can philosophically organize and make sense of these different kinds of souls and regimes, one will be better positioned to live well despite the presence of negative forces that threaten to misshape one's own or others' characters. It is helpful to be able to diagnose the specific illness of one's own city if one desires to respond to it skillfully in such a way that one does not succumb to the disease onself. Thus, it will be useful not just at a contemplative level, but also at a practical one, to know whether one lives in a city that overvalues money, or honor, or freedom (or perhaps is a mixed type).

A timocracy comes to be when faction takes place in the guardians and auxiliaries and the lower classes become interested in moneymaking and the possession of land, gold, silver, and houses. The rulers and guardians of the city remain interested in only virtue, but when the divided city cannot agree on what they value, they compromise, allowing private land and housing when it was previously forbidden. Thus private life and its concerns become the root of degeneration in public life.[8] Its citizens mostly occupy themselves with honor and war, guarding against faction. This same regime will also begin to desire wealth, though not as much as the oligarchic regime. Analogously, the timocratic soul loves honor and victory, and is a lover of hearing but without rhetorical skill. He loves gymnastics and the hunt, is brutal to slaves yet obedient to rulers. He has a strong sense of hierarchy but does not consider the importance of the lowest classes for the good of the whole city, unlike the best guardians. While younger, he will despise money but then as he ages he will love it more and more.

The formation of the timocratic man comes about through a mixture of experiences: his father's correctly leading him toward a life of reason, coupled with social forces outside the family that influence him toward money-based desires (549e–50b). The timocratic soul, then, is a kind of compromise between these two kinds of orientations to life (550b).

The oligarchy is focused around money; in this polity, those who hold property are given office and the rest excluded (550c–d). The more that the citizens pursue wealth, the less that they care for honor, and the more likely that they are to break the law, or to rewrite the law so that it favors their own financial gain rather than what is good for the city. Socrates states that this polity is deficient in two ways: first, it is like the pilot of a ship being chosen by wealth and not skill. This city will lack leaders that have knowledge and will mistake wealth as the mark of a good ruler, when wealth is not particularly relevant. In his image of the pilot of a ship, Socrates uses a familiar example of a technical skill that requires knowledge for successful running of the ship in order to separate technical skill from the honor or money. Even in a democratic context that does not value hierarchy, the specialized skill of a pilot is understood to be a significant difference in ability. Since knowledge of how to sail a ship has disastrous consequences if lacking in the one commanding its naviation, Socrates's audience has an accessible model of the ways in which knowledge is independent of a person's possession of either honor or money. According to Socrates, the oligarchic city is no longer one, but rather two cities, the rich and the poor fighting against one another. Faction dominates. Because the rulers fear arming the many, the city will not be proficient at war and will be less able to defend itself against outsiders. The wealthy will love money so much that they will not want to contribute funds to the wars that ought to be fought.

Socrates next uses the imagery of bees, stating that in an oligarchy, a useless man, who is neither a ruler nor a maker but simply wealthy, can become a mere "consumer of goods," like a drone that never contributes his work to the city at all. Unlike the worker bees, he may still have the danger of "stinging" his compatriots, offering nothing to the city but taking from them as he sees fit. As commentators have noted, this same term, drone (*kēphēn*), is also used by Hesiod in the *Theogony* to refer negatively to women who take the money of the men to whom they are married and spend it, although they have not contributed to its being earned.[9] While Socrates's allusion may not be directly to Hesiod, such past usage ties Socrates back to a larger tradition of using the term as a metaphor for those who take without giving, lacking a concern for the common good.

The oligarchic soul arises when the son of a timocrat sees his father suffer the loss of his honor and property in court. Since he lives in a state where there is no guarantee of justice, when he sees the loss of honor, he decides that honor is insecure and cannot be valued as highly as his father honored it. Instead, he spends all his energy on thrift and the acquisition of money, presumably to protect himself from the same change in fortune that his father had experienced. Again, because he does not care for virtue and did not hear his father speak of virtue as a philosopher would, he does not care for the rational principle or for spirit but only allows these parts of the soul to thrive in a way that supports his extreme desire for money, which he lets grow uncontrolled. The moneymaking part of the soul becomes the driving force of the soul when the oligarchic soul places it on the soul's "throne" like a king (553c). He does, however, restrain his other appetites so that he is not dominated by them. In this respect, he still has more restraint than the democratic soul will have. But he does not seek what is good or rational for its own sake, does not love victory and so is unwilling to put his money toward competitions, and does not care about education or culture, which requires some expenditure of money.

In both his accounts of the timocratic and oligarchic soul, Socrates offers an acute psychology. That is he offers a logical account as to what motivates each kind of person to choose a good that is not the greatest good as if it were the best. The oligarchic soul, for example, does not really love money as much as he seeks security, but he names money as a form of security. Thus even a form of desire that is, strictly speaking, irrational in that it arises from the lowest part of the soul and not the highest, has a kind of rational motivation to it. Such a diagnosis of the psychological ills of the soul allows Socrates to give rational form to what might otherwise be named solely as irrational. Moreover, those who listen to Socrates may also examine their own motivations. If they are moneymakers (like Cephalus or Polemarchus), perhaps they can identify with the desire for security as a motivating force. These models can potentially become means by which to increase one's self-knowledge.

Democracy arises after oligarchy. Socrates says that because oligarchies do not promote reason or honor, but allow appetites to grow, they can also lead to a number of impoverished people who are in debt or disenfranchised. This impoverished class comes to hate and to conspire against those who have property and power, since they now have nothing—neither virtue, honor, nor money. When the poor, who are disenfranchised but athletic, see the rich, unhealthy oligarchs act in a confused and unskilled manner in war, they come to think that they would be better off ruling than the oligarchs, and civil war may ensue (556c–e). Democracy arises when the oligarchs are put to death or exiled, or put on equal footing with the rest of the citizenship. In a democracy—as was the case in Athenian democracy—all have an equal share in government. This city possesses a great deal of freedom (*eleutheria*) and free speech (*parrhēsia*). Because of this freedom of the individual, each man can choose to organize his life as he wishes, and so many different sorts of individuals arise in the democratic state, more conditions, in fact, than in any other state. Socrates describes this democratic regime as the most beautiful (*kallistē*) of all regimes, like a many-colored cloak. Moreover, Socrates adds, "Because, thanks to its license, it contains all species of regimes, it is probably necessary for the man who wishes to organize a city, as we were just doing, to go to a city under a democracy" (557d).

Here, Socrates speaks critically of democracies. Democracies lack a sufficient care for knowledge and do not place power in the hands of those who know the most about any matter of skill, let alone justice or any of the other virtues. Here, it is helpful to keep in mind that Socrates is not speaking of representative democracies, which have often attempted to combine features of both democracy and oligarchy, in the hope that elected representatives will be more skilled than the average citizen and yet accountable to the people as a whole. Socrates's object of criticism is the pure democracy of a city such as Athens, in which even higher offices are assigned by lottery (557a).[10] In such democracies, particular kinds of knowledge and the possession of office are not correlated, nor are there even elections of those who would be more skilled—and indeed Athens itself in Socrates's time elected only very few of its officials, such as generals. To this extent, democracy as a model of government is far from the ideal just city since it lacks wisdom in rulers, does not possess shared agreement about who should rule, and does not exhibit justice, since some unskilled members end up doing work for which they are not especially qualified. At the same time, Socrates says that this sort of plurality and diversity provides the maker of a city an opportunity to choose from among many different soul types that are required in order to compose the just city. The just city is both pluralistic and well ordered, both a one and many.[11] In democracy, plurality overcomes unity.

Several commenators have noted this description of democracy most closely mimics the action of the *Republic* itself.[12] According to them, the democratic city allows philosophy to flourish, in part because of its freedoms and allowance of free speech. Indeed, the Athens in which Socrates has this philosophical conversation that is the substance of the dialogue is a democratic one, though one in turmoil. At the same time, Socrates's earlier remarks about democracy as the greatest "sophist" suggest that he is considerably more skeptical about the possibility of a philosopher surviving the appeals of praise and blame that can corrupt and destroy the greatest natures in a democracy than this more optimistic reading warrants. While Socrates does not name particular individuals, one might think of individuals such as Alcibiades, who felt unable to escape the desire for honor that the democracy meted out only to those that pleased it. Even the historical Socrates's influence on Alcibiades was insufficient. Moreover, Socrates himself is killed by the democrats, who do not treat him as a benefit to the city. Indeed, dramatic presentation of Socrates across many dialogues showcases both his capacity to do philosophy in the democratic city and the harmfulness of democratic social forces on the possibility of philosophcial conversions to justice. As Socrates presents democracy here, the pursuit of individual private ends leads to a sense in which the city as a unified whole does not even exist but becomes merely a collection of private individuals with disparate interests. In the purely democratic city, there is a lack of genuine community.

Socrates describes the democracy by an image: it is akin to a varied (*poikilon*) cloak that is embroidered with flowers. As Rosenstock has argued, Socrates may also be alluding to the cloak of Athena.[13] In the Athenian celebration of the Panathenaia, the city presented a statue of Athena with a newly embroidered cloak. A group of representatives of the city processed formally to the temple of Athena in order to make the presentation. The cloak thus represents a kind of civic unity under the goddess. However, Socrates's claim that the democratic city is like a decorated cloak here suggests an emphasis on the superficiality of its embroidery and décor. In suggesting that a city that has the appeal of a multicolored cloak is only appealing to boys and women, and not to the city as a whole, Socrates implicitly denigrates the practice (557c).[14] The democratic city may attempt to find unity through its ceremonies and its presentation of ancient myths, but this unity is perhaps only "covering up" a deeper disunity.

The democratic soul is analogous to the democratic city. The democratic soul is not necessarily a representative of how all people within the democratic city are formed, but as Santas has argued, a democratic soul might well prefer a democratic city in which he could exercise his desires for freedom.[15] Rather, the democratic soul is one that cannot choose between competing desires, because it possesses no hierarchy of goods, and is insistent upon making all goods in life equal. While the other imperfect souls do not choose the good as their overriding end, at least they have an end toward which all of their choices are directed.[16] The oligarchic man loves money more than excellence, but at least he is willing to prioritize his choices in life so that they are oriented toward moneymaking. He therefore must restrain at least some of his appetites in order to attain what he desires. The democratic soul, however, has no principle according to which he orders his choices. What the good is for him changes from day to day. He does not distinguish betweeen necessary (*anankaios*) and unnecessary desires. Thus, he can make choices that are bad, such as indulging in unhealthy foods, enacting inappropriate sexual behavior, or otherwise acting immoderately (559b–d). He is ruled by these unnecessary desires instead of ruling over them. Moreover, because he moves from one activity to another without prioritzing any, he possesses no expertise—for example, he becomes a dabbler in pratices like philosophy (561c–d). Thus the democratic soul is unhealthy, not particularly developed in any particular skill, and unable to find a clear, discernable end in the project of living itself. We can contrast this kind of soul with someone like Socrates, who devotes his life to the practice of philosophy and bringing others to care for their souls—a practice that both brings happiness to Socrates's life and orders his desires.

Again, Socrates offers a model of democracy that allows those who might reside in one to make a diagnosis of its potential ills. As explained in the earlier chapter on Book One, the drama of the dialogue is set at a time in which democracy was just about to give way to the rise of tyranny. Polemarchus will be killed by the tyrants who overthrew the democracy and Socrates by the democracy who saw his philosophical practice as a threat. The drama of the dialogue mirrors, to some extent, its content about the limits of democracy, and especially the ways in which democracy can suddenly turn into the far more dangerous distortions of tyranny. At the same time, the drama also shows that philosophy and justice can exist in a democracy: Socrates, most notably, is its philosophical hero, but the very fact that all of these characters can continue to grow in learning about justice also demonstrates that philosophy can occur in this context. The private setting of Polemarchus's house provides the shelter necessary for the philosophical discussion to take place.

Paradoxically, tyranny arises from a democracy in part because the populace objects so vehemently to hierarchy. In a democracy that is the height of freedom, we find the conditions for the rise of tyranny, which is the height of slavery. This can take place when those in charge of the city take for themselves profit from the merchants and the farmers who are the remaining productive members of society. They redistribute wealth, mostly with a view to themselves, but in the outward name of equality. Those who object to this are called oligarchs and become perceived as opponents of democracy. Finally a man emerges who claims to be a protector of the people, who then ends up taking over power for himself. Socrates says that often, such a man uses the court system to kill another, supposedly on behalf of the people, but in the act of killing, becomes less like a human being and more like a wolf (565d–66a). If he is not himself killed or exiled, he may receive bodyguards and slowly consolidate power until he is the city's tyrant. He then purges the body of the city from what is best in it, leaving only what is worst.

Not surprisingly, the city suffers under the tyrant, but Socrates's even more important point is to claim that the tyrant himself suffers. This is explicitly an answer to Thrasymachus's earlier claims that those who act against the city's laws and only for their own advantage are happier. Socrates's claim will be that the tyrant is unhappy both for reasons essentially internal (the state of his soul) and external (e.g., he lacks friends and exists in a social situation in which he must fear and cannot genuinely love). In contrast to the aristocratic soul, who is both fully human and a person who experiences internal balance as well as fulfillment, the tyrant's very humanity is distorted and he lacks the happiness that accompanies harmony and the satisfaction of his soul.

The healthy soul is hardly deprived on Socrates's model: he entertains "beautiful words and thoughts" (*logôn kalôn kai skepseôn*) (571d). His appetites are neither deprived nor overfed so that they are still, and his spirit is soothed (571e–72a). With the lower parts of his soul well cared for, the highest part can then grasp the truth, such that even when he goes to sleep he is less likely to dream unsoundly. The person who pursues the highest pleasures of reason also is satiated with what is most real (585d). In describing the just person's soul, Socrates stays with language that emphasizes his humanity. However, when he turns to the soul of the tyrant, Socrates uses the imagery of the drone again, speaking of the "buzz" of other bees that surround the young tyrant in the course of his development, placing a love (*eros*) in the soul of the man, a huge drone (*kêphēn*) that is indulged by the whole rest of the soul until this drone within leaves the young person with the "sting of longing" (573a). In contrast to the longing of the rational part of the philosophical soul, which has a kind of desire for the forms that leads to happiness when fulfilled, the tyrant's soul is drunken, erotic, and melancholic (573c). Through relying on the language of the drone, Socrates describes the soul of the tyrant as akin to one who is under a kind of attack—only unlike the external stings of a bee that a body might suffer, the attack of the dronelike *eros* stings from within. This soul can never be fully satisfied, since his desires only continue to grow larger. In this way, this soul is set in opposition to the just soul, who has a soul that has been well educated such that all of its parts are balanced and fulfilled.

Tyrannical souls can also exist even in a regime of relative peace and quiet, where they can do damage at a smaller scale. Here, Socrates names conventionally unjust acts: stealing, robbery, theft, taking bribes, and even the enslavement of other men (575b). They are flatterers; Socrates implies that this sort of flattery is dishonorable and beneath a free person. Tyrants lack true friendships of equality, since they either flatter others (and so in a sense are enslaved to the others' desires, which they wish to please) or manipulate them (575e–76a). A city ruled by such a soul is unhappy, and so is the tyrannical soul himself. Socrates adds to the internal discord suffered by the tyrannical soul a lack of external goods that many ordinary people might desire: friendship, the benefits of a flourishing city, and a kind of freedom unavailable to sycophants and flatterers. In making these claims, Socrates offers a counterargument to Thrasymachus's claim that the tyrannical soul is "happy and blessed" (*eudaimones kai makarioi*) (344b). He also does so through the way in which he images the model of the tyrannical soul, in describing the very nature as a degeneration and a diseased version of the just soul. Socrates uses many negative images of the tyrant's soul: a man who contains a winged drone implanted with the sting of longing (572d–e), a drunken man (573c), a man willing to strike his own parents (574b–c), a slave (577d), a soul drawn by a gadfly (577e), like one bound in prison (579b), like a gourmand (579b), one who "lives like a woman" (579b), a "flatterer of base men" (579e). Thus, while Socrates does offer an argument based on how far the model of the tyrant's soul departs from the ideal and smooth-functioning just soul, he also paints a negative mental picture for his audience of the tyrant. Many of the preceding images in particular concern negative instances of being overcome with lower desires. If a person listening to Socrates were motivated primarily by an interest in the pleasures of appetites, she would find in Socrates's descriptions negative experiences surrounding appetite or physicality: being stung by a bee, being imprisoned, longing without satisfcation, or feeling drunk. Socrates's images not only speak to a rational judgment about which life is better, but they also make appeals to natural aversions of appetites and the body. Thus his image can speak not only to the just person, but also to the soul of a person who values appetitive goods and may potentially find the life of the tyrant appealing.

The dialogue itself has characters who share some features of the soul types described herein: for example, Socrates would seem to be a philosophical soul, Glaucon a timocratic one driven by honor,[17] and Cephalus the oligarch. However, Socrates is careful *not* to treat individuals as being exactly like the models of soul given here. For example, when Adeimantus says that Glaucon is a kind of timocratic soul, Socrates names some differences: Glaucon is not as stubborn as in the ideal and is more musical than the timocrat (548d–e). Socrates goes out of his way to emphasize that these models are not exact descriptions into which every soul can be precisely placed. Rather, we once again see a set of general patterns that are idealized models that help to make the visible, ordinary world intelligible, and yet in which the multiplicity and variability of the world of ordinary people and things is not fully capturable by the model.

Accordingly, Socrates's way of speaking to Glaucon is far more nuanced than the straight application of a model. He does often appeal to Glaucon's sense of honor, for example, noting the poetry that has been written in his honor, but also tries to draw upon Glaucon's rational capacity to imagine and understand ideas like the forms. Likewise, while Cephalus may be best placed among the oligarchic souls as a resident metic, he does not seem to simply be a greedy moneymaker, but one who rather understands his craft to be a mode of contribution to the city, and who has a concern with fairness as well as with moneymaking. Plato's own characters may have some features of one type but also features of another, participating in the model of justice to varying degrees and in a variety of modalities. Indeed, insofar as Socrates's words throughout the dialogue have been to a mixed audience of many types of people, Socrates does not rule out the possibility that *any* kind of soul might experience a reawakening of reason. Socrates does not treat even Thrasymachus as a "hopeless case." Similarly, the city and the causal origins of any given city may not perfectly map onto the typology of cities that Socrates has developed. As Pappas says, in Plato's own adulthood the Tyrants were replaced by a democracy. So upward movement as well as downward degeneration is possible, and Plato as author must have known this.[18]

Philosophically, however, Socrates's approach here is distinct from the earlier approach that he took with Thrasymachus in which they traded paradigms of technical expertise, unable to agree as to which kind of paradigm of expertise was most appropriate to the task at hand. Here Socrates still uses an idealized model to make his argument. Even the tyrannical soul is an ideal, in that it represents a typology of persons that may not perfectly map onto any particular unjust individual. Socrates does not argue, for example, by pointing to particular tyrants who have claimed to be unhappy, or by making personal appeals to Thrasymachus to examine whether he himself is happy—even though Plato dramatically gives us some good evidence that Thrasymachus is easily upset and even beastlike (336b). Instead, Socrates works out of the abstract model of justice that has been argued for throughout the dialogue; justice is made visible through such a model. Since the tyrannical soul is a diseased version of the ideal soul, the *typos* of the unjust soul also becomes visible, as a kind of failure to achieve the fullness of justice in a human soul. Much like an ideal model of health in which all parts of the body are in balance, such that sickness is relative deviation from this model, the tyrannical soul is a derivative type of soul, a diseased version of the healthy balance that the just soul possesses.[19]

As Ferrari has argued, the city-to-soul analogy also makes the nature of the city more clearly visible, insofar as the compression of a regime into a single soul lets us view the whole in a way that we usually cannot see the city.[20] To the extent that the soul is also like the city, it also makes visible elements of imperfect cities that are in practice messy and perhaps hard to grasp, by giving it the organization of a single person who has a predominant desire, for example, for honor or wealth or licentious freedoms.

Socrates is explicit that with this typology, whether a tyrant is happy or not also becomes more visible than simply observing actual tyrants. He asks Glaucon, "Would I also be right in suggesting that the one to whom we should all listen is the one who has the power to judge, who has dwelled with a tyrant, seen his conduct at home, and observed in person how he is with those in his household, where he has been stripped of his dramatic costume, and has likewise seen him in the dangers of public life?" (577a). By abstracting from the external trappings of particular tyrants in particular cities, which can be deceptive because of the sham appeals of clothing, power, and other public displays, Socrates's models get to what is essential about the tyrant—his soul. His psychology, in the most literal sense of being a series of *logoi* about various types of souls, focuses the sight of his audience on the happiness of the person through a kind of clarity that an abstract model can provide. While this use of abstract models may not be surprising in light of the last hundred years of psychology and an even longer philosophical tradition, Socrates's approach here stands in contrast to the work of both comedians and tragedians who also criticized different kinds of political figures. A comedy might mock or ridicule a particular politician and so act to humiliate or at least humble. However, it does not seek logically to identify the causes of the soul problems of the politician. Through offering his own models, Socrates also offers a causal account of *why* the acquisition of power, money, and other external goods does not lead to happiness. At the same time, by making it a derivative model dependent upon the ideal of which it is the degenerate type, Socrates does not simply present two equal paradigms but rather gives an ontological priority to the just soul.

The final segment of Socrates's argument rests upon one last image of the soul, an image that further develops and elaborates upon the image of the soul developed in Book Four. At the end of Book Nine, Socrates slightly reformulates his manner of speaking about reason, spirit, and the appetites in terms of three kinds of love that also characterize three kinds of human beings: "the lover of wisdom, the lover of victory, and the lover of gain" (581c). What were considered once only as aspects of the individual soul now come to characterize the whole of a particular kind of person, through an act of metonymy. These three kinds of persons are used functionally in the argument in order to move toward a final judgment about the relative happiness of the just and unjust souls. In Socrates's analysis so far, there is still one problem that remains: it is quite possible that even after listening to Socrates's arguments, any particular tyrant might make a claim that he is happy. Socrates's typology of souls that match or depart from the ideal just soul still does not address the basic empirical question: who experiences the most pleasure? Here, Socrates says that the pleasures of each kind dispute one another about which is most pleasurable since each kind of person takes his own preferred pleasure to be the best (581e). Pleasure would seem to be relative to what one loves most, but if one loves most whatever one finds most pleasurable then the resolution of the problem might seem to be impossible. Perhaps one could only say that whatever any given person actually prefers as the greatest pleasure, is the most pleasurable to him.

Socrates's model of the just soul is meant to avoid exactly this kind of relativistic approach, by arguing for a hierarchy within the soul. Socrates acknowledges that people may still dispute the relative pleasure of different kinds of lives. However, Socrates's point here is not to say merely that the philosopher subjectively thinks his own pleasure is the best. Rather, the philosopher has the proper *range* of experience to be able to make the better judgment that the life of contemplation really is the most pleasant.[21] In a sense, the objective judgment is available to anyone who undertakes to examine the question by partaking of all three kinds of pleasure, but only the wisdom-loving soul has, in fact, done so. Socrates argues that those who have tasted all three kinds of pleasure will know that the most pleasing kind is found in the pursuit of wisdom. Only the wisdom-loving person knows this, since only she has partaken of the "vision of what is" (582c). Qualitatively speaking, the pleasure of contemplation outweighs all of the rest. Moreover, as Klosko notes, intellectual pleasures are further increased when shared with others, and so may have additional social value.[22] The difficulty is that those who have not partaken of contemplation lack any experience of it, and so may mistake the limits of their own experience for what is possible. As Rosen points out, the argument is not completely persuasive, since it is possible that those who have not tasted the highest kinds of pleasures might find the lower pleasures to be subjectively more intensely pleasurable than those who have tried all three kinds.[23] But Socrates still thinks that a judgment can still be made as to which is the most pleasurable good to those who have experienced all three kinds of pleasures since they will always report back the same conclusion. So while happiness is not defined by pleasure alone, pleasure completes the happiness of the soul.

Socrates's final word on the tyrant's soul, until its mention in the myth of Er, is a new image of the soul. Socrates describes the tyrant's soul as one that is dominated by a many-headed beast that cows the soul's other aspects: a lion and shrinking man. As Gastaldi has argued, the roots of the image of the *thērion* (beast) with multiple heads comes from archaic poetry—for example, Heracles was reputed to have slain the water creature, the Hydra.[24] This monster is unambiguously bad and in need of being defeated because it is dangerous. Euripides's *Heracles* describes the Hydra as "murderous" (419).[25] Yet because the heads regrow when cut off absolutely, another way must be found to defeat it. The monster's heads are only succesfully prevented from regenerating by Heracles's companion, who is able to burn the wound immediately so that they are sealed off. In Socrates's own image, he builds on a longer poetic tradition in comparing the appetites to a Hydra, emphasizing the potentially monstrous nature of appetites. Unlike the Hydra, however, the appetites cannot be fully removed from a human being, nor ought they be. Indeed, Socrates's limiting of this image to the unjust man suggests that the appetites do not have this Hydralike nature in all souls, but only in the case of a soul whose formation has encouraged their growth. Once they have reached monstrous proportions, their defeat is not as easy as merely fighting against them. Here, Socrates captures one of the difficulties with moderation, which is that once the appetites have been habituated in a partiuclar way, change is difficult. Thus, educating the appetites over a long period of time through rational rule is essential.

A lion is associated with *thumoeidēs* or the spirited part of the soul. Michael Clarke has linked back this image to Homer, demonstrating that the simile of a lion is an extended one used in multiple ways over the whole of the *Iliad*, especially in the presentation of Achilles.[26] For example, Achilles responds to Hector's request that the body of the defeated man be returned for proper mourning with a refusal on the grounds that there can be "no oaths to be trusted between lions and men, nor do wolves and sheep have like-thinking minds."[27] In this comparison, Achilles names himself as the lion and the wolf, one who treats even his human opponent as mere prey.[28] Clarke notes that Homer uses the imagery of the lion widely to describe other warriors, such as Menelaos and Agamemnon, and in doing so does not use the lion to separate out the human being from beasts but rather to emphasize a certain commonality between them. For example Clarke notes that "courage, rejoicing, desiring, and fear" are all attributed to animals and that such thinking can easily be assimilated to the warrior's own state of mind on the battlefield. Yet this similarity between the human and the animal is not altogether unambiguous. For example, the *menos* of the warrior that can lead to the exercise of valor can also lead to dangerous *mania*. At times the imagery of the lion is used to this effect, as when Diomedes and Odysseus are described as "like a pair of lions" in their slaughter of Trojans as they sleep.[29] Achilles's self-description as akin to a lion at numerous points also communicates an abandonment of civilized, human values.

Keeping with the earlier approach, Socrates's image of the lion presents *thumoeidēs* as holding the possibility of either courageous valor or inhuman destructiveness. At the same time, through the "lion" being situated within the soul of a person whose rationality can potentially control its strength, or the soul of one who is dominated by the many-headed beast, Socrates also offers a way of describing how *thumoeidēs* can be allied with reason. The effect of this reincorporation of the archaic is striking. First, such an image affirms a limited truth within the archaic tradition, while also bringing it into the framework of philosophical thinking that gives priority to the rational. Second, such an image helps to address the difficulty of how to persuade the nonphilosopher who does not already love the forms, and has not tasted such pleasures, of the desirability of such a life. While not providing strong epistemic justification for why the life of justice is most desirable—at least not at the level of knowledge—Socrates nonetheless provides a minature poetic vision of the human soul that allows his audience to "see" something of the undesirability of the rule of the appetites. His image communicates characteristics of the soul in ways that are affectively persuasive: a monster is frightening, and a lion is both a potential source of admiration or fear. The image functions in part through its taking up the affective aspects of these elements of the archaic traditon, but situating them within the larger context of a rational argument about pleasure and the relative values of different kinds of pleasure. As Segal argues, metaphors and similes in Plato often both instruct and impart knowledge, through "bringing diverse acts into a common genus," much as Arisotle describes such rhetorical devices (*Rhet.* 3.10, 2–3).[30] Here, too, we see an effort to instruct through imagery of the soul in a way that also classifies and gives shapes to the movements of the tyrant's soul, as diverse and seemingly chaotic as those energies may sometimes appear to be.

Socrates's image of the tyrannical soul at the end of Book Nine is described as one that is "molded" in speech (588c). He speaks of "molding a single *idea*" for each of the three parts of beast, lion, and man within the soul. Thus, he clearly understands his own practice of creating this image in terms of a verbal *poiēsis*, a making of an image in a way that is analogous to craft. Thus, it is all the more perplexing when, in Book Ten, Socrates criticizes image-making. How are the criticisms of making images compatible with Socrates's own practices, not only in Book Nine, but throughout the *Republic*? In answering this question, we must assume that Socrates is well aware of the problem, especially since he self-consciously employs this language of molding and creating images that have considerable artifice. One might try to argue that the mathematical divided line is a very close resemblance of the nature of being, insofar as it is an intellectual image. It is harder to make the same sort of case for the far more poetic image of spirit as akin to a lion. Thus, however we interpret Book Ten, we must assume that Socrates does also see a legitimate place for images in philosophy, even those that are grounded in the poetic tradition, or that are mythopoetic in quality.

Socrates's next topic is to expand on his criticisms of *mimēsis* beyond the scope of his earlier criticisms in Book Three. Its placement within the *Republic* as a whole demands some explanation. If the criticisms are intended to be a simple furthering of the problems with traditional poetry, then they would seem to belong in the earlier discussion of Homer and tragic *mimēsis*. Why wait so long to introduce them here if the criticisms are only about traditional poets in distinction from Socrates's own approach to what is best for the just city? Moreover, Socrates has already given an account of the limits of images (*eikasia*) and their relation to higher objects of thought in the divided line and the cave. If Socrates only wants to say that the shadows and images of this ordinary world are not the full reality of the forms, he has already asserted this in the central books. Book Ten, however, makes a return to the question of *mimēsis* rather late in the game. But there is a good reason for Socrates to do so near the end of their discussion: given that Socrates's argument has been full of images, paradigms, and models of justice, different types of cities, different types of souls, and even the forms themselves, it is important that the nature of these images not be misunderstood.

In the course of their discussion, Socrates has been clear that while they have been able successfully to "catch sight" of justice through their images and paradigms, the project of understanding the forms more generally is hardly complete. Socrates has already stated the need for a "longer way." This late introduction of a further criticism of poetry and its image-making as a way then, further helps Socrates to differentiate his own philosophical practice of image-making and that of the traditional poets, who do not test their images through argument, and do not even understand the distinction between image and form. At the same time, Socrates also places images, even his own, as lesser creations than those of the divine craftsmen, who makes the forms. Socrates's use of images reflects a middle state in between the ideal of complete knowledge of the forms and an approach to image-making that is content to remain in the realm of appearances without concern for truth.

This way of looking at the criticisms of poetry in Book Ten, I believe, helps to make sense of both its late placement in the dialogue and the greater expansiveness with which Socrates treats the notion of *mimēsis*, beyond the criticisms of poetic education in Books Two and Three. Here, Socrates is not only concerned with whether the traditional poetic education is the best educator for those who reside in an ideal city in which the citizens will be educated to be just. Rather, Socrates takes up the question of how we understand image-making in general, even and perhaps especially for human beings in nonideal cities, who often rely on images to try to further understand reality, or to teach it to others. It makes good sense for Socrates's discussion of image-making in general to take place after the main philosophical imagery of the dialogue has been discussed, as a way of looking back on its use of imagery as a whole.

Socrates's main criticism of the poets is that they *seem* to know but do not know, and to explain that they seem to know because they create mere appearances of what is. This distinction between appearance and knowledge could not easily have been discussed in the earlier books, since the forms had not yet been introduced. As Jera Marušič has argued, Socrates's claim that the poets are only concerned with appearances and therefore lack knowledge is not a widespread assumption about poetry that Socrates reports, but rather is a novel claim that Socrates here makes.[31] Those who admire Homer "cannot perceive that they are at three removes from what is true" (599a). Socrates is making the case not only that the poets are thrice removed from the truth, but also that their audiences do not even recognize that there *is* a distinction to be made between images and what they represent. His aim is to help his own audience to recognize the distinction between what something is and how it may be represented through images, whether visual or verbal. Socrates's criticism of painting is not especially persuasive, insofar as few people expect of a painter that he possess substantive wisdom of the subject matter of his painting, whether it be knowing how to build a table or to understand the art of war, just because he can paint a table or a battle scene. However, as argued in earlier chapters, the poets *were* often treated as repositories of wisdom about the cosmos in matters both divine and human, and are Socrates's true objects of criticism.

In order to demonstrate that the poets lack knowledge of their subject matter, Socrates first sets up a description of the relationship between poetry and other imitative arts by drawing analogies between poetry and painting. He then draws a disanalogy between poetry and other arts. Socrates says that when it comes to the craft of a couch, there are three types of making that are possible: the making of the form or idea of the couch by a divine craftsman; the making of a particular, actual couch in the world by a technical artisan, the couch-maker; and the making of the painting of a couch (597b–c). Socrates returns to the ontology that he had previously set out in the middle books, a division between forms and ordinary material things and their images, but now additionally suggests that there are not only forms of moral or aesthetic goods (beauty, justice, and so on), but also forms of everyday objects. Socrates substantially enlarges his approach to *mimēsis*: no longer is he only concerned with the imitation on stage of bad men by actors (or poets) but rather *any* sort of deliberate making of one thing that is like another thing.[32] Like a mirror that only reflects an imperfect image of that which it is attempting to reflect, but is not the "real" thing, the mimetic arts in general lack the fullness of being of that which they imitate (596d–e).

Socrates enlarges the scope of his earlier criticisms. Rather than limiting himself to how and why imitations of bad men are morally bad for performers and audiences alike, he now considers how image-making *as such* is epistemologically limited.[33] The two accounts might seem to conflict, if our consideration focuses on which kinds of poetry should be allowed or forbidden in the ideal city. The earlier books seem to separate *mimēsis* from narration, where the latter is allowed as an acceptable *lexis*, but then Book Ten seems to include all of poetry, even narration, as mimetic and therefore bad (see 599e, 601a, 603b).[34] However, even if the difficulty cannot be completely resolved, at least the tension can be somewhat relaxed, if we consider that Socrates's two sets of arguments have two different purposes.[35] In the earlier books, Socrates is responding to poetry as an educational process and hypothesizing what kinds of poetry would be best to banish from the ideal city's educational practices. His main focus is children, while the relevance or danger of poetry for adults is more prominent in Book Ten.[36] Naming imitation and narration as two different kinds of *logoi* draws a distinction that helps to name what is wrong with the influence of poetry on its audience as well as on the actors who perform it. Narration is not as problematic as the imitation of bad men when considering this matter.

By the time Book Ten comes along, however, the context for the discussion of poetry has shifted. By now, Socrates has himself used a variety of images, and one as yet unanswered question is how philosophical image-making might be distinct from the images of poets. Socrates clearly is not a rhapsode, and his practice in leading the discussion at Polemarchus's house is easily distinguished from such performances. However, his use of images could still be confused with that of the traditional poets.

Socrates says to Glaucon that they must either reject poetry or make an *apologia* on its behalf so that we do not fall prey to its charms like foolish lovers (608a): "Just like those who have fallen in love with someone, when they think the love is not beneficial, by force, stay away all the same, so we, too—on account of the love for this poetry that has arisen from the nurture of these beautiful cities—we will gladly have what appears to be best and truest. But as long as it's not able to make its defense (*apologēsasthai*), when we listen to it, we'll chant this argument we are making as a countercharm, taking care against falling back again into the childish love of the many" (607e–8a).

The question naturally arises, then, as to what an *apologia* on behalf of philosophical poetry might look like. By explicitly criticizing the epistemological status of the poet and, in particular, the poet's self-understanding of himself *as an image-maker*, Socrates can distinguish philosophical from nonphilosophical poetry. Philosophers understand the nature of their own image-making and the distinction between an image and that which it represents, while the traditional poets do not. Unlike philosophical image-makers such as Socrates, who does reflect on how images relate to originals, the poets themselves do not undertake any meta-reflection on what it means to make an image. Like painters, the poets present their poetry without any commentary on how to regard the relationship between image and original—even though theirs is also a verbal enterprise. The image can therefore be taken to imitate accurately what it represents. In the case of painting, the adequacy of an image and its relationship to the original might be whether it is convincing to the person who views the painting. A poet who convincingly imitates a battle in words such that his audience has a vivid imaginal experience of the battle between Achilles and Hector might be deemed successful. Here, the audience member's *feeling* as though she is in some way experiencing something of what the poet's words name is the measure of its adequacy. By placing the emphasis on whether the poet not only represents what he claims to know (for example, the nature of courage in war), by asserting the poet's distance from the truth of the forms, Socrates shifts the locus of concern from audience experience to the epistemological state of the poet: both what he knows about the specific topic of his poetry as well as his understanding of what an image is.[37] This knowledge or lack of it in turn affects those who listen, who receive the appearance of knowledge and mistake it for its real possession. The poet lacks knowledge of the forms of what he describes, and he does not even know that he ought to care about such objects of knowledge in the first place.

Socrates's use of images is different. He also uses images in a wide variety of ways, as paradigms of justice, as ways of organizing into types souls and cities, and even to allow his listeners to imagine phenomena like being educated to contemplate the forms, something of which they have no firsthand experience. Moreover, he also sometimes denies possessing full knowledge of the forms, such as the form of the good. However, Socrates also frequently undertakes higher order reflection on the notion of image-making as such and also asks for such reflection from his interlocutors. When Socrates uses images in the the middle books, he does so with considerable attention to what it means to use an image, and with explicit claims that the image is *not* the original form *that* it images. For example, Socrates stated that he can only give an image of the good as if it is the "child" of the good and that this imagery of the sun does not reflect complete knowledge on his part. He describes the model of the just city as a way to "catch sight" of the form of justice but never claims that it is a *logos* that captures all that can be said about justice itself.

While a craftsman is only one "remove" from the truth, that is, one remove from that which is and is unchanging—the form of the couch—the painter is two removes: he does not construct a physical, usable couch, but only a picture of one. The painter only imitates but does not create. The painter imitates the appearance of something (*phainomenēn ge*) but lacks the knowledge of how to make the real object (596e). The painter is deliberate in his attempt to show how the bed appears to the person who is looking at the painting, that is, he is concerned with the perspective of the viewer more than with a care for the whole of the object itself. Yet he may deceptive appear to be an expert when he is not.[38] Moreover, if one were to ask a painter to make a couch, he would be unable to do so qua painter, even if he is a master of imitation and can make a realistic looking painting of a couch. Thus, the painter's limit is not only an epistemological limit, but also a creative one. He cannot create the forms of artifacts as does the divine craftsman. He cannot even bring into being ordinary couches in the same way that a craftsmen does. This is an easy claim to grasp, and makes possible grasping a somewhat more contentious claim, that the poet or rhapsode also does not bring into being that which he imitates. After all, a poet might well claim to be inspired, such that the gods are working in and through his *logoi*. In a certain sense, he might claim to bring Achilles, Hector, or others into being. After all, they are not historical figures but inventions of the poet. According to a view of poetry as powered by divine inspiration, the poet might even claim to express something divine and to act as a kind of conduit for the divine. Here, Socrates rejects this view of poetry as inspired and replaces it with a much more mundane view of the poet as a painterlike imitator, whose work is about mimicking appearances rather than revealing hidden realities or possessing great creative powers.

Signficantly, however, Socrates does not offer a wholescale rejection of all "making" (*poiēsis* in the broader sense of the Greek term). Instead, he develops a hierarchy of three different kinds of making: the divine, the craftsman, and the painter/poet. The "makings" of the divine craftsman are lauded as good and not at all deficient, since the ideas form the foundation of what is, from the point of view of human life, stable and enduring.[39] The skilled craftsman who knows how to make specific objects, like a table, is a more modest kind of a maker but nonetheless has a kind of useful, human knowledge. Although Socrates characterizes this craftsman's state as correct opinion (*doxa*) or trust (*pistis*), it is still clear that his opinions are enough to assist him in making the chair, table, or whatever object well. In contrast, the poets claim too much for themselves while also lacking even the craftsman's humble knowledge. While we know that there is no human being who is a master of all crafts, or who even have good opinions about how to make items that belong to specific crafts, some poets seem to make knowledge claims that range over many realms of expertise. Poets such as Homer attempt to imitate many things: warriors, kings, poor men, politicians, women, children, slaves, all sorts of people, and the many sorts of activities that these different people might undertake. Moreover, these poets make *moral* claims about the thoughts, words, and actions of the characters whom they portray. They even represent the gods and attribute to the gods a variety of words and internal motivations, as well as actions. The force with which they can convey their ideas may dazzle the audience who listens, for they bring an aesthetic power to their imitations. Instead of different colors of paint, the "colors" of the poet are rhythm, meter, and harmony, which make beautiful the things that he describes (601a).

Socrates reminds his listeners, however, that the poets are no more capable of understanding the moral and theological realm than any other ordinary person. The strongest evidence of this is that a poet who really knew of all these things should be able to *act* in a way that demonstrates such knowledge, Socrates asserts. But we have no evidence that Homer, Thales, or Anacharsis could govern a city, help to write its laws, win wars, educate, or even make shoes, although he can describe them being made (599c–600a). Deeds would seem to demonstrate knowledge more than words alone, and yet Homer and others are not renowned for their deeds. This imitator not only lacks knowledge but even lacks right opinion, because he has no one who does know to guide him in his artistry. At the same time, poets are powerful with respect to their capacity to arouse human affect. Yet they tend to arouse the worst parts of human nature, such as excessive grief, rather than its best aspects (603c–5c).

So, although Socrates's initial images are those of the painter whose artwork merely imitates an object in a way that does not convey the fullness of its being, his main target is the poets and their verbal imitations.[40] While the leap from the imitations of the painters to the poets leaves open many questions about whether their respective forms of imitation are similar[41]—not to mention the question of whether the main aim of either poet or painter really is the imitation of particular objects or people—Socrates's main concern is that the poet is not even committed to seeking to know, all while *seeming* to be an authority on subjects about which he speaks. Like the person still inside the cave casting shadows and creating echoes, the poet is not properly oriented to what he ought to care about most.

While the introduction here of a divine craftsmen is somewhat puzzling—especially given the absence of such a craftsmen from the schemata of the cave and divided line—perhaps we can see the divine craftsman as an ideal against which we must measure the knowledge of human beings: to the extent that we did not create the forms, our knowledge of them must be qualitatively different from the knowledge that a creator would have of their being. No human being can know the forms the way that one who brought them into being would know them. Rather, a human being can be either like the craftsman, who has opinions about the forms and tries to create reality in response to those opinions, or an inferior sort of maker, who merely *seems* to know but neither knows nor even cares to know the form. Socrates is not exactly like the craftsman; after all, his is not a "how-to" kind of knowing, and he seeks to know, not just to have opinions about the forms. Nonetheless, in an analogous way, Socrates's images of the forms are an in-between sort of *poiēsis*, images that seek to express what Socrates thinks of the forms, but which are more limited than the divine knowledge that the hypothetical divine craftsman has of the forms. Like real craftsmen, Socrates is not perfect or divine in his knowledge, but at least his aim is for the models to reflect the forms, which as a philosopher he loves and seeks to know.

What distinguishes Socrates's image-making from that of the painter or poet in Book Ten is in part how he understands the objects that are being imaged. Socrates thinks that there is a single, uniform form that is to be sought, rather than only a variety of many individual beautiful things.[42] The poets and painters do not seek this unity. Socrates understands that the images he offers are images rather than originals, and he is quite clear about this; thus his poetry does not attempt to deceive others. Socrates seeks an understanding of justice that is stable and unchanging. Although he uses a variety of images to discover the nature of justice, he is unlike Thrasymachus, who wanted to make justice dependent upon who is in power. Justice in its essence does not depend on the particular regime in which one lives. In this sense, Socrates is also willing to be subject to a truth outside of his own invention. He is not a relativist even while he retains the notion that how we see the form is perspectival due to our own human limits. These human limits, however, are not determinative of justice but rather set in contrast to the unchanging nature of the forms, against which this human limit is measured.

Socrates offers images that he thinks really can show something of the forms that these images describe. However, Socrates does not claim to speak with a godlike knowledge, but often disavows it, especially speaking of the highest objects of knowledge such as the form of the good. His claims about his own epistemic state are far more modest. More importantly, as previous chapters have argued, the *Republic* uses imagery but also draws its audience into self-reflection and critical distance about the use of images as they are being constructed.[43] Socrates argues for his models and paradigms, and allows his interlocutors to disagree with the adequacy of such models, as when Glaucon objected to the city of sows as inadequate as an ideal of justice. Moreover, the central books strongly assert that images of the forms are not identical to the forms that they image. Socrates's audience is not asked to passively receive these images, much less to be dazzled by them, but rather to maintain a sense of both their utility and their limitedness. The use of multiple images (sun, divided line, cave) to image the forms further reinforces the limited quality of each individual image.

Given the highly idealized nature of the best city, it is especially important that Socrates' image of the just city be subject to this kind of a criticism, that is, treated *as* an image. Socrates emphasizes once again at the end of Book Nine that what matters is not whether the city in speech exists anywhere on earth, but rather that a heavenly pattern of justice exists for the person who wishes to found such a "city" in himself. Like the craftsman who tries to create the real couch on the basis of the form, Socrates hopes his listeners will care to create something that looks like justice itself, in themselves. Even more than instantiating a political reality, Socrates desires for his interlocutors to care about justice, to seek to know it, and to seek to become just themselves. His images are overwhelmingly oriented toward these goals.[44] Socrates's images allow his interlocutors—and Plato's readers—to reimagine the possible structures and aims of a city. That is, through actively imagining the nature of the ideal city in speech, we are invited to do at least three things. First, a reader ought to learn something further about the nature of justice and injustice. Second, she ought to model Socrates and his interlocutors and subject these models of justice to philosophical criticism. Third, she might compare this ideal city in speech to her own city and its political arrragements, and so come to see justice and injustice in her own lived context. But all of these actions depend upon the capacity to imagine a city that is different from one's own city; they do not require that this city come into being in order for the philosophical understanding of justice to take place. Neither must such a city exist in order to act justly in one's own city—for example, one might care for his own soul and develop reason's command over spirit and the appetites, or seek to improve education for his fellow citizens.

Socrates's use of imagery is set apart from other kinds of poetry, insofar as his myths explicitly promote a philosophical stance. As Moss has argued, there are ethical consequences when the poet copies the mere appearance of excellence rather than genuine excellence and his listeners take these appearances as models: they will go away with souls that are contradictory, unstable, and lacking in virtue.[45] Still, Socrates's images, such as a philosopher emerging from the cave, appeal not only to logic but also to affect. The affective of appeal of images can be problematic, and so the distinction between poetry that attempts to unify reason and affect—as Socrates's images do—and those that only arouse affective responses, is crucial. Affect can be educated, and the right kinds of images are conducive to a proper affective response, when affect is aligned with knowledge.[46]

Good poetry is grounded in knowledge (598e). However, we may also need to discuss matters about which we do not have perfect knowledge. In the myth of Er, we will also see that myth can appropriately take up matters that are not knowable in a strong sense of the term (e.g., what one experiences, if anything, after death). Philosophical poetry as used by Socrates in the dialogue does not overcome the problems of epic or tragic poetry by displaying omniscience of the whole, or image-free knowledge. Instead, Socrates's philosophical poetry incorporates its own limits within it. That is, Socrates uses philosophical imagery to point to realities that he admits to being difficult to know, such as the forms. But his images do not eliminate questions but instead continue to deepen our questions further. Philosophical poetry attempts to awaken the rational aspect of the soul rather than the worst, not by claiming that its author is fully wise or accomplished but rather by orienting us to critical reflection and questioning of realities, such as the forms, whose reality is not exhausted by our inevitably incomplete accounts of them.[47]

While much of the *Republic* concerns itself with an ideal city and just action within it, the final myth turns to human choice and action in the context of political and social imperfection and evil. The myth of Er is a cosmic myth. It not only uses poetic language, but also speaks about a topic about which it is difficult to grasp the truth, despite Socrates's objections to poetry that it imitates the truth poorly as it is (598b). As Segal has argued, even the *Republic* as a whole has an epic quality, insofar as it articulates heroic ideals, and a vision of what is best and noble for the human person, on a grand scale.[48] The myth of Er presents a similarly cosmic view in the final section of the dialogue, like a miniature epic. Myth is a form of speech that is responsive to human *eros*, as that within us that yearns to understand fundamental matters about which we as humans lack understanding, and to possess goods that we lack the means fully to attain.[49] That is, myth addresses the longing of the soul for truth and for goodness in light of human limits with respect to knowledge and power.[50] Poetry can appropriately play the role of the pedagogue if the limits of what it offers are also part of its teaching. The human soul is not a closed off composite which is self-sufficient but rather includes needy and erotic elements that lead the soul to look outside of itself and to the world, to matters both accessible to human beings, and to those beyond what human capacities can reach.[51] The nature of soul is to seek and to become, and not only to be.[52] Philosophical poetry for Socrates encourages the human person to turn her *eros* toward its proper objects—the forms—and toward the cultivation of virtue in the soul.[53] Myth and imagery are appropriate ways to speak of difficult matters such as the origins of the city; the meaning of suffering and death; human responsibility in light of cosmic necessity; and the forms of justice, goodness, and beauty.

A few brief words might be said about myth here, although it is beyond the scope of this work to give a full account of Platonic myth in the dialogues as a whole. First, a myth is neither literally true, in the sense of being a precise account of that which it describes, but neither is it merely something like a fairy tale, despite some of the connotations associated with the English term "mythology." Instead, a *mythos* is a kind of a story; that is, a myth has narrative form. Unlike the image of the soul as a city, which is essentially static in its structure, a myth has temporal dimensions: for example, souls make a journey (as in the myth of Er), or the creation of the world by a demiurge is described (*Timaeus*), or the process of coming to recollect over the course of learning is described (*Meno*).

Second, Platonic myths tend to be cosmic in scale: myths such as the myth of Er, that in the Palinode of the *Phaedrus* or the *Timaeus* situate the human being in a larger cosmic context. While this cosmic context is presented as if from an omniscient view, as the teller of the tale describes it, in fact the human beings within the myth are not capable of having this omniscient view themselves. For example, within the myth of the *Phaedrus*, only a few of the souls, those who follow Zeus, get a glimpse of the forms, but the myth itself is told from the point of view of a narrator who sees all the different types of souls as if looking down on them with a view of the whole. In the myth of Er, individual souls only learn about the rewards and punishments that others suffer through conversation, but Socrates narrates the myth from the vantage point of one who observes the whole of the comsos, from the spindles of necessity, to the vast groups of souls ascending and descending, to an entire series of choices that individual souls will make.

This gap between the narrator's omniscience and the actual range of experience available to the persons within it cautions us against interpreting the myth as if Socrates or the narrator really is omniscient. Instead, the myth is an act of the imagination, yet one that attempts to convey a larger context for its topical material that communicates the larger whole in which human actions, seekings, and choices take place. Typically, Platonic cosmic myths concern areas of human life that are both inaccessible to full human knowledge, and yet crucial to our desire to know the meaning of our lives: for example, what happens after we die or where we were before we were born; what role the gods have in our existence and formation; or how and why the world itself exists. These topics remain significant to us because they inform our sense of life's meaning: that life ends is a central consideration for how to live well and leads us to treat our own lives differently than if we thought ourselves to be immortal. This is true regardless of whether life were to continue in some new form after death or not. As Pieper has argued, myths frequently concern stories "between the realm of the divine and the human."[54] And yet, at least in the case of Platonic myths, they are told by human beings and not by gods; even the inspired poetry described in the *Ion* is not told by a god but rather by a divinely inspired human being, and many Platonic myths have no indication of divine inspiration at all.[55]

Still, we may have glimpses of how birth, death, learning, forgetting, and the creation of the larger cosmos affect us. People do report what it feels like to come near to death themselves, or recollect the births or deaths of others; these subjects of conversation become occasions to explore fundamental questions of meaning, such as what it means to live if life does not go on forever, or what it would mean if life were lived over and over again. In this sense, such myths address liminal spaces still suitable for philosophcal exploration: we cannot fully know what it means to die, and yet the dying process is not simply a "wall" that we hit or an abrupt termination. Rather, dying constitutes part of human experience, while at the same time what happens when death occurs remains mysterious. Socrates is curious to know from Cephalus what old age is like, and Cephalus reports his own experience of growing old and considering the meaning of his life in light of the inevitability of death. Yet neither of them can even in principle know what death is like while still alive.

The myth of Er, however, is not primarily an explanation of death but rather is about the meaningfulness of choice of life. On my reading, the myth carves out space for political freedom and responsibility for human freedom. Individuals who live in the ordinary polis that may lack many qualities of the ideal city nonetheless are shown to be responsible for the kinds of lives that they lead, insofar as these lives are chosen by them and not the consequence of external necessity.[56] While much of the *Republic* concentrates on the development of an ideal city in speech, that city is a model developed in order for Socrates and his friends to learn something about political and individual justice. It presents a highly idealized image of justice. And yet the characters of the *Republic* live in a city with pressing and concrete political problems. They live in a world of suffering, where both Polemarchus and Socrates will die as the result of political turmoil. The myth not only restores to justice the good effects that come from leading a just life at a conceptual level, although this is an important piece of what Socrates had said about justice in Book Two, when it was classified as a good that is good both for its own sake and for its effects.[57] The myth of Er is also a reflection upon moral choice for those who reside in the ordinary and imperfect city, and not the ideal one. Its emphasis on a degree of personal freedom in the midst of disorder and circumstances beyond one's control can be understood as a political claim about the place of individual choice in a world that is constrained by both political and cosmic "necessity."

Death, of course, is something of which we have no direct experience. While we may have experiences related to dying, the totality of that experience remains a mystery to all who are still alive, including Socrates, who narrates the myth. Socrates does not fully comprehend the cosmic context. Instead, Socrates sets his sights upon the cosmic whole in light of the reality of death. His story about death as a primary truth that is unknown, yet fundamental to our human condition, sets the limits of the dialogue, as death sets a limit to life. The myth contextualizes human life within a larger scheme of the cosmos. Human life is presented in terms of a divine scheme, rather than only in terms of the needs of this particular city now, or the one person's particular goals at a single moment in his or her life. That is, the myth presents human life as possessing its fullest meaning only in view of a larger sense of the whole, but a whole not completely available to us. Socrates's earlier discussion of the perfect city in speech suggested the possibility of grasping the whole of justice. In contrast, this final myth offers Socrates's audience a picture of human life that is oriented toward human *limit* in a cosmos that exceeds human comprehension. The myth of Er points us to human limit and imperfection and not ideals. Thus the myth serves as a powerful example of critical poetry that encourages and engenders critical reflection, as some forms of poetry might not.

Critics are often puzzled by the myth of Er and its sudden introduction of cosmological themes in a dialogue so far that has limited itself to the scope of human justice. Annas, for example, characterizes the myth as a "messy" end to the dialogue.[58] Her criticism is not only aesthetic but rather deeply philosophical: the dialogue seems to undo the prior conclusion that just living is good regardless of external consequence. Moreover, it is disappointing that all reward and punishment seems to be temporary and fleeting, such that the universe really does not seem to care at all about what happens to human beings. At most, the myth seems only to reemphasize Socrates's original point that the just life is the happiest because the soul is in harmony and ordered when it is ruled by reason. Furthermore, the myth does not actually describe the particular rewards and punishments that the just and unjust receive after death. As Ferrari phrases it, it only "describes describings of them."[59] Thus if the point of the myth is to give a precise account of what specific external rewards justice produces, it fails to do so. Instead, we get a much more general picture of a cosmos that is bound by necessity, and yet one in which the choices of souls that take up particular lives exhibit a kind of freedom within those bounds of necessity.

The myth occurs in the context of finalizing Socrates's argument about the superiority of the just life to the unjust life. The myth returns to justice what had been taken away from it in Book Two for the sake of argument. While Glaucon had insisted that Socrates examine justice apart from its consequences, both for this life and after, Socrates is insistent that we do not have a complete picture of justice until we *do* add back the consequences. Those who are just will not only be happy in their souls' being harmonious, but will also be rewarded.[60] Glaucon's desire for the examination of pure justice, in and of itself, even "on the torture rack," needs to be tempered by the recognition that justice mostly *does* "pay," while injustice does not.[61] However, the myth is not only oriented to the past decisions of those who have acted justly or unjustly, but also to the future choices of the ensouled lives *after* they have suffered reward or punishment and learned from their past actions. My focus here will be on how the passages concerning the souls' choices of "new life" illuminate a Socratic concern with freedom in light of human limit.

Rather than taking the myth to be a literal description of what happens after death, we can understand it as a mythopoetic mode of speaking about a signficant human experience about which we cannot have exacting knowledge—at least not in advance.[62] It seems fair to think that Socrates is genuine in believing that justice and injustice will be rewarded or punished in some way after death, since these claims are what allow justice to be a good that is both intrinsically good for the person who possesses it, and good for its external rewards. But his mythical language, nearly omniscient standpoint in narrating the myth, and emphasis on the forgetful nature of reentering into life all suggest that this is not intended to be an exacting description of what that life looks like. After all, when we have truly and fully experienced death, there is no return to make a story. Er's exceptional experience in which he is allowed to return only reinforces the notion that within the context of human life, death remains a mystery. Even a person who hears the report of Er, or Socrates, may doubt whether the reality of the experience is true or not, since he or she cannot personally test its truthfulness.[63] Yet mortality remains a meaningful experience for living beings, even if death as such cannot be experienced or fully known in advance. Knowing *that* we will die sets conditions for the meaningfulness of life. Socrates presents death as a boundary condition, in which the actions of our life inform both what happens to us after we die and how we make subsequent choices in determining a next life. But these themes of choice and consequence are also relevant to how we live well before we die: justice often has consequences in our ordinary world, and how well we are able to choose in the midst of relatively novel circumstances in life has much to do with how we have made choices in the past. By using the language of myth, Socrates does not pretend to give a precise account of death per se, but rather one that offers a more holistic account of the relationship between human freedom and choice, and the consequences of the just and unjust lives.

Er, unlike the other souls he meets, experiences his own death and then returns to the world of living human beings in order to tell about it.[64] Er is not required to drink from the river, Lethe, a river of forgetfulness from which all others must drink. He does not forget his origin, while the rest of humanity must forget. These themes of life, death, rebirth, memory, and the loss of memory are best presented in mythic form since they all concern human limitation. The myth focuses on three kinds of human limit: the limits of knowledge, the limits of mortality as the end of life, and the limits of external necessity that constrain human control over external events. Facing death embodies each of these three kinds of limits. We do not know what it means to die, and what—if anything—follows death. We are limited in the length of life and have nearly no control over the timing or manner of its end. The circumstances that the dying encounter is generally a matter of external necessity: whether dying is short or drawn out, expected or sudden, the manner of death, and so on.

The structure of the myth parallels this lived experience of mortality, for the myth presents human beings as faced with a cosmos dominated by the forces of necessity (*anankē*) and an order that is not subject to their own control at the time of death. The human beings who choose new lives must live within the cosmological limits set out within it. All must follow the directions of the judges who direct them either through the heavens or below the earth. Except for Er, all must drink and forget their past lives after they choose new ones. These souls are allotted a lottery number that narrows the range of lives that remain from which they might choose.

The three daughters of Fate each attend to different kinds of limit on human life. Lachesis, whose name is derived from *lanchanô*, or "to get by lot," allots the time of each person's life, measuring the thread that delimits its length. Clothe spins the thread, turning the outer revolution of the Spindle, and Atropos turns the inner portion, after which the thread is cut. Lots are chosen that determine the order in which souls might choose lives. Once a life is chosen, that life is bound to a soul by Necessity (*Anankê*). The limits set upon the souls' choice of a next life are substantial. Yet within this larger realm of Necessity, the human being has a range of choices available to him in response to his memory and past experiences that allow him to choose his own character in the future. Er hears a spokesperson for the Fates announce that the ultimate responsibility for choosing that life lies with the souls who choose: "A demon will not select you, but you will choose a demon. Let him who gets the first lot make the first choice of a life to which he will be bound by necessity. Virtue is without a master; as he honors or dishonors her, each will have more or less of her. The blame belongs to him who chooses; god is blameless" (617e).

The myth emphasizes that it is not the gods who are responsible for our choosing lives of justice and injustice but rather we ourselves who choose. Although the judges direct just souls upward and unjust souls downward for a thousand years, the next years are in the power of the individual souls and not the gods. To this extent, Socrates sets himself apart from the tradition of Greek tragedy that had emphasized fate as the primary cause of human suffering or misfortune. While the Fates do run the larger cosmological system in which human actions occur, Socrates emphasizes that human beings bear a certain responsibility for ourselves and for our choices. Indeed the root of this freedom is virtue. In the preceding passage, Socrates personifies Virtue along with the Fates. Yet, virtue is not subject to the same kinds of limits found in the rest of the procedures of choosing a life. Virtue is without a master (617e).

Socrates's story also argues for the importance of philosophy in making good judgments about how to choose.[65] The decision by the man with the first allotted choice underscores the importance of not only knowing what is good, but also *why* it is good. This man who is habitually just has only seen a thousand years of beautiful and pleasant things, after his life of avoiding injustice. However, such a man is the same individual who chooses the life of the tyrant who eats his own children: "The man who had drawn the first lot came forward and immediately chose the greater tyranny, and, due to folly and gluttony, chose without having considered everything adequately; and it escaped his notice that eating his own children and other evils were fated to be a part of that life. When he considered it at his leisure, he beat his breast and lamented the choice, not abiding by the spokesman's forewarning. For he didn't blame himself for the evils but chance, demons, and anything rather than himself. He was one of those who had come from heaven, having lived in an orderly regime in his former life, participating in virtue by habit, without philosophy" (619b–d). The man who is just through habit alone lacks adequate grounds for choosing a new life. Er's account highlights two problems in particular with that man's capacity to choose. First, this man is apt to blame others rather than himself in refusing to take responsibility for his eventual choice of the life of a tyrant. In this way, his actions as a tyrant actually mirror the orientation of the soul that first chose the tyrannical life in the lottery. The same soul who refuses to take responsibility for his choice of new life will also express disdain for responsibility when he acts as a tyrant. This man understands his life as subject to external necessity rather than to the internal rule of virtue, and he chooses a life accordingly.

Second, the man chooses from "folly (*aphrosunē*) and greed" and "without having considered everything adequately (*anaskepsamenon*)" (619b–c). Although this man has been to the heavens and witnessed the rewards allotted to the just, he still lacks an adequate preparation to consider, that is, more literally, he is not capable of "looking around" to understand the totality of the life of the tyrant, its losses as well as its seeming appeals. He does not know how to see.

Habit proves to be insufficient for virtue insofar as the future presents us continually with novel situations. While habit is perhaps a sufficient guide for the child who learns to share his toys with others when they share play space, some further examination of generosity is needed when exploring more complex political situations. It is not always clear what constitutes generosity in the particular moment when the scenario is new and unfamiliar. And yet this is precisely what the characters of the *Republic* themselves must face in the new conflicts between oligarchs and democrats.

Socrates himself navigates these novel situations remarkably well. In the *Apology*, he offers the jurors examples of two different situations in which he chose a just act rather than an unjust one. Under the democracy, Socrates reminds them, the assembly decided to judge as a group the ten generals who had failed to retrieve bodies after a naval battle, although it was not lawful to judge them without individual trials (*Apol.* 32b). Socrates had opposed their action as unjust. Although the situation was novel and tempted many of those who voted that the generals be killed, Socrates spoke out against their actions and could identify these actions as unjust, despite the novelty of the particulars. Under the rule of the Thirty Tyrants, Socrates refuses to take Leon of Salamis and to arrest him unjustly, though it could easily have meant his own death to refuse (32d). His explanation is that he did not care about death as a motivating factor in his decisions (32d). For, as Socrates will go on to say in his trial, he understands that death is an inevitable limit of human life; whether one acts justly or unjustly, eventually death will come. Socrates's philosophical reflections on death prepare him for addressing the novelty of these new moral challenges, and they are successful because Socrates is both oriented in a stance that embraces the goodness of justice itself, while also acknowledging his own human limit and mortality. Socrates, when faced with the choice to kill Leon of Salamis, simply went home, a quiet choice that preserved his own integrity in the midst of political chaos. Socrates is not being apolitical, but rather he is making a decisive political choice in a quiet way that acknowledges his own limit to affect the current conflict. The soul that chooses the life of the tyrant does not acknowledge his own limit, perhaps even rejects such quiet actions, instead choosing a life that seems to illustrate an inhuman desire for limitlessness.

Still, Socrates does hold out one way in which the living can learn beyond the limits of their own lives: through listening to the narratives of others' lives. In the myth of Er, the dead souls who have just arrived after their journey in the heavens or under the earth set up camp together in a field, and spend a week in talk: "All those who were acquaintances greeted one another; and the souls that came out of the earth inquired of others about the things in the other place, and those from heaven about the things that had happened to those from the earth. And they told their stories to one another, the ones lamenting and crying, remembering how much and what sorts of things they had suffered and seen in the journey under the earth . . . and those from heaven, in their turn, told of the inconceivable beauty of the experiences and the sights there" (615a–b). Er specifies that these souls learn from one another how the impious and unjust are punished, and those who are incurable are continually so, unable to come back up even after a thousand years. The sharing of stories about the lives and experiences of the just and unjust alike are central to the process by which these imperfect souls become better prepared to choose their subsequent lives. Indeed, such narratives expand the range of moral scenarios available to the moral actor. Those who have heard others' accounts of the consequences of particular good or bad choices are less likely to come unprepared to situations like those they have heard. In other words, they learn how to discern through considering and reflecting upon others' narratives.

Socrates argues that such practice of discernment ought to be the lifelong practice of souls well before the choice of a new life; it is the task of the living and not only of the dead. Especially because lives are mixed with health and sickness, wealth and poverty, and varying levels of honor, the difficulties of discerning just from unjust actions, and desirable from undesirable lives, are considerable (618b). Socrates continues: "And on this account each of us must, to the neglect of other studies, above all see to it that he is a seeker and student of that study by which he might be able to learn and find out who will give him the capacity and the knowledge to distinguish the good and the bad life, and so everywhere and always to choose the better from among those that are possible. . . . From all this he will be able to draw a conclusion and choose—in looking off toward the nature of the soul—between the worse and the better life, calling worse the one that leads it toward becoming more unjust, and better the one that leads it to becoming juster. He will let everything else go. For we have seen that this is the most important choice for him in life and death" (618e–19a). While most people are distracted by wealth, honor, or health, it is more fundamental to the good life to seek to better understand justice. But coming to know *that* justice is more important than other goods is only gained through the experiences of seeing examples of poverty, wealth, beauty, ugliness, different habits of soul and stations in life and comparing the outcomes of these lives (618d). Certainly personal experience can offer some limited experiences of the wide range of such goods and their relative lack of import compared with justice. But Socrates emphasizes that the observation of the lives of others and listening to the accounts of others' lives, can also produce learning. The possibility of freedom and genuine responsibility arises through reflecting not only on one's own life choices, but also carefully observing a wide range of human values and choices made in accordance with those values. Arguably, the dialogue form itself is one way in which the lives of others can be both observed and learned from. While Socrates criticizes tragic poetry for its simple presentations of unjust men, the presentation of Thrasymachus, his beliefs, the reasons behind his beliefs and the violence of his character as he rages, blushes, and calls Socrates names, together provide one model of a human life. Socrates and his care for justice even at the risk of his own death, provides a different model.

We might read the myth of Er not only as a tale about death, but also about violence in the city and the chance to make new choices after violence. By the time that Plato wrote the *Republic*, its dramatic events were long over. Democracy had been restored. Some of the oligarchs and their supporters had been tried and executed, but others continued to live in the city and exercised their citizenship. While the harmony of the ideal city was never achieved, a kind of restoration of order after civil war did occur. In Athens's own history, a "new life" could only be chosen when the past life was forgotten in one sense. War and its divisive violence can only be healed when a certain degree of forgetting is possible. To this extent, the fact that souls must drink from the river Lethe has a political as well as cosmological relevance. Good, just choices must take account of the mistakes of the past, but it is also in light of a forgetfulness of the past that the future is allowed to enter. Just as the individual souls in the myth both choose these new lives, in light of what they have learned from their old lives, and then drink to forget the past, so, too, did Athens have to learn how to forget some of its past divisions. Its own citizens must have remembered what they learned from their past actions but then also chose to forget these past lives so that they might fully embrace their current reality as a postwar polis composed of both those who sympathized with the democrats and those who had oligarchic commitments.

The myth of Er thus expresses a kind of political reality about the movement of the polis through time: to live in time means to embrace the change that comes with being a temporal being: the gains and losses of cities, friends, opinions, even one's self. The *Republic* displays this kind of loss of the old self in the picture of the enslaved, chained resident of the cave who leaves the cave and has to forget his former life. The cave's philosopher, too, must forget at least something about contemplation in the midst of activity within the cave. His focus must be on the ordinary world, at least at that moment. Such forgetting is made possible because each one of us as individuals is not the end of the universe, as Socrates presents it. Rather, the cosmos is ruled by necessity and a reason that transcends any individual reasoner. Even heaven and hell are themselves subject to a higher rational principle; they are not just arbitrary places to which souls are sent but are governed by the goddess Ananke, who determines the universe according to a rational necessity.[66] Justice has a cosmological dimension that transcends our individual lives and our individual cities. So we cannot in the end regard the individual in isolation from the greater picture of the whole.

Plato's approach also differs from that of Homer in its mythological treatment of the character of Odysseus. In Homer, Odysseus's story is told to King Alcinous. There, Odysseus recounts many of his travels, and in particular his descent into Hades and his return from it, precedes his true voyage home. Until he speaks to Alcinous and Arete, Odysseus still wanders and is not yet oriented toward home. Plato also offers us an image of Odysseus in the *Republic*. We see the character Odysseus not only overtly in the myth of the man who chooses the next life as a private life, but also perhaps in the figure of the freed philosopher who goes down into the cave, or in the character of Socrates himself, who "goes down" to the Piraeus at the beginning of the dialogue.[67] In Homer's account, Odysseus's account emphasizes the terribleness of death. Among the most memorable characters in his description, we find the description of Odysseus trying to grasp the ghost of his mother, who is only a shade, and so who cannot be grasped, and the glaring eyes of Aias who is still angry that Odysseus won a battle for honor and for arms on the beach at Troy and who remains eternally in the state in which he died. Odysseus also describes Agamemnon, who is forever angry at his wife's betrayal while he is away at war, and the capstone of the whole section, Achilles, who laments that he would rather be a poor laborer breaking the earth for a little food than be the honored king of all of Hades. In Homer, we find the permanence of death, and characters who never escape the choices that they made in their lives. No one learns anything new about justice or virtue, and even the punishments that they receive seem to teach them little.

But those who "descend" in the *Republic* are all people who *do* learn from the descent because in each case their descent is connected with a prior ascent. Er learns from his experience and his life does not end on the battlefield. He comes back to tell about the choices he saw, and to make evaluations for others who will listen to him, for example, in his recognition that Odysseus's choice seems to have been the finest of all. Er was part of the community of the dead, but also takes his own experiences and even his own losses and uses them for the good of the larger, living community. The philosopher who descends back into the cave has seen the forms; he is different from those who never ascended out of the cave, and whatever trials he might face in the return to the mundane world of politics, he at least has the comfort of having seen the forms, and being permanently changed by the sight of them. He frees others so that they, too, might know this good that he has loved. Socrates, too, goes down to Piraeus, but he does not encounter characters who are permanently wedded to their views of the world: Glaucon and Adeimantus seem genuinely to learn about justice, and even Thrasymachus becomes a sort of a "friend" midway through the dialogue. Reason and myth alike contain within themselves the possibility of a real transformation of the soul, although they do not guarantee it.

Odysseus's choice is clearly the culmination of the myth, and it is an important counterpart to the idealistic and utopian qualities of the earlier books. Odysseus is not returning to a perfect world governed by philosopher-kings. Having lived a life attached to war and to honor, this man who was skilled in many ways (*polutropos*) chooses a simple and private life, one that involves neither eating his own children, nor the glory of an Achilles, or the escapism of being an animal rather than a human being. Instead, he chooses the life of a man who "minds his own business," the life of a just man content to lead that just life even in an imperfect and an unjust world.

In certain ways Socrates is like Odysseus: not involved in politics at its most formal level of rule. Yet Socrates is political in a different way, engaging in political dialogue and demanding that others care for their souls. Socrates's life takes place in the real, not ideal, city. Yet it is arguably a happy one because Socrates lives justly and philosophically. The myth of Er points to the possibility of a just and happy life even within the limits of the imperfect, real world, and not only the utopia set out earlier in the *Republic*. Like many of Socrates's images, it is an image that is meant not only to educate, but also to encourage his interlocutors to pursue a philosophcial life rather than to remain with received opinions. It is a call to responsibility for their own lives. In this way, we can easily enough imagine Socrates at the end of the discussion finally making his ascent back up from the Piraeus to Athens on a path that might seem somewhat less rugged and steep than the path leading out of the cave.

Notes

Introduction

1. Translations are my own unless otherwise noted. The Greek text translated is from *Platonis Respublica*, ed. R. S. Slings (Oxford: Oxford University Press, 2003). Some sections use the Bloom translation in cases of previously published material, where this use is noted. I have benefited especially from the assistance of Bloom's translation and that of Joe Sachs.

2. The pervasiveness of such language in the *Republic* and its link to Homer has been widely acknowledged. See Charles Segal, "The Myth Was Saved: Reflections on Homer and the Mythology of Plato's Republic," *Hermes* 106 (1978): 323–24. Howland makes this myth central to interpretation of the text. Jacob Howland, *The Republic: The Odyssey of Philosophy* (Philadelphia: Paul Dry Books, 2004). Howland writes that Socrates is the hero of "a philosophical epic cast in the form of a philosophical drama" (32). He links these opening words to those of Odysseus in the *Odyssey* at 23.252 (see Howland, 48). See also Claudia Baracchi, *Of Myth, Life and War in Plato's Republic* (Bloomington: Indiana University Press, 2001), 40–42, and C. D. C. Reeve, *Blindness and Reorientation: Problems in Plato's Republic* (New York: Oxford University Press, 2013), 35–52.

3. Lines from the *Republic* are marked solely by line number; references to all other dialogues are noted with title as well as line parenthetically.

4. Whether the divided line is drawn vertically or horizontally is never made clear by Socrates, but its placement vertically would fit well with the mention of higher and lower parts of the line, and the movement of the journey in the image of the cave.

5. Rosen and Dorter also give attention to Plato's images as models or paradigms. See Kenneth Dorter, *The Transformation of Plato's Republic* (Lanham, MD: Lexington Books, 2006), Stanley Rosen, *Plato's Republic: A Study* (New Haven, CT: Yale University Press, 2005). See also Nicholas D. Smith, "Plato's Book of Images," in *Philosophy in Dialogue: Plato's Many Devices*, ed. Gary Scott (Evanston,

IL: Northwestern University Press, 2007), 3–14. See also a more general discussion of philosophy as *theōria* in Gerald Press, "Knowledge as Vision in Plato's Dialogues," *Journal of Neoplatonic Studies* 3, no. 2 (1995): 61–90. Kastely examines the rhetoric of Platonic imagery and its political value. James L. Kastley, *The Rhetoric of Plato's Republic* (Chicago: University of Chicago Press, 2015). Patterson explores the relationship between word and image in Richard Patterson, "Word and Image in Plato," in *Presocratics and Plato: Festschrift at Delphi in Honor of Charles Kahn*, ed. Richard Patterson, Vassilis Karasmanis, and Arnold Hermann (Las Vegas: Parmenides, 2012), 429–55. See also John Sallis, *Being and Logos: Reading the Platonic Dialogues*, 3rd ed. (Bloomington: Indiana University Press, 1996).

6. See Kastely, *Rhetoric*. See also Manuela Tecusan, "Speaking about the Unspeakable: Plato's Use of Imagery," *Apeiron* 25, no. 4 (1992): 69–87.

7. See especially Leo Strauss, *The City and Man* (Chicago: University of Chicago Press, 1978) but also David Roochnik, *Beautiful City: The Dialectical Character of Plato's Republic* (Ithaca: Cornell University Press, 2003). For a clear account of Platonic irony itself, see Charles L. Griswold, "Irony in the Platonic Dialogues," *Philosophy and Literature* 26, no. 1 (2002): 84–106.

8. In this work, I use Socrates rather than Plato to describe whatever Socrates does, and Plato when talking about authorial choices such as the decision to write in dialogue form or to stage the discussion at a particular time.

9. Jill Frank, *Poetic Justice: Rereading Plato's Republic* (Chicago: University of Chicago Press, 2018), 9–11.

10. Andrea Nightingale, *Genres in Dialogue: Plato and the Construct of Philosophy* (Cambridge: Cambridge University Press, 2000).

11. See Press, "Knowledge as Vision," who explicitly connects understanding knowledge as *theoria* to a perspectival model of knowledge. I understand my reading of the *Republic* to be largely in keeping with Press's broader account of *theoria* as well as Gonzalez's development of perspectivism. See Francisco Gonzalez, "Plato's Perspectivism," *Plato Journal* 16 (2016): 31–48, and Marina McCoy, "Perspectivism and the Philosophical Rhetoric of the Dialogue Form," *Plato Journal* 16 (2016): 49–57.

12. Here, I do not explore the question of whether Plato conceives of other forms of argumentation that are image free in other dialogues. On the one hand, Socrates clearly alludes to a form of dialectic that is not reliant on images. On the other hand, the *Republic* does not show us what it looks like, and we might argue that at least some other forms of dialectic—such as division and collection as found in the *Sophist* or *Statesman*—still do use imagery as part of their methodology. Arguing for these points, however, is beyond the scope of this work.

13. Gadamer views the *Republic* as a paradigm of justice in which the just soul can recognize itself rather than as a political plan. See Hans-Georg Gadamer, "Plato and the Poets," in *Dialogue and Dialectic: Eight Hermeneutical Studies on Plato*, trans. P. Christopher Smith (New Haven: Yale University Press, 1980), 39–72. Jill Frank argues that the very act of reading and rereading encourage us not to take

Plato as an authority but rather to engage with the text in a process of questioning and wonder. Frank, *Poetic Justice*, 15–16.

Chapter 1. Poetry and the *Republic*

1. Evidence that this may have been true of the historical Socrates can be found in Aristophanes's *Frogs* when the Chorus alludes to Socrates's desire to "cast out all the arts" and to ignore the greatness of tragedy (1491–1494).

2. For authors who see a positive role for poetry, see, for example, Drew Hyland, "Taking the Longer Road: The Irony of Plato's *Republic*," *Revue de Métaphysique et de Morale* 93, no. 3 (1988): 317–35, and Pierre Destrée, "Happiness, Justice, and Poetry in Plato's *Republic*," in *Proceedings of the Boston Area Colloquium in Ancient Philosophy*, volume 25, ed. Gary Gurtler SJ and William Wians (Leiden: Brill, 2009), 243–69. See also Nightingale's extensive work on the relationship of the form of the dialogue to earlier genres in *Genres in Dialogue* for a fuller discussion of the Platonic dialogue and its dual reliance upon and departure from a variety of Greek poetic genres. Ruby Blondell's work on character and drama of the dialogues shows Plato's large indebtedness to his predecessors. See Ruby Blondell, *The Play of Character in Plato's Dialogues* (Cambridge: Cambridge University Press, 2002). For more on the form of the dialogue, see also essays in Charles L. Griswold, ed., *Platonic Writings, Platonic Readings* (New York: Routledge, 1988).

3. Charalambopolous makes a strong case for the performative nature of the dialogues on the basis of historical evidence. See Nikos Charalambopolous, *Platonic Drama and Its Ancient Reception* (Cambridge: Cambridge University Press, 2012). Charles Kahn argues that Xenophon may even have been influenced by Plato to write dialogues. See Charles Kahn, *Plato and the Socratic Dialogue: The Philosophical Use of a Literary Form* (Cambridge: Cambridge University Press, 1998), 76–79.

4. Charalambopolous, *Platonic Drama*, 24–26.

5. Charalambopolous, *Platonic Drama*, 60–64.

6. See also Nails, who gives additional evidence for the widespread availability of styles in Plato's time, despite the relatively recent rise in literacy. Debra Nails, *Agora, Academy, and the Conduct of Philosophy* (Dordrecht: Kluwer Academic, 1995), 215–18. Havelock is perhaps the best known of those who link Platonic writing to the influence of comedy. See Eric Havelock, *Preface to Plato* (Cambridge, MA: Harvard University Press, 1982), 158–62.

7. Winslow, for example, finds the question of style to be more significant than content. See Russell Winslow, "On Mimetic Style in Plato's *Republic*," *Philosophy and Rhetoric* 45, no. 1 (2012): 46–64.

8. Mitscherling comprehensively lays out the wide range of interpretations. See Jeff Mitscherling, *The Image of the Second Sun: Plato on Poetry, Rhetoric, and the Technē of Mimēsis* (Amherst, NY: Humanity Books, 2009), 15–113. Nehamas,

for example, argues that in Book Three, the emphasis is on Homeric poetry and its specific effects on children. See Alexander Nehamas, "Plato on Imitation and Poetry in *Republic* 10," in *Plato on Beauty, Wisdom, and the Arts*, ed. J. M. E. Moravcsik and P. Temko (Totowa, NJ: Rowman & Littlefield, 1982), 47–78.

9. Havelock also argues for the centrality of education as that which offers unity to the criticism of poetry in the *Republic*. See Havelock, *Preface to Plato*, 3–15. However, Havelock also takes the criticisms of poetry to be not just Socrates's, but also Plato's own view. This approach, however, does not provide an explanatory account of why Platonic dialogue includes poetic elements as part of its substance. Commentators who wish to claim that Plato really wants to banish all poetry from education must provide some sort of an account of how the dialogue form educates and why the poetic and mythic elements persist, particularly given the great care and attention that Plato gives to *lexis*. Once one takes into account the form of Platonic dialogue, Havelock's claim that for Plato "reality is rational, scientific and logical, or it is nothing" is difficult to sustain (Havelock, 25).

10. See Mitscherling, *Image of the Second Sun*, 41. Mitscherling goes on to argue that the real target of the criticism of poetry is more specifically the sophists and their *technē* of *mimēsis*. While I agree that at moments, the sophists are a subject of Socratic criticism, the discussion is more squarely focused on poets rather than sophists.

11. See, however, Pappas's work on imitation and inspiration in the *Laws*, in which he shows how these two kinds of criticism can form a coherent whole. Nickolas Pappas, "Plato on Poetry: Imitation or Inspiration?," *Philosophy Compass* 7, no. 10 (2012): 669–78.

12. Roochnik lays out the numerous tensions between the ideal city and the action of the *Republic* in Roochnik, *Beautiful City*, 70–73.

13. See Patrick Lake's 2011 dissertation, "Plato's Homeric Dialogue: Homeric Quotation, Paraphrase, and Allusion in the *Republic*." See also Geoffrey Bakewell, "The Voice of Aeschylus in Plato's *Republic*," in *Voice and Voices in Antiquity*, ed. Niall Slater (Boston: Brill, 2016), 260–76, who argues for a variety of Platonic references to Aeschylus, as well as for a Platonic redemption of tragedy in new form.

14. See Marina Berzins McCoy, "Socrates on Simonides: The Use of Poetry in Socratic and Platonic Rhetoric," *Philosophy and Rhetoric* 32, no. 4 (1999): 349–67, and Nicholas D. Smith, "Socrates and Plato on Poetry," *Philosophic Exchange: Annual Proceedings* 37 (2006–2007): 42–54.

15. See Grace Ledbetter, *Poetics Before Plato* (Princeton, NJ: Princeton University Press, 2002).

16. Ledbetter, *Poetics Before Plato*, 3.

17. Ledbetter, *Poetics Before Plato*, 13.

18. Ledbetter, *Poetics Before Plato*, 18.

19. Stuart G. P. Small, "On Allegory in Homer," *Classical Journal* 44, no. 7 (April 1949): 423–30.

20. In contrast to those who read the dialogue as simply opposing poetic interpretation, I have argued that Socrates's interpretations of the Simonides poem allow him to set forth his own philosophical thinking, such that the inclusion of the poetry and its discussion in the dialogue reflects a Platonic reappropriation of poetry. See McCoy, "Socrates on Simonides," 349–67.

21. My interpretation of Book Ten's criticisms of imagery is reserved for a later chapter along with the rest of the analysis of Book Ten, but I generally follow Moss and Nehamas. They argue that the poets are mistakenly thought to be experts in virtue, but they imitate only the appearance of virtue in their presentation of heroes. This interpretation is consistent with Book Three's reasons for criticizing poetry and also explains why Plato can still present characters in dialogical form: because according to Plato, Socrates is a true image of virtue in a way that Homeric heroes are not. See Jessica Moss, "What Is Imitative Poetry and Why Is It Bad?," in *The Cambridge Companion to Plato's Republic*, ed. G. R. F. Ferrari (New York: Cambridge University Press, 2007), 415–44, and Nehamas, "Plato on Imitation and Poetry."

22. Commentators disagree as to how much beauty is even a consideration in the *Republic*. Christopher Janaway asserts that because the focus of the *Republic* is moral and political concerns, questions of aestheticism are being deliberately set aside. Plato is not offering a theory of aesthetics at all but rather looking at the educative value of his poetry, although he recognizes its aesthetic power. See Janaway, *Images of Excellence: Plato's Critique of the Arts* (Oxford: Clarendon Press, 1995).

23. See Gabriel Richardson Lear, "Plato on Learning to Love Beauty," in *The Blackwell Guide to Plato's Republic*, ed. Gerasimos Santas (Oxford: Blackwell, 2006), 104–23, and Destrée, "Happiness, Justice, Poetry," 253–58.

24. Lear, "Plato on Learning to Love Beauty," 113.

25. See Silvia Gastaldi, "Poetry: *Paideia* and *Mimēsis*," in *The Painter of Constitutions: Selected Essays on Plato's Republic*, ed. Mario Vegetti, Franco Ferrari, and Tosca Lynch (Sankt Augustin: Academia Verlag, 2013), 33.

26. My translation.

27. Peter Struck, *The Birth of the Symbol: Ancient Readers at the Limits of Their Texts* (Princeton, NJ: Princeton University Press, 2004), especially 4–5 and 77–110.

28. Gastaldi, "Poetry: *Paideia* and *Mimēsis*," 33, n. 47.

29. Struck, *Birth of the Symbol*, 1–20.

30. Bernard Freydburg, "Homeric *Methodos* in Plato's Socratic Dialogues," in *Philosophy in Dialogue: Plato's Many Devices*, ed. Gary Scott (Evanston, IL: Northwestern University Press, 2007), 118.

31. Along quite different lines, Frank argues that poetry can often lead to conflicting interpretations of its content, or deference to poetic authority when its meaning is not clear, as when Polemarchus cites Simonides. Frank, *Poetic Justice*, 55–60.

32. Urmson asserts that the problem with mimetic poetry is for those who do not recognize that the poetry is removed from reality, that is, it is problematic for

nonphilosophers. James Urmson, "Plato and the Poets," in *Plato's Republic: Critical Essays*, ed. Richard Kraut (Lanham, MD: Rowman & Littlefield, 1997), 223–37.

33. Roochnik, *Beautiful City*, 71.

34. Blondell says that even the presence of silent interlocutors reminds us that Socrates's arguments might not be accepted by his audience. See Blondell, *Play of Character*, 192.

35. Jill Frank undertakes an extensive exploration of what it means to be able to read and to reread the Platonic text. Frank, *Poetic Justice*, 19–49.

36. For a further elaboration on the different layers of reading a dialogue, including the notion of multivocity, see McCoy, "Perspectivism," 49–57. Frank also discusses the multivocality of words especially in relation to the *Phaedrus*'s discussion of writing in *Poetic Justice*, 21–27.

37. Although Plato's *Laws* is critical of multiple characters' voices (*Laws* 719c–e), the concern there is with lawmakers' need to proclaim and enact a single law. Poetry does not carry the burden of lawmaking in its artistic setting, and neither does philosophy as such.

38. Blondell, *Play of Character*, 206–9.

39. Frank, *Poetic Justice*, 29–30.

40. Blondell, 201–2. Here, I side with Blondell against Frank, who sees less resistance among the dramatized characters and places all the work of criticism on the part of the reader. However, if one includes Glaucon and Adeimantus's objections to Socrates's failure to win the argument against Thrasymachus, or Glaucon's rejection of the "city of sows" in favor of some other city, I think we see a bit more resistance on the part of Socrates's interlocutors, rather than total compliance.

41. Segal, "The Myth Was Saved," 316.

42. Segal, "The Myth Was Saved," 317–20. As Segal says, the use of similes and metaphors give a kind of coherence to the world in the midst of a flood of events, such as deaths on the Homeric battlefield, that might otherwise lack such unity. Repeated similes offer a sense of an eternal present and qualities that endure (e.g., "rosy fingered dawn," or the "life-giving" earth, see Segal, 319).

43. The next chapter discusses more extensively the dramatic dating of the dialogue and its sociopolitical context in the course of examining the arguments of Book One.

44. Marina Berzins McCoy, *Rhetoric of Philosophers and Sophists* (Cambridge: Cambridge University Press, 2008), 46.

45. Others who argue for the relevancy of the dialogue form to encourage better living and not only the holding of better ideas include Pierre Hadot, *Philosophy as a Way of Life: Spiritual Exercises from Socrates to Foucault* (Oxford: Wiley-Blackwell, 1995), especially 89–93, and Harvey Yunis, "The Protreptic Rhetoric of the *Republic*," in *The Cambridge Companion to Plato's Republic*, ed. G. R. F. Ferrari (New York: Cambridge University Press, 2007), 1–26.

46. Here I depart from Rowe, who sees the role of character primarily as a chance to enter into the argument from different perspectives, while continuing to emphasize only the different logical, and not only psychological, perspectives. See Christopher Rowe, "The Literary and Philosophical Style of the *Republic*," in *The Blackwell Guide to Plato's Republic*, ed. Gerasimos Santas (Oxford: Blackwell, 2006), 7–24.

47. Frank argues along similar lines for this antiauthoritative approach to poetry. See Frank, *Poetic Justice*, 50–62.

48. Here, I dissent from the interpretation that Socrates intends to describe the lie to the citizens as a kind of beneficial *pharmakon* that is necessary to politics, and even for the development of virtue. For an example of such an interpretation, see Carl Page, "The Truth about Lies in Plato's *Republic*," *Ancient Philosophy* 11 (1991): 1–33, and a thoughtful response by Daniel Dombrowski, "On the Alleged Truth about Lies in Plato's *Republic*," *Polis* 21 (2004): 93–106.

49. Along similar lines, Frank argues that the mimetic poetry of the dialogue encourages a disidentification that encourages reflection by the reader on the distance between the object and its mimetic representation, and thus opens up the reader to question and to seek to become good. Frank, *Poetic Justice*, 78–80.

50. Gabriel Lear argues that the common link between *mimēsis* in Books Two, Three, and Ten is the common emphasis on appearance: the poet-rhapsode appears to be a character while he is not, just as the painting appears to be the couch while it is not. See Lear, "Mimesis and Psychological Change in *Republic* III," in *Plato and the Poets*, ed. Pierre Destrée and Fritz-Gregor Herrmann (Leiden: Brill, 2011), 195–216. My suggestion here is that the Greek term *mimēsis* is itself already broad enough to incorporate *both* the senses of making copies and imitating characters. Conceptually, the two are not distinct in terms of a vocabulary, although Socrates does shift his attention from one aspect of what it means to imitate in Book Ten.

51. See Leon Golden, "Plato's Concept of *Mimesis*," *British Journal of Aesthetics* 15 (1975): 118–31, and Jera Marušič, "Poets and Mimesis in the *Republic*," in *Plato and the Poets*, ed. Pierre Destrée and Fritz-Gregor Herrmann (Leiden: Brill, 2011), 222–26.

52. Gerald F. Else, *Plato and Aristotle on Poetry*, ed. with notes by Peter Burian (Chapel Hill: University of North Carolina Press, 1986), 26.

53. Else, *Plato and Aristotle on Poetry*, 26–27.

54. See Havelock, *Preface to Plato*, 21–22, and Nickolas Pappas, "*Mimēsis* in Aristophanes and Plato," *Philosophical Inquiry* 21 (Summer–Fall 1999): 63.

55. Havelock similarly acknowledges the same. See Rosalind Thomas, "Prose Performance Texts: *Epideixis* and Written Publication in the Late Fifth and Early Fourth Centuries," in *Written Texts and the Rise of Literate Culture in Ancient Greece*, ed. Harvey Yunis (Cambridge: Cambridge University Press, 2003), 162–87, and Havelock, *Preface to Plato*, 37–40. Plato's *Phaedrus* treats the form of writing as

a reminder of the written word (275c–d), while Alcidamas similarly sees writing as valuable primarily when it reminds others of the oral skillfulness of the author for the sake of his later reputation. Thus, our own sense of how these distinctions "must" be experienced may not apply in Plato's own cultural milieu.

56. For example, Aristophanes's *Frogs* alludes to the audience's possession of a *biblion* of the play. See *Frogs* 1114.

57. Thomas, "*Epideixis*," 175–80.

58. Havelock comes to a similar conclusion: the author's aim is to make his audience come to a sympathetic identification with his "content." Havelock, *Preface to Plato*, 45. I would nuance this slightly to say the audience is asked to sympathetically identify with a *character*, insofar as the formative mirroring of emotions and ideas arises more naturally through interpersonal imitation rather than only the imitation of ideas.

59. Similarly, one who beholds a painting that misrepresents its objects will *imagine* the object in a skewed way, that is, have a bad *eikōn* of it.

60. Pappas, "*Mimēsis* in Aristophanes," 61–78.

61. Pappas notes that Aristophanes also treats *mimēsis* in a quite pejorative sense, for example, in *Birds*, *Frogs*, and *Clouds*. See Nickolas Pappas, "Plato's Aesthetics," 2.1, *Stanford Encyclopedia of Philosophy* (Fall 2016), ed. Edward N. Zalta, https://plato.stanford.edu/archives/fall2016/entries/plato-aesthetics/, accessed January 30, 2017.

62. Winslow takes this passive, uncritical reception of mimetic poetry to be Socrates's primary objection. Style, rather than poetic content, makes our inherited concepts problematic—and such a problem with *mimēsis* is not limited only to poets. See Winslow, "On Mimetic Style in Plato's *Republic*," 46–64.

63. By Socrates, I mean only the views of the character in the dialogue. Perhaps the historical Socrates also held some of these views, but in the absence of specific evidence, it is important to remain neutral. It might just as easily be the case that Plato thought these problems through with poetic education, and discovered through the process of writing ways to address them.

64. All three of these devices have been explored by commentators on Platonic dialogues, but my aim here is specifically to link them back to how the dialogues encourage a *mimēsis* of Socrates that provides an alternative to the total ban on poetry.

65. For key discussions of Platonic and Socratic irony, see Griswold, "Irony"; Hyland, "Longer Road"; and Jill Gordon, *Turning Toward Philosophy: Literary Device and Dramatic Structure in Plato's Dialogues* (University Park: Penn State Press, 2010), 117–33; and Gregory Vlastos, "Socratic Irony," *Classical Quarterly* 37, no. 1 (1987): 79–96.

66. For a fuller discussion of Platonic irony, see Hyland, "Longer Road," and Griswold, "Irony." More recently, see Christopher Long, *Socratic and Platonic Political Philosophy: Practicing a Politics of Reading* (Cambridge: Cambridge University Press,

2014), for a nuanced examination of differences between the Socratic and Platonic standpoint, especially in the contrast between the spoken and written word.

67. Hyland, "Longer Road," 319.

68. Roochnik, *Beautiful City*, and Howland, *Odyssey*.

69. Pappas briefly considers a similar line of inquiry in the difference between the Platonic dialogue and traditional poetry. Nickolas Pappas, *The Routledge Guidebook to Plato's Republic* (New York: Routledge, 2013), 257–59.

70. Todd Mei, following Gadamer, argues that the point of such Platonic irony is to show that *all* human understanding is hermeneutical; first, there must be an establishment both of the fact that the literal meaning of a poem is insufficient, and then the recognition that a deeper hermeneutic of opening up any given limit to a further question is necessary. See Todd Mei, "Justice and the Banning of the Poets: The Way of Hermeneutics in Plato's *Republic*," *Review of Metaphysics* 60 (June 2007): 755–78.

71. Along similar lines, Press describes the dialogues as "enacted," insofar as the dialogue creates effects in its own audience through the imagination and emotions, and not only through its propositional content. See Gerald Press, "Plato's Dialogues as Enactments," in *The Third Way: New Directions in Platonic Studies*, ed. Francisco Gonzalez (Lanham, MD: Rowman & Littlefield, 1995), 133–52.

72. For the argument that Plato's works were likely read aloud, see Blondell, *Play of Character*, 22–23, and Yunis's analysis of the popular character of Platonic works, "Protreptic Rhetoric," 9–15. See also Alcidamas, a contemporary of Plato's, who compares written speeches to statues that are mere imitations of real objects, in his work "On Those Who Write Written Speeches," in *Alcidamas, the Works and Fragments*, ed. J. Muir (London: Bristol Classical Press, 2001).

73. See also Blondell, *Play of Character*, 246. Blondell argues that a reader who is most like any one of the characters can better access the material through that character's engagement. To this, I add that the taking on of voices *different* than one's own also provides for a more expansive understanding of the problem of justice, by allowing one to go beyond the confines of personal experience.

74. Hyland, "Longer Road," 318–19; Rosen, *Plato's Republic*, 101–2; Howland, *Odyssey*, 10–11; Baracchi, *Of Myth, Life, and War*, 101.

75. Blondell agrees that Plato shows an awareness of his own literary works and how such criticisms might apply back to them, but then she argues that his exclusion of such characters after Book One suggests a Platonic rejection of such *mimēsis*. Blondell, *Play of Character*, 232. But Book One is part of the dialogue, and Adeimantus also practices *mimēsis* of poetic passages of material that goes against the regulations of the city. See also Roochnik, *Beautiful City*, 71.

76. Blondell notes the difference between mere imitation and a kind of imitation that becomes formation, through learning how to do what one begins by only imitating. Blondell, *Play of Character*, 236–38.

77. Schultz argues that the dialogue shows limits with the model of self-mastery of the emotions as a sufficient model for being responsive to the emotions, laying out the different ways in which Cephalus, Polemarchus, and Thrasymachus attempt to master their emotions, and the ways in which each of their attempts fails. See Anne-Marie Schultz, *Plato's Socrates as Narrator: A Philosophical Muse* (Lanham, MD: Lexington, 2013), 141–65.

78. Of course, as Pappas and others have remarked, even the ideal city is not exactly utopian, in passing over the simple city to accommodate Glaucon's desire for more, a desire that many human beings will share. See Pappas, *Plato's Republic*, 85.

79. See Karl Popper, *The Open Society and Its Enemies, Volume I: Plato* (New York: Routledge, 1963), 270–71.

80. Jonathan Lear also argues for the possibility that one's understanding of myth can deepen. For example, those educated philosophically might hear the noble lie and understand it in one way as children but then later, once they have seen the forms, understand its deeper sense. See Jonathan Lear, "Allegory and Myth in Plato's *Republic*," in *The Blackwell Guide to Plato's Republic*, ed. Gerasimos Santas (Oxford: Blackwell, 2006), 33–34.

81. Carmola notes that the use of the term *gennaion pseudos* points to the intergenerational tensions in politics, in Socrates's choice of *gennaios* rather than *kalos* to describe this myth of how nobility is generated across generations. See Kateri Carmola, "Noble Lying: Justice and Intergenerational Tension in Plato's *Republic*," *Political Theory* 31, no. 1 (February 2003): 39–62.

82. As Long has argued, the dialogue attempts to create a kind of musical harmony in which unity and plurality are balanced, and musical language found throughout the dialogue serves as a metaphor for such reconciliation through discussion. See Christopher Long, "Socrates and the Politics of Music: Preludes of the *Republic*," *Polis* 24, no. 1 (2007): 70–90.

83. Patricia Fagan, *Plato and Tradition: The Poetic and Cultural Context of Philosophy* (Evanston, IL: Northwestern University Press, 2013), 60–61. Howland, *Odyssey*, 105. See Hesiod, *Theogony and Works and Days*, trans. Kimberly Johnson (Evanston, IL: Northwestern University Press, 2017), 106–201.

84. Howland, *Odyssey*, 106; Pappas, *Plato's Republic*, 96; Carmola, "Noble Lying," 53–56; Fagan, *Plato and Tradition*, 60.

85. While my interpretation is distinctive from others in its particulars, I more or less align with those who see the myth not as a totalitarian exercise in control, but rather an attempt to educate its citizens in critical self-understanding. See Kerry Burch, "Plato's Myth of the Noble Lie and the Predicaments of American Civic Education," *Studies in Philosophy and Education* 26 (2007): 111–25; Eva Brann, "Music of the *Republic*," *Agon* 1 (1967): 114.

86. While he offers a different interpretation, Jonathan Lear also argues for the centrality of learning to understand allegories as allegories in "Inside and Outside the *Republic*," *Phronesis* 37, no. 2 (1992): 184–215.

87. Roochnik notes that the noble lie is designed to control *eros*, insofar as the objects of *eros* are particular: erotic love leads us to love one person more than another, but the city here is pushed away from such particular *eros* toward love of all other citizens equally. Roochnik, *Beautiful City*, 44.

88. Pappas makes a similar point but in the opposite direction, suggesting that a child who is told that the memories that he has of his origin are illusory, while the myth is real, will also grow to question what other assumptions he might have made as illusory. See Pappas, *Plato's Republic*, 97. Here I depart from Page, who argues that Plato understands lying to be just in some cases.

89. Along similar lines, Golden argues that *mimēsis* has a place to play since the total reality of the forms is not accessible to us and therefore "ascension to reality through various stages of mimesis is the only path open to us" (124).

Chapter 2. Visioning and Reenvisioning Justice

1. Portions of this chapter were originally presented at the Plato's Technical Animal workshop in ancient philosophy at St. Francis Xavier University in October 2015. I am grateful for comments and feedback received at the conference.

2. For a discussion of contemporary difficulties with settling on the language of mental imagery or representation in describing the work of the imagination, see Nigel Thomas, "Mental Imagery," in *Stanford Encyclopedia of Philosophy* (Summer 2016), ed. Edward N. Zalta, http://plato.stanford.edu/entries/mental-imagery/#Exp Rep, accessed 26 September 2016. Moreover, many cognitive scientists today use "mental imagery" as shorthand for any quasi-perceptual experience.

3. The claim that images are understood as images even at the lowest level of the divided line is argued for in the chapter on the image of the divided line (chapter 8).

4. Eventually, Socrates will also claim that the just life is identical for men and women, but at the outset, the descriptions seem to assume just men and their activities as the object of conversation.

5. Of course, Socrates also contrasts the visible world and invisible, and the lovers of sight and true philosophers. However, as I will argue, the visual model of knowledge remains central for the philosopher who is said to love the "spectacle" or sight of the truth (475e).

6. Press also argues for the dialogues more generally to be understood as about the presentation of *theōria*, understood as visions. See Press, "Plato's Dialogues as Enactments," 133–52.

7. Andrea Nightingale, *Spectacles of Truth in Classical Greek Philosophy* (Cambridge: Cambridge University Press, 2004), 94–138.

8. Segal, "The Myth Was Saved," 324.

9. Press, "Knowledge as Vision," 61–90.

10. Marina McCoy, *Wounded Heroes: Vulnerability as a Virtue in Ancient Greek Literature and Philosophy* (Oxford: Oxford University Press, 2013).

11. Homer, *Iliad* X.224.

12. Vlastos is perhaps the most famous proponent of such a view, in his work on the Socratic elenchus, in which he argues that with a typical interlocutor, Socrates's practice is to take an interlocutor's claim p, introduce an additional claim q to which the interlocutor assents, and then show that p and q are logically incompatible, such that the interlocutor must reject p. See Gregory Vlastos, "The Socratic Elenchus: Method Is All," in *Socratic Studies* (Cambridge: Cambridge University Press, 1994), 1–28.

13. Ruby Blondell lays out the evidence for the centrality of character in her chapter "A Changing Cast of Characters: *Republic*," in *Play of Character*, 165–250.

14. Segal, "The Myth Was Saved," 315–36.

15. Blondell argues that the various characters in the *Republic* also represent those who have been educated more or less conventionally, or more in a way akin to the ideal education of the philosophers in the ideal city. Those who have an education that is more philosophical display greater autonomy and philosophical progress. Cephalus is relatively conventional and unphilosophical on Blondell's reading, wedded to a traditional poetic view. See Blondell, *Play of Character*, 165–73.

16. As Howland puts it, each soul naturally loves what is its "own," so the question is whether Socratic discourse can affect such natural attachments. Howland, *Odyssey*, 60.

17. Carl Page, "The Unjust Treatment of Polemarchus," *History of Philosophy Quarterly* 7, no. 3 (1990): 245. Steinberger calls this an instance of "retrospective irony," borrowing the term from Halperin. Peter J. Steinberger, "Who Is Cephalus?," *Political Theory* 24, no. 2 (May 1996): 184. As Reeve notes, it is precisely the wealth that Cephalus thinks lends him security that leads the Tyrants to kill his family. See Reeve, *Blindness and Reorientation*, 37–38.

18. Polemarchus's brother Lysias, in his courtroom speech against Eratosthenes in response to the death of Polemarchus, uses this very language of considering the city an enemy when it ought to have been considered a friend in "Against Eratosthenes," 12.51.

19. This assumes the later dramatic date of 411 BCE, although the point still applies if the dramatic date is 421. Nails argues that neither 411 nor 421 serves adequately as an account of the dramatic date, but in either case, the Platonic audience would recall Polemarchus's death. See Debra Nails, "The Dramatic Date of Plato's *Republic*," *Classical Journal* 93 (1998): 383–96.

20. See Lysias, "Against Eratosthenes," 12.4, 12.20.

21. Blondell, *Play of Character*, 165–68. Some metics were former slaves, so while they were free citizens, they might have retained some of the lower social status associated with slavery. Others were merchants or artisans who had immigrated. Socrates's failure to address trade and the status of metics in his city is glaring, but

Plato's inclusion of them as author raises for his own audience significant questions about the just status of metics in the city.

22. Page argues that although it is playful, this "mask of tyranny" might well become reality in a person such as Polemarchus under the right conditions. Page, "Unjust Argument," 246–49.

23. Jacob Howland, *Glaucon's Fate: History, Myth, and Character in Plato's Republic* (Philadelphia: Paul Dry Books, 2018), 7.

24. Schultz argues that Polemarchus seeks to exert social control over others, and even if this seems to be done playfully here with Socrates, his joke still suggests a desire for mastery and control over others on Polemarchus's part that is in keeping with his later definition of justice as helping friends and harming enemies. See Schultz, *Plato's Socrates as Narrator*, 154–56.

25. David Schindler, *Plato's Critique of Impure Reason: On Goodness and Truth in the Republic* (Washington, DC: The Catholic University of America Press, 2008), 49.

26. Thanks to Nickolas Pappas for pointing this out.

27. Lattimore translation, Book 22.59–62. Bloom makes the connection. See Allan Bloom, trans., *The Republic of Plato*, 2nd ed. (New York: Basic Books, 1991), 441.

28. For this reason, I cannot agree with McPhee, who draws a connection between the teacher in the myth of Er in Book Ten who can teach souls which new lives are best to choose, and Cephalus, as this kind of teacher. Cephalus places his life's value in passing on his fortune and argument to Polemarchus, but neither expectation comes to fruition. See Patrick McKee, "Surprise Endings: Cephalus and the Indispensable Teacher of *Republic* X," *Philosophical Investigations* 31, no. 1 (January 2008): 68–82. Steinberger suggests the opposite, following Bloom, in arguing that the soul who chooses the life of the tyrant due to living a conventional life of virtue is akin to Cephalus. See Steinberger, "Who Is Cephalus?" What seems clear, however, is that Cephalus's choices, because they are not grounded in philosophy, have value but limited value. They do not allow him to know how to act in novel cases. Thus he is neither the teacher nor the tyrant, but potentially either one, depending on what circumstances face him. Philosophical reflection alone could move him to be a teacher, but he abandons this option when he leaves the room.

29. Bloom, for example, names Cephalus's piety as "extreme selfishness" (315). Schulz says he fears what will happen to him in the afterlife for past injustices and therefore sacrifices to the gods. See Schulz, *Plato's Socrates as Narrator*, 152–53. Howland sees Cephalus's desire to live justly as rooted in a fear of death and punishment, such that Cephalus's definition is "self-centered" and his sacrifices undertaken instrumentally. See Howland, *Odyssey*, 60–62. Kenneth Dorter, in *The Transformation of Plato's Republic* (Lanham, MD: Lexington Books, 2006), 25–26, sees Cephalus as a man of appetites. Reeve, in contrast, notes Cephalus's moderation. See C. D. C. Reeve, *Philosopher-Kings: The Argument of Plato's Republic* (Princeton, NJ: Princeton University Press, 1988), 5–6.

30. Douglas Gerber, trans., *Greek Elegiac Poetry from the Seventh to Fifth Centuries BC* (Cambridge, MA: Loeb Classical Library, 1999).

31. I am indebted to David Roochnik's work on wonder in Plato's *Theaetetus*. See David Roochnik, "Self-Recognition in Plato's *Theaetetus*," *Ancient Philosophy* 22 (2002): 37–52.

32. See Hesiod, *Theogony*, 265–67. For the chaotic role that the monstrous plays in Hesiod's mythology, see Jenny Strauss Clay, "The Generation of Monsters in Hesiod," *Classical Philology* 88, no. 2 (1993): 105–16.

33. The question of whether Socrates is poor or not is controversial, but he seems not to have had wealth or to have pursued its acquisition.

34. Contrast this to the view of Sobel, who sees the example of the madman as Plato's attempt to show that no actions are always right or always wrong, but must be tied to a kind of Platonic teleology and moral consequentialism. Jordan Howard Sobel, "Republic 331c–d," *History of Philosophy Quarterly* 4, no. 3 (July 1987): 281–90.

35. Howland argues that Cephalus is a person whose view of *eros* is one that begins and ends with sexual lust and who is essentially self-centered in his concern for money and family. Howland, *Odyssey*, 59–60. Rosen argues that Cephalus is a "moderate hedonist who spends within his means," interested in pleasure but mostly temperate and conventional in his pursuit of it. Rosen, *Plato's Republic*, 29. While Cephalus is not especially philosophically inclined, I take his own description of being happy in his old age and affirmation of the values of honesty and fair exchange to characterize the way that he has lived his own life. Cephalus does not seem anxious in his old age, but content that he has lived his life well according to his own model of justice. Still, his view is limited with respect to the mercantile domain in which it mostly remains.

36. Roochnik argues extensively and persuasively for the centrality of *eros* to philosophical practice. *Eros*, if properly understood, includes a desire for wisdom and not only bodily desires. Roochnik, *Beautiful City*, 52–53. Jill Gordon further develops the place of *eros* in Platonic philosophy in *Plato's Erotic World: From Cosmic Origins to Human Death* (Cambridge: Cambridge University Press, 2012).

37. D. Campbell, *Greek Lyric III*, 2nd edition (Cambridge, MA: Harvard University Press, 1991), 359. Of course, such a view of Simonides may well be inaccurate, given that so many sources for his work are indirect and incomplete.

38. As Kimon Lycos has argued, Book One moves the reader from an action-oriented view of justice to a more theoretical conception. See Kimon Lycos, *Plato on Justice and Power: Reading Book I of Plato's Republic* (Albany: State University of New York Press, 1987).

39. Aristotle also examines this form of argument in *Prior Analytics*, 69a. Commentators on Aristotle disagree as to whether this form of argument moves straight from one part to another, or from part to universal and back to part. My argument here does not depend on resolving the problem in Aristotle, since Soc-

rates here uses parts in order to talk explicitly about universals. For more on this controversy and a textual argument for the inclusion of the universal, see William Benoit, "Aristotle's Example: The Rhetorical Induction," *Quarterly Journal of Speech* 66, no. 2 (1980): 183–89. Hauser argues for the possibility of an intuitive connection from part to part, in which reasoners are not always aware of the universal in an explicit sense. My own view follows Hauser in thinking that both kinds of paradigmatic reasoning can occur. An argument that includes the universal is more logically complete, but connecting particulars to one another is a means by which the universal can come to light and be grasped. The universal can become clearer in the very course of making sense of how particulars relate. See Gerard A. Hauser, "Aristotle's Example Revisited," *Philosophy and Rhetoric* 18, no. 3 (1985): 171–80, and Hauser, "Reply to Benoit," *Philosophy and Rhetoric* 20, no. 4 (1987): 268–73.

40. See Maria Jose Martin-Velasco, "The Paradigm in Aristotle's *Rhetoric* and Its Use in Judicial Speeches," Institute of Classical Studies talk, December 9, 2010.

41. Martin-Velasco, "Paradigm in Aristotle's *Rhetoric*," 3.

42. As Martin-Velasco points out, Lysias himself uses this structure of arguing from *paradeigma* in his speech "On the Property of Aristophanes." See Martin-Velasco, "Paradigm in Aristotle's *Rhetoric*," 8–12.

43. Of course, this is also true of Aristotelian *epagōgē* in the presentation in the *Prior Analytics* where attending to particulars leads to insight into a universal. The Aristotelian account of induction (*epagōgē*) is controversial, since there are several variations on exactly *how* insight into the universal is acquired. I follow Engberg-Pederson's account that it is *nous* that does the work of grasping the general point, but that the general point may be true or false. See Engberg-Pederson, "More on Aristotelian Epagoge," *Phronesis* 24, no. 3 (January 1979): 301–19. However, my point here is that Socrates's discussion with Polemarchus and Thrasymachus is not simply a case of inductive argument that persuades or fails to be persuasive because his interlocutors are either good reasoners or bad ones. Rather, the claim is that these interlocutors choose their particular examples from the basis of their own lived experiences, and they disagree as to which universals *can* be legitimately inferred from those particulars.

44. Page, "Unjust Argument," 252.

45. Blondell notes that Polemarchus is an elenctic success, yet may be almost too pliable in his willingness to change views so quickly, and a certain deficiency in the elenchus that it does not always encourage independent thinking on the part of an interlocutor. Blondell, *Play of Character*, 178–79. But Page reminds us of the line from the *Phaedrus* in which Polemarchus is said to have been "turned toward philosophy" (*Phaedrus* 257b). Page, "Unjust Argument," 245.

46. As Kastely says, persuasion is not manipulation, since the aim of manipulation is to impose one's order on another, while in persuasion the goal is for "the audience to understand and embody the order that is proposed to it." Kastely, *Rhetoric*, 5.

Chapter 3. Paradigmatic Argument and Its Limits

1. As Blondell has argued, there is a gradual deepening of the challenge to tradition in the three interlocutors: Cephalus unreflectively embraces tradition, Polemarchus wonders about its value, and Thrasymachus rejects it outright. See Blondell, *Play of Character*, 189.

2. The separation of Plato as author from the characters in this dialogue has a long history in the works of figures such as Klein, Hyland, Sallis, Howland, Blondell, and Roochnik, who in a variety of ways note that how Plato writes is separable from what his characters say. For a recent analysis of the meaning of Platonic writing as technological innovation and as a form of political practice, see Long, *Socratic and Platonic Political Philosophy*.

3. Kastely notes the congruity. Kastely, *Rhetoric*, 38.

4. See Marina McCoy, "Sophistry and Philosophy in Plato's *Republic*," *Polis* 22, no. 2 (2005): 265–86.

5. T. D. J. Chappell, "Thrasymachus and Definition," *Oxford Studies in Ancient Philosophy* 18 (2000): 101–7.

6. Julia Annas helpfully lays out the terms conventionalism and immoralism here and argues that Thrasymachus is an immoralist. See Annas, *An Introduction to Plato's Republic* (Oxford: Oxford University Press, 1981). Others who see Thrasymachus as an immoralist include Pappas, *Plato's Republic*, 59–70, and Rachel Barney, "Socrates' Refutation of Thrasymachus," in *The Blackwell Guide to Plato's Republic*, ed. Gerasimos Santas (Malden, MA: Wiley-Blackwell, 2006), 44–62. In contrast, Bloom takes the point of view that Thrasymachus is a conventionalist, writing that "Thrasymachus' definition of justice is really the same as the city's and . . . he acts as its representative." See Bloom, *Republic*, 326. A. E. Taylor, *Plato, the Man and His Work* (New York: Meridian, 1960 rpt.) argues that Thrasymachus is an ethical nihilist. For a different take, see T. J. Henderson, "In Defense of Thrasymachus," *American Philosophical Quarterly* 7 (1970): 218–28, who argues that the "advantage of the stronger" means that in any interaction, if one party acts justly he is left vulnerable to the actions of the other party. G. B. Kerferd, "The Doctrine of Thrasymachus in Plato's *Republic*," *Durham University Journal* 9 (1947): 19–27, suggests that justice always means "another's good" for both ruled and ruler, and that the initial definition Thrasymachus proposes is a "deliberate paradox framed in terms such as to arrest the attention" of those present (26). Cross and Woozley, *Plato's Republic: A Philosophical Commentary* (London: MacMillan, 1964), 38–41, argue that Thrasymachus is simply inconsistent. See also Theodore L. Putterman, "Socrates/Thrasymachus: The Extent of Their Agreement," *Polis* 17 (2000): 79–90, who argues that Thrasymachus is initially a conventionalist but later is amoral (if not immoral) in his approach to human nature.

7. Barney and Santas also see Thrasymachus's view as an empirical, descriptive statement, and not as normative. See Rachel Barney, "Callicles and Thrasymachus,"

Stanford Encyclopedia of Philosophy (Winter 2011), ed. Edward N. Zalta, https://plato.stanford.edu/archives/win2011/entries/callicles-thrasymachus, accessed August 20, 2015, and Gerasimos Santas, "Methods of Reasoning about Justice," in *The Blackwell Guide to Plato's Republic*, ed. Gerasimos Santas (Malden, MA: Blackwell, 2006), 125–45. Pappas similarly uses the term "naturalistic" to describe the Thrasymachean position. See Pappas, *Plato's Republic*, 60. Hourani sees instead a legalistic view, seeing Thrasymachus's real definition of justice as "obedience to the laws." See George F. Hourani, "Thrasymachus' Definition of Justice in Plato's *Republic*," *Phronesis* 7 (1962): 110–20.

8. As Anderson argues, Socrates and Thrasymachus do not even have the same sorts of ideas about what it means to talk about justice. Socrates wants to attribute stable claims to the nature of justice, while Thrasymachus dislikes even that assumption, preferring to treat justice descriptively and in terms of changing histories that contribute to what it means in different cities at different times. Still, this knowledge can guide our ideas as to how best to act. See Merrick E. Anderson, "Thrasymachus' Sophistic Account of Justice in Republic I," *Ancient Philosophy* 36 (2016): 151–72.

9. Long notes the language of music used in the dialogue, and he argues that while Thrasymachus threatens to disrupt civic unity and Adeimantus to impose it without allowing for difference, Socrates develops a vision of harmony in which both unity and difference are preserved. See Long, "Socrates and the Politics of Music," 70–90.

10. Kimon Lycos persuasively argues that the aim of Book One is to support a movement away from justice and its external effects, as per the traditional Greek view, and toward the Socratic-Platonic understanding of justice as internalized as the condition for a good life. See Kimon Lycos, *Plato on Justice and Power: Reading Book I of Plato's Republic* (Albany: State University of New York Press, 1987).

11. Santas takes Thrasymachus simply to be making a purely empirical argument that generalizes across a number of different kinds of regimes in asserting that justice is the advantage of the stronger. In contrast, I argue that Thrasymachus is immediately normative about his claims: a ruler who is knowledgeable will seek his own advantage (or if a group rules, they will seek their own advantage), and this is for the best, for him (or them). See Gerasimos Santas, *Understanding Plato's Republic* (Malden, MA: Wiley-Blackwell, 2010), 16–19.

12. Here Socrates and Thrasymachus agree on a fundamental point: the true ruler possesses knowledge. See Barney, "Socrates' Refutation of Thrasymachus," 48. Santas argues that Plato is trying to show the logical gap between the laws of particular societies and justice, since the former can be mistaken, but it is Thrasymachus and not Socrates who offers the idea of the true ruler as one who knows and does not make mistakes. See Santas, *Understanding Plato's Republic*, 19–20.

13. Rosen argues that Socrates cannot favor a view of justice as a *technē*, because a *technē* can be used well or badly, while justice is clearly about what is

beneficial. However, Socrates does not assume that a *technē* cannot be used to describe activities that include value judgments: for example, a doctor here cares for the good of his patient and does not just know how to produce health. See Rosen, *Plato's Republic*, 44. At the same time, I am sympathetic to Roochnik's claim that the nature of philosophical practice will later be considerably widened beyond the realm of the technical as a dialectical development of the text. See Roochnik, *Beautiful City*. However, just because justice is more than an ordinary *technē* as it is developed in later books, does not mean that there is no value at all in Socrates's comparison of justice to a *technē*: if justice requires knowledge, then it makes sense to look at other instances of knowledge that care about the good of those over which they rule.

14. See, for example, Cross and Woozley, *Plato's Republic*, chapter 2.

15. Robert Neil in his appendix to Aristophanes's *Knights* notes that the work of the *balaneus* was among the lowest public roles of both men and women, and so is used as a term of insult in that work. See Aristophanes's *Knights* (Cambridge: Cambridge University Press, 1901), 1403. Socrates's use is as an insult as well, despite the fact that Thrasymachus has argued in a manner consistent with Socrates's mode of argumentation, albeit with radically different conclusions. Of course, Thrasymachus does not hear these thoughts of Socrates, only the narrative audience. See Schultz, *Plato's Socrates as Narrator*, 156–59, for more on how Socrates's narration gives the Platonic audience insight into Thrasymachus's character and the limits of self-restraint as a response to emotional regulation.

16. C. E. Graves notes the parallels to the similar sounding phrase at *Republic* 344d in his appendix to a Cambridge Greek edition of Aristophanes's *Wasps* (Cambridge: Cambridge University Press, 1899), 130.

17. Reeve, *Philosopher-Kings*, 20, likewise sees Socrates's argument as weak, noting that other competitors in crafts such as boxing try to "outdo" their opponents all the time.

18. Moore argues for the significance of the blush: on Thrasymachus's view, excellence is a result of both knowledge and victory, but Socrates forces him to choose between the two leading to Thrasymachus's shame. See also Holly Moore, "Why Does Thrasymachus Blush? Ethical Consistency in Socrates' Refutation of Thrasymachus," *Polis* 32 (2015): 321–43.

19. Howland, *Glaucon's Fate*, 125.

20. Dorter takes the arguments of Book One to be insufficient because they remain only at the level of *eikasia*, as Dorter applies back the structure of the divided line to the dialogue as a whole. See Dorter, *Transformation of Plato's Republic*, 45–46.

21. Pappas argues that Book One represents a view more like the Socrates that Plato had known, while the remainder of the dialogue is a more distinctively Platonic thesis. Pappas, *Routledge Guidebook*, 70.

22. Lycos, *Plato on Justice and Power*. Lycos also notes that the *technē* analogy is only an analogy, insofar as one can be the giver or recipient of the art of

medicine, but justice is different: everyone participates in justice, like it or not, in being part of a city. See Lycos, *Plato on Justice and Power*, 168.

23. Dusty Hoesly and Nicholas D. Smith, "Thrasymachus: Diagnosis and Treatment," *Dialogues on Plato's Politeia (Republic): Selected Papers from the Ninth Symposium Platonicum* (Sankt Augustin: Academic Verlag), 60–65. Along similar lines, Howland argues that Thrasymachus shows himself to esteem the truth in his argument with Socrates, and yet his claims about injustice would seem to support a covert and self-serving approach to speechmaking that Thrasymachus does not, in fact, really admire. See Howland, *Odyssey*, 74–75. See also Peter J. Hansen, "Thrasymachus and His Attachment to Justice," *Polis* 32 (2015): 344–68.

24. See Debra Nails, *The People of Plato: A Prosopography of Plato and Other Socratics* (Indianapolis: Hackett, 2002), 154–56, who lays out the evidence clearly.

25. Nails, *People of Plato*, 251. See also Lysias, "Against Eratosthenes," in *Greek Orators—I* (Aris and Philips, 1985).

26. As a further complication, in 403 Lysias was briefly awarded the status of citizen, but then the decree was revoked.

27. Either in a few years or in twenty, depending on the dating of the dialogue.

28. This Euthydemus cannot be identified with Euthydemus of Chios, the sophist, who is named in the dialogue the *Euthydemus*. See Nails, *People of Plato*, 151–52.

29. Jacob Howland, "Plato's Reply to Lysias: *Republic* 1 and 2 and *Against Eratosthenes*," *American Journal of Philology* 125, no. 2 (2004): 179–208.

30. Howland, "Plato's Reply to Lysias," 185–88.

31. Howland, "Plato's Reply to Lysias," 196–99.

32. Socrates himself is an interesting contrast, for in the *Apology* he claims not to have acted against Leon of Salamis or to have followed the council's bad decision about killing the generals without a trial. The *Apology* tries to present Socrates as not taking sides in the democratic-oligarchic factions: he cares for everyone's soul and refuses to act unjustly no matter who is in charge. But this is not enough to rescue Socrates from the charge of not really supporting the democracy either, although one might argue that dramatically situating Socrates in conversation with these characters in the Piraeus is Plato's attempt to show his alliances to them.

33. See Long, *Socratic and Platonic Philosophy*, 180–85, for his reflections on imaginative response.

Chapter 4. Narrative, Poetry, and Analogical Strategies of Argument

1. Kastely, *Rhetoric*, 48. Kastely sees Socrates's arguments as rhetorical and not epistemological, but I argue that the persuasiveness that Socrates seeks is of a philosophical kind. However, to the extent that he also carefully chooses images

that help his particular interlocutors to learn about justice in a way that is especially suitable for them, there are rhetorical dimensions to Socrates's practice. The same idea can be learned about from different perspectives and Socrates's images are suitable to Glaucon and Adeimantus's concerns, which form part of their characters.

2. Portions of this chapter were presented at the Ancient Philosophy Society annual meeting in April of 2016 and published as "Myth and Argument in Glaucon's Account of Gyges's Ring and Adeimantus's Use of Poetry," in *Logoi and Muthoi*, ed. William Wians (Albany: State University of New York Press, 2019), 266–78. See also Long, "Socrates and the Politics of Music," for an account of the musical movement of the *Republic*'s arguments.

3. See Haydn Ausland, "Socrates' Argumentative Burden in the *Republic*," in *Plato as Author: The Rhetoric of Philosophy*, ed. Ann N. Michelini (Leiden: Brill, 2003), 123–24.

4. In contrast, Weiss takes Glaucon and Adeimantus really to favor the unjust life. See Roslyn Weiss, "Wise Guys and Smart Alecks in Republic 1 and 2," in *The Cambridge Companion to Plato's Republic*, ed. G. R. F. Ferrari (New York: Cambridge University Press, 2007), 99–106.

5. Despite many attempts by commentators to connect these three categories to contemporary philosophical categories, such as consequentialism or deontology, Annas rightly says that the categorical formulations are not quite identical to any such theories and need to be taken on their own terms. Annas, *Introduction*, 60–63.

6. For example, Aristotle relies on this distinction in the *Topics* 118b20–22 and implicitly in the framing of the *Nicomachean Ethics* as well in considering whether happiness is chosen for its own sake or for the sake of other goods.

7. Rosen notes that the language used here is both reminiscent of Aristotle and of Platonic language of the forms. At 357b, Glaucon refers to *toionde ti agathon*, which Rosen translates as "a good of such a kind" and later *triton ti eidos*, "a third kind of form," at 357c. See Rosen, *Plato's Republic*, 61–62.

8. While the exact dating of the *Dissoi Logoi* is controversial, most scholars date it prior to 420 BCE on the basis of its reference to Polyclitus the sculptor's son. Plato's *Protagoras* refers to a second son, but the *Dissoi Logoi* to only one, thus suggesting that if the dramatic date of the *Protagoras* is around 420 BC, the *Dissoi Logoi* must have been written before a second son was born. See T. M. Robinson, *Contrasting Arguments: An Edition of the Dissoi Logoi* (New York: Arno Press, 1979), 34–35. At any rate, the fifth century is generally agreed upon as the time frame, such that Glaucon's argumentative suggestion is in keeping with other thinkers' practices at the time.

9. See, for example, Poulakos, who argues that the *Dissoi Logoi* is a sophistic work that emphasizes the capacity to argue either side of any argument. See John Poulakos, *Sophistical Rhetoric in Classical Greece* (Columbia: University of South Carolina Press, 1995), 57–58.

10. See Ausland, "Socrates' Argumentative Burden in the *Republic*," 123–51.

11. Ausland, "Socrates' Argumentative Burden in the *Republic*," 128. Moreover, Ausland notes Glaucon's language here makes reference to *krisis* at 360e, and to praise, *encomiazomenon*, at 358d.

12. For a fuller argument that Glaucon's initial argument here is contractarian, see Santas, *Understanding Plato's Republic*, 37–41. Santas takes this contractarian view to be Glaucon's own, but it seems clear to me that Glaucon offers it as part of building up a Thrasymachean case with the hope that Socrates will be able to demolish it by giving a counterargument.

13. Jacob Howland also argues extensively for the view that *mythos* is indispensable to the *Republic* and its *logos*. See Jacob Howland, "Storytelling and Philosophy in Plato's *Republic*," *American Catholic Philosophical Quarterly* 79, no. 2 (2005): 213–32.

14. Thanks to Jacob Howland for pointing this out to me.

15. Here, I am arguing that the example of the shepherd and the ring is not merely a thought experiment, insofar as the question of self-knowledge in enacting any given thought experiment is not necessarily paramount. Plato is not only after our moral intuitions, but also displaying the power of *mythos* and especially its mimetic powers. Two authors who treat this as a thought experiment in a way to which I am generally friendly are Shields and Miščević. See Christopher Shields, "Plato's Challenge: The Case Against Justice in Republic II," in *The Blackwell Guide to Plato's Republic*, edited by Gerasimos Santas (Malden, MA: Wiley-Blackwell, 2006), 63–83, and Nenad Miščević, "Plato's *Republic* as a Political Thought Experiment," *Croatian Journal of Philosophy* 35 (January 2012): 153–65.

16. As Sonja Tanner argues in her book *In Praise of Plato's Poetic Imagination*, Horace later explicitly links poetry's emotional effects on its audience to *mimēsis*, and Plato's Ion connects the partial mimetic identification of the actor to the character whom he imitates as fundamental to his ability to act well (*Ion* 535c). See Tanner, *In Praise of Plato's Poetic Imagination* (Lanham, MD: Lexington Books, 2010), 77.

17. Schultz argues that Socrates's narration and his frequent inclusion of his feelings about the situation at hand, such as responses of fear, models a form of self-mastery in which Socrates shows the listener how to be responsive to emotions in which one neither ignores emotions nor is ruled by them, but rather is responsive to them. See, for example, her helpful reflections on Socrates's *aporia* in Book Two, and his capacity to regulate his desire for answers to questions about justice in *Plato's Socrates as Narrator*, 179.

18. See, for example, Rosen, *Plato's Republic*, 12; Howland, *The Republic*, 78–83; Roochnik, *Beautiful City*, 55–57; and Schultz, *Plato's Socrates as Narrator*, 160. More recently, Howland has argued that Glaucon's political ambition may have led him to involvement with the Thirty Tyrants. See Howland, *Glaucon's Fate*, 22–51.

19. Here I am thinking of Socrates's refusal to harm the generals and Leon of Salamis.

20. As Howland writes, "Like Socrates, we attempt to move by means of imagination and inference from the visible exterior of Plato's *dramatis personae* to their invisible interior." Howland, "Storytelling and Philosophy," 217.

21. In the *Sophist*, the distinction between eikastics and phantastics helps to further elucidate the difference between a positive and negative use of the imagination, as Tanner has argued. See Tanner, *In Praise of Plato's Poetic Imagination*, 92–103, for more on eikastics and phantastics in the *Sophist*.

22. Tanner, *In Praise of Plato's Poetic Imagination*, 103.

23. Lake, "Plato's Homeric Dialogue," 126.

24. Ausland also notes the use of epideictic, forensic, as well as deliberative elements in Adeimantus's speech, in "Socrates' Argumentative Burden," 133–43.

25. As Annas says, the two brothers' speeches are different but their desire for Socrates to show why justice is good in itself is the same. Annas, *Introduction*, 66.

26. Similarly, in Plato's *Protagoras* Socrates protests the value of the interpretation of poetry in contrast to speaking on behalf of one's own ideas, but then also offers an interpretation of Simonides that is reflective of Socratic concerns. See McCoy, "Socrates on Simonides."

27. In contrast, Stanley Rosen argues in *Plato's Republic: A Study* that the poets are for Adeimantus a "powerful contribution to the corruption of the many" and even pandering to the many (67–68). They may well be, but this is in part due to how the material of the poets is received and treated, which is not the only way in which one can respond to poetry.

28. The Hesiodic reference is to *Works and Days*, 232–34, and clearly concerns the benefits accorded to an entire land, not only an individual, when the ruler makes just judgments.

29. Howland, "Storytelling and Philosophy," 216, notes the brothers' openness to the question of the good life as what Socrates names as "divine."

30. Rosen asserts that one's own soul is closer to oneself than the external city is, and therefore the soul should have greater priority here. See Rosen, *Plato's Republic*, 70–71. However, the soul is not directly visible even to oneself, but only indirectly through actions, desires, and conflicts between desires, as Book Four will make clear.

31. Pappas argues that the analogy is a hypothetical one: it is tentative, and relies on many ideas already in Book One as its basis, but Socrates is open to seeing whether the analogy will help us to better understand justice. Before the analogy is explored, its success is uncertain. See Pappas, *The Routledge Guidebook to Plato's Republic*, 80. My explorations here are compatible with that view and seek to articulate how it functions as a possible (but not certain) mode of discovery.

32. See Bernard Williams, "The Analogy of City and Soul in Plato's *Republic*," in *Plato's Republic: Critical Essays*, ed. Richard Kraut (Lanham, MD: Rowman &

Littlefield, 1997), 49–94. In contrast, Lear argues that the city-soul isomorphism is causal, that is, that the processes of internalization and externalization produce the isomorphism between justice in the city and justice in the soul. See Lear, "Inside and Outside the *Republic*."

33. Rosen also notes the tentative nature of the identification, as also seen in Socrates's use of the term *"pou* (perhaps)" at 368d. See Rosen, *Plato's Republic*, 70.

34. Though one can try to save the argument by stating that the craftsmen are ruled over by the guardian's rationality, in being obedient to it, this solution changes the idealized image of the just soul as ruled by its own reason.

35. Christopher Long, "Who Let the Dogs Out?," in *Plato's Animals*, ed. Jeremy Bell and Michael Naas (Bloomington: Indiana University Press, 2015), 131–45.

36. The vast majority of images that Plato as author uses in the *Republic* are not analogies but rather similes and metaphors. For a thorough list of the stunning diversity and frequency of such images, see Dorothy Tarrant, "Imagery in Plato's *Republic*," *Classical Quarterly* 40, no. 1 (1946): 27–34.

37. As Bloom notes in this commentary, n. 24, 448.

38. At least until Socrates's interlocutors insist on further exploring the political problems that interest them.

39. Bartha argues that this second kind of argument from analogy, from similarity, is far more like what we commonly name as analogical argument today than is argument from paradigm. See Paul Bartha, "Analogy and Analogical Reasoning," *Stanford Encyclopedia of Philosophy* (Fall 2013), ed. Edward N. Zalta, http://plato.stanford.edu/archives/fall2013/entries/reasoning-analogy/, accessed June 11, 2015.

40. Commentators are divided on whether Socrates's assumption that justice is easier to see in the city than in the soul is a reasonable one. Santas notes that no one can look into another's soul but all can look at the just city, emphasizing the public accessibility of justice in the polis. See Santas, *Understanding Plato's Republic*, 56. Rosen points out that one's personal soul is easier to access than the nature of any city outside of us. See Rosen, *Plato's Republic*, 71. Given the complexity and difficulty of the task of characterizing the nature of the soul, even in Book Four, however, whether one's own soul can be known with precision seems questionable.

41. Rosen suggests that Socrates hopes that the trait will somehow emerge through the course of their discussion. Rosen, *Plato's Republic*, 71.

42. As Santas notes, Thrasymachus did not assume any such isomorphism between the just individual and the just city. The just person obeys the city's laws and the unjust one disobeys them, but there is no shared characteristic or cause that leads us to call both by the name of justice. See Santas, *Understanding Plato's Republic*, 57. Benardete takes the lack of argument for the isomorphism even further: "Socrates' proposal is on the face of it absurd" (45). See Seth Benardete, *Socrates' Second Sailing: On Plato's Republic* (Chicago: University of Chicago Press, 1989).

43. See G. E. R. Lloyd, *Polarity and Analogy* (Cambridge: Cambridge University Press, 1966), and Bartha, "Analogy and Analogical Reasoning."

44. As Lear argues, the soul portrayed later is not a psychic unity; most souls such as the oligarchic soul are fragmented psyches that are unable to achieve the kind of union that would result in true psychological wholeness. See Lear, "Inside and Outside the *Republic*," 184–215. However, although there is only one class in the simple city, there are different kinds of specialized work, and so analogously there is also potential for conflict between those different kinds of work of the soul. As Annas points out, even the simple city already demonstrates the growth of both justice and injustice (369a). See Annas, *Introduction*, 78.

45. Here one can easily see why Plato pursues the possibility of recollection in the *Meno*.

46. One might object that Socrates (or at least Plato) already knew the features that were in common between city and soul and is simply teaching these features to the others, but at some point he had to make the connection between city and soul and make such an imaginative leap himself. Moreover, if we see the analogy as already developed before Socrates teaches his friends, then Socrates's claim that they are using the "bigger letters" to learn what the smaller ones say would not really be true.

Chapter 5. Images of Justice

1. To the extent that this argument depends on a particular way of reading images of the forms in the middle books, its full defense cannot be made until later chapters.

2. Portions of this discussion are reprinted with permission from "The City of Sows and Sexual Differentiation in Plato's *Republic*," in *Plato's Animals*, ed. Jeremy Bell and Michael Naas (Bloomington: Indiana University Press, 2015), 149–60. (Translations of the *Republic* in this material are Allan Bloom's.) As an example of commentators who take the city of sows to point to animality, see also Christopher Berry, "Of Pigs and Men: Luxury in Plato's *Republic*," *Polis* 8 (1989): 2–24.

3. Walter Burkert, *Greek Religion* (Cambridge, MA: Harvard University Press, 1987), 242.

4. H. S. Versnel, "The Festival for Bona Dea and the Thesmophoria," *Greece & Rome* 39 (1992): 34.

5. Walter Burkert, "The Myth of Kore and Pig-Sacrifice," in *Homo Necans: The Anthropology of Ancient Greek Sacrificial Ritual and Myth*, trans. Peter Bing (Berkeley: University of California Press, 1983), 257.

6. Burkert, *Greek Religion*, 242.

7. Versnel, "Festival for Bona Dea," 34.

8. Burkert, *Greek Religion*, 242.

9. For more on the nature of such primitivism in the festival itself, see Versnel, "Festival for Bona Dea," 37–38.

10. Versnel, "Festival for Bona Dea," 35.

11. Burkert, *Greek Religion*, 244.

12. Catherine McKeen, "Swillsburg City Limits (the 'City of Pigs': 'Republic' 370C–372D)," *Polis* 21 (2004): 72.

13. Burkert, *Greek Religion*, 244.

14. Jeffrey Henderson, *The Maculate Muse: Obscene Language in Attic Comedy* (Oxford University Press, 1991), 131–32.

15. Henderson, *Maculate Muse*, 131–32.

16. Burkert, *Homo Necans*, 259.

17. Burkert, *Homo Necans*, 260.

18. Susan Guettel Cole, "Demeter in the Ancient Greek City and Its Countryside," in *Oxford Readings in Greek Religion*, ed. Richard Buxton (Oxford: Oxford University Press, 2000), 139.

19. Cole, "Demeter," 137.

20. Howland, *Odyssey*, 90–91.

21. Of course, the reading of the soul as tripartite is the standard view. See, for example, Christopher Bobonich, *Plato's Utopia Recast: His Later Ethics and Politics* (Oxford: Clarendon Press, 2002), 528–30; John Cooper, "Plato's Theory of Human Motivation," *History of Philosophy Quarterly* 1, no. 1 (1984): 3–21; George Klosko, *The Development of Plato's Thought* (New York: Methuen, 1986), 64–71; Nicholas White, *A Companion to Plato's Republic*, 2nd edition (Indianapolis: Hackett, 1979), 123; and Santas, *Understanding*, 79–89, though Santas is quite careful to examine different options for what is meant by part or power.

22. See Roochnik, *Beautiful City*, especially 17–20. Annas also notes the development of reason with the later additional clarification that reason desires to know the forms, distinguishing it from a Humean view of reason. Annas, *Introduction*, 141.

23. Ludwig shows the difficulty with reconciling *eros* (even bodily *eros*, not only intellectual *eros*) in the *Republic* with *eros* in dialogues such as the *Symposium*. See Paul Ludwig, "Eros in the *Republic*," in *The Cambridge Companion to Plato's Republic*, ed. G. R. F Ferrari (New York: Cambridge University Press), 202–31.

24. Pappas, *Plato's Republic*, 111.

25. Similarly, Blössner argues that the aristocratic, timocratic, oligarchic, and other soul types of Book Nine are only that: "types" and not real people. This fact should be central to our interpretation of them. See Norbert Blössner, "The City-Soul Analogy," in *The Cambridge Companion to Plato's Republic*, ed. G. R. F. Ferrari (New York: Cambridge University Press, 2007), 345–85.

26. Long, "Socrates and the Politics of Music."

27. While one might wish to locate spirit as the seat of the emotions, only some emotions fit well into spirit. Anger, fear, patriotism, and a desire to compete fit well. But the loving affection that is held for friends, distinct from both *eros* and from a rational judgment about another's good, is harder to fit into the threefold

analysis. Even the love of sight and sound, later contrasted with true philosophy, seems to belong neither to the appetites nor to reason.

28. Various names have been given to this principle. Bobonich calls it the PNC, principle of noncontradiction. Here, I follow Klosko and Reeve with "principle of opposites." See Bobonich, *Plato's Utopia Recast*, 529; Klosko, *Development of Plato's Thought*, 66; and Reeve, *Philosopher-Kings*, 118–23. Annas correctly argues that this is not a principle of noncontradiction, which would concern propositions, but more like a Principle of Conflict that concerns how aspects of the soul can relate. See Annas, *Introduction*, 137. Price argues that the text is ambivalent as to whether the parts of the soul are more like psychological subjects or aspects of a soul, but leans toward the latter. See Anthony Price, "Are Plato's Soul-Parts Psychological Subjects?," *Ancient Philosophy* 29, no. 1 (2009): 1–15.

29. Charles H. Kahn, "Plato's Theory of Desire," *Review of Metaphysics* 41, no. 1 (1987): 77–103. For a slightly different take on the soul while also affirming the centrality of motivation, see Cooper, "Plato's Theory of Human Motivation," who argues that reason desires to rule over the other soul parts. Thus reason is neither mere intellectual curiosity, nor a bare rational principle, but has its own kind of desires.

30. Thus the distinction between Socrates's theory and that of Kant or Hume is apparent.

31. Kahn, "Plato's Theory of Desire," 81.

32. As Roochnik argues, however, the attention given to the soul as desiring rather than only as calculative develops over the course of the dialogue. Book Four in itself says relatively little about the desiring nature of reason.

33. For example, see Annas, *Introduction*, 124; Roochnik, *Beautiful City*, 27–28, Klosko, *Development of Plato's Thought*, 66. As Annas notes, the translation of Greek into readable English has led to the need to use the language of parts, kinds, things, and so on, in ways not present in the original Greek.

34. Or, where Socrates simply uses the term *pleiō* (more) (436c), a translator might render "plurality" for the sake of good English grammar, which suggests more precise ontology than in the Greek.

35. In addition, Socrates says that the "same forms" are present in the soul as in the city when describing the civic and individual virtues (435c).

36. For example, whether the parts of the Platonic soul are agents or faculties of the soul is a question of contemporary philosophical discourse, but not the kind of philosophical distinction that Socrates himself draws—even though Socrates says he is trying to be "precise" about the soul at 436c! For a clear summary of the debate, see Santas, *Understanding*, 81–88.

37. Jonathan Lear argues for the changeable nature of the soul and the ways in which city shapes soul and vice versa through processes of internalization and externalization in "Inside and Outside the *Republic*," 184–215. Lear's solution is elegant and contains many psychological truths to which Socrates might well be

amenable, but as Ferrari argues, Socrates does not invoke internalization or other causal processes when he applies the city-soul analogy. See Giovanni R. F. Ferrari, *City and Soul in Plato's Republic* (Sankt Augustin: Academia Verlag, 2003), 50–53.

38. And even in cases of strong internal conflict, there is a deeper unity to the soul that is experiencing the conflict, as Rosen rightly notes. Rosen, *Plato's Republic*, 157.

39. Bobonich objects that understanding the parts of the soul as a metaphor is too weak, since it then does not tell us what the underlying reality of the soul is. Bobonich, *Plato's Utopia Recast*, 254. However, a paradigmatic image is stronger than a metaphor, but weaker than a claim to be a precise account of the soul's nature.

40. While he argues in favor of tripartition, Burnyeat argues that Plato goes out of his way not to rely on the theory of forms or any strong metaphysical commitments in his theory of soul, precisely so that he can develop a hypothesis about the just soul to show that it is happier. He writes, "The weaker the substantive theoretical commitments of those reasons, the better from Plato's point of view." Myles F. Burnyeat, "Presidential Address: The Truth of Tripartition," *Proceedings of the Aristotelian Society* 106 (2006): 4.

41. Malcolm Schofield, "Euboulia in the *Iliad*," *Classical Quarterly* 36 (1986): 6–31.

42. Schofield, "Euboulia in the *Iliad*," 6.

43. Schofield, "Euboulia in the *Iliad*," 16.

44. For example, Blössner rightly says that even if justice in both the soul and city is doing one's own, it still does not follow that justice in the soul is each part of the soul doing its own work. It could be that the individual soul as a whole does its own work. Thus we must look to a different way of understanding the working of the analogy than as a logical proof. See Blössner, "The City-Soul Analogy," 345–85.

45. Annas, *Introduction*, 111.

46. See Ferrari, *City and Soul*, 59–83.

47. Annas, *Introduction*, 153–69.

48. Of course, this presents a different problem, as Sachs has argued. If justice is a state of the soul, then how can it be shown that the just person is also just in the sense of the ordinary or "vulgar" conception of justice discussed in Book One? In some ways, Socrates seems to change the model of justice so much that the focus becomes on internal harmony and not external action. Singpurwalla gives a persuasive argument that the well-ordered and balanced soul will also act justly in the more conventional sense. Love of learning and intellectual pursuits will itself help to moderate the desires of lower parts of the soul. Moreover, the just soul who knows and loves the good will be motivated to bring about the good. On my view, both of these reasons have considerable merit, but Singpurwalla adds the important point that being unified with others is also part of happiness, and so the just person will be motivated to perform just actions. See David Sachs, "A Fallacy in Plato's

Republic," *Philosophical Review* 72 (1963): 141–58, and Rachel Singpurwalla, "Plato's Defense of Justice in the *Republic*," in *The Blackwell Guide to Plato's Republic*, ed. Gerasimos Santas (Malden, MA: Wiley Blackwell, 2006), 263–82.

49. Ferrari, Kastely, and Blössner all take the image of the city to be rhetorical in various ways. See Ferrari, *City and Soul*; Blössner "The City-Soul Analogy"; Kastely, *Rhetoric*, 93–97. Blössner, for example, shows that the language of the city and its analogical application to the soul allows for Plato to speak about aspects of the soul in a time that his work lacked a sufficient language to describe them. Tecusan offers a more extensive argument that images are always rhetorical and never heuristic. See Tecusan, "Speaking about the Unspeakable," 69–87.

50. Tecusan makes the suggestion that the link between city and soul is tested through the principle of opposition. See Tecusan, "Speaking about the Unspeakable," 84.

51. Mitchell Miller, "Platonic Provocations: Reflections on the Soul and the Good in the *Republic*," in *Platonic Investigations*, ed. Dominic O'Meara (Washington, DC: The Catholic University of America Press, 1985), 172–73. Klosko takes reason to be purely instrumental in determining a "plan of life" for a person, in which case reason could be understood self-evidently to be the only faculty that can organize and discipline a life. See Klosko, *Development of Plato's Thought*, 73–75. While I take philosophical reason to be more than instrumental for Socrates—as becomes especially clear when Socrates describes it as oriented to the forms that it loves—even on Klosko's reading the point stands that there must be some act of recognition that reason is well suited to rule, rather than to be ruled by, other aspects of the soul. This act of recognition is a moment of insight into justice in the soul that is not already found in seeing justice in the city.

52. Ferrari, *City and Soul*, 62–65.

53. Ferrari, *City and Soul*, 63.

54. Plato certainly would have been aware of the limits to language and the possibility that language could be either wholly detached from reality, even deliberately by a sophistical speaker. Neither must we assume that Plato is the naïve rationalist he is sometimes stereotyped as being. Essays such as Gorgias's "On Non-Being" make clear that in the larger intellectual context, there was plentiful discussion of language and its limits in capturing reality, as the *Republic*'s criticism of poetry also makes clear.

55. Popper, *Open Society*. Taylor helpfully distinguishes between different forms of totalitarianism, ranging from the Orwellian to the paternalistic. Taylor sees Plato's approach as paternalistic. See C. C. W. Taylor, "Plato's Totalitarianism," in *Plato's Republic*, ed. Richard Kraut (Lanham, MD: Rowman & Littlefield, 1997), 31–48.

56. Taylor, "Plato's Totalitarianism."

57. Roochnik, *Beautiful City*, chapter 2.

58. Here, I follow Kraut, who sees the forms themselves as the ultimate good and a good life as one that understands, loves, and imitates the forms (319).

See Richard Kraut, "The Defense of Justice in Plato's *Republic*," in *The Cambridge Companion to Plato's Republic*, ed. G. R. F. Ferrari (New York: Cambridge University Press, 2007), 311–37.

59. Rosen also notes the lack of attention to philosophical desire in the model of soul in Book Four. Rosen, *Plato's Republic*, 154.

60. Of course, Socrates tends to emphasize the opposite: the tendency of appetites to be uncontrolled. But he does not quite call them entirely bad, so much as in need of the guidance of reason.

61. Williams, "Analogy of City and Soul in Plato's *Republic*," 49–59.

62. Williams, "Analogy of City and Soul in Plato's *Republic*." See also Roochnik, *Beautiful City*, 15–16.

63. See also Pappas, *Plato's Republic*, 101–2, who notes that the courage needed for soldiers in the perfect city is not yet the full-fledged courage of knowing good and evil in the perfectly just soul. Santas, too, notes that a just person who performs his function in the city is not yet the just soul that Socrates describes. Santas, *Understanding*, 101–2.

64. And even this more expansive philosophical education is laid out later. As Annas points out, the initial "wisdom" of the guardians is more like practical wisdom or the capacity to plan the city. Annas, *Introduction*, 112–13. But by Books Five and Six, it becomes clear that the philosopher-kings will need to be wise in a sense more like intellectual or theoretic wisdom, and not only practical wisdom. See Annas, *Introduction*, 134, and Hendrik Lorenz, "The Analysis of the Soul in Plato's *Republic*," in *The Blackwell Guide to Plato's Republic*, ed. Gerasimos Santas (Oxford: Blackwell, 2006), 153–58.

65. Rosen, *Plato's Republic*, 136.

66. See Rosen, *Plato's Republic*, 132–33. Likewise, Roochnik argues that the dialogue implicitly argues that democracy is the best of all possible forms of rule, since it allows for the flourishing of philosophy, although it is not ideal. See Roochnik, *Beautiful City*.

67. One thinks of members of religious orders today whose needs are met such that they do not ordinarily suffer from hunger or lack of shelter, but who give up most personal property and family in order to pursue a different kind of work.

68. Annas, *Introduction*, 116–17.

69. For the view that the city exists as a model for the soul such that the moral lessons can be held independently of its political claims, see Julia Annas, *Platonic Ethics, Old and New* (Ithaca, NY: Cornell University Press, 1999), 72–95. As Annas writes, the virtuous person does not need to live in the ideal state in order to be happy but can be happy through being virtuous (88).

70. Santas describes the model as a "heuristic" device. Santas, *Plato's Republic*, 102.

71. Ferrari rejects the need for isomorphism: in the just city, people are just by each doing his or her own work to contribute to the well-being of the city, and a

just soul is one that exercises self-rule where each part does its own work. Although this separates political justice from individual justice, it does solve the problem. See Ferrari, *City and Soul*, 41. Jonathan Lear also rejects Williams's premise that the city is just if and only if all of its citizens are just. Lear, "Inside and Outside," 194–95. But Lear makes this claim for a different reason: a city is spirited if its spirited citizens are "successful in shaping the polis in their own image" (195).

72. Ferrari quite rightly denies that the analogy functions in a way that requires that the citizens of the just city each individually be just, wise, and so on. Ferrari, *City and Soul*, 43–44. He notes, for example, that a good statesman certainly could know what is good for the state but not know what is good for himself!

73. Pappas, *Plato's Republic*, 106.

74. Rosen argues that it is not particularly appealing in the just city, either. If only a few possess the rule of reason, then everyone else ends up being ruled by force, if we include rhetorical persuasion as a version of force, he says. Rosen, *Plato's Republic*, 144.

75. Lear likewise emphasizes that how an appetitive soul comes to be appetitive is through a cultural shaping process. See Lear, "Inside and Outside," 184–215. Lear's article captures well the nuances of how city and soul are mutually affecting while also affirming the isomorphism of city and soul. However, any such reading must take account of the nature-based division of natures as the reason for separate classes that Socrates emphasizes early on in the *Republic*, an approach that seems to be abandoned in the myth of the cave and even in the genesis given to the timocratic, oligarchic, democratic, and tyrannical persons who are shaped by family structures and not simply nature. Thus, the claim that different images are used for different argumentative purposes seems to me a better option.

Chapter 6. Image, Argument, and Comedy in the Ideal City

1. Sallis also reads this section as essentially comic but sees its comedy in the disruption of the erotic that is necessary for philosophy. See Sallis, *Being and Logos*, 371–78.

2. Nightingale notes the critical function of comedy and Plato's own borrowing this feature from comedy. While she argues for a complex relationship between comedy and poetry, she sees Plato as more hostile to Aristophanes here than I do. See Nightingale, *Genres in Dialogue*, 172–92.

3. The term "comic hero" is controversial. Rosen locates its first use in a 1964 book by Cedric Whitman, *Aristophanes and the Comic Hero*, and acknowledges some difficulties with Whitman's conclusions. Nonetheless, Rosen argues that the notion is a useful construct for looking at Greek comedy if not too narrowly constrained. The comic hero is heroic because the author of the comedy declares him to be such; from there, nearly any character type is capable of taking on this role. See Ralph

Rosen, "The Greek 'comic hero,'" in *The Cambridge Companion to Greek Comedy*, ed. Martin Revermann (Cambridge: Cambridge University Press, 2014), 222–40.

4. For an overview of the political role of comedy, see Alan Sommerstein, "The Politics of Greek Comedy," in *The Cambridge Companion to Greek Comedy*, ed. Martin Revermann (Cambridge: Cambridge University Press, 2014), 291–305.

5. Greene gives a number of examples of funny moments in Platonic dialogues, such as Socrates's claim that Heraclitus thinks the cosmos is like a leaky ship or a man with a runny nose. William Chase Greene, "The Spirit of Comedy in Plato," *Harvard Studies in Classical Philology* 31 (1920): 63–123.

6. Arlene Saxonhouse, "Comedy in Callipolis: Animal Imagery in the *Republic*," *American Political Science Review* 72, no. 3 (1978): 889. Howland, *Odyssey*, 113.

7. Naming this section as comic goes back to at least the middle of the eighteenth century, as Adam shows. See J. Adam, *Plato's Republic*, translated with an appendix and commentary (Cambridge: Cambridge University Press, 1902), 345. Greene does not specifically call the proposals of Book Five comedic but argues more generally for a reading of the dialogue in which the ideal and actual are contrasted in the manner of comedy—for example, in the nuptial number that he terms a "mathematical comedy." See Greene, "Spirit of Comedy," 97–106. See Saxonhouse, "Comedy in Callipolis," 888–909. Saxonhouse, however, focuses on the *Birds* while acknowledging the links back to the *Assemblywomen*.

8. Pappas, *Plato's Republic*, 127–45; Santas, *Understanding Plato's Republic*, 110–19; Klosko, *Development of Plato's Thought*, 133–58.

9. Aristotle's own way of naming Socrates's proposals in this section is to call them the ideas of *Socrates* as described in Plato's *Republic*. See Aristotle, *Politics* 2.1261aff.

10. Leo Strauss, *The City and Man* (Chicago: University of Chicago Press, 1964); Bloom, *Republic*; Rosen, *Plato's Republic*, 171–97; Mary P. Nichols, *Socrates and the Political Community: An Ancient Debate* (Albany: State University of New York Press, 1987), 99–151; Drew Hyland, "Plato's Three Waves and the Question of Utopia," *Interpretation* 18, no. 1 (1990): 91–109; Howland, *Glaucon's Fate*, 169–77; Arlene Saxonhouse, "The Philosopher and the Female in the Political Thought of Plato," *Political Theory* 4, no. 2 (May 1976): 195–212; Howland, *Odyssey*, 107–18; Roochnik, *Beautiful City*, 157–77; Kastely, *Rhetoric*, 98–108.

11. Jeffrey Henderson, "The Dēmos and Comic Competition," in *Nothing to Do with Dionysos? Athenian Drama in Its Social Context*, ed. John J. Winkler and Froma I. Zeitlin (Princeton, NJ: Princeton University Press, 1990), 271–313.

12. Henderson, "Dēmos and Comic Competition."

13. Jeffrey Henderson, "Comic Hero vs. Political Elite," in *Tragedy, Comedy, and the Polis: Papers from the Greek Drama Conference, Nottingham, 18–20 July 1990*, ed. Allan Sommerstein (Bari: Levante, 1993), 307–20.

14. Henderson, "Comic Hero." Bernard Freydberg has also argued for a serious commitment to *logos* by the comic playwright. He argues that Aristophanes'

Assemblywomen ridicules men and their generally poor use of political power not because of a total Aristophanic dismissal of *logos* but rather because of an even deeper respect for it: were there not a respect for *logos*, there would be no reason to find the crazy absence of it in the comedic city so funny. See Bernard Freydberg, *Philosophy as Comedy: Aristophanes, Logos, and Eros* (Bloomington: Indiana University Press, 2008), 111–57.

15. Greene, "Spirit of Comedy," 67. Saxonhouse, "Comedy in Callipolis," 889.

16. As Halliwell argues, laughter is the central defining feature of Greek comedy according to ancient Greek reflections on the form. See Stephen Halliwell, "Laughter," in *The Cambridge Companion to Greek Comedy*, ed. Martin Revermann (Cambridge: Cambridge University Press, 2014), 189–205.

17. For the use of the stage naked in comedy, see Alan Hughes, *Performing Greek Comedy* (Cambridge: Cambridge University Press, 2012), 87. Hughes notes this use of the cloak by the Chorus in early comedy, and its use both to conceal and to reveal, for example, in order to conceal the mechanism of a "dolphin" on which an actor might ride on stage.

18. Nightingale notes the use of abuse and invective as devices of criticism in comedy. Nightingale, *Genres in Dialogue*, 181–85.

19. Other authors have also linked the *Republic* back to Aristophanes's *Clouds*. See Claudia Baracchi, "Beyond the Comedy and Tragedy of Authority," *Philosophy and Rhetoric* 34, no. 2 (2001): 151–76, and Nichols, *Socrates and the Political Community*.

20. See Ian Ruffell, "Utopianism," in *The Cambridge Companion to Greek Comedy*, ed. Martin Revermann (Cambridge: Cambridge University Press, 2014), 206–21. As Ruffell shows, this utopian thinking is found even earlier in Homer, Hesiod, and across other genres, but Aristophanes is considerably less nostalgic than others in his portrayal of such ideals.

21. Sommerstein, "The Politics of Greek Comedy," 296.

22. Nightingale argues that the Platonic critical stance toward social norms is itself borrowed from Greek comedy. See Nightingale, *Genres in Dialogue*, 190–92.

23. Adam lists the parallel passages, for example, *Rep.* 457c and *Ass.* 614ff.; *Rep.* 458b and *Ass.* 583; *Rep.* 463c and *Ass.* 635–37; *Rep.* 462a and *Ass.* 594, *Ass.* 673–75; *Rep.* 464d and *Ass.* 657–72; *Rep.* 465aff. and *Ass.* 641–43; and *Rep.* 468c and *Ass.* 679–81. See Adam, *Plato's Republic*, 350–51.

24. Lake, "Plato's Homeric Dialogue."

25. Nightingale, *Genres in Dialogue*.

26. John S. Kieffer, "Philoctetes and *Arete*," *Classical Philology* 37, no. 1 (January 1942): 38–50.

27. Nightingale, *Genres in Dialogue*, 100.

28. Robin Henry-Reames, *Seeming and Being in Plato's Rhetorical Theory* (Chicago: University of Chicago Press, 2018).

29. Whether commentators wish to order and date the dialogues or not, that the *Republic* was composed after the death of Socrates is widely agreed upon.

My interpretation here does not depend on any particular dating of the dialogue after 391 BCE.

30. For a full discussion of both sides of the argument in early scholarship, see Adam, *Plato's Republic*, 345–48. Adam notes that Aristotle's remarks at *Politics* 2.1266a that "nobody else" has introduced the innovation of children and women in common" implies that Plato must the originator of the idea, but Adam thinks Aristotle must be excluding comedy, since he does not say Plato was the first, but the only, and the presence of these same ideas in comedy shows this is simply not true.

31. Robert Usher, *Aristophanes' Ecclesiazusae* (Oxford: Clarendon Press, 1973). Adam also considers earlier commentators who hypothesize that the material of Book Five was published earlier than the rest of the *Republic*, but this hypothesis has no independent support other than the supposition that Aristophanes must have been looking to Plato for inspiration. See Adam, *Plato's Republic*, 352–54.

32. Adam, *Plato's Republic*, 354.

33. Nightingale sees the comic material as derivative from a prior sophistic or philosophical source common to Plato and Aristophanes, on the grounds that at *Rep.* 452a–d Socrates says comedy was written in response. But what Socrates says in that passage is that the play was written in response to Cretan and Spartan practices, not a prior manuscript or performance.

34. While some take the comedy to be pure parody of the very idea of women in rule, Ruffell disagrees. Indeed, he suggests that the unwillingness of commentators to see an Aristophanic influence on Plato has little basis. See Ruffell, "Utopianism," 216. Indeed, Praxagora is one of the least unseemly and most competent among comic figures who propose political solutions.

35. Ludwig, "Eros in the *Republic*," 212; Klosko, *Development of Plato's Thought*, 142.

36. Nightingale, *Genres in Dialogue*, 177–78.

37. For further discussion, see David Kawalko Roselli, "Social Class," in *The Cambridge Companion to Greek Comedy*, ed. Martin Revermann (Cambridge: Cambridge University Press, 2014), 241–58.

38. Translations are from *Aristophanes: The Birds and Other Plays*, trans. David Barrett and Alan Sommerstein (London: Penguin, 1978).

39. Hughes, *Performing Greek Comedy*, 157–58.

40. Allan Bloom, "Response to Hall," *Political Theory* 5, no. 3 (August 1977): 315–30.

41. Here, I depart from Kremer, who sees Praxagora's solutions as repulsive rather than ridiculous, and the play as a clear rebuke of communism. See Mark Kremer, "Aristophanes' Criticism of Egalitarianism: An Interpretation of *The Assembly of Women*," *Interpretation* 21, no. 3 (1994): 261–74.

42. See Nightingale, *Genres in Dialogue*, 175–80. But Nightingale argues that Plato engages with the *Assemblywomen* not in order to parody it, but rather to challenge Aristophanes's mockery of ideas that Plato thinks ought to be taken seriously.

43. As should be clear from the discussion, comic form is not reducible to that which provokes laughter, but Halliwell gives a clear account of the centrality of laughter to the form of comedy. See Halliwell, "Laughter."

44. Saxonhouse, "Comedy in Callipolis," 890.

45. Trivigno argues that the *Republic* only treats powerful laughter as problematic, while the *Laws* creates space for the educational benefits of comedy. Franco V. Trivigno, "Plato on Laughter and Moral Harm," in *Laughter, Humor, and Comedy in Ancient Philosophy*, ed. Pierre Destrée and Franco V. Trivigno (Oxford: Oxford University Press, 2019), 13–34.

46. For an interpretation that emphasizes the criticism of democracy, see Kremer, "Aristophanes' Criticism of Egalitarianism."

47. Bloom's translation nicely captures Socrates's animallike language.

48. Roselli, "Social Class," 251.

49. As an example of a conversation between a fifteen-year-old newlywed and her husband, see Xenophon's *Oikonomikos*. There, Xenophon portrays women as better suited to indoor tasks, and men to outdoor ones.

50. Exceptions were prostitutes and the better respected *heterai*, a well-educated courtesan class of women who had considerably more freedom.

51. For a full argument, see Helene P. Foley, "Performing Gender in Greek Comedy," in *The Cambridge Companion to Greek Comedy*, ed. Martin Revermann (Cambridge: Cambridge University Press, 2014), 259–74.

52. Gregory Vlastos, "Was Plato a Feminist?," in *Feminist Interpretations of Plato*, ed. Nancy Tuana (University Park: Pennsylvania State University Press, 1994), 11–26. Moreover, Kochin shows that the traditional notion of masculinity is as much under revision as is the notion of the feminine, in Socrates's emphasis on self-control. See Michael Kochin, *Gender and Rhetoric in Plato's Political Thought* (Cambridge: Cambridge University Press, 2002), 37–59.

53. See Julia Annas, "Plato's *Republic* and Feminism," *Philosophy* 51, no. 197 (July 1976): 307–21, and Annas, *Introduction*, 181–85.

54. Moreover, as Penelope Murray shows, the dialogue often excludes the feminine from the city, as in its excision of the lamentations associated with women and feminine aspects of tragedy. Penelope Murray, "Tragedy, Women and the Family in Plato's *Republic*," in *Plato and the Poets*, edited by Pierre Destrée and Fritz-Gregor Herrmann (Leiden: Brill, 2011), 175–93.

55. Ludwig, "Eros in the *Republic*."

56. Saxonhouse notes that *ocheuō* or "to cover" or "to mate" is applicable only to animals. Saxonhouse, "Comedy in Callipolis," 896. Howland, *Republic*, 114–15.

57. Henderson, *Maculate Muse*, 127, 133. Henderson notes play on the dog imagery in comedy. For example, *Lysistrata* describes female masturbation as "flaying the flayed dog" (*Lysistrata* 158).

58. Roochnik argues for a tension between the arithmetical and the erotic, and places philosophical activity on the side of the erotic, which the arithmetical cannot justly contain. Roochnik, *Beautiful City*, 51–77. Kastely, *Rhetoric*, 105–6.

59. While one might object that the reaction of an audience member of the Platonic dialogue cannot be known, the same is true of any dramatic work, including comedy and its capacity to inspire laughter. Aristophanes even offers a meta-analysis of humor in the *Frogs*. See Halliwell, "Laughter," 191–92. Yet we still willingly state which points of an Aristophanic comedy are meant to be funny despite our distance from that audience; speaking of audience response in Platonic dialogue is not all that different.

60. Ruffell, "Utopianism," 215. This moment occurs in the *Assemblywomen*, when one character refuses to give up his money to be held in common. Polemarchus plays a significantly more restrained, but similar, role in the *Republic*.

61. Henderson, "Dēmos and Comic Competition," 271–313, argues for this role for the comic hero, though he does not extend his interpretation to Plato's Socrates.

62. Rosen, "The Greek 'comic hero,'" 232–33.

63. Of course, representative democracies maintain both the grounding of the authority of rule in the people and give over actual practice of such rule to elected and appointed representatives. But Athens had a pure democracy that sometimes succumbed to populism. Not all forms of democracy treat this modulation between demos and elite in identical ways.

64. Hughes discusses the way in which a male's manipulation of his own body, for example, an enlarged costume "phallus," plays a role in Greek comedy. See Hughes, *Performing Greek Comedy*, 156, 180–82.

65. Trivigno, "Plato on Laughter."

66. Freydberg, *Philosophy as Comedy*, 121.

67. Nightingale, *Genres in Dialogue*, 176–77.

68. Nightingale, *Genres in Dialogue*, 179–80. Nightingale has a different understanding of how Platonic comedy is to function, however, seeing Plato as far more critical of the comedians than in my analysis.

69. Nightingale connects the *Laws* to this section of the *Republic*. See Nightingale, *Genres in Dialogue*, 175–77.

70. Hughes, *Performing Greek Comedy*, 119.

71. Hughes, *Performing Greek Comedy*, 118.

72. As Hughes notes, Stanislavski and method acting were unknown. *Performing Greek Comedy*, 114–15.

73. Hughes, *Performing Greek Comedy*, 180–83. Hughes notes that even actors playing female characters wore the undergarment and the phallus.

74. Howland interprets the stripping off of the outer garment to reveal the inner as an act of removing *nomos* in order to get to *physis*. Howland, *Odyssey*, 114.

75. As Kochin puts it, the question of whether such political proposals is "possible" must be asked not only abstractly, but also more specifically: "'possible' need not mean 'possible for me.'" Kochin, *Gender and Rhetoric*, 85.

76. Donald Morrison, "The Utopian Character of Plato's Ideal City," in *The Cambridge Companion to Plato's Republic*, ed. G. R. F. Ferrari (New York: Cambridge University Press, 2007), 234–35. Santas, *Understanding Plato's Republic*, 121.

77. Annas thinks this unlikely to satisfy Plato, and she takes him to be dissatisfied with moderate changes on the basis of his radicalism. Annas, *Introduction*, 186. However, if we take into account the presence of comic elements, then one reasonable response is precisely to temper Socratic idealism with the realism injected by comic elements.

Chapter 7. The Image of the Sun

1. Exceptions include John Sallis, who examines the role of the image as facilitating access to the intelligible through a "double seeing"; Nicholas Smith, who argues that images function in order to provoke thought (*dianoia*); and Jill Frank, who argues that part of the truth of a mimetic image *is* its partial and perspectival nature. See Sallis, *Being and Logos*, 312–454; Smith, "Plato's Book of Images," 3–13; and Frank, *Poetic Justice*, 62–69. Kastely also argues for the political need to show the nonphilosopher the value of philosophy. See Kastely, *Rhetoric*, 131–46.

2. Here, I follow Gonzalez's approach to the dialogues as perspectival. See Gonzalez, "Plato's Perspectivism," 31–48, and McCoy, "Perspectivism," 49–57. Similarly, Frank uses the language of "partial" and "perspectival" to describe the "truth of mimēsis." Frank, *Poetic Justice*, 67.

3. As Gerald Press argues, Plato is neither a skeptic nor a dogmatist, and knowledge as *theōria* allows for such middle ground. See Press, "Knowledge and Vision," 61–89.

4. Nightingale offers an excellent account of the theoretical journey that the middle books present, in which visual metaphors dominate, and the journey for truth is coupled with a need to return home after the journey, as with the traditional *theōros*. See Nightingale, *Spectacles of Truth*, especially 107–18.

5. Nightingale, *Spectacles of Truth*, 111.

6. Frank also argues for the centrality of *aisthēsis* in the sun-good analogy. Frank, *Poetic Justice*, 181–83. She goes on to argue that *doxa* or opinion can help to stabilize *aisthēsis* insofar as *logoi* are public, while sensations and perceptions are private. Frank, *Poetic Justice*, 183–91.

7. See Sallis, *Being and Logos*, 383; Frank, *Poetic Justice*, 67.

8. See, for example, Gorgias's "On Non-Being."

9. While this chapter cannot argue for a more comprehensive view of the forms, I take Platonic forms to be independent existing substances prior to sensible reality in which sensible reality participates. Aristotle also takes Plato to say that the forms are "separate" (*echōrise*) (*Metaphysics* M, 9 1086b). However, one need not commit to a radical version of the Two Worlds theory in order to think that the forms are ontologically prior and separate. To the extent that the sensible world participates in the ideal, the sensible world *is* an extension of the ideal one. As Press argues, the material world is that *through* which we gain insight into the ideal,

which is partially accessible and yet never fully grasped. See Press, "Knowledge as Vision," 80–81. See also Frank, *Poetic Justice*, 67–69.

10. Rosen helpfully lays out different senses of paradigm. Rosen, *Plato's Republic*, 201–3.

11. Rosen, *Plato's Republic*, 208.

12. Of course, once we use Socrates as a "model" of justice, the account of who Socrates is becomes part of this middle level of paradigm. Socrates himself, though, still remains in flesh and blood only an instance of the form of justice. Here, I depart somewhat from Rosen's way of categorizing paradigms. However, Rosen also asserts that constructed models are only copies or images of unconstructed Ideas. Rosen, *Plato's Republic*, 207.

13. Commentators often dismiss the ontological priority of the form of the good. Cross and Woozley take the priority of the form of the good to be rather limited, such that the forms are only known fully when known in their relation to the good. They also rightly point out that not as much is said about the good as the cause of intelligibility as one might desire. See Cross and Woozley, *Plato's Republic* (1964), chapter 9. Santas takes the form of the good to provide for knowing features of the forms such as their permanence. See Gerasimos Santas, "The Form of the Good in Plato's *Republic*," *Philosophical Inquiry* (1980): 374–403. But for an argument that this really means beyond being, and not only beyond essence, see Rafael Ferber and Gregor Damschen, "Is the Idea of the Good Beyond Being? Plato's *'epekeina tēs ousias'* Revisited (*Republic* 6 509b8–10)," in *Second Sailing: Alternative Perspectives on Plato*, ed. Debra Nails, Harold Tarrant, Mika Kajava, and Eero Salmenkivi (Espoo: Wellprint Oy, 2015), 197–203. In general, treating the forms as properties rather than entities leads to some conclusions that do not fit very well with Socrates's strong, if too brief, metaphysical claims. For example, Fine concludes that the form of the good must be the teleological structure of things. She takes it to have less substance than the forms as such. But when Socrates names it as a causal agent of the *ousia* of the forms, the most direct interpretation is that it is not *merely* a substance of the sort that the forms are, but beyond even the being of any particular form—while not personal in nature, more like the nature of God who is "beyond being" and the cause of being, but not merely *a* being. Of course, Plato's influence on later religious thinkers stems from this kind of an approach to his ontology.

14. Strauss, *City and Man*, 120–21.

15. If one needs evidence to take seriously the role of the divine in the image of the form of the good, Themistius and Alexander in antiquity held opposing positions as to whether Aristotle in *De Anima* III.5 agreed or disagreed with the need for a divine cause for human thinking. While they disagree about Aristotle, they both see the role of divinity in the Platonic account. See Eli Diamond, "Aristotle's Appropriation of Plato's Sun Analogy in *De Anima*," *Apeiron* 47, no. 3 (2014): 365–89.

16. Here, I depart from Santas, *Understanding Plato's Republic*, 143, who sees a correct definition as the perfection of a form, rather than recognizing the separation between an insight and its later articulation in language, as I think is more defensible a position in considering the ongoing revision of language about justice beginning early on in Book One. Santas does not fully embrace the visual nature of Plato's images of the forms, preferring an algebraic or digital model, but Plato of course did not have algebra, but rather geometry, which retains a visual component as a discipline that binds together the visual with the intellectual. Moreover, Plato rejects the view that the good is knowledge (505b). If we place knowledge and its articulation in language on the same level as one another, then the forms are prior to not only what we know about them, but also what we can say about them, or our intellection of them.

17. This is Kastley's approach. Kastley, *Rhetoric*, 131–46.

18. Aristotle's claim that Plato's lecture on the form of the good ended up being about mathematics (found in Aristoxenes's *Elementa Harmonica* II.30–31) is not an exception. Without access to the original speech, we can only hypothesize whether Plato meant by "the good is one," a unity as such, perfection, a numerical conception, or other possible meanings.

19. Rosen, *Plato's Republic*, 207. As Rosen says, the city in speech is imperfect for this reason.

20. Verity Hart, "Beware of Imitations: Image Recognition in Plato," in *New Essays on Plato: Language and Thought in Fourth Century Philosophy*, ed. Fritz-Gregor Herrmann (Swansea: Classical Press of Wales, 2006), 21–42. Hart also nicely connects passages on recollection from dialogues such as the *Phaedo* to these passages in the *Republic*: one can be reminded of something by that which is both like and unlike it, for example, an image.

21. Fine argues against a Two Worlds theory, although her distinction rests on a differentiation between true propositions and a mix of true and false propositions as characteristic of the contrast between knowledge and belief. Gail Fine, *Plato on Knowledge and the Forms: Selected Essays* (Oxford: Clarendon Press, 2003), 215–46. However, Socrates does not use the language of propositions and such an approach overlooks the manner in which Socrates conceptualizes knowing and opining according to visual metaphors, which nuance the nature of those concepts.

22. Press, "Knowledge as Vision," 73. See also Gonzalez, "Plato's Perspectivism," who argues that each dialogue in relation to the others offers a partial perspective that is "conditioned by the specific context, aim, and characters" (33), and my own response, McCoy, "Perspectivism," 49–57.

23. Fine argues that it is possible to have belief about the forms. As she shows, Socrates says that in order to have knowledge, one must know forms, but this is a weaker claim than saying that there is knowledge only of forms. See Fine, *Plato on Knowledge and Forms*, 67.

24. Smith notes the strong contrast between contemporary epistemologists' understanding of knowledge as justified belief and Socrates's assignment of knowledge and belief as two different powers. Smith, "Plato's Book of Images," 6.

25. However, it does not follow that the sensible world would be unknowable, since sensible things participate in the forms, and so it could still be known by knowing the forms in which the sensible world participates. However, any aspect of the sensible world that does not participate in the forms might not be an object of knowledge. But such a claim would not be too far from Aristotle's idea that the material cause of a thing is not knowable in the same strong sense as a formal or final cause.

26. Fine, *Plato on Knowledge and Forms*, 86.

27. Klosko, *Development of Plato's Political Theory*, 84.

28. As Schindler says, the philosopher loves the whole of that which he seeks and is unwilling to rest with only one part. Schindler, *Plato's Critique*, 102.

29. Annas and Fine both reject the existential interpretation on the grounds that to talk about the existence of nonbeing makes no sense, but here I try to explain how and why it can be sensible as a conceptual distinction. Of course, in the *Sophist*, the Stranger takes up exactly the problem of nonbeing, but does not draw the same kinds of distinctions between existential, veridical, and predicative uses of *einai* that contemporary thinkers see as crucial. See Annas, *Introduction*, 195–98; Cross and Woozley, *Plato's Republic*, 162. But as Chen points out, for Plato, to exist is to already to be qualified and vice versa. Socrates describes ontically, not propositionally. See Ludwig Chen, *Acquiring Knowledge of the Ideas: A Study of Plato's Methods in the Phaedo, Symposium, and the Central Books of the Republic* (Stuttgart: Franz Steiner Verlag, 1992), 66, n. 14.

30. Mitchell Miller, "Beginning the 'Longer Way,'" in *The Cambridge Companion to Plato's Republic*, ed. G. R. F. Ferrari (New York: Cambridge University Press, 2007), 322.

31. See Herman Sinaiko, *Love, Knowledge and Discourse in Plato: Dialogue and Dialectic in Phaedrus, Republic, Parmenides* (Chicago: University of Chicago Press, 1965), 137.

32. Some commentators seem to take the form of the good to be mostly conceptual: for example, Denyer says, "Having a teleological explanation is seeing what is good about it" (307). See Nicholas Denyer, "Sun and Line: The Role of the Good," in *The Cambridge Companion to Plato's Republic*, ed. G. R. F. Ferrari (New York: Cambridge University Press, 2007), 284–309. Cooper takes the desire for the good to be "equivalent to the desire on the part of reason to work out the ends of life on one's own and to achieve them." On this view, reason determines what the good is rather than looking at its nature to see what it is and to allow its life to be determined by the good. See Cooper, "Plato's Theory of Human Motivation," 8. However, insofar as the form of the good is the causal origin of the other forms, I

NOTES TO CHAPTER 7

take Socrates to be positing something ontologically much stronger: an entity that is uniquely "beyond being" not because it lacks being or is merely conceptual, but because its being exceeds the being of all the other forms of which it is a cause. If so, then Socrates seems to be pointing toward a deep yearning for a transcendent Good that implicitly characterizes all of human action, and not only an explanatory sense of what is good.

33. Kastely, in *Rhetoric*, argues that Socrates is speaking rhetorically in using this analogy (116–18). In his view, the philosopher needs to be able to tell the nonphilosopher about his superior understanding, but the nonphilosopher cannot understand it, so he must resort to analogies. Kastely suggests that a dialectical account of the form of the good would be different (137), but then does not tell us where this dialectical account is found, only that it would not use images and would transcend history and even all temporality (140). Thus it seems safer for the purposes of interpretation here to restrict our commentary to what Socrates actually does show us is a way to describe the forms in ways that help us to understand how we can learn and know, namely, to use images.

34. As Fine notes. See Fine, *Plato on Knowledge and Forms*, 87.

35. Hart, "Beware of Imitations," 22–23.

36. Miller argues that the reason the longer way that would give a more precise account of the form of the good is not taken is because Glaucon is not ready. This may be true, but Socrates directly states his own (relative) ignorance as well. See Miller, "Beginning the 'Longer Way,'" 310–11. See also Tecusan, "Speaking about the Unspeakable," 80–81.

37. Bloom translation.

38. Here, Socrates anticipates, in different form, Descartes's noting of the difference between the scope of the intellect and the scope of the will. Howland also notes the gap between the seeking of the good and knowledge of the form of the good. See Howland, *Republic*, 121.

39. Liddell Scott.

40. Jacob Howland argues that Socrates's religious language "lacks the clarity, precision, and certainty" of other types of knowledge, such as mathematical knowledge. Howland, *Odyssey*, 125.

41. Rosen, *Plato's Republic*, 254.

42. This is why Aristotle's own solution to the problem is not to claim that there is a good itself, but only to talk about specific goods for specific kinds of things. If the good for the human being is happiness, then the stopping point is more easily articulated when he gives an account of happiness. For example, in Aristotle's account of the work of the human person in Book One, chapter 7 of the *Nicomachean Ethics*, he gives an account of human faculties and how their flourishing activity is happiness for the human being.

43. As Ross notes, Eucleides stated that Plato's view is that the good is one, but called by many names: god, wisdom, reason, among others. See Diogenes

Laertius, ii.106, iii.6. In David Ross, *Plato's Theory of Ideas* (Oxford: Clarendon Press, 1953), 44.

44. Chen sees a similar priority of vision over predication and description in the *Symposium*. Vision comes before reasoning about what one sees. See Chen, *Acquiring Knowledge of the Ideas*, 52.

45. Richard Patterson, "Word and Image in Plato," in *Presocratics and Plato: Festschrift at Delphi in Honor of Charles Kahn*, ed. Richard Patterson, Vassilis Karasmanis, and Arnold Hermann (Las Vegas: Parmenides, 2012), 439.

46. Denyer gives an account of the good and how it allows us to understand not only artifacts, but also mathematicals apart from sensory experience. See Denyer, "Sun and Line," 284–309.

47. Sallis argues that the good makes images of itself, with the sun being a primary such instance. Sallis, *Being and Logos*, 405.

48. As Rosen argues in *Plato's Republic*, this sense of causation cannot mean ordinary genesis through time or any kind of change, since the particular forms are eternal and therefore cannot come into being. Rather, he says, "the Good is a necessary condition for the being of ideas, but a condition that always obtains" (262). This seems right in order to make the theory coherent.

49. See Miller, "Beginning the 'Longer Way,' " and "Platonic Provocations," 163–93. See also Hyland's critique in Hyland, "Longer Road," 163–67. White also takes up this idea of the good as perfection in *A Companion to Plato's Republic*, 101.

50. Miller, "Beginning the 'Longer Way,' " 333. Similarly, Gonzalez argues that the forms are ideals and the form of the good is the ideal of being "best" that all particular forms, such as the form of beauty, represent insofar as they are ideals. See Francisco J. Gonzalez, *Dialectic and Dialogue: Plato's Practice of Philosophical Inquiry* (Evanston, IL: Northwestern University Press, 1998), 216–17, 232–33.

51. Rosen argues that the form of the good is not moral or political in nature, and that Plato sees moral virtue as closer to the body than to the soul (267). However, Socrates claims it is the source of *all* the forms, and the form of justice is surely a political form, such that the form of the good must also have *some* quality of goodness that also can be a sufficient cause of all the moral and political forms. But its goodness surely exceeds what inheres in any one of the other forms. In a sense, Socrates implies that being itself is good, or at least the being of the forms.

52. Thus, views that see the forms as merely a regulative ideal will not suffice, since these do not explain their causal power. For this view of the form as a regulative ideal, see David Lachterman, "What Is the Good of Plato's *Republic*?," *Saint John's Review* 39, nos. 1 and 2 (1989–1990): 157–60.

53. I recognize that Miller's point is to say that the good is perfection, not that perfection is separable from the good, but my point is that the generation of the *existence* of other forms cannot be achieved through the category of perfection, even if the "perfect" nature of the forms can be, unless one means by perfect something quite ontologically robust, such as the perfection of God.

54. Sallis connects the unity of the good not to divinity but to the name of the One, also linked to the good in the *Philebus*. If what is intended is an ultimate causal unity, this view is compatible with my own. Sallis, *Being and Logos*, 411.

55. Mark McPherran, "The Gods and Piety of Plato's *Republic*," in The *Blackwell Guide to Plato's Republic*, ed. Gerasimos Santas (Oxford: Blackwell, 2006), 95. McPherran demonstrates the continued presence of religious practice throughout the ideal city, which never abandons such practice. See also Pappas, *Plato's Republic*, 167.

56. Hyland takes this phrase likewise strongly and argues that knowledge is always of being, such that the sun is beyond capacity to know. See Hyland, "Aporia, the Longer Road," 158–59. I agree that the form of the good is not graspable, that is, cannot be known comprehensively. However, this need not mean it is inaccessible. Socrates's image of the sun is again useful here: as Hyland says, the sun is too bright to look at directly, but in another sense, in every act of vision, the sun is present and visible. Knowledge of the good in the sense of mastery is beyond human capacity, while access to the good as a human being is part of what it means to be one who learns and grows in knowledge.

57. To this extent, the causal power of the good is potentially different than the causal power of other forms. Beauty causes the beauty in beautiful things, but the good causes the being of all else even though it is beyond being. Therefore its causal agency must be different in kind, though Socrates does not take up this point.

58. Miller, "Platonic Provocations," 191.

59. For an excellent account of the relationship between sight and touch in the *Timaeus*, see Luc Brisson, "Plato's Theory of Sense Perception in the 'Timaeus': How It Works and What It Means," *Proceedings of the Boston Area Colloquium in Ancient Philosophy*, ed. John Cleary and Gary Gurtler, 13 (1997): 147–75, especially 169–74.

60. As noted in the commentary by Lamb in Plato, *Plato in Twelve Volumes*, vol. 9, trans. W. R. M. Lamb (Cambridge, MA: Harvard University Press; London: William Heinemann Ltd., 1925).

61. Gosling argues against the idea of two different faculties as well, saying that the same faculty is at work. J. G. Gosling, "*Doxa* and *Dunamis* in Plato's *Republic*," *Phronesis* 12 (1968): 129–30.

62. Gordon similarly disputes the interpretation that the realms of rational grasp of the forms and the encounter with the sensible world are two separable processes. She analyzes a passage from the *Phaedo* in which Socrates shows that looking at particular sensible objects and comparing them to one another helps us to understand equality itself, through the added intervention of the process of recollection of the forms as seen in the *Meno*. See Jill Gordon, *Turning Toward Philosophy: Literary Device and Dramatic Structure in Plato's Dialogues* (University Park: Penn State Press, 2010), 139–41.

63. Here I depart from Cooper, who reads the distinction between stable knowledge and unstable opinion to map onto the distinction between the stability of the forms and the instability of sense experience. But this does not explain what

Socrates is doing with the metaphor of relative darkness and relative illumination of the forms. See Neil Cooper, "Between Knowledge and Ignorance," *Phronesis* 31, no. 3 (1986): 229–42.

64. Socrates seems to readily accept Glaucon's use of "opinion" to describe what he himself names as "trust" when describing the second lowest section of the divided line. This seems to be a case of Plato's typical ease with using ordinary Greek a bit more loosely than is the case in contemporary philosophy. Socrates seems to recognize that "opinion" in its ordinary usage can refer to many things, from unstable beliefs arrived at after some inquiry, to beliefs we passively receive, or matters that we take for granted. Socrates's use of "trust"/*pistis* helps to resolve some of these ambiguities.

65. Sallis argues similarly, that there are not two regions of things that differentiate knowledge and opinion but the same thing showing itself differently. Sallis, *Being and Logos*, 406–7, though he characterizes the nature of the subject's encounter differently.

66. Along similar lines, Schindler argues that Plato has an intentional view of consciousness, such that the encounter that leads to being able to characterize an epistemic state as knowledge or opinion is about an event that takes place between consciousness and its object. Schindler, *Plato's Critique*, 98–99.

67. Schindler, *Plato's Critique*, 114.

68. As Schindler says, "While appearance is in some respect opposed to being, being is not opposed to, but rather inclusive of, appearance." Schindler, *Plato's Critique*, 114.

69. Santas also takes this to be a central motivation for Socrates's distinction between these two states. See Santas, *Understanding Plato's Republic*, 125.

70. Rosen, in *Plato's Republic*, makes essentially the same point: "Logos itself cannot be simply discursive; if it were, the Ideas would be linguistic entities and the whole significance of the metaphor of the sun would be lost. Instead, pure logos speaks about what it has seen or grasped noetically. If there were no speech, we would not know what we had seen. But if there were nothing to see prior to speaking, we would not know what we were talking about" (265). To this we might add that sensory experience is also not reducible to its verbal description: for example, describing the experience of listening to music at a concert afterward is different than the initial experience of the music itself. *Nous* also grasps prior to the articulation in language of what one knows or "sees."

71. Sallis, *Being and Logos*, 392–93.

72. Miller, "Beginning the 'Longer Way,'" 322–23.

73. See Smith, "Plato's Book of Images," 11.

74. See Press, who in "Plato's Dialogues as Enactments" argues for *theōria* rather than proposition as central to Platonic epistemology. See also Gordon, *Turning Toward Philosophy*, 155, who notes the emphasis on image, not proposition, in the *Sophist*, especially in the distinction between eikastics and phantastics.

75. Roochnik in *Beautiful City* emphasizes this aspect of the image even above the ontological and epistemological aspects. For him, the *eros* to know the good exists only for the philosopher, however, and not the nonphilosopher (66–67). However, given that Socrates has said that the good is something that everyone seeks, even the nonphilosopher is always implicitly seeking it as she or he lives out an ordinary life. But perhaps it is fair to say that the philosopher is intentional in this quest, and aware of his own *eros* and its true objects. Nightingale also emphasizes the erotic quality of the love of the forms. See Nightingale, *Spectacles of Truth*, 116.

76. Klein, *Commentary on Plato's Meno*, 114.

77. Here, I depart slightly from Jill Gordon, who takes the forms to be images. See Gordon, *Turning Toward Philosophy*, 167.

78. Smith also argues that some images, such as those of the mathematicians mentioned in the divided line, are made possible *because* of their knowledge. See Smith, "Plato's Book of Images," 6–9. Rosen takes a different point of view, arguing that if the idea of the beautiful has properties that are unique to it, and that individuate it from particular beautiful things, then it cannot be seen through these particular beautiful things. Rosen, *Plato's Republic*, 257. For a well-developed view of Platonic individuation, see Mary Margaret McCabe, *Plato's Individuals* (Princeton, NJ: Princeton University Press, 1999).

79. Smith, "Divided Line." Contrast this view with Kastley, who in *Rhetoric* argues that not only dialectic but also philosophy is free of images on a Platonic account: those who practice true philosophy "have no need of an image" (141).

80. Miller, "Beginning the 'Longer Way,'" 318–23.

Chapter 8. The Divided Line and the Cave

1. Howland, *Odyssey*, 127.

2. I am particularly indebted to insights offered by Smith, who argues for the centrality of the image of the divided line to its interpretation, although some of the details of my interpretation differ from his. See Nicholas D. Smith, "Plato's Divided Line," *Ancient Philosophy* 16, no. 1 (1996): 25–46.

3. Baracchi calls attention to the need for discerning what is beneath any given analogy, that is, how the connection between the visible and invisible world itself is made possible by what she calls a "logic of desire," an even more basic coming together of desires that guide the origins of analogies. My attention here is to the argumentative elements of images, but for her analysis of these dimensions, see Baracchi, *Of Myth, Life, and War*, 18–35.

4. As Howland says in *Odyssey*, "The intelligible and visual domains are now depicted as part of *one and the same line*" (127).

5. Annas notes the differences between the divided line and the cave and especially the difficulty with understanding *eikasia* consistently across both images. Annas, *Introduction*, 254–55.

6. Denyer, "Sun and Line," 293.

7. Of course, often words do use imagery. Howland writes, "*Logos* is by nature imagistic: it images what is *seen*" (131), which acknowledges that some images work better than others. But to this I would add that some experiences are not easily expressible in a *logos* at all, and elements of many experiences exceed what words can capture—for example, the beauty of a piece of music to which one listens. The forms, too, seem to exceed the *logoi* that can be given of them.

8. Pappas, *Plato's Republic*, 171–72.

9. Klosko makes this argument but assumes that since only forms can be known and the sensible world is not composed of forms, the sensible world is not knowable. See Klosko, *Development of Plato's Political Theory*, 88–89. But my claim here is that in understanding the likeness of the form, insofar as a sensible thing participates in the form, that sensible thing may give insight, if properly understood for what it is (what is caused by forms), and what it is not (not itself a form).

10. Klein, *Commentary on Plato's Meno*, 114–15. Howland, *Odyssey*, 129–30.

11. Klein, *Commentary on Plato's Meno*, 115.

12. Smith, "Plato's Divided Line," 40–42.

13. Richard Robinson, *Plato's Earlier Dialectic*, 2nd edition (Oxford: Clarendon Press, 1953), 93–94.

14. F. M. Cornford, "Mathematics and Dialectic in the Republic, VI–VII," in *Studies in Plato's Metaphysics*, ed. R. E. Allen (London: Routledge & Kegan Paul, 1965), 64–66.

15. Robinson, *Earlier Dialectic*, 95.

16. Robinson, *Earlier Dialectic*, 105–13.

17. Robinson, *Earlier Dialectic*, 107.

18. Likewise, Fine argues that Platonic moral argument belongs to the realm of *dianoia*. Fine, *Plato on Knowledge and Forms*, 107.

19. Gonzalez, following Robinson, offers an overview of major views of how commentators have interpreted the practice of dialectic. See Gonzalez, *Dialectic and Dialogue*, 220–23. Dorter gives a helpful overview of multiple passages across dialogues in describing the nature of dialectic and how many aspects described abstractly in other dialogues as dialectical occur within the *Republic* itself. See Dorter, *Transformation of Plato's Republic*, 8–18.

20. Miller sees the central books as giving a kind of abbreviated overview of the longer way. Miller, "Beginning the 'Longer Way,'" 310–44. In contrast, see Hyland, "Aporia, the Longer Road," *Graduate Faculty Philosophy Journal* 31, no. 2 (2011): 145–75. Hyland argues that the way of the *Republic* is a mistaken way, not simply a shorter one. The disagreement rests on the question of the severity of Socrates's claim to "not know" the good: is it fundamental to being human, as Hyland argues, or not? Here I try to argue for the idea of partiality of vision rather than either presence or absence.

21. Kastely therefore argues that the images only teach Glaucon about dialectic, but that we do not see dialectic take place in the dialogue. Kastely, *Rhetoric*, 135.

22. Here, I follow Cornford's approach to *noēsis* as a synthetic, intuitive grasp of its objects. See Cornford, "Mathematics and Dialectic in the Republic, VI–VII," 61–95.

23. Robinson understands *nous* in terms of intuition but then adds the claim that such knowledge must be certain. But as Gonzalez rightly points out, Socrates does not give certainty as a criterion of knowledge here. See Gonzalez, *Dialectic and Dialogue*, 222. But it is possible to think that one has had an insight into the forms and not to be certain that one has seen correctly. Socrates seems to think that one way to test whether one has seen well is to discuss what one has seen with others, that is, to engage in philosophical conversation. My use of the term "intuition" here is not meant to convey certainty or the elimination of doubt, as per Robinson's analysis.

24. See Klosko, *Development of Plato's Political Theory*, 90. While there are important questions about the authenticity of the Seventh Letter, Socrates's language here in the *Republic* about "catching sight" of the forms supports the notion that Plato thought such kind of knowledge exists and can be experienced. Joseph also argues for the forms as an invisible world, suggesting it is no less foolish than scientific claims about the relativity of space and time that are not captured by ordinary sense experience. See Horace W. B. Joseph, *Knowledge and the Good in Plato's Republic* (Westport, CT: Greenwood Press, 1981, reprint of Oxford University Press, 1948 edition), 61–73. For an excellent account of the genre of letters such as the Seventh Letter and why they are not the "real" Plato any more than a dialogue, see Julia Annas, *Platonic Ethics, Old and New*, 74–78. I agree with Annas, and my only very limited claim here is to show a continuity between the letter tradition and the dialogue with respect to this language of sight.

25. For others who see vision as key to *nous*, see Cornford, "Mathematics and Dialectic in the Republic, VI–VII," 61–95.

26. Gonzalez, *Dialectic and Dialogue*, 228.

27. Here I am in agreement with Gonzalez, who argues that for Plato knowledge is neither the result of giving a *logos*, nor does it require giving a *logos*, but rather only the more limited claim that one is *capable* of giving a *logos* if one has knowledge. Gonzalez notes the same relation is held up in the *Protagoras* 336b. See Gonzalez, *Dialectic and Dialogue*, 223–24.

28. See Annas, *Introduction*, 282–84. Elias states that the myth itself does not make clear whether anyone can, in fact, know in the way that is reserved for the highest portion of the divided line. See Julius Elias, *Plato's Defense of Poetry* (Albany: State University of New York Press, 1984), 202.

29. As Fine argues, Socrates frequently discusses the capacity to give an account of something as a marker of being a dialectician (e.g., 511b–c, 533a–d). See Fine, *Plato on Knowledge and Forms*, 113. But here I distinguish between dialectic as argument and the noetic insight into the forms per se.

30. Rosen, *Plato's Republic*, 207. Gonzalez, *Dialectic and Dialogue*, 224. While Gonzalez understands the forms quite differently than I do, I agree with his account of dialectic as not a proof but rather the capacity to give an account and to speak to others about what one knows.

31. Here, I depart from Kastely, who thinks that the philosopher/dialectician would not need images at all and that his way of doing philosophy is beyond them. Kastely, *Rhetoric*, 141.

32. Pappas, *Plato's Republic*, 177–78. Rosen also notes in a general way the lack of a fit between the city and the world inside the cave because the cave lacks any real form of community. Rosen, *Plato's Republic*, 270.

33. See Marina McCoy, "Sophistry and Philosophy in Plato's *Republic*," *Polis* 22, no. 2 (2005): 265–86. Howland, *Odyssey*, 138, argues that the puppeteers are the sophists, while Bloom takes them to be the poets. Reeve takes them to be moneymakers fixed on the man-made in another respect altogether. See Reeve, *Philosopher-Kings*. Rosen takes them more generally to be illusion-makers. Rosen, *Plato's Republic*, 272. Destrée sees them as poets and painters. Destrée, "Poets in the Cave," 337.

34. Kastely, *Rhetoric*, 133.

35. Ellen Wagner, "Compulsion Again in the *Republic*," *Apeiron* 38, no. 3 (2005): 87–101.

36. Brown comprehensively lays out the range of positions taken on this passage in Eric Brown, "Justice and Compulsion for Plato's Philosopher-Rulers," *Ancient Philosophy* 20 (2000): 1–17.

37. Strauss, *City and Man*, 124. See also Bloom, *Republic*, 407–8; Roochnik, *Beautiful City*, 74–77; Rosen, *Plato's Republic*, 277–78; and Kastely, *Rhetoric*, 148–50.

38. Terence Irwin, *Plato's Moral Theory* (Oxford: Oxford University Press, 1977), 164–74.

39. Annas, for example, says that the contemplative philosopher must consider the ordinary world to be nothing more than "trash." Annas, *Introduction*, 264–65. Burnyeat, however, argues that reason persuades the philosopher to make a return, in repayment for the debt of education that they received from the city. See Myles F. Burnyeat, "Sphinx without a Secret," *New York Review of Books* (May 30, 1985), 30–36, http://www.nybooks.com/articles/1985/05/30/sphinx-without-a-secret/. Brown argues that it is just to obey the laws, and the law that the philosophers must rule is enacted in order to guarantee the maximal happiness of the city. Brown, "Justice and Compulsion," 9–12.

40. Howland likewise says that the philosopher who has been outside the cave is not detached from his humanity and so returns to the cave willingly. Howland, *Odyssey*, 144–45.

41. Brown rightly argues that an interpretation of this section must take account of three elements of the text: why the philosophers prefer not to rule, that

they are compelled to rule, and also why they nonetheless choose to do what is just. Here, I argue that these three elements can be made compatible in that the philosopher's reactions change over time: at first they must be compelled because they prefer not to rule and love contemplation, but later they can integrate contemplation and political action when they can "see" the connections between the forms and political life anew. See Brown, "Justice and Compulsion," especially 9–10.

42. Rosen takes the first prisoner to be freed "by nature" (515c) but I take the reference to nature to be about the whole of the prisoner's experience of initial confusion and discomfort. The image clearly states that another drags the released prisoner along the road (518e). See Rosen, *Plato's Republic*, 270.

Chapter 9. Images of Imperfection

1. Griswold argues that the response to the injustice of the ordinary city in the *Republic* is essential to turn one's back on it, and to focus on harmonizing one's own soul. See Charles L. Griswold, "Longing for the Best: Plato on Reconciliation with Imperfection," *Arion* 11, no. 2 (Fall 2003): 101–36. Here, I argue that Socrates is not arguing for quietism so much as asserting that even in the worst of regimes, to live justly affords greater happiness than living unjustly. It is an argument against people like Thrasymachus, who seem to capitulate to injustice as the "way of the world," not to be resisted, where Socrates favors resisting injustice through becoming a just type of person. This need not mean that the just person is completely inactive, only that the *approach* to enacting justice in the world is primarily through becoming a just sort of person whose actions will either benefit, or at least avoid harming, others around her. See also Ferrari, who contrasts Plato to Isocrates's far more political orientation. Ferrari, *City and Soul*, 88–90.

2. Here, I agree with Annas, who has argued that the moral and political aspects of the text can be separated. That is not to say that the political elements of the text are irrelevant, but rather that it is possible to consider the ethical question of whether to be just apart from whether one lives in a perfectly just or terribly unjust city, and in either case, Socrates's claim is that the just life is the happiest and best life. See Annas, *Platonic Ethics, Old and New*, 72–95.

3. While it is beyond the scope of this work, such a typology may also explain how Socrates is able to speak differently to different kinds of souls in his own *psychagōgia* and teaching of others.

4. Baracchi, *Myth, Life, and War*, 206.

5. Sara Brill, "Political Pathology in Plato's *Republic*," *Apeiron* 49, no. 2 (2016): 127–61. Brill argues that the medical language lays out a critical theory in which the practitioner of philosophy must also embark on self-criticism, just as a doctor learns in part from suffering from some of the diseases that he wishes to cure (408d–e).

6. Roochnik especially develops this line of argument in *Beautiful City*, particularly 51–77. Baracchi similarly writes that one finds the "irruption of life (in its death-bringing fluctuation) in the midst of the discourse aimed at controlling it." Baracchi, *Myth, Life, War*, 78.

7. Ferrari therefore takes the images of city and soul to be proportional analogies, and not causally related. See Ferrari, *City and Soul*, 60. I agree with Ferrari that the main force of the analogy is comparative, not causal. Still, sometimes Socrates does seem to say that more people in a given city are of the sort that the city is, for instance, democratic souls flourish in the democratic regime but are not to be found in the aristocratic one.

8. Brill, "Political Pathology," 131.

9. Danielle S. Allen, "Angry Bees, Wasps, and Jurors: The Symbolic Politics of ὀργή in Athens," in *Ancient Anger: Perspectives from Homer to Galen*, ed. Susanna Braund and Glenn W. Most (Cambridge: Cambridge University Press, 2003), 94–98. Bruce Rosenstock, "Athena's Cloak: Plato's Critique of the Democratic City in the *Republic*," *Political Theory* 22, no. 3 (1994): 379.

10. Of course, as only male citizens were part of the democracy, it was hardly an instance of universal suffrage, especially with the presence of slaves, but the point is that it is not the mixed system of representative democracy, which attempts to guard against problems with populism. As Rosen says, we should not confuse Socrates with a "contemporary liberal." Rosen, *Plato's Republic*, 317.

11. Segal, "The Myth Was Saved," 316–17.

12. Most notably, see Roochnik, *Beautiful City*, 77–93. Roochnik identifies the city's possession of free speech, the expression of *eros*, privacy, and the capacity to engage freely in philosophy as characteristics of the democratic city, while also acknowledging many of its limits.

13. Rosenstock, "Athena's Cloak," 364.

14. Murray, "Tragedy, Women," 188–89. Murray also connects Socrates's uses of *theōmai* here to the theatrical.

15. Gerasimos Santas, "Plato's Criticism of the 'Democratic Man' in the 'Republic,'" *Journal of Ethics* 5, no. 1 (2001): 65.

16. Santas thus takes this section to be a criticism of a version of a desire satisfaction theory. See Santas, "Plato's Criticism," 67–68.

17. Ferrari, *City and Soul*, 69.

18. Pappas, *Plato's Republic*, 193.

19. For a cogent critique of problems with the adequacy of the analogy to health in the form that it is set out in the *Republic*, see Santas, *Understanding*, 208–11.

20. Ferrari, *City and Soul*, 77.

21. Annas, *Introduction*, 307–9.

22. Klosko, *Development of Plato's Political Theory*, 105.

23. Rosen, *Plato's Republic*, 335.

24. Silvia Gastaldi, "The Image of the Soul and the Happiness of the Just Man," in *The Painter of Constitutions: Essays on Plato's Republic*, ed. Mario Vegetti, Franco Ferrari, and Tosca Lynch (Sankt Augustin: Academia Verlag, 2013), 293–94. See Hesiod, *Theogony*, 313–5.

25. Gastaldi, "Image of the Soul," 294.

26. See also Gastaldi, "Image of the Soul," 294.

27. Michael Clarke, "Between Lions and Men: Images of the Hero in the *Iliad*," *Greek, Roman, and Byzantine Studies* 36, no. 2 (Summer 1995): 143.

28. Clarke, "Between Lions and Men," 144.

29. Clarke, "Between Lions and Men," 148–49.

30. Segal, "The Myth Was Saved," 318.

31. Jera Marušič, "Poets and Mimesis in the *Republic*," in *Plato and the Poets*, ed. Pierre Destrée and Fritz-Gregor Herrmann (Leiden: Brill, 2011), 220–221.

32. Here, I follow Marušič's cogent way of unifying the concept of *mimēsis*. See Marušič, "Poets and Mimesis in the *Republic*," 222–26.

33. Janaway argues that while the sense of *mimēsis* changes, the reference to poetry as the object of the critique remains stable. Janaway, *Images of Excellence*, 107. Nehamas argues that Book Ten is the first time that Plato is systematic in his treatment, and that the earlier books really say little more than that good characters alone should be imitated. See Nehamas, "Plato on Imitation and Poetry," 51–52. Halliwell argues that the sense shifts in Plato's works. See Stephen Halliwell, *The Aesthetics of Mimesis: Ancient Texts and Modern Problems* (Princeton, NJ: Princeton University Press), 25.

34. Halliwell, *Aesthetics of Mimesis*, 126.

35. Belfiore argues that the presentations are remarkably alike, especially considering that Plato's aim is not to classify different kinds of mimetic practice but to discuss moral and psychological problems associated with it. See Elizabeth Belfiore, "A Theory of Imitation," *Transactions of the American Philological Association* 114 (1984): 121–46.

36. Pappas, *Plato's Republic*, 250.

37. Nehamas argues that the very use of the painting comparison shifts the focus away from *mimēsis* as acting like someone else, its common meaning before Plato, and to the question of the appearance rather than the reality that is being imitated. Nehamas, "Plato on Imitation and Poetry," 55–58.

38. Moss, "What Is Imitative Poetry?,"423.

39. Griswold notes a series of problems with the introduction of the divine craftsmen, for example, that this seems to both anthropomorphize God and comically introduces ideas for beds and other artifacts. See Charles Griswold, "The Ideas and the Criticism of Poetry in Plato's *Republic*, Book Ten," *Journal of the History of Philosophy* (April 1981): 19, 2, 135–150. Addressing this point is beyond the scope of this work, but I do not take Socrates to be ironic so much as demonstrating that *even if* the ideas themselves have a higher cause, the sort of *poiēsis* that poets and

painters partake in is still not at the level of the divine, but removed from it. Poets are not inspired by the gods but rather are their poor imitators. Their makings are of an inferior sort when compared to divine action, rather than an instance of it.

40. Griswold, "Ideas and the Criticism," 137.

41. Annas, *Introduction*, 340–41; Moss, "What Is Imitative Poetry?," 415–16.

42. Moss, "What Is Imitative Poetry?," 427.

43. Baracchi says the difference between Homer and Socrates on this point is that Socrates acknowledges the limits and shadows of his mythology while Homer does not. Socrates gives up the poets' claims to mimetic immediacy, that is, where there is no gap between the imitation and what it purports to describe. Baracchi, *Of Myth, Life, and War*, 122–25. See also Pappas, *Plato's Republic*, 259.

44. Kastely, *Rhetoric*, 201.

45. Moss, "What Is Imitative Poetry?," 430. Similarly, Nehamas argues that poets present vicious characters as if they are virtuous, thus providing a bad model for those who imitate them. Nehamas, "Plato on Imitation and Poetry," 68. Other explanations of the reason for the ethical problems with imitation include Ferrari's claim that the poet only imitates the words and deeds, but not inner reality of human beings. G. R. F. Ferrari, "Glaucon's Reward, Philosophy's Debt: The Myth of Er," in *Plato's Myths*, ed. Catalin Partenie (Cambridge: Cambridge University Press, 2009), 129.

46. As Kastely has argued, for this reason rhetoric has a place in the practice of philosophy. Kastely, *Rhetoric*, 225–26. In my view, Kastely rightly emphasizes the role of affect in Socrates's images and the need for its education. However, he sees the dialogue as oriented toward nonphilosophers, while I have been arguing that these images seek to educate philosophically. As I have argued, many of them educate one about a specific philosophical topic, such as justice, while others prepare one for the practice of philosophy (e.g., the cave image).

47. Lear sees the myth of Er as having both argumentative and therapeutic aspects. See Lear, "Allegory and Myth in Plato's *Republic*," 38–43.

48. Segal, "The Myth Was Saved," 324.

49. Gordon, *Plato's Erotic World*, 172–73.

50. In contrast, Levin has argued that while we cannot take poetry to be a *technē*, since philosophy alone is the true art that has access to the truth, nonetheless poetry can play a pedagogical role in the formation of children and in the poetry associated with public festivals that bind together members of the state. Poetry as it is currently written is not beneficial to those who listen to it, or to those who speak it, but it might be written differently in order to become of benefit. See Susan B. Levin, *The Ancient Quarrel between Philosophy and Poetry Revisited* (Oxford: Oxford University Press, 2000), chapter 5. Along similar lines, Greene argues that the primary problem with poetry is that the poet occupies himself with the world of the senses, thus shutting himself off from the intelligible world. Greene argues that philosophical poetry exists, but it must give "knowledge of the truth" by

choosing "images in such a way that the reader or hearer shall be reminded by the particulars of the universals." See William Chase Greene, "Plato's View of Poetry," *Harvard Studies in Classical Philology* 29 (1918): 28.

51. Roochnik notes that the philosophically erotic soul is even "mad" for what is other than itself, that is, the forms and their unifying structure. See Roochnik, *Beautiful City*, 90.

52. Baracchi, *Myth, Life, and War*, 197–99.

53. Segal writes that Platonic myth functions as a way of educating *eros*. See Segal, "The Myth Was Saved," 330–32. Of course, myth is not the only thing that can so function. Socrates also argues that the proper sort of music will also shape *eros* appropriately, but myths also have their place in such formation.

54. Josef Pieper, *The Platonic Myths*, trans. Dan Farrelly (South Bend, IN: St. Augustine's Press, 2011), 9.

55. In this respect, Platonic myths are quite different than the divine inspiration that religious traditions ascribe to sacred scripture.

56. Portions of this chapter were previously published in Marina McCoy, "Freedom and Responsibility in the Myth of Er," *Ideas y Valores* 61, no. 149 (2012): 125–41. Translations from the sections on the myth are from Bloom.

57. Baracchi draws attention to Socrates's use of the term *apologia* in returning to justice what the argument still owes it. Baracchi, *Of Myth, Life, and War*, 93.

58. Annas, *Introduction*, 353.

59. Ferrari, "Glaucon's Reward," 127.

60. Annas, *Introduction*, 122.

61. Ronald Johnson, "Does Plato's Myth of Er Contribute to the Argument of the *Republic*?," *Philosophy and Rhetoric* 32, no. 1 (1999): 3. Ferrari also offers a quite convincing argument that the myth is primarily addressed to Glaucon, who respects the intrinsic value of justice but still greatly desires that the just person receive honor and respect. Ferrari, "Glaucon's Reward," 116–33.

62. Here, I depart from interpreters such as Michael Inwood, who take the myth to be a more precise account of reincarnation. Again, I do not dispute that Socrates may believe in a general picture of reincarnation, especially since this theme recurs across many dialogues and is also shared by a number of religious people today. However, the metaphorical and symbolic aspects of mythic language are significant and ought to inform how we read the details of the myth, and what we take to be beyond the scope of knowledge. See Inwood, "Plato's Eschatological Myths," 28–50.

63. Thus, while I take near death experiences in the contemporary as well as ancient context seriously, insofar as they occur across many times, cultures, and religious beliefs, it is also notable that the particular images of those who experience them are partially informed by the cultural context in which they occur and partially often counter to the experiencer's cultural expectations. See, for example, a myriad of reports at www.nderf.org.

64. Fascinatingly, the myth of Er shares much in common with near death experiences as reported in many different cultures. This myth may indeed have some of its roots in being a near death experience. However, Socrates's exposition of it cannot simply be a report of an actual experience, since he also weaves into the myth characters that have formed part of the language of the *Republic* as a whole: for example, Odysseus, who like Socrates engages in ascent and descent. The language of the myth is also reminiscent of the ascent and descent of the cave. Thus, clearly at least some of its elements are actively constructed by Plato rather than being a straightforward report of an actual near death experience.

65. H. S. Thayer, "The Myth of Er," *History of Philosophy Quarterly* 5, no. 4 (1988): 371–72. Baracchi, *Myth, Life, and War*, 202.

66. Johnson, "Does Plato's Myth?," 8–9.

67. Baracchi, *Myth, Life, and War*, 180.

Bibliography

Adam, J. *Plato's Republic.* Translated with an appendix and commentary. Cambridge: Cambridge University Press, 1902.

Alcidamas. "On Those Who Write Written Speeches." In *Alcidamas, the Works and Fragments.* Edited by J. Muir. London: Bristol Classical Press, 2001.

Allen, Danielle S. "Angry Bees, Wasps, and Jurors: The Symbolic Politics of ὀργή in Athens." In *Ancient Anger: Perspectives from Homer to Galen,* edited by Susanna Braund and Glenn W. Most, 76–98. Cambridge: Cambridge University Press, 2003.

Allen, R. E., ed. *Studies in Plato's Metaphysics.* London: Routledge & Kegan Paul, 1965.

Altman, William. *Plato the Teacher: The Crisis of the Republic.* Lanham, MD: Lexington Books, 2013.

Anderson, Merrick. "Thrasymachus' Sophistic Account of Justice in *Republic* I." *Ancient Philosophy* 36 (2016): 151–72.

Annas, Julia. *Platonic Ethics, Old and New.* Ithaca, NY: Cornell University Press, 1999.

Annas, Julia. "Plato's Myths of Judgment." *Phronesis* 27, no. 2 (1982): 119–43.

Annas, Julia. *An Introduction to Plato's Republic.* Oxford: Oxford University Press, 1981.

Annas, Julia. "Plato's *Republic* and Feminism." *Philosophy* 51 (July 1976): 307–21.

Aristophanes. *Aristophanes: The Birds and Other Plays.* Translated by David Barrett and Alan Sommerstein. London: Penguin, 1978.

Aristophanes. *Knights.* Cambridge: Cambridge University Press, 1901.

Asmis, Elizabeth. "Plato on Poetic Creativity." In *Cambridge Companion to Plato,* edited by Richard Kraut, 338–64. Cambridge: Cambridge University Press, 1992.

Ausland, Haydn. "Socrates' Argumentative Burden in the *Republic.*" In *Plato as Author: The Rhetoric of Philosophy,* edited by Ann N. Michelini, 123–25. Leiden: Brill, 2003.

Bakewell, Geoffrey. "The Voice of Aeschylus in Plato's *Republic.*" In *Voice and Voices in Antiquity,* edited by Niall Slater, 260–76. Boston: Brill, 2016.

Baracchi, Claudia. "Beyond the Comedy and Tragedy of Authority." *Philosophy and Rhetoric* 34, no. 2 (2001): 151–76.

Baracchi, Claudia. *Of Myth, Life, and War in Plato's Republic*. Bloomington: Indiana University Press, 2001.

Barney, Rachel. "Callicles and Thrasymachus." *Stanford Encyclopedia of Philosophy*, edited by Edward N. Zalta. Winter 2011. https://plato.stanford.edu/archives/win2011/entries/callicles-thrasymachus/. Accessed August 21, 2015.

Barney, Rachel. "Socrates' Refutation of Thrasymachus." In *The Blackwell Guide to Plato's Republic*, edited by Gerasimos Santas, 44–62. Malden, MA: Wiley-Blackwell, 2006.

Barney, Rachel. "Platonism, Moral Nostalgia, and the 'City of Pigs.'" *Proceedings of the Boston Area Colloquium in Ancient Philosophy* 17 (2001): 207–27.

Bartha, Paul. "Analogy and Analogical Reasoning." *Stanford Encyclopedia of Philosophy*, edited by Edward N. Zalta. Fall 2013. http://plato.stanford.edu/archives/fall2013/entries/reasoning-analogy/. Accessed June 11, 2015.

Belfiore, Elizabeth. "A Theory of Imitation." *Transactions of the American Philological Association* 114 (1984): 121–46.

Bell, Jeremy, and Michael Naas, eds. *Plato's Animals*. Bloomington: Indiana University Press, 2015.

Benardete, Seth. *Socrates' Second Sailing: On Plato's Republic*. Chicago: University of Chicago Press, 1989.

Benoit, William. "Aristotle's Example: The Rhetorical Induction." *Quarterly Journal of Speech* 66, no. 2 (1980): 182–92.

Berry, Christopher. "Of Pigs and Men: Luxury in Plato's *Republic*." *Polis* 8 (1989): 2–24.

Blondell, Ruby. *The Play of Character in Plato's Dialogues*. Cambridge: Cambridge University Press, 2002.

Bloom, Allan, trans. *The Republic of Plato*, 2nd edition. New York: Basic Books, 1991.

Bloom, Allan. "Response to Hall." *Political Theory* 5, no. 3 (August 1977): 315–30.

Blössner, Norbert. "The City-Soul Analogy." In *The Cambridge Companion to Plato's Republic*, edited by G. R. F Ferrari, 345–85. New York: Cambridge University Press, 2007.

Bobonich, Christopher. *Plato's Utopia Recast: His Later Ethics and Politics*. Oxford: Clarendon Press, 2002.

Brann, Eva. "The Music of the *Republic*." *Agon* 1 (1967): 1–117.

Braund, Susanna, and Glenn W. Most, eds. *Ancient Anger: Perspectives from Homer to Galen*. Cambridge: Cambridge University Press, 2003.

Brill, Sara. "Political Pathology in Plato's *Republic*." *Apeiron* 49, no. 2 (2016): 127–61.

Brisson, Luc. "Plato's Theory of Sense Perception in the 'Timaeus': How It Works and What It Means." *Proceedings of the Boston Area Colloquium in Ancient Philosophy*, edited by John Cleary and Gary Gurtler, 13 (1997): 147–75.

Brown. Eric. "Justice and Compulsion for Plato's Philosopher-Rulers." *Ancient Philosophy* 20 (2000): 1–17.

Burch, Kerry. "Plato's Myth of the Noble Lie and the Predicaments of American Civic Education." *Studies in Philosophy and Education* 26, no. 2 (2007): 111–25.

Burkert, Walter. "Thesmophoria." In *Greek Religion*. Cambridge, MA: Harvard University Press, 1987.

Burkert, Walter. "The Myth of Korē and Pig-Sacrifice." In *Homo Necans: The Anthropology of Ancient Greek Sacrificial Ritual and Myth*, translated by Peter Bing, 256–64. Berkeley: University of California Press, 1983.

Burkert, Walter. *Homo Necans: The Anthropology of Ancient Greek Sacrificial Ritual and Myth*. Translated by Peter Bing. Berkeley: University of California Press, 1983.

Burnet, John. *Platonis Opera, Volume Four*. Oxford: Oxford University Press, 1903.

Burnyeat, Myles F. "Presidential Address: The Truth of Tripartition." *Proceedings of the Aristotelian Society* 106 (2006): 1–23.

Burnyeat, Myles F. "Sphinx without a Secret." *New York Review of Books*, May 30, 1985, 30–36. http://www.nybooks.com/articles/1985/05/30/sphinx-without-a-secret/. Accessed January 20, 2017.

Campbell, D. *Greek Lyric III*, 2nd edition. Cambridge, MA: Harvard University Press, 1991.

Carmola, Kateri. "Noble Lying: Justice and Intergenerational Tension in Plato's *Republic*." *Political Theory* 31, no. 1 (February 2003): 39–62.

Chappell, T. D. J. "Thrasymachus and Definition." *Oxford Studies in Ancient Philosophy* 18 (2000): 101–7.

Charalambopolous, Nikos. *Platonic Drama and Its Ancient Reception*. Cambridge: Cambridge University Press, 2012.

Chen, Ludwig. *Acquiring Knowledge of the Ideas: A Study of Plato's Methods in the Phaedo, Symposium, and the Central Books of the Republic*. Stuttgart: Franz Steiner Verlag, 1992.

Clarke, Michael. "Between Lions and Men: Images of the Hero in the *Iliad*." *Greek, Roman, and Byzantine Studies* 36, no. 2 (Summer 1995): 137–59.

Clay, Jenny Strauss. "The Generation of Monsters in Hesiod." *Classical Philology* 88, no. 2 (1993): 105–16.

Cole, Susan Guettel. "Demeter in the Ancient Greek City and Its Countryside." In *Oxford Readings in Greek Religion*, edited by Richard Buxton, 199–216. Oxford: Oxford University Press, 2000.

Cooper, John. "Plato's Theory of Human Motivation." *History of Philosophy Quarterly* 1, no. 1 (1984): 3–21.

Cooper, Neil. "Between Knowledge and Ignorance." *Phronesis* 31, no. 3 (1986): 229–42.

Cornford, F. M. "Mathematics and Dialectic in the Republic, VI–VII." In *Studies in Plato's Metaphysics*, edited by R. E. Allen, 61–95. London: Routledge & Kegan Paul, 1965.

Cornford, F. M., trans. *The Republic of Plato*. Translated with an introduction and notes. London: Oxford University Press, 1941.

Cross, R. C., and A. D. Woozley. *Plato's Republic: A Philosophical Commentary.* London: MacMillan, 1964.

Denyer, Nicholas. "Sun and Line: The Role of the Good." In *The Cambridge Companion to Plato's Republic*, edited by G. R. F. Ferrari, 284–309. New York: Cambridge University Press, 2007.

Desjardins, Rosemary. *Plato and the Good.* Leiden: Brill, 2003.

Destrée, Pierre. "Poets in the Cave." In *Dialogues on Plato's Politeia (Republic): Selected Papers from the Ninth Symposium Platonicum*, edited by Noboru Notomi and Luc Brisson, 336–40. Sankt Augustin: Academia Verlag, 2013.

Destrée, Pierre. "Happiness, Justice, and Poetry in Plato's *Republic.*" In *Proceedings of the Boston Area Colloquium in Ancient Philosophy*, volume 25, edited by Gary Gurtler SJ and William Wians, 243–69. Leiden: Brill, 2009.

Destrée, Pierre, and Fritz-Gregor Herrmann, eds. *Plato and the Poets.* Leiden: Brill, 2011.

Detienne, Marcel. "The Violence of Well-Born Ladies: Women in the Thesmophoria." In *The Cuisine of Sacrifice Among the Greeks*, edited by Marcel Detienne and J. P. Vernant, 129–47. Chicago: University of Chicago Press, 1989.

Detienne, Marcel, and J. P. Vernant, eds. *The Cuisine of Sacrifice Among the Greeks.* Chicago: University of Chicago Press, 1989.

Devereux, Daniel. "Socrates' First City in the *Republic.*" *Apeiron* 13, no. 1 (June 1979): 36–40.

Diamond, Eli. "Aristotle's Appropriation of Plato's Sun Analogy in *De Anima.*" *Apeiron* 47, no. 3 (2014): 365–89.

Dombrowski, Daniel. "On the Alleged Truth about Lies in Plato's *Republic.*" *Polis* 21 (2004): 93–106.

Donahue, Brian. "The Dramatic Significance of Cephalus in Plato's *Republic.*" *Teaching Philosophy* 20, no. 3 (September 1997): 239–49.

Dorter, Kenneth. *The Transformation of Plato's Republic.* Lanham, MD: Lexington Books, 2006.

Edwards, Michelle, trans. *Greek Orators I: Antiphon and Lysias.* Oxford: Aris and Philips, 1985.

Elias, Julius. *Plato's Defense of Poetry.* Albany: State University of New York Press, 1984.

Else, Gerald F. *Plato and Aristotle on Poetry.* Edited with an introduction and notes by Peter Burian. Chapel Hill: University of North Carolina Press, 1986.

Engberg-Pederson, Troels. "More on Aristotelian Epagoge." *Phronesis* 24, no. 3 (January 1979): 301–19.

Fagan, Patricia. *Plato and Tradition: The Poetic and Cultural Context of Philosophy.* Evanston, IL: Northwestern University Press, 2013.

Ferber, Rafael, and Gregor Damschen. "Is the Idea of the Good Beyond Being? Plato's *"epikeina tēs ousias"* Revisited (*Republic* 6 509b8–10)." In *Second Sailing: Alternative Perspectives on Plato*, edited by Debra Nails, Harold Tarrant, Mika Kajava, and Eero Salmenkivi, 197–203. Espoo: Wellprint Oy, 2015.

Ferrari, Giovanni R. F. *City and Soul in Plato's Republic.* Sankt Augustin: Academia Verlag, 2003.

Ferrari, Giovanni R. F. "Glaucon's Reward, Philosophy's Debt: The Myth of Er." In *Plato's Myths*, edited by Catalin Partenie, 116–33. Cambridge: Cambridge University Press, 2009.

Ferrari, G. R. F., ed. *The Cambridge Companion to Plato's Republic.* New York: Cambridge University Press, 2007.

Fine, Gail. *Plato on Knowledge and Forms: Selected Essays.* Oxford: Clarendon Press, 2003.

Flew, G. N. "Responding to Plato's Thrasymachus." *Philosophy* 70, no. 273 (July 1995): 437–47.

Foley, Helene P. "Performing Gender in Greek Comedy." In *The Cambridge Companion to Greek Comedy*, edited by Martin Revermann, 259–74. Cambridge: Cambridge University Press, 2014.

Frank, Jill. *Poetic Justice: Rereading Plato's Republic.* Chicago: University of Chicago Press, 2018.

Freydberg, Bernard. *Philosophy as Comedy: Aristophanes, Logos, and Eros.* Bloomington: Indiana University Press, 2008.

Freydburg, Bernard. "Homeric *Methodos* in Plato's Socratic Dialogues." In *Philosophy in Dialogue: Plato's Many Devices*, edited by Gary Scott, 111–29. Evanston, IL: Northwestern University Press, 2007.

Friedlander, Paul. *Plato*, 3 vols. Translated by Hans Meyerhoff. Princeton, NJ: Princeton University Press, 1964.

Fussi, Alessandra. "The Myth of the Last Judgment in the *Gorgias*." *Review of Metaphysics* 54, no. 3 (2001): 29–52.

Gadamer, Hans-Georg. "Plato and the Poets." In *Dialogue and Dialectic: Eight Hermeneutical Studies on Plato*, translated by P. Christopher Smith, 39–72. New Haven: Yale University Press, 1980.

Gastaldi, Silvia. "The Image of the Soul and the Happiness of the Just Man." In *The Painter of Constitutions: Essays on Plato's Republic*, edited by Mario Vegetti, Franco Ferrari, and Tosca Lynch, 291–307. Sankt Augustin: Academia Verlag, 2013.

Gastaldi, Silvia. "Poetry: *Paideia* and *Mimesis*." In *The Painter of Constitutions: Selected Essays on Plato's Republic*, edited by Mario Vegetti, Franco Ferrari, and Tosca Lynch, 25–71. Sankt Augustin: Academia Verlag, 2013.

Gerber, Douglas, editor and translator. *Greek Elegiac Poetry from the Seventh to Fifth Centuries BC.* Cambridge, MA: Loeb Classical Library, 1999.

Gerson, Lloyd. "Platonic Dualism." *Monist* 69 (1986): 352–69.

Golden, Leon. "Plato's Concept of *Mimesis*." *British Journal of Aesthetics* 15 (1975): 118–31.

Gordon, Jill. *Plato's Erotic World: From Cosmic Origins to Human Death.* Cambridge: Cambridge University Press, 2012.

Gordon, Jill. *Turning Toward Philosophy: Literary Device and Dramatic Structure in Plato's Dialogues*. University Park: Penn State Press, 2010.

Gonzalez, Francisco. "Plato's Perspectivism." *Plato Journal* 16 (2016): 31–48.

Gonzalez, Francisco. *Dialectic and Dialogue: Plato's Practice of Philosophical Inquiry*. Evanston, IL: Northwestern University Press, 1998.

Gonzalez, Francisco, ed. *The Third Way: New Directions in Platonic Studies*. Lanham, MD: Rowman & Littlefield, 1995.

Gosling, J. G. "*Doxa* and *Dunamis* in Plato's *Republic*." *Phronesis* 12 (1968): 119–30.

Greene, William Chase. "The Spirit of Comedy in Plato." *Harvard Studies in Classical Philology* 31 (1920): 63–123.

Greene, William Chase. "Plato's View of Poetry." *Harvard Studies in Classical Philology* 29 (1918): 1–75.

Griswold, Charles L. "Longing for the Best: Plato on Reconciliation with Imperfection." *Arion* 11, no. 2 (Fall 2003): 101–36.

Griswold, Charles L. "Irony in the Platonic Dialogues." *Philosophy and Literature* 26, no. 1 (2002): 84–106.

Griswold, Charles L. "Plato's Metaphilosophy: Why Plato Wrote Dialogues." In *Platonic Writings, Platonic Readings*, edited by Charles Griswold, 143–67. New York: Routledge, 1988.

Griswold, Charles. "The Ideas and the Criticism of Poetry in Plato's *Republic*, Book 10." *Journal of the History of Philosophy* 19, no. 2 (1981): 135–50.

Hadot, Pierre. *Philosophy as a Way of Life: Spiritual Exercises from Socrates to Foucault*. Oxford: Wiley-Blackwell, 1995.

Halliwell, Stephen. "Laughter." In *The Cambridge Companion to Greek Comedy*, edited by Martin Revermann, 189–205. Cambridge: Cambridge University Press, 2014.

Halliwell, Stephen. "The Life and Death Journey of the Soul: Interpreting the Myth of Er." In *The Cambridge Companion to Plato's Republic*, edited by G. R. F. Ferrari, 445–73. Cambridge: Cambridge University Press, 2007.

Halliwell, Stephen. *The Aesthetics of Mimesis: Ancient Texts and Modern Problems*. Princeton, NJ: Princeton University Press, 2002.

Hansen, Peter J. "Thrasymachus and His Attachment to Justice." *Polis* 32 (2015): 344–68.

Hart, Verity. "Beware of Imitations: Image Recognition in Plato." In *New Essays on Plato: Language and Thought in Fourth Century Philosophy*, edited by Fritz-Gregor Herrmann, 21–42. Swansea: Classical Press of Wales, 2006.

Hauser, Gerard A. "Reply to Benoit." *Philosophy and Rhetoric* 20, no. 4 (1987): 268–73.

Hauser, Gerard A. "Aristotle's Example Revisited." *Philosophy and Rhetoric* 18, no. 3 (1985): 171–80.

Havelock, Eric. *Preface to Plato*. Cambridge, MA: Harvard University Press, 1982.

Henderson, Jeffrey. *The Maculate Muse: Obscene Language in Attic Comedy.* Oxford: Oxford University Press, 1991.

Henderson, Jeffrey. "The Dēmos and Comic Competition." In *Nothing to Do with Dionysos? Athenian Drama in Its Social Context,* edited by John J. Winkler and Froma I. Zeitlin, 271–313. Princeton, NJ: Princeton University Press, 1990.

Henderson, Jeffrey. "Comic Hero vs. Political Elite." In *Tragedy, Comedy, and the Polis: Papers from the Greek Drama Conference, Nottingham, 18–20 July 1990,* edited by Allan Sommerstein, 307–20. Bari: Levante, 1993.

Henderson, T. J. "In Defense of Thrasymachus." *American Philosophical Quarterly* 7 (1970): 218–28.

Hesiod. *Theogony and Works and Days.* Translated by Kimberly Johnson. Evanston, IL: Northwestern University Press, 2017.

Hoesly, Dusty, and Nicholas D. Smith. "Thrasymachus: Diagnosis and Treatment." In *Dialogues on Plato's Politeia (Republic): Selected Papers from the Ninth Symposium Platonicum,* 60–65. Sankt Augustin: Academic Verlag.

Hourani, George F. "Thrasymachus' Definition of Justice in Plato's *Republic.*" *Phronesis* 7 (1962): 110–20.

Howland, Jacob. *Glaucon's Fate: History, Myth, and Character in Plato's Republic.* Philadelphia: Paul Dry Books, 2018.

Howland, Jacob. *The Republic: The Odyssey of Philosophy.* Philadelphia: Paul Dry Books, 2004.

Howland, Jacob. "Storytelling and Philosophy in Plato's *Republic.*" *American Catholic Philosophical Quarterly* 79, no. 2 (2005): 213–32.

Howland, Jacob. "Plato's Reply to Lysias: *Republic* 1 and 2 and *Against Eratosthenes.*" *American Journal of Philology* 125, no. 2 (2004): 179–208.

Hughes, Alan. *Performing Greek Comedy.* Cambridge: Cambridge University Press, 2012.

Hyland, Drew. "Aporia, the Longer Road, and the Good." *Graduate Philosophy Journal* 32, no. 1 (2011): 145–75.

Hyland, Drew. "Plato's Three Waves and the Question of Utopia." *Interpretation* 18, no. 1 (1990): 91–109.

Hyland, Drew. "Taking the Longer Road: The Irony of Plato's *Republic.*" *Revue de Métaphysique et de Morale* 93, no. 3 (1988): 317–35.

Inwood, Michael. "Plato's Eschatological Myths." In *Plato's Myths,* edited by Catalin Partenie, 28–50. Cambridge: Cambridge University Press, 2009.

Irwin, Terence. *Plato's Moral Theory.* Oxford: Oxford University Press, 1977.

Isager, Signe. *Ancient Greek Agriculture: An Introduction.* Edited by Jens Erik Skydsgaard. London: Routledge, 1992.

Janaway, Christopher. *Images of Excellence: Plato's Critique of the Arts.* Oxford: Clarendon Press, 1995.

Johnson, Ronald. "Does Plato's Myth of Er Contribute to the Argument of the *Republic?*" *Philosophy and Rhetoric* 32, no. 1 (1999): 1–13.

Joseph, Horace W. B. *Knowledge and the Good in Plato's Republic*. Westport, CT: Greenwood Press, 1981, reprint of Oxford University Press, 1948 edition.

Kahn, Charles H. *Plato and the Socratic Dialogue: The Philosophical Use of a Literary Form*. Cambridge: Cambridge University Press, 1998.

Kahn, Charles H. "Plato's Theory of Desire." *Review of Metaphysics* 41, no. 1 (1987): 77–103.

Kahn, Charles H. "The Meaning of 'Justice' and the Theory of Forms." *Journal of Philosophy* 69, no. 18 (1972): 567–79.

Kastley, James L. *The Rhetoric of Plato's Republic*. Chicago: University of Chicago Press, 2015.

Kerferd, G. B. "The Doctrine of Thrasymachus in Plato's *Republic*." *Durham University Journal* 9 (1947): 19–27.

Kieffer, John S. "Philoctetes and *Arete*." *Classical Philology* 37, no. 1 (January 1942): 38–50.

Klein, Jacob. *A Commentary on Plato's Meno*. Chicago: University of Chicago Press, 1965.

Klosko, George. *The Development of Plato's Thought*. New York: Methuen, 1986.

Kochin, Michael. *Gender and Rhetoric in Plato's Political Thought*. Cambridge: Cambridge University Press, 2002.

Konstan, David. *The Emotions of the Ancient Greeks*. Toronto: University of Toronto Press, 2006.

Kraut, Richard. "The Defense of Justice in Plato's *Republic*." In *The Cambridge Companion to Plato's Republic*, edited by G. R. F Ferrari, 311–37. New York: Cambridge University Press, 2007.

Kraut, Richard, ed. *Cambridge Companion to Plato*. Cambridge: Cambridge University Press, 1992.

Kremer, Mark. "Aristophanes' Criticism of Egalitarianism: An Interpretation of *The Assembly of Women*." *Interpretation* 21, no. 3 (1994): 261–74.

Lachterman, David. "What Is the Good of Plato's *Republic?*" *Saint John's Review* 39, nos. 1 and 2 (1989–1990): 139–72.

Lake, Patrick. "Plato's Homeric Dialogue: Homeric Quotation, Paraphrase, and Allusion in the *Republic*." Doctoral dissertation, Fordham University, 2011.

Lamb, W. R. M., trans. *Plato in Twelve Volumes*, vol. 9. Cambridge, MA: Harvard University Press; London: William Heinemann Ltd., 1925.

Lattimore, Richmond, trans. *Homer, Odyssey*. New York: Harper and Row, 1968.

Lear, Gabriel Richardson. "Mimesis and Psychological Change in *Republic* III." In *Plato and the Poets*, edited by Pierre Destrée and Fritz-Gregor Herrmann, 195–216. Leiden: Brill, 2011.

Lear, Jonathan. "Allegory and Myth in Plato's *Republic*." In *The Blackwell Guide to Plato's Republic*, edited by Gerasimos Santas, 25–43. Oxford: Blackwell, 2006.

Lear, Gabriel Richardson. "Plato on Learning to Love Beauty." In *The Blackwell Guide to Plato's Republic*, edited by Gerasimos Santas, 104–23. Oxford: Blackwell, 2006.

Lear, Jonathan. "Inside and Outside the *Republic*." *Phronesis* 37, no. 2 (1992): 184–215.

Ledbetter, Grace. *Poetics Before Plato*. Princeton, NJ: Princeton University Press, 2002.

Levin, Susan B. *The Ancient Quarrel between Philosophy and Poetry Revisited*. Oxford: Oxford University Press, 2000.

Lloyd, G. E. R. *Polarity and Analogy*. Cambridge: Cambridge University Press, 1966.

Long, Christopher. "Who Let the Dogs Out?" *Plato's Animals*, edited by Jeremy Bell and Michael Naas, 131–45. Bloomington: Indiana University Press, 2015.

Long, Christopher. *Socratic and Platonic Political Philosophy: Practicing a Politics of Reading*. Cambridge: Cambridge University Press, 2014.

Long, Christopher. "Socrates and the Politics of Music: Preludes of the *Republic*." *Polis* 24, no. 1 (2007): 70–90.

Lorenz, Hendrik. "Plato on the Soul." In *The Oxford Handbook of Plato*, edited by Gail Fine, 243–66. Oxford: Oxford University Press, 2008.

Lorenz, Hendrik. "The Analysis of the Soul in Plato's *Republic*." In *The Blackwell Guide to Plato's Republic*, edited by Gerasimos Santas, 146–65. Oxford: Blackwell, 2006.

Ludwig, Paul. "Eros in the *Republic*." In *The Cambridge Companion to Plato's Republic*, edited by G. R. F. Ferrari, 202–31. New York: Cambridge University Press.

Lycos, Kimon. "Aristotle and Plato on 'Appearing.'" *Mind* 73, no. 292 (1964): 496–514.

Lycos, Kimon. *Plato on Justice and Power: Reading Book I of Plato's Republic*. Albany: State University of New York Press, 1987.

Lysias. *Selected Speeches (Cambridge Greek and Latin Classics)*. Cambridge: Cambridge University Press, 2002.

Martin-Velasco, Maria Jose. "The Paradigm in Aristotle's *Rhetoric* and Its Use in Judicial Speeches." Institute of Classical Studies talk, December 9, 2010.

Marušič, Jera. "Poets and Mimesis in the *Republic*." In *Plato and the Poets*, edited by Pierre Destrée and Fritz-Gregor Herrmann, 217–40. Leiden: Brill, 2011.

McCabe, Mary Margaret. *Plato and His Predecessors: The Dramatisation of Reason*. Cambridge: Cambridge University Press, 2000.

McCabe, Mary Margaret. *Plato's Individuals*. Princeton, NJ: Princeton University Press, 1999.

McCoy, Marina. "Myth and Argument in Glaucon's Account of Gyges's Ring and Adeimantus's Use of Poetry." In *Logoi and Muthoi*, edited by William Wians, 266–78. Albany: State University of New York Press, 2019.

McCoy, Marina. "Perspectivism and the Philosophical Rhetoric of the Dialogue Form." *Plato Journal* 16 (2016): 49–57.

McCoy, Marina. "The City of Sows and Sexual Differentiation in Plato's *Republic*." In *Plato's Animals*, edited by Jeremy Bell and Michael Naas, 149–60. Bloomington: Indiana University Press, 2015.

McCoy, Marina. "Freedom and Responsibility in the Myth of Er." *Ideas y Valores* 61, no. 149 (2012): 125–41.

McCoy, Marina. *Wounded Heroes: Vulnerability as a Virtue in Ancient Greek Literature and Philosophy*. Oxford: Oxford University Press, 2013.

McCoy, Marina. *Rhetoric of Philosophers and Sophists*. Cambridge: Cambridge University Press, 2008.

McCoy, Marina. "Sophistry and Philosophy in Plato's *Republic*." *Polis* 22, no. 2 (2005): 265–86.

McCoy, Marina. "Socrates on Simonides: The Use of Poetry in Socratic and Platonic Rhetoric." *Philosophy and Rhetoric* 32, no. 4 (1999): 349–67.

McKee, Patrick. "Surprise Endings: Cephalus and the Indispensable Teacher of *Republic* X." *Philosophical Investigations* 31, no. 1 (January 2008): 68–82.

McKeen, Catherine. "Swillsburg City Limits (the 'City of Pigs': 'Republic' 370C–372D)." *Polis* 21 (2004): 70–92.

McPherran, Mark. "The Gods and Piety of Plato's *Republic*." In *The Blackwell Guide to Plato's Republic*, edited by Gerasimos Santas, 84–103. Oxford: Blackwell, 2006.

Mei, Todd. "Justice and the Banning of the Poets: The Way of Hermeneutics in Plato's *Republic*." *Review of Metaphysics* 60 (June 2007): 755–78.

Michelini, Ann, ed. *Plato as Author: The Rhetoric of Philosophy*. Leiden: Brill, 2003.

Miller, Mitchell. "Beginning the 'Longer Way.'" In *The Cambridge Companion to Plato's Republic*, edited by G. R. F. Ferrari, 310–44. New York: Cambridge University Press, 2007.

Miller, Mitchell. "Platonic Provocations: Reflections on the Soul and the Good in the *Republic*." In *Platonic Investigations*, edited by Dominic O'Meara, 163–93. Washington, DC: The Catholic University of America Press, 1985.

Miščević, Nenad. "Plato's *Republic* as a Political Thought Experiment." *Croatian Journal of Philosophy* 35 (January 2012): 153–65.

Mitscherling, Jeff. *The Image of the Second Sun: Plato on Poetry, Rhetoric, and the Technē of Mimēsis*. Amherst, NY: Humanity Books, 2009.

Moore, Holly. "Why Does Thrasymachus Blush? Ethical Consistency in Socrates' Refutation of Thrasymachus." *Polis* 32 (2015): 321–43.

Moore, Holly. "The Psychagogic Work of Examples in Plato's *Statesman*." *Philosophy and Rhetoric* 49, no. 3 (2016): 300–22.

Moravcsik, J. M. E., and Philip Temko, eds. *Plato on Beauty, Wisdom, and the Arts*. Totowa, NJ: Rowman & Littlefield, 1982.

Morgan, Kathryn. *Myth and Philosophy: From the Presocratics to Plato*. Cambridge: Cambridge University Press, 2000.

Morrison, Donald. "The Utopian Character of Plato's Ideal City." In *The Cambridge Companion to Plato's Republic*, edited by G. R. F Ferrari, 232–55. New York: Cambridge University Press, 2007.

Morrow, Glenn. "Plato and Greek Slavery." *Mind* 48, no. 190 (1939): 186–201.

Moss, Jessica. "What Is Imitative Poetry and Why Is It Bad?" In *The Cambridge Companion to Plato's Republic*, ed. G. R. F. Ferrari, 415–44. New York: Cambridge University Press, 2007.

Murray, Penelope. "Tragedy, Women and the Family in Plato's *Republic*." In *Plato and the Poets*, edited by Pierre Destrée and Fritz-Gregor Herrmann, 175–93. Leiden: Brill, 2011.

Nadoff, Ramona. *Exiling the Poets*. Chicago: University of Chicago Press, 2002.

Nails, Debra. *The People of Plato: A Prosopography of Plato and Other Socratics*. Indianapolis: Hackett, 2002.

Nails, Debra. "The Dramatic Date of Plato's *Republic*." *Classical Journal* 93 (1998): 383–96.

Nails, Debra. *Agora, Academy, and the Conduct of Philosophy*. Dordrecht: Kluwer Academic, 1995.

Nails, Debra, Harold Tarrant, Mika Kajava, and Eero Salmenkivi, eds. *Second Sailing: Alternative Perspectives on Plato*. Espoo: Wellprint Oy, 2015.

Nehamas, Alexander. "Plato on Imitation and Poetry in *Republic* 10." In *Plato on Beauty, Wisdom, and the Arts*, edited by J. M. E. Moravcsik and Philip Temko, 47–78. Totowa, NJ: Rowman & Littlefield, 1982.

Nichols, Mary P. *Socrates and the Political Community: An Ancient Debate*. Albany: State University of New York Press, 1987.

Nightingale, Andrea. *Spectacles of Truth in Classical Greek Philosophy*. Cambridge: Cambridge University Press, 2004.

Nightingale, Andrea. *Genres in Dialogue: Plato and the Construct of Philosophy*. Cambridge: Cambridge University Press, 2000.

Notomi, Noboru. "Image-Making in *Republic* X and the *Sophist*: Plato's Criticism of the Poet and the Sophist." In *Plato and the Poets*, edited by Pierre Destrée and Fritz-Gregor Herrmann, 299–326. Leiden: Brill, 2011.

Notomi, Noboru, and Luc Brisson, eds. *Dialogues on Plato's Politeia (Republic): Selected Papers from the Ninth Symposium Platonicum*. Sankt Augustin: Academia Verlag, 2013.

Nussbaum, Martha. *The Fragility of Goodness: Luck and Ethics in Greek Tragedy and Philosophy*, 2nd ed. Cambridge: Cambridge University Press, 2001.

Osborne, Robin. "Women and Sacrifice in Classical Greece." *Classical Quarterly* 43, no. 2 (1993): 392–405.

Page, Carl. "The Truth about Lies in Plato's *Republic*." *Ancient Philosophy* 11 (1991): 1–33.

Page, Carl. "The Unjust Treatment of Polemarchus." *History of Philosophy Quarterly* 7, no. 3 (July 1990): 243–67.

Pappas, Nickolas. "Plato's Aesthetics." *Stanford Encyclopedia of Philosophy*, edited by Edward N. Zalta. Fall 2016. https://plato.stanford.edu/archives/fall2016/entries/plato-aesthetics/. Accessed January 30, 2017.

Pappas, Nickolas. *The Routledge Guidebook to Plato's Republic*. New York: Routledge, 2013.

Pappas, Nickolas. "Plato on Poetry: Imitation or Inspiration?" *Philosophy Compass* 10 (2012): 1–11.

Pappas, Nickolas. "*Mimēsis* in Aristophanes and Plato." *Philosophical Inquiry* 21 (Summer–Fall 1999): 61–78.

Partenie, Catlin, ed. *Plato's Myths*. Cambridge: Cambridge University Press, 2009.

Patterson, Richard. "Word and Image in Plato." In *Presocratics and Plato: Festschrift at Delphi in Honor of Charles Kahn*, edited by Richard Patterson, Vassilis Karasmanis, and Arnold Hermann, 429–55. Las Vegas: Parmenides, 2012.

Patterson, Richard, Vassilis Karasmanis, and Arnold Hermann. *Presocratics and Plato: Festschrift at Delphi in Honor of Charles Kahn*. Las Vegas: Parmenides, 2012.

Patterson, Richard. "Diagrams, Dialectic, and Mathematical Foundations in Plato." *Apeiron* 40, no. 1 (2007): 1–33.

Patterson, Richard. "*Philosophos Agonistes*: Imagery and Moral Psychology in Plato's *Republic*." *Journal of the History of Philosophy* 35 (1997): 327–54.

Patterson, Richard. "Plato on Philosophic Character." *Journal of the History of Philosophy* 25, no. 3 (1987): 325–50.

Pieper, Josef. *The Platonic Myths*. Translated by Dan Farrelly. South Bend, IN: St. Augustine's Press, 2011.

Plutarch. *Plutarch's Lives*. Translated by Bernadette Perrin. Cambridge, MA: Harvard University Press, 1914.

Popper, Karl. *The Open Society and Its Enemies, Volume I: Plato*. New York: Routledge, 1963.

Pulakos, John. *Sophistical Rhetoric in Classical Greece*. Columbia: University of South Carolina Press, 1995.

Press, Gerald. "Knowledge as Vision in Plato's Dialogues." *Journal of Neoplatonic Studies* 3, no. 2 (1995): 61–90.

Press, Gerald. "Plato's Dialogues as Enactments." In *The Third Way: New Directions in Platonic Studies*, edited by Francisco Gonzalez, 133–52. Lanham, MD: Rowman & Littlefield, 1995.

Price, Anthony. "Are Plato's Soul-Parts Psychological Subjects?" *Ancient Philosophy* 29, no. 1 (2009): 1–15.

Putterman, Theodore L. "Socrates/Thrasymachus: The Extent of Their Agreement." *Polis* 17 (2000): 79–90.

Reames, Robin Henry. *Seeming and Being in Plato's Rhetorical Theory*. Chicago: University of Chicago Press, 2018.

Reeve, C. D. C. *Blindness and Reorientation: Problems in Plato's Republic*. New York: Oxford University Press, 2013.

Reeve, C. D. C. *Philosopher-Kings: The Argument of Plato's Republic.* Princeton, NJ: Princeton University Press, 1988.

Revermann, Martin, ed. *The Cambridge Companion to Greek Comedy.* Cambridge: Cambridge University Press, 2014.

Robinson, Richard. *Plato's Earlier Dialectic,* 2nd edition. Oxford: Clarendon Press, 1953.

Robinson, T. M. *Contrasting Arguments: An Edition of the Dissoi Logoi.* New York: Arno Press, 1979.

Roochnik, David. *Beautiful City: The Dialectical Character of Plato's Republic.* Ithaca: Cornell University Press, 2003.

Roochnik, David. "Self-Recognition in Plato's *Theaetetus.*" *Ancient Philosophy* 22 (2002): 37–52.

Roselli, David Kawalko. "Social Class." In *The Cambridge Companion to Greek Comedy,* edited by Martin Revermann, 241–58. Cambridge: Cambridge University Press, 2014.

Rosen, Ralph. "The Greek 'comic hero.'" In *The Cambridge Companion to Greek Comedy,* edited by Martin Revermann, 222–40. Cambridge: Cambridge University Press, 2014.

Rosen, Stanley. *Plato's Republic: A Study.* New Haven, CT: Yale University Press, 2005.

Rosen, Stanley. *The Quarrel between Philosophy and Poetry.* New York, NY: Routledge, Chapman, and Hall, 1988.

Rosenstock, Bruce. "Athena's Cloak: Plato's Critique of the Democratic City in the *Republic.*" *Political Theory* 22, no. 3 (1994): 363–90.

Ross, David. *Plato's Theory of Ideas.* Oxford: Clarendon Press, 1953.

Rowe, Christopher. "The Literary and Philosophical Style of the *Republic.*" In *The Blackwell Guide to Plato's Republic,* edited by Gerasimos Santas, 7–24. Oxford: Blackwell, 2006.

Ruffell, Ian. "Utopianism." In *The Cambridge Companion to Greek Comedy,* edited by Martin Revermann, 206–21. Cambridge: Cambridge University Press, 2014.

Sachs, David. "A Fallacy in Plato's *Republic.*" *Philosophical Review* 72 (1963): 141–58.

Sachs, Joe, trans. *Plato's Republic.* Translation, glossary, and introductory essay. Newburyport: Focus Philosophical Library, 2007.

Sallis, John. *Being and Logos: Reading the Platonic Dialogues,* 3rd ed. Bloomington: Indiana University Press, 1996.

Santas, Gerasimos. *Understanding Plato's Republic.* Malden, MA: Wiley-Blackwell, 2010.

Santas, Gerasimos. "Methods of Reasoning about Justice." In *The Blackwell Guide to Plato's Republic,* edited by Gerasimos Santas, 125–45. Malden, MA: Blackwell, 2006.

Santas, Gerasimos, ed. *The Blackwell Guide to Plato's Republic.* Malden, MA: Wiley-Blackwell, 2006.

Santas, Gerasimos. "Plato's Criticism of the 'Democratic Man' in the 'Republic.' " *Journal of Ethics* 5, no. 1 (2001): 57–71.

Santas, Gerasimos. "The Form of the Good in Plato's *Republic.*" *Philosophical Inquiry* (1980): 374–403.

Saxonhouse, Arlene. "Comedy in Callipolis: Animal Imagery in the *Republic.*" *American Political Science Review* 72, no. 3 (1978): 888–901.

Saxonhouse, Arlene. "The Philosopher and the Female in the Political Thought of Plato." *Political Theory* 4 (2) (1976): 195–212.

Schindler, David. *Plato's Critique of Impure Reason: On Goodness and Truth in the Republic.* Washington, DC: The Catholic University of America Press, 2008.

Schofield, Malcolm. "Euboulia in the *Iliad.*" *Classical Quarterly* 36 (1986): 6–31.

Schultz, Anne-Marie. *Plato's Socrates as Narrator: A Philosophical Muse.* Lanham, MD: Lexington Books, 2013.

Segal, Charles. "The Myth Was Saved: Reflections on Homer and the Mythology of Plato's *Republic.*" *Hermes* 106 (1978): 315–36.

Shields, Christopher. "Plato's Challenge: The Case against Justice in *Republic* II." In *The Blackwell Guide to Plato's Republic,* edited by Gerasimos Santas, 63–83. Malden, MA: Wiley-Blackwell, 2006.

Shorey, Paul, ed. and trans. *Plato's Republic,* volume 1. London: Heinemann, 1930.

Shorey, Paul, ed. and trans. *Plato's Republic,* volume 2. London: Heinemann, 1935.

Sinaiko, Herman. *Love, Knowledge and Discourse in Plato: Dialogue and Dialectic in Phaedrus, Republic, Parmenides.* Chicago: University of Chicago Press, 1965.

Singpurwalla, Rachel. "Commentary on Santas: Plato on the Good of the City-State in the *Republic.*" *Proceedings of the Boston Area Colloquium in Ancient Philosophy* 30 (2015): 63–70.

Singpurwalla, Rachel. "Plato's Defense of Justice in the *Republic.*" In *The Blackwell Guide to Plato's Republic,* edited by Gerasimos Santas, 263–82. Malden, MA: Wiley-Blackwell, 2006.

Slater, Niall, ed. *Voice and Voices in Antiquity.* Boston: Brill, 2016.

Slings, R. S. ed. *Platonis Respublica.* Oxford: Oxford University Press, 2003.

Small, Stuart G. P. "On Allegory in Homer." *Classical Journal* 44, no. 7 (April 1949): 423–30.

Smith, Nicholas D. "Plato's Book of Images." In *Philosophy in Dialogue: Plato's Many Devices,* edited by Gary Scott, 3–14. Evanston, IL: Northwestern University Press, 2007.

Smith, Nicholas D. "Socrates and Plato on Poetry." *Philosophic Exchange: Annual Proceedings* 37 (2006–2007): 42–54.

Smith, Nicholas D. "Images, Education, and Paradox in Plato's *Republic.*" *Apeiron* 32, no. 4 (1999): 125–41.

Smith, Nicholas D. "Plato's Divided Line." *Ancient Philosophy* 16, no. 1 (1996): 25–46.

Sobel, Jordan Howard. "Republic 331c–d." *History of Philosophy Quarterly* 4, no. 3 (July 1987): 281–90.

Sommerstein, Alan. "The Politics of Greek Comedy." In *The Cambridge Companion to Greek Comedy*, edited by Martin Revermann, 291–305. Cambridge: Cambridge University Press, 2014.

Sprague, Rosamond Kent. *Plato's Philosopher-King*. Columbia: University of South Carolina Press, 1976.

Steinberger, Peter J. "Who Is Cephalus?" *Political Theory* 24, no. 2 (May 1996): 172–99.

Strauss, Leo. *The City and Man*. Chicago: University of Chicago Press, 1978.

Struck, Peter. *The Birth of the Symbol: Ancient Readers at the Limits of Their Texts*. Princeton, NJ: Princeton University Press, 2004.

Tanner, Sonja. *In Praise of Plato's Poetic Imagination*. Lanham, MD: Lexington Books, 2010.

Tarrant, Dorothy. "Imagery in Plato's *Republic*." *Classical Quarterly* 40, no. 1 (1946): 27–34.

Tate, J. "Plato and Imitation." *Classical Quarterly* 26 (1932): 161–69.

Taylor, A. E. *Plato, the Man and His Work*. New York: Meridian, reprint 1960.

Taylor, C. C. W. "Plato's Totalitarianism." In *Plato's Republic*, ed. Richard Kraut, 31–48. Lanham, MD: Rowman & Littlefield, 1997.

Tecusan, Manuela. "Speaking about the Unspeakable: Plato's Use of Imagery." *Apeiron* 25, no. 4 (1992): 69–87.

Thayer, H. S. "The Myth of Er." *History of Philosophy Quarterly* 5, no. 4 (1988): 369–84.

Thomas, Nigel. "Mental Imagery." In *Stanford Encyclopedia of Philosophy*, edited by Edward N. Zalta. Summer 2016 edition. http://plato.stanford.edu/entries/mental-imagery/#ExpRep. Accessed September 26, 2016.

Thomas, Rosalind. "Prose Performance Texts: *Epideixis* and Written Publication in the Late Fifth and Early Fourth Centuries." In *Written Texts and the Rise of Literate Culture in Ancient Greece*, edited by Harvey Yunis, 162–87. Cambridge: Cambridge University Press, 2003.

Trivigno, Franco V. "Plato on Laughter and Moral Harm." In *Laughter, Humor, and Comedy in Ancient Philosophy*, edited by Pierre Destrée and Franco V. Trivigno, 13–34. Oxford: Oxford University Press, 2019.

Tuana, Nancy, ed. *Feminist Interpretations of Plato*. University Park: Pennsylvania State University Press, 1994.

Urmson, James. "Plato and the Poets." In *Plato's Republic: Critical Essays*, ed. Richard Kraut, 223–37. Lanham, MD: Rowman & Littlefield, 1997.

Usher, Robert. *Aristophanes' Ecclesiazusae*. Oxford: Clarendon Press, 1973.

Vegetti, Mario, Franco Ferrari, and Tosca Lynch, eds. *The Painter of Constitutions: Selected Essays on Plato's Republic*. Sankt Augustin: Academia Verlag, 2013.

Versnel, H. S. "The Festival for Bona Dea and the Thesmophoria." *Greece & Rome* 39 (1992): 31–55.

Vlastos, Gregory. "The Socratic Elenchus: Method Is All." In *Socratic Studies*, 1–28. Cambridge: Cambridge University Press, 1994.

Vlastos, Gregory. "Was Plato a Feminist?" In *Feminist Interpretations of Plato*, edited by Nancy Tuana, 11–26. University Park: Pennsylvania State University Press, 1994.

Vlastos, Gregory. *Socratic Studies*. Cambridge: Cambridge University Press, 1994.

Vlastos, Gregory. "Socratic Irony." *Classical Quarterly* 37, no. 1 (1987): 79–96.

Vlastos, Gregory. "Does Slavery Exist in Plato's *Republic*?" *Classical Philology* 63, no. 4 (October 1968): 291–95.

Wagner, Ellen. "Compulsion Again in the *Republic*." *Apeiron* 38, no. 3 (2005): 87–101.

Weiss, Roslyn. *Philosophers in the Republic: Plato's Two Paradigms*. Ithaca: Cornell University Press, 2012.

Weiss, Roslyn. "Wise Guys and Smart Alecks in *Republic* 1 and 2." In *The Cambridge Companion to Plato's Republic*, edited by G. R. F. Ferrari, 90–115. New York: Cambridge University Press, 2007.

White, Nicholas. *A Companion to Plato's Republic*, 2nd ed. Indianapolis, IN: Hackett, 1979.

Wild, John. *Plato's Modern Enemies and the Theory of Natural Law*. Chicago: University of Chicago Press, 1953.

Williams, Bernard. "The Analogy of City and Soul in Plato's *Republic*." In *Plato's Republic: Critical Essays*, edited by Richard Kraut, 49–94. Lanham, MD: Rowman & Littlefield, 1997.

Winkler, John J., and Froma I. Zeitlin, eds. *Nothing to Do with Dionysos? Athenian Drama in Its Social Context*. Princeton, NJ: Princeton University Press, 1990.

Winslow, Russell. "On Mimetic Style in Plato's *Republic*." *Philosophy and Rhetoric* 45, no. 1 (2012): 46–64.

Woodruff, Paul. "What Could Go Wrong with Inspiration?" In *Plato on Beauty, Wisdom, and the Arts*, edited by J. M. E. Moravcsik and Philip Temko, 137–50. Totowa: Rowman & Littlefield, 1982.

Yunis, Harvey. "The Protreptic Rhetoric of the *Republic*." In *The Cambridge Companion to Plato's Republic*, edited by G. R. F. Ferrari, 1–26. New York: Cambridge University Press, 2007.

Index

abstraction, 8, 17, 23–24, 44–45, 49, 51, 62–63, 82, 102, 122, 124, 142, 183, 185, 190, 198, 218–19, 251–52

Achilles, 18–20, 25, 28–29, 31, 135, 254–55, 260–61, 276–77

Aeschylus, 1, 12, 26, 159–60

analogy, 9, 44–46, 60–61, 72, 77, 85, 88, 101–8, 111–15, 124–28, 137–38, 140–42, 149, 160, 182–83, 195, 199–216, 223–24, 231, 243, 247, 252, 256–58, 263, 296n22, 300n30, 301n36, 302n44, 305n44, 308n72, 318n33, 322n3, 327n7; analogical reasoning, 103–8, 112, 138

aporia, 37, 63, 299n17

aristocracy, 165, 241–42, 249, 303n25, 327n7

Aristophanes, 14, 24, 156–63, 169, 308n2, 311n31; *Assemblywomen*, 153–65, 309n14, 311n42, 313n60; *Clouds*, 100, 158, 160, 175, 310n19; *Frogs*, 31, 159–60, 281n1, 286n56, 313n59; *Knights*, 165, 296n15; *Lysistrata*, 24, 118, 158, 160, 165, 312n57; *Wasps*, 74, 165, 296n16

Aristotle, 5, 12, 61–62, 108, 137, 151, 191, 195, 197, 220, 292n39, 298nn6–7; *De Anima*, 5, 315n15;

Nicomachean Ethics, 191, 298n6, 318n42; *Rhetoric*, 61–62, 256; *Topics*, 108, 298n6

audience, 5, 8–10, 14–26, 29–38, 51–54, 61–62, 69, 74, 79–81, 88–95, 102, 142, 156–68, 173, 176–77, 221, 229–31, 244, 250–52, 255, 258–64, 268, 286n58, 287n71, 290n19, 296n15, 299n16, 313n59

band of thieves, image of, 77

beauty, 14, 18, 49, 151, 163, 169, 175, 178, 184–88, 195, 198, 202, 205, 208, 225, 235, 246, 258–59, 263, 266, 274, 283n22, 320n57, 323n7

bees, 98, 244, 249–50, 329n9

being, 2–3, 7, 20, 160, 178, 181–85, 189, 195–98, 202–4, 209, 212–15, 230, 315n13, 319n51, 320n57; images and, 3, 10, 42, 201, 207, 212, 224, 237, 256–58, 262; nature of, 2, 182, 198, 206, 226, 256

body, 24, 29, 40, 63–64, 71, 93–94, 120, 135, 141–42, 162–65, 168, 174, 184, 200, 249–50, 252, 254–55, 313n64, 319n51

cave, image of, 1, 3, 6, 7, 9–10, 44–47, 124, 138–39, 146, 151–52,

CPSIA information can be obtained
at www.ICGtesting.com
Printed in the USA
LVHW020754010621
689025LV00004B/82